The DRURY Family of Maryland

and

Descendants in Virginia, Kentucky, Pennsylvania, Ohio, Illinois, and Missouri

Donald William Drury

Heritage Books
2025

HERITAGE BOOKS

AN IMPRINT OF HERITAGE BOOKS, INC.

Books, CDs, and more—Worldwide

For our listing of thousands of titles see our website
at
www.HeritageBooks.com

Published 2025 by
HERITAGE BOOKS, INC.
Publishing Division
5810 Ruatan Street
Berwyn Heights, MD 20740

Heritage Books by the author:

French Families in the Mississippi Valley:
Some Descendants of the Aubuchon, Bequette, Creely, Delisle, Hubert,
Langlois, Marechal, Ouimet, Payant, and Tesson Families

The Brewer Family of Maryland and Descendants in Kentucky and Missouri

The Drury Family of Maryland and Descendants in Virginia,
Kentucky, Pennsylvania, Ohio, Illinois, and Missouri

International Standard Book Number
Paperbound: 978-1-68034-629-9

Contents

Preface

Preface

The name Drury derives from Drieu, a French knight who came to England with William the Conqueror in 1066. Over the centuries some branches of the family prospered while others fared not as well. These differences stemmed mainly from religious and political prejudices that combined to reinforce each other. By the sixteen hundreds when the European powers were expanding to the Americas there were two main branches of the family – those who remained Catholic and those who did not. The Protestant Drurys came mainly to New England. The Catholic Drurys came instead to George Calvert's colony of Maryland where they were promised freedom to practice their religion unhindered.

This book explores the lives of some of those Drurys in Maryland and the associated families into which they married. As time passed their descendants spread into Virginia, Kentucky, Pennsylvania, Ohio, Illinois, and Missouri. It is not a completely typical genealogical work with family lists and pedigree charts that show relationships. It attempts rather to place these people into their social and historical context giving us some idea how they lived and what their life was like.

We begin by discussing conditions leading to the development of colonization in Maryland. Then the earliest Drury colonists are introduced and we discuss what is known about them. Their lives and those of their descendants are examined in relation to the economic, political and military events that helped to shape them. This ambitious attempt is sure to have flaws, but hopefully they will be outweighed by the positive features.

We must acknowledge a number of people who have helped greatly in the writing of this work. Several major contributors should be acknowledged. Linda Reno, genealogist, author, and expert on St. Mary's County, Maryland history, has provided extensive information and advice over many years. Peter Himmelheber, an expert on the history of land ownership in Colonial Maryland was also extremely helpful providing numerous maps showing locations of colonial plantations and correcting a number of misunderstandings that might have caused confusion.

Kathleen Simons, a descendant of the Ann Arundle Drurys, helped with extensive material and a review of Chapter Five. Much of the material in Chapter Six dealing with John Drury and Susanna Hayden was obtained from many years of research by Patricia Obrist. James Gangler of Washington D.C. provided information and photos of descendants of Michael Drury in Chapter Nine. Another descendant, Steve Driver, provided similar assistance for Chapter Twelve dealing with his ancestor Joseph Drury. Many others have helped in ways too numerous to mention, but their combined assistance was instrumental in making this book possible.

Chapter One

Background of Immigration

This work deals with those Catholic Drurys who eventually settled in Maryland. It will show how the Drurys fared in the new world and what their life was like. Initially we need to consider the conditions prevailing in England that caused them to consider leaving England at all. Many Englishmen were well content with the state of their society and their country. G. R. Elton writes in discussing the background of colonization.

> *"We are not talking about ignorant men; we are talking about men who, having seen both sides, were content to believe that the country they had been born into was especially blessed.... [These] conditions I speak of were widely diffused in popular consciousness, among the aristocracy, the gentry, and the people at large, whether travelers or stay-at-homes"*[1]

Against these attitudes we can cite a number of obvious factors that could possibly provide incentive to leave. There was a severe depression during most of the sixteenth century with consequent loss of jobs and poor health due to starvation.[2] This was aggravated with two episodes of Bubonic plague in 1557-8 and again in the 1590's and a severe Influenza epidemic at the end of the century.[3] The job market was further glutted with recently discharged soldiers returning from the War with Spain.[4]

Another cause of dissention was religious persuasion. This caused much strife during the period but was mainly used in the struggle to attain political power and wealth. Religious prejudice and persecution was endemic throughout the old world in the sixteenth and seventeenth centuries. Every Christian sect believed that all others who did not subscribe to their beliefs were heathen or blasphemers who were in league with the devil. Since religion and politics were intimately tied together in their view, anyone not agreeing with their faith was also a subversive spy intent on overthrowing the state by any means available. As Ernest Smith wrote in *Religion under the Barons of Baltimore* in 1896, "In their day the duty of tolerating religious error was a part of no man's creed. No preacher of true toleration had yet arisen among men. Nor was the world ready for such a prophet. Neither the Church of England, the Puritans, nor the Catholics believed in religious liberty at that time. All believed in a State church established by law, and each was intent on establishing its own faith to the exclusion of every other."[5]

Additional insight is provided by James Anthony Froud.

> They *"clamoured against persecution, not because it was persecution, but because truth was persecuted by falsehood; and however furiously the hostile factions exclaimed each that the truth was with them and the falsehood with their enemies, neither the one nor the other disputed the obligation of the ruling powers to support the truth in itself."*[6]

Smith continues,

"It was precisely the same in the early Seventeenth Century when James I was king. Then, too, men considered it the business of government to prescribe a religion for its subjects. They also held that the more perfect the government, the more conscientiously and effectually it would do this. Whatever a man's private opinions might be, he had no right outwardly and publicly to assert them, and should he be so unreasonable as to do so he deserved to be severely punished. Accordingly, Sir George Calvert himself, when secretary of state, Roman Catholic though he was, made no scruple of sending even his own co-religionists to prison..."[7]

These views had been held for at least 50 years by the time the Maryland Proprietorship was founded. For centuries the Kings of England had been at odds with the Pope regarding the authority of the Catholic Church over the Crown. Henry VIII was convinced that the Pope would use Catholics in England to attempt a revolution overthrowing his reign. This fear climaxed a few years after Henry VIII became King with a series of events and proclamations culminating in the formal establishment of the Church of England with Henry as its head in 1531. The English clergy rejected the authority of the Pope in 1535 and declared the Pope's authority in England void the following year.

As a prince, Henry did not expect to become King, for he had an elder brother, Arthur, who was heir to the throne. A marriage was made between Arthur and a Spanish Princess, Catherine of Aragon, but Arthur presently died. The royal houses of Spain and England wished to repair the connection, and the obvious way to do it was to marry the young widow to Henry, now heir in Arthur's place. But Spain and England were Christian monarchies and Christian law forbade a man to marry his brother's widow.[10]

To be a Christian was to be a Churchman and there was only one Church (though plagued with many heresies), and the Pope was its head. At the request of both Spain and England the Pope dispensed with the Christian law forbidding a man to marry his brother's widow, and when in due course Prince Henry ascended the English throne as Henry VIII, Catherine was his Queen.

For some years the marriage was successful; they respected and liked one another, and Henry took his pleasures elsewhere but lightly. However, at length he wished to divorce her. The motives for such a wish are presumably as confused, inaccessible, and helpless in a King as any other man, but here are three which make sense: Catherine had grown increasingly plain and intensely religious; Henry had fallen in love with Anne Boelyn, one of her ladies in waiting; and the Spanish alliance had become unpopular. None of these absolutely necessitated a divorce but there was a fourth that did. Catherine had not been able to provide Henry with a male child and was now presumed barren. There was a daughter, but competent statesmen were unanimous that a Queen on the throne of England was unthinkable. Anne and Henry were confident that between them they could produce a son; but if that son were to be his heir, Anne would have to be Henry's wife.

The Pope was once again approached, this time by England only, and asked to declare the marriage with Catherine null on the grounds that it contravened the Christian law which forbade marriage with a brother's widow. But England's insistence that the marriage should be nullified was balanced by Spain's insistence that it shouldn't. And at that moment Spain was well placed to influence the Pope's deliberations. Rome, where the Pope lived, had been very thoroughly sacked and occupied by Spanish Troops. In addition, one imagines a natural disinclination on the part of the Pope to have his powers turned on and off like a tap. At all events, after much ceremonious prevarication while Henry waited with a rising temper, it became clear that so far as the Pope was concerned, the marriage with Catherine would stand.[11]

To the ferment of a lover and the anxieties of a sovereign Henry now added a bad conscience, and a serious matter it was for him and those about him.

The Bible, he found, was perfectly clear on such marriages as he had made with Catherine; they were forbidden. And the threatened penalty was exactly what had befallen him, the failure of male heirs. He was in a state of sin. He had been thrust into this state of sin by his father with the active help of the Pope, and the Pope now proposed to keep him in a state of sin. The man who would do that, it began to seem to Henry, had small claim to being the Vicar of God.

And indeed, on looking into the thing really closely, Henry found -- what various voices had urged for centuries off and on -- that the supposed Pope was no more than an ordinary Bishop, the Bishop of Rome. This made everything clear and everything possible. If the Pope was not the Pope at all, but merely a Bishop among Bishops, Henry reasoned, then these special powers he had as Pope did not exist. In particular, of course, he had no power to dispense with God's rulings as revealed in Leviticus 18, but equally important, he had no power to appoint other Bishops; and here an ancient quarrel stirred.

For if the Pope had not the power to appoint Bishops, then who did have, if not the King himself --- King by the Grace of God. Henry's ancestors, all those other Henrys, had been absolutely right he decided. The Bishop of Rome, without a shadow of legality, had succeeded over the centuries in setting up a rival reign within the kingdom, a sort of long drawn usurpation of power. The very idea of it used to throw Henry into terrible rages. It should go on no longer!

He looked about for a good bishop to appoint to Canterbury, a Bishop with no ambitions to modify God's ruling on deceased brother's wives, yet sufficiently spirited to grant a divorce to his sovereign without consulting the Bishop of Rome. The man was found in Thomas Crammer. Catherine was divorced, Anne married, and the Established Church of England was off on its singular way.

Catholics were stripped of their estates and titles, refused opportunity for advancement and, in general, became second-class citizens. They were denied the right to openly practice their religion. Laws were passed which stripped them of any right to participate in governing the country or to hold office.[12] Conditions were ripe for dissent. The power of the nobility was increasingly challenged by the mercantile interests of the rising middle class, just as Henry had challenged the Roman Catholic Church when he established the Church of England and confiscated Church holdings for distribution to his adherents. Towns were now becoming the center of life and trade, as had the Manors and Castles in Medieval times. Merchants and trading companies continued to increase their influence over Parliament as they sought advantage for themselves and their partners.

The merchants and nobles looked for quick profits in the new world. After all, they had the example of Spain who had plundered shiploads of gold and jewels from Central and South America. When similar wealth was not found they turned to other profitable commodities such as timber and fish. Initially they had no thought of creating permanent settlements. [13]

But a second motive for colonization soon arose. This was for the land itself. By the beginning of the seventeenth century land was becoming scarce in England. The Law of Primogeniture in which all the property of a deceased landowner went to the eldest son, left many younger sons without resources or means to acquire them in England. A man had to be a landowner in order to maintain status, be able to vote, and, in general, be considered a gentleman. Those with no land of their own were considered lower class.

Even here some were still hesitant. Would this new land be habitable? In the early stages the promoters had difficulty in recruiting settlers. Bossy tells us…

"…it seems exceptionally clear that English Catholics simply did not want to move out of England. In the 1580's when the legal repression of Catholicism in England was becoming severe, two Catholic gentlemen developed a scheme to take up a patent of colonization and make a settlement on the New England coast that would in fact be a refuge for Catholics. The main reason why the idea failed to materialize does not seem to have been that Queen Elizabeth's government opposed it; indeed, even so strict a Protestant as Sir Francis Walsingham seems to have thought it a good idea. The real problem, it seems to me [Bossey], was that Catholics did not want to go. According to [Jesuit Robert] Parsons, they viewed the project as a disguised form of forcible transportation – an "exportation to a barbarous country" -- and as a kind of cowardly flight for which the Protestants would sneer at them. …This tells us a good deal about the Catholic frame of mind, at least among the gentry; for men of honor, it was a dishonorable thing to consider; for men with a heavy stake in their country, deeply embedded in its civilization, it was a brutal uprooting from which they flinched." [14]

George Calvert was one of many who sought favor and attempted to advance his fortunes in this era. Though some have written of his inherited greatness, Smith informs us that Calvert's ancestral home was a farmhouse near the town of Danby Wiske in the valley of the swale in Yorkshire, and his ancestors were probably Flemish artisans. His elevation to the nobility came through service to King James I. But even here his peerage was Irish and did not command the status of English nobility. [15]

Sir George Calvert, first Lord Baltimore, was born about 1579 in Yorkshire. One pedigree states he was the son of Leonard Calvert and Grace Crossland. This is impossible because Grace Crossland was not born until February 1572/3. She would not be bearing children at age seven. A pedigree compiled by Benedict Leonard Calvert lists Leonard Calvert's wife as Alice. The possibility does exist that Grace was Leonard's second wife even though she was twenty years his junior. [16]

George graduated from Trinity College, Oxford in 1597 and then spent several years traveling on the continent. When he returned he became secretary to Sir Robert Cecil. He held several minor posts in government and by 1608 had become clerk of the Privy Council. The next year he became a member of Parliament. King James I, who held him in high regard, sent him on several missions abroad including one to Ireland to investigate complaints of persecution of the Catholic population.

In 1617 he was knighted, in 1619 he became a principal secretary of State, and in 1621 he was again a member of Parliament. He resigned as Principal Secretary when he informed the King he had become a Catholic in 1625, but was persuaded to remain as a member of the Privy Council and was made Baron of Baltimore. Baronies in this reign, and especially Irish Baronies, were very cheap affairs. They were actually put up for sale. How high he might have gone no one knows, but he continued to be trusted by the King and was honored and respected by those who knew him.

The statement is often made, as here, that Calvert resigned his office because he had become a Roman Catholic. This is inconsistent with admitted facts:

First, Roman Catholics were not debarred from employment at court under James I.

Second, it was known that Calvert himself was a Roman Catholic when he received his appointment. *The office of treasurer was put in Commission, and Secretary Winwood dying about the same time, his place was divided between Naunton and Calvert, the first of whom was a Protestant and the other a Papist."* This was in 1616. (See Smollet, volume V, p. 40) Moreover, in 1620 he was expressly mentioned by name along with the Earls of Arundle and Worcester, Lord Digby, and others as "popishly affected." (Kennedy, p. 38) Why should he have thought it necessary to resign, even if he had been recently converted? The only motive that could compel him to such a course for conscious' sake was the necessity of taking the oaths of supremacy and allegiance, and these he had already taken.

Third, when Calvert avowed his Romanism in 1625 Archbishop Abbott said of him: "He apparently turneth Papist, which he now professeth, this being the third time he hath been to blame that way."

Fourth, in 1624 Calvert's eldest son Cecil was in his 18th year; Leonard, who came next, in his 16th. They were both Roman Catholics, as were all his children. When did they become so? Was Cecil "converted" when his father was? Was Leonard? This allegiance of all his family to Rome, together with the fact that his mother was of the Roman obedience, and that his own adherence to it was well known long before his acknowledgement of it, has even suggested the question: Was he ever anything else than a Roman Catholic?

Fifth, again, the king, who entertained the most violently unreasonable feelings of hatred towards "perverts" but who was kind and considerate for those who were born Roman Catholics, always retained his affection to Calvert to the last, even making him a peer of the realm only a few months after his supposed conversion, and willingly granting to him on his own terms the charter of his Newfoundland plantation.[17]

George Calvert's interest in the New World was long standing. He was a member of the East India Company and of the Virginia Company. In 1621 he became a member of the

Council for New England. His first independent venture was in Newfoundland, the source of fish and oil from the Grand Banks. A number of attempts to colonize there had been attempted without success. George Calvert bought his land in Newfoundland from Sir William Vaughn who had established a colony there in 1618. By 1627 Baltimore had received a grant for additional acreage, but after spending a season in the Colony he became convinced that the climate was too harsh and the growing season too short to be successful. In addition there was the increasing threat of war between the Canadian French and the English Colonists.[18]

He requested that the King grant him a charter to move his settlement farther south to the milder climate of Virginia. He went to Virginia in October of 1629. He was courteously received by the governors of the Colony but was insulted by at least one member of the Colony for refusing to take the oath of supremacy and allegiance. But no matter what they thought of him personally, his wealth, and the fact that he was Baron of Baltimore by royal proclamation could be an asset to the colony that they had no qualms about using to advantage.

This refusal to take the oath must have perplexed them. They knew of his shifting religious preferences according to the needs of the moment. Even so, as an educated nobleman, he was well aware of the limitations of the oath and, at any rate, had taken it before in England. So what was he up to? Their well-founded suspicion that he coveted territory in Virginia was more responsible for the hostility, especially by William Claiborne Secretary of the Colony, than his simple refusal to take the oath. These suspicions were substantiated immediately on Calvert's return to England when he requested the King to move his charter from Newfoundland to land below the James River.[19]

Claiborne followed soon after to lobby vigorously against granting any charter that would take land from Virginia. William Claiborne obtained a trading license in the 1620s covering the entire area that eventually became Maryland. He and other Protestant investors from England had developed a profitable trade in beaver pelts with the Indians that would be jeopardized if the Calverts were granted land anywhere in Virginia. He developed excellent relations with the Susquehannock Indians who were the dominant tribe in the area and also supplied the highest quality beaver pelts. His business was becoming very profitable by the time the Calvert charter was granted. Claiborne went to England to lobby Parliament to nullify the charter but was unsuccessful. Calvert's connections at court proved more powerful, and the site of the charter was moved to the Chesapeake region where Claibourne had his trading venture. This was the beginning of the twenty-five year feud between Claibourne and the Calvert family. It was born, as we see, from a combination of commercial competition, religious prejudice, and personal animosity. These were compounded by misunderstandings and missed opportunities for their resolution.

Claiborne backers in England, especially Sir William Stanley Earl of Stirling and Proprietor of Nova Scotia, and William Cloberry a Puritan merchant and lobbyist, had eagerly funded Claiborne's endeavors as one way to recoup losses suffered when Charles I ceded Canada to the French. Now it seemed to them that the whim of this Catholic King would once again snatch what they considered rightfully theirs from their grasp. Stanley had provided a Scottish trading license to Claiborne for the same areas where the Calvert Charter was sited. Claibourne argued that Kent island and its Trading Post were his because the Calvert Charter specified that it included only unsettled lands and Claibourne had been on the island for over two years before the charter was granted, built dwellings there, and had people living there permanently. Cecil Calvert naturally contended that the island was part of the Maryland Proprietorship as granted in the charter. Claiborne's trading license had been issued by the Protestant parliament, and the Calvert charter was granted by the Catholic King Charles I.

English courts were unable to resolve the issue of whether Virginia or Maryland owned the land and, with support in Parliament divided evenly, the only thing for the parties to do, as had always been the case, was for each to enlist the native Indian tribes to try to force the other out of the territory. Claiborne had the advantage here of being on excellent terms with the Susquehanocks, the most powerful tribe in the area. This alliance remained in place for many years due to Claiborne's friendship with, and trust of, the Indians; and also because the Susquehanocks needed a secure southern border to their territory in order to deal with hostile Iroquois neighbors to the north. In response the Maryland colonists organized with the Piscataways, the dominant tribal group in Southern Maryland. This tribe headed a loose confederation of small bands numbering in total some seven thousand people. Each tribe went by different names at times because of their practice of naming themselves after the area where they settled. This caused much confusion at first. Their languages were similar so the colonists considered them as somewhat related. The Indians eagerly set up this alliance in order to get help from the settlers in fighting the Susquehanocks who were raiding both the Indians and the Whites in the territory at the urging of Claiborne. He was adamant about removing the Maryland colonists stating, "He would drive out the new arrivals even if he had to do it with the Indians in a canoe."

Driving this conflict was the European trade in beaver pelts that had become hugely popular in the making of men's hats. Cecil Calvert (2nd Lord Baltimore) in England heavily emphasized the huge profits possible by trading in beaver without including mention of the associated risks. Both sides knew that the key to the beaver trade was the possession of Kent Island and Maryland. Claiborne had the advantage here. He was on the scene in America several years before the establishment of the Maryland Proprietorship. He had good contacts in England with Protestant businessmen who had the ear of Parliament and, most importantly, he was on excellent terms and was trusted by the Susquehannock tribes who controlled most of the territory where the prime pelts could be found. For the Maryland colonists the critical task to accomplish was the destruction of the Kent Island trading station that everyone saw as a threat. This assumed greater importance as beaver along the Potomac became scarcer and of inferior quality. This conflict was the cause of much strife throughout the first three decades of Maryland history.[20]

In the meantime Henry Fleet, a colonial trader and competitor of Claiborne's who worked for Maryland, intercepted and captured a ship belonging to Claiborne claiming it was trading illegally in Maryland waters. Claiborne retaliated by attacking two Maryland ships in Chesapeake Bay. Two Virginians were killed in this second battle and the Virginia assembly blamed Thomas Harvey, the governor of Virginia. They drove him out of the colony sending him to England and threatened to shoot him if he returned. Parliament and the King could not let this flouting of their authority stand. They returned Harvey to Virginia where he removed the ringleaders from office and sent them to England for trial. He also removed Claibourne from office and took away Claibourne's other positions.

Encouraged by these events and by the placement on the Virginia Council of several men favorable to the Calverts, Maryland officials invaded Kent Island in February of 1638 and confiscated large quantities of trade goods and other property. They executed some of the rebels and allowed others to swear allegiance to Governor Calvert and immigrate to Maryland, but Claibourne was charged with piracy, mutiny, sedition, and various other crimes.

Unfortunately this did Governor Calvert little good in trying to secure beaver pelts. When Claibourne was forced to leave, the Susquehannocks remained true to their friend and refused to trade with the Marylanders. Instead they traveled many miles to trade at the newly established trading post at Fort Christina (Wilmington, Delaware). This refusal effectively stopped the beaver trade in Maryland even though Lord Baltimore was still promoting it in England. It was this more than any other single thing that started the trend toward tobacco production in Maryland.

Over the next decade a number of events on both sides of the Atlantic affected the fortunes of Maryland. In 1641 the Irish rebellion threatened Lord Baltimore's lands and revenues in Ireland. The English civil war (1642-1645) reduced royal patronage and diminished his influence in Parliament. At the same time in Maryland several of his major supporters became dissatisfied with the way things were going. The Jesuit priests were trying to obtain grants of land directly from the Indians to circumvent his control over patents and their income, and the Susquehannocks began raiding in Maryland driving out some of his Indian allies. In the middle of all these troubles was the Calvert's old enemy William Claibourne. He aided and befriended anyone who would attack or cause problems for Maryland. During his absence from Virginia, Claibourne became a partner in the Providence Island Company and became close to its Puritan owners and their friends in Parliament. At the conclusion of the war when Protestants took over in England, Claibourne was fully prepared to take advantage of the situation to regain Kent Island and ruin the Calverts.[21]

Richard Ingle was a sea captain who worked with William Claiborne. Maryland authorities arrested him in 1644 for violating a Virginia prohibition against trading in Maryland waters that he refused to recognize. With the help of Thomas Cornwallis, an Anglican and a member of the Maryland government, he managed to escape and went to England. While there Ingle obtained letters of marque from the Protestant parliament and recruited a group of adventurers from Virginia. Ingle returned to Maryland and began raiding plantations, freeing indentured servants, looting towns, and generally terrorizing the population. Governor Leonard Calvert was even forced to flee to Virginia for a time. Ingle and his men took what they wished by force from the settlers who remained. By doing this he was both exacting revenge for former mistreatment by the Calverts and carrying out the wishes of Parliament who had branded Calvert a traitor for collecting taxes for King Charles I in 1644.

While in Virginia, Leonard Calvert hired an army of Puritan mercenaries led by Richard Bennett. This was possible in part because the Anglicans in Virginia had persecuted Puritans as well as Catholics. Because of this they were sympathetic to other victims and, of course, this was a good chance to make money. Also they were not averse to helping an adversary of Virginia. From Leonard Calvert's point of view they were the largest effective military force available at the time.

In 1645 Governor Calvert retook the colony with the help of Bennett's mercenaries. He died shortly after Bennett's army had driven Ingle out of Maryland but before the mercenaries could be paid. On his deathbed he appointed Margaret Brent, a prominent woman property owner, as his executrix and charged her with seeing that the soldiers were paid from his estate. There was much unrest because there was a shortage of food in addition to their lack of pay. She bought corn to feed them and then began selling property and cattle to obtain funds to pay the soldiers. When Leonard Calvert's money ran out she used the governor's position as agent for his brother to sell part of Cecil Calvert's cattle to pay the rest of the soldiers.[22]

Cecil Calvert objected strenuously from England and accused her of wasting his estate. But the colonists defended her actions stating that no one else could have handled the situation as well. It is speculated that perhaps Cecil Calvert objected as strongly as he did to impress the Protestants in Parliament that he was not being too lenient with Catholics in his colony. Opposition in Parliament by the new Protestant government forced him to appoint a number of Protestants to the council in Maryland including the new governor William Stone who replaced his dead brother, and Richard Bennett, staunch friend of Claibourne, fanatic Puritan, and commander of the militia. The large number of Protestants who migrated from Virginia and settled along the Potomac gradually changed the balance of power in the colony.

With Claibourne and his friends firmly in control in both Virginia and Maryland a peaceful period seemed likely, especially as hostilities with the Susquehannocks also were ended through Claibourne's influence. Unfortunately this was the beginning of the end as both Europeans and Indians began a series of wars that lasted twenty years and totally destroyed the coastal beaver trade. Once this was gone there was little to fight over. The Puritan repression in Maryland resulted finally in the bloody 1665 Sabbath day battle on the Severn River. Maryland forces were led by Governor Stone; the Puritan forces by Josias Fuller. This battle may have been one of the reasons why the Cromwell government in England restored Maryland to the more moderate Calverts.

Against this background of manipulation and intrigue Cecil Calvert, second Lord Baltimore, was arranging to populate his proprietorship. In spite of assertions by later historians that Maryland was set up as a haven for persecuted Roman Catholics, only about a third of the initial colonists were Catholic. Calvert issued instructions to his

_____

brother Leonard who accompanied the group as the first governor of Maryland that Catholic services should be as private as possible and not to discuss religion with others. Even though two Jesuit priests were among the initial immigrants and a mass was said on arrival in Maryland, it is clear from the records of the early proprietary government that Cecil Calvert was most interested in populating this huge tract of land he had been granted and that his actions were intended to further this aim above all else. After all, rents from this land were to be his income and the source of his wealth for the rest of his life. He could not really afford to make mistakes.[23]

Much has been made of the "Acts of toleration" enacted in 1649 which were supposedly aimed at preventing persecution of Catholics in Maryland. Actually this was a shrewd political move on Calvert's part. It assured Catholics that they would not be persecuted while at the same time assuring Protestants that they would not suffer reverse discrimination at the hands of the Catholic Proprietors. In addition it partially mollified the Protestant Parliament in England whose members were having misgivings by this time about giving so generous a grant to a Catholic.

But if we examine this legislation more closely we will see that it was not as tolerant as we might be expected to believe. This act contained five sections. Under the first section it was provided that those who denied the Godhead of any person of the Trinity, or uttered reproachful words concerning the Trinity, should be punished by death and their property confiscated. Under the second section those who spoke reproachfully of our Lord's Mother, or of any of the Apostles or Evangelists, were liable to be fined, imprisoned, or whipped. By the third section it was settled that whipping and fining likewise awaited those who styled their neighbors heretics, Schismatics, Puritans and the like. In the fourth section fines, imprisonments and whippings were decreed against profaners of the Sabbath or Lord's Day. The fifth section was of an entirely different character. It was enacted and ordained that no person should suffer molestation on account of the free exercise of his religion except as had been set forth in the earlier sections. Even by the standards of the time three hundred and fifty years ago this was a step back into the darkness. [24]

A more sympathetic view of the Act and its history can be found in Edwin Beitzel's *The Jesuit Missions of St. Mary's County* where he quotes from Andrew Matthews "*History of Maryland*." Matthews writes:

"The enactment of this Act is often mistakenly celebrated as the beginning of Religious tolerance in Maryland. Actually the Act formally limited the complete freedom of conscience established by Lord Baltimore with the founding of the province in 1634, because, under its provisions, penalties were provided against Jews, unbelievers, and Deists or Unitarians, although in actual practice there seems to have been no discrimination. This so-called Toleration Act was but a delimiting expression forced upon the ideals or wishes of the proprietary and the actual practice of the early settlers. It was the response to the threat of a powerful outside force inimical to the principles of toleration; and this force was, for a while, held off by means of this enactment. Rightly, therefore, the act of 1649 is a compromise between the liberal practices in the province during the preceding 15 years, and the drastic restrictions which were subsequently instituted." Even the toleration formally instituted by this Act was far in advance of other states.[25]

No matter which view we accept, this was the world to which colonists were enticed. Pamphlets and advertisements emphasized the dual inducements of quick riches and free land for those who could bring settlers. In modern terms what was happening was land speculation by the nobility and the upper classes; buying land for rent or resale for a quick profit. Glowing descriptions from various sources fueled this fervor.

A typical description of Maryland in the early seventeenth century can be found in John Smith's second book of the history of Virginia as quoted in John Leeds Bozeman's *History of Maryland.*

"The sommer is hot as in Spaine; the winter cold as in France and England... The winds here are variable, but the like thunder and lightning to purifie the ayre I have seldome either seene or heard in Europe...Sometimes there are great droughts, other times much raine, yet great necessitie of neither, by reason we see not but that all the raritie of needful fruits in Europe, may be there in great plenty... within is a country that may have the perogative over the most places knowne, for large and pleasant navigable rivers, heaven and earth never agreed better to frame a place for man's habitation;...Here are mountains, hills, plaines, valleys, rivers and brookes, all running most pleasantly into a faire bay, compassed but for the mouth, with fruitful and delightsome land."[26]

Another enthusiastic account is provided on pages seven and eight of *The Old Line State* where an anonymous author of "An account of the colony of the Lord Baron of Baltimore in Maryland" speaks of the "great quantity of fish to be had in the bay and its tributaries, the great oaks from which beams sixty feet long and two and a half feet wide are cut, the great cypresses which do not deign to branch until they have reached a height of eighty feet, the mulberries for silkworms and the cedars equaling those of Lebanon itself. The small growth included grapes for wine, plums, cherries, gooseberries, chestnuts, walnuts, strawberries, and raspberries."

Morris Radoff adds the following:
"The wonder of the land is something almost impossible for twentieth Century man to understand; he takes it for granted that anyone may own land. But that was surely not the case in Europe in the Sixteenth and Seventeenth centuries, where it was the Lord of the manor who owned the land, and even when it was occupied and tended by others the fish and game, and the timber were normally reserved for his Lordship's use. It was, of course, true that even in Maryland men did not at first own land in fee simple: the quitrent or it's equivalent had to be paid -- and the Calvert's were strict about this --; the land might revert under certain circumstances, such as doedands which violate present day concepts of absolute ownership of property. But in the great majority of cases men were not disturbed in their tenancy; they could sell their land and crops, mortgage them, leave them to their heirs, plant and plan for the future. From time to time, the acreage allowed to each settler changed, but during the earliest period it was a generous amount and more could be had by purchase subsequent to settlement."[27]

Not only was there much land available, it was much richer so they were told. The fertile topsoil had been accumulating layer on layer for thousands of years. By the time the immigrants arrived in 1634 it averaged two to three feet thick. Indian cultivation did not disturb the soil as much as European methods. The large anchor roots of the giant trees made it difficult to clear land for cultivation. Instead, Indians piled the soil into mounds above the general level and planted their crops in these elevated hills of loose soil.

These high expectations were not entirely pipedreams, but there was much to learn in adapting to the new surroundings. The local Indians taught the settlers about survival in this new land and their first years were considerably easier because of this. Unlike the Virginia shortages in its early years, the Maryland settlers were even able to export a shipload of corn to New England the first year.[28] The forests were full of game. There were deer, elk, bear, bison, beaver, and among the smaller animals there were squirrel, opossum, raccoon, and turtles. Of course there were also the predators such as bobcats and wolves. Quail, turkeys, coots and loons were plentiful as well as waterfowl like Canada Geese, Canvasbacks, Mallards, Teal, and even Cormorant. Seafood was also abundant. Popular choices were Drum, Sheepshead, Bass, Perch, Catfish, Sturgeon, and Gar. Oysters, crabs and other shellfish were also on the menu. Unfortunately there were also mosquitoes and other insects that spread debilitating diseases like malaria until the settlers learned to cope with them. This initial period was known as seasoning. Most of the plantations were sited along the rivers for ease of transportation. Proximity to water and swampy areas made these dangers worse.[29]

When the colonists arrived in 1634 they found these Indians living peacefully in what is now southern Maryland. Even though the English considered all this territory their own according to the royal charter, Leonard Calvert, as leader of the Colony, met with the chiefs and "bought" a thirty mile strip of land from them for cloth, axes, and trade goods. It is doubtful that the Indians understood what the transaction involved as no Indian, even as late as the nineteenth century in the west, had any concept of "ownership of land". They probably thought they were conferring hunting and fishing rights in this territory.

He obtained the services of Henry Fleet as interpreter and met with the Indian leaders. Some accounts tell us he took over an Indian village where St. Mary's city now stands. Others say he bought the land and the dwellings from the natives. Still other accounts leave us with the impression that the Indians took advantage of him in that they were ready to move on to another site before he arrived and that they accepted all he was willing to give them for the site they were about to abandon. At any rate the deal was made, and the settlers immediately moved into about half the village. The Indians showed them their native ways of agriculture and introduced the settlers to maize (corn), squash, beans, and tobacco. Most of these Indians were peaceful and lived by hunting and by farming small plots of land. The Yacomico, who the new settlers first met, had to rely on their environment for their survival. Everything that they used was made from what they could find in the woods and rivers around them or what they could grow.

Frame

Completed unit

Yacomico Witchott

They lived in a type of longhouse that they called a **witchott**. The frames of these houses were made from young trees, or saplings. The saplings were cut down and the bark was peeled off the outside. The ends of the poles were buried in holes in the ground the other ends tied together to make arches. A series of arches were built together to make a large oval frame. Once the frame was done, it was covered with mats that were woven out of grasses that grew in the nearby marshes.[30]

Father White, one of the Jesuit Priests accompanying the voyage, described them in his journal as having excellent sight, good hearing, and an acute sense of smell.

They were proper and tall men, swarthy and painted a dark red "which they doe to keep away the gnats…" They wear their hair in diverse fashions and adorn themselves with hawk bills, talons of eagles, or the teeth of beasts. "Their apparel is deere skins and other furs which they wear loose like mantles, under which all their women and those which are come to man's stature wear perizomata of skins, which keep them decently covered from all offence of sharp eyes. All the rest are naked and sometimes men of the younger sort wear nothing at all." He further describes them as pleasant, agreeable and chaste. "If these were once Christian they would doubtless be a virtuous and renouned nation. In any case they yielded themselves like lambs "giving us houses, land, and livings for a trifle."[31]

When the colonists took over the Yacomico village they renamed it St. Maries City and started living temporarily in the Indian huts. The Indians even helped them by teaching the Indian method of cultivation and which were the most beneficial plants and animals to hunt and cultivate.

13

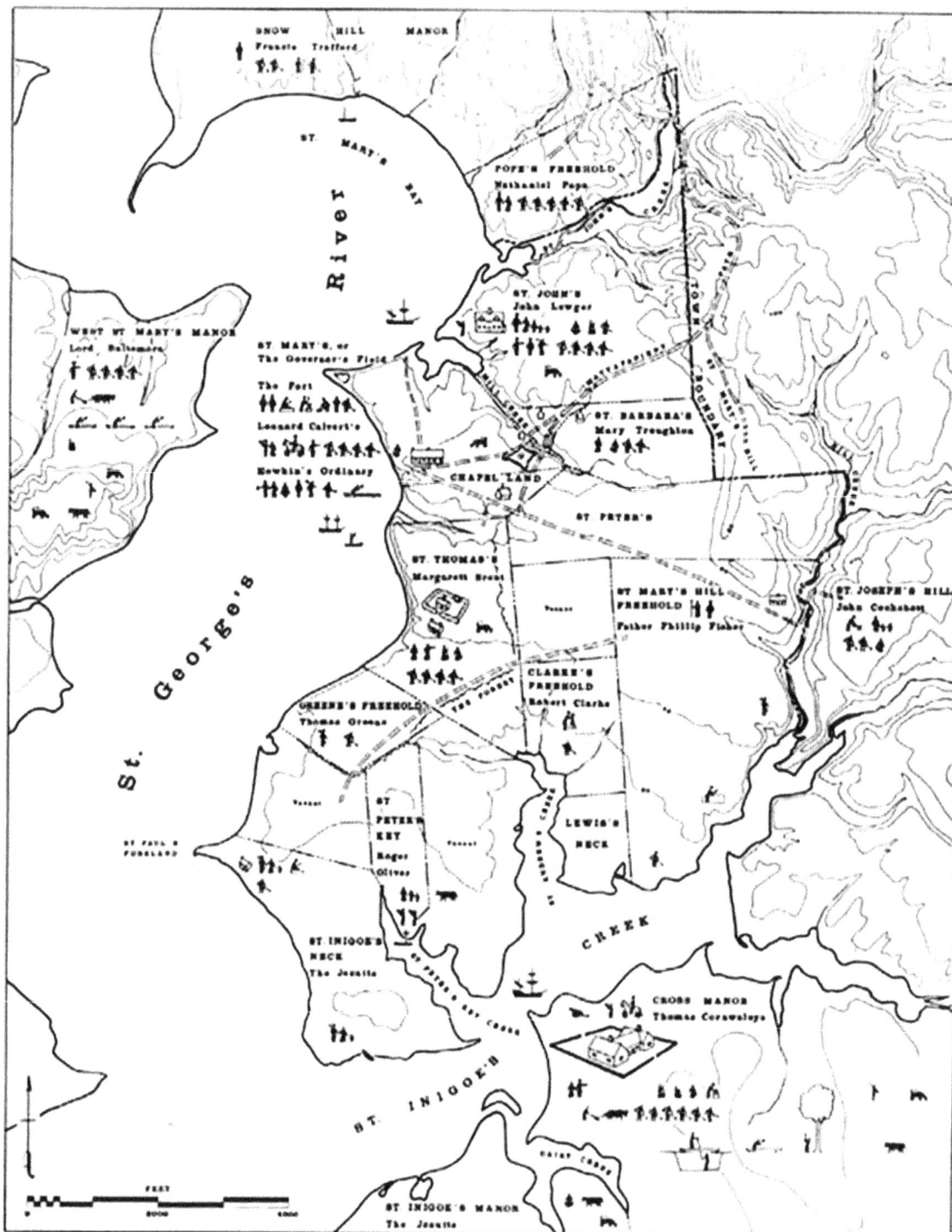

St. Mary's City - 1642

Most of the settlers who came to Maryland were between sixteen and twenty four years old. This was true of both men and women. Life was hard and many died either of disease or injury by the time they were thirty-five. If they managed to live beyond this age they would probably be able to live to be sixty or more. The critical factors in becoming successful and powerful after immigrating were having money available to take advantage of opportunity, and to have political connections both in Maryland and in England. The Calverts intended their proprietorship to be very much a feudal domain as had been the case in England hundreds of years earlier. Their charter from King Charles gave them almost more power than Parliament and they and their other Noble investors hoped to enrich themselves through the rents from the plantations. Cecil Calvert actually had almost as much power in Maryland as had the King in England.

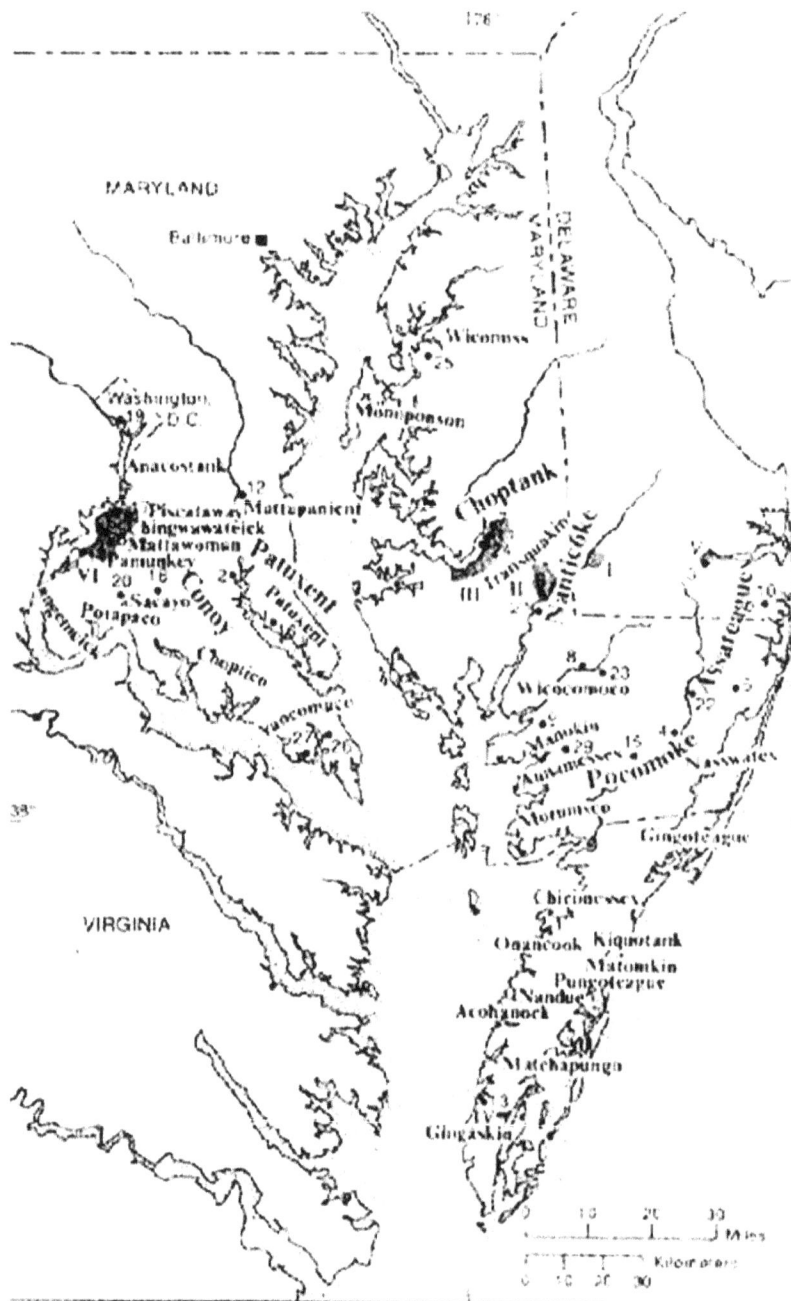

Tribes and Villages, 1620 – 1837. Locations of some Villages are tentative. [32]

Endnotes

[1] Elton *G. R.*, *Contentment and discontent on the eve of colonization* p. 112 in Quinn, David B., Early Maryland in a Wider World Wayne State University Press Detroit, Mi. 1982

[2] Nolan, John S., *The Militarization of the Elizabethan State* in Journal of Military History Vol. 58 No. 3 (7/1994) URL: www.jstor.org/stable/2944132 : See also Innes, Arthur D. , *A History of England*: The British Empire Vol. II Macmillan 1913, and Lunt, William Edward, *History of Englan*d Harper & Brothers 1945

16

[3] Twigge, Graham, *Plague in London: Spatial and temporal aspects of mortality in Endemic diseases in London*, in Center for metropolitan working papers series No 1 1993, Ed. John L. Champion.

[4] <http://www.royal.gov.uk/HistoryoftheMonarchy/KingsandQueensofEngland/thetudors/ElizabethI.aspx>

[5] Smith Ernest, *Religion under the Barons of Baltimore* 1896, p. 10

[6] Froude James Anthony, *History of England from the fall of Woolsey to the defeat of the Spanish Armada 1870,* p 480

[7] Op Cit

[10] The Holy Bible, King James Version, Leviticus 18

[11] Grun, Bernard, *The Timelines of History ,* Simon and Shuster 1971, 1505, 1527

[12] *Elizabethan Recusants and the Recusancy Laws*: <www.elizabethan-era.org.uk/elizabethan-recusants-recusancy-laws.htm>

[13] Radoff, Morris L., *The Old Line State: A History of Maryland* 1971, p 1

[14] Bossy, John, *Reluctant Colonists: The English Catholics confront the Atlantic,* p 158 in Quinn, David B., Early Maryland in a Wider World, Wayne State University Press Detroit, Mi. 1982

[15] Smith, *Ernest, Religion under the Barons of Baltimore* 1896, pp 33, 104

[16] Barnes Robert, *Maryland Genealogies* Vol. One

[17] Op Cit, p 32

[18] Bossy, John, *Reluctant Colonists: The English Catholics confront the Atlantic,* pp 32-33 in Quinn, David B., Early Maryland in a Wider World, Wayne State University Press Detroit, Mi. 1982

[19] Smith, *Ernest, Religion under the Barons of Baltimore* 1896, p. 86

[20] Fausz, J. Fredrick, *Merging and Emerging Worlds: Anglo-Indian Interest Groups and the Development of the Seventeenth Century Chesapeake* in Colonial Chesapeake Society, Carr, Lois Green, Morgan, Philip D, and Russo, Jean B., Ed. University of North Carolina Press 1988, pp 59-62

[21] Ibid pp 79, 80

[22] Henretta, James et al. *"Margaret Brent: A Woman of Property "* in America's History 3rd Ed. Worth 1997

[23] Op Cit.

[24] Smith, Ernest, *Religion under the Barons of Baltimore* 1896, p. 318, 319

[25] Andrews, Mathew P, *A History of Maryland*

[26] Bozeman, John L. *History of Maryland*, Vol. 1 p 137

[27] Radoff, Morris L., *The Old Line State: A History of Maryland* 1971, p 8

[28] Ibid p 12

[29] Ibid pp 7, 8

[30] Shoemaker Sandy, *Where Maryland Began...The Colonial History of St. Mary's County 2000*, pp 2,3

[31] Radoff, Morris L., *The Old Line State: A History of Maryland* 1971, p 8

[32] Trigger Bruce G. ed., *Indians of North America*, Smithsonian Institute, V. 15 p 241

Note: For more about William Claiborne and his feud with the Calverts see Hale, Nathaniel Claiborne, *Virginia Venturer: A Historical Biography of William Claiborne 1600 – 1677. 1951*
    For more from the Calvert perspective see Radoff, Morris L., *The Old Line State – A History of Maryland. 1971*

Chapter Two
Drurys to America
1650 - 1700

These then were the conditions our Drury ancestors would have found when they arrived in America. From the earliest records available we can assume that they were first transported to Maryland or Virginia either as indentured servants or in exchange for land grants. Those from Virginia who chose to leave went to Maryland at some later time. We can also assume from the discussion in Chapter One that they were younger sons who did not always share in the family estates and who, even though we can assume they were educated, had little chance to make lives for themselves in England. Contrary to our modern concepts of transport as applying only to convicts or other prisoners who were sent off with no control over their destination, most transportees negotiated their passage. This was an accepted way for those wishing to go to America to obtain passage and pay for it later. [1]

It is clear from historical research that at least seventy percent of the immigrants arrived as servants bound by some sort of contract to serve long enough to pay their passage and earn a profit for all involved in the transaction. They had a good deal of control over where they went and on the length of the indenture. Those with education such as our ancestors would probably have negotiated a shorter term because their services were more valuable than those of ordinary laborers. [2]

By the early seventeenth century the Drury families in England had divided into several branches. Originally Catholic, as all Christians were through the Middle Ages, some converted to Anglican after Henry VIII established the Church of England. Motives for these conversions are unclear but some appear to be political. Many Drury families were wealthy. Others held high public office. Conversion was often the price for retaining power and privileges. Other branches of the family considered this price too high and refused to renounce their faith even though at that time Catholics were considered spies and saboteurs under the control of the Pope in Rome. Some, though not all, Catholics became involved in such plots, but they all came under suspicion and were subject to capricious confiscation of their estates and fortunes. Some of the Drurys who became Anglicans felt in time that even this faith had too many "Popish Trappings" and shifted to more austere beliefs such as Puritanism

William Drury

The earliest date that any Drurys are documented in Maryland is 1650 when William Drury witnessed a lease between Francis Barnes and William Winchester in what was then Kent County in northern Maryland.[3] A second William Drury made a deposition in 1664 when he witnessed the drowning of Charles Hodges in Ann Arundel County.[4] These two men cannot be the same. A person had to be at least 21 years old to witness a legal document. This fact places the birth of the first William at 1629 at the latest. The second William was 26 in 1664 placing his birth in 1638. It is unlikely, though not impossible, that this second William could be the one who was transported into Maryland from Virginia in 1663.[5] If this William was the same one transported the previous year it makes it less likely that he managed to travel to Ann Arundel County, woo, and marry Christian Merriken after 1665. It is most likely that it was this second William Drury who married Christian Merriken and by whom he had a daughter also named Christian.[6]

Christian Merriken, the widow of John Merriken, patented the 50 acre tract known as "Merriken," lying in Broad Neck Hundred in Ann Arundel County shortly before her marriage to William Drury.[7] She predeceased her second husband, however, and Drury afterwards married Alice Savage Gill, widow of John Gill.[8] After William Drury died in 1676, Christian's son by her first marriage, Hugh Merriken, petitioned the court on 29 June 1679, to recover "New Scotland," the 50 acres of land his father patented in 1659. The court found in his favor and the land was returned to him as his right of inheritance. After appraisement the land was found to be of little or no value owing to continual use for more than three years with no care of the soil. It was valued at only 150 pounds of tobacco. The plantation had on it two tobacco houses, one old dwelling house, a small hog house, and an apple orchard.[9] Two main reasons can be cited for this lack of attention to care of the soil. First, it was easier to move to another vacant area than to spend time rotating crops that were not as profitable as tobacco. A second and probably more important reason was that merchants said that fertilizing the land made the tobacco smell like dung and they refused to buy it.

William's will caused considerable controversy. He left the bulk of the estate to his daughter Christian who was to receive her inheritance at age 16. Alice, his widow, who had since remarried, sued to have the will overturned because by law she was entitled to one third of the estate. The suit was settled two years later on 18 June 1678 with Alice and her new husband receiving 6143 pounds of Tobacco as her share of the estate.[10]

Charles Drury

Charles is reported in some genealogies as being born about 1700. There are also references to a Charles Drury being transported by one Benjamin Brasseur to Virginia in 1653 and patenting land in Anne Arundel County Maryland ten years later in 1663.[11] Charles Drury and his family were well to do. He would have been unlikely to resort to being transported in order to obtain passage.[12] There is a third Charles Drury who gave a deposition in 1736 and stated at that time that he was about 60 years old.[13] That document confirms his birth as about 1675 but gives us no clue as to where he was born. This Charles could not be either of the ones mentioned above. It is not clear which of these men is the initial immigrant. If his birth could be confirmed as being in 1700 then this Charles and the one born in 1675 could not be the same person, but it raises the question of whether they could be father and son. At this time no relation has been established.

Recorded events in early eighteenth century Maryland create a timeline that suggests that the Charles Drury born in 1675 may possibly be the one referred to by Andrews and the Rameys.[14] No matter which Charles we accept as the immigrant, there is confusion about the order of his marriages. Both Andrews and the Rameys state that he married Alice Adney, and then a Miss Cole of Sudley after Alice died.[15] There is a Mary Drury who witnessed an appointment of Charles Drury as attorney for Walter Hoxton in 1729, five years before the marriage to Alice Adney.[16] We have no record of what happened to Mary Drury after 1729 if, in fact, this was the same Charles Drury; but she must have died before his second marriage. She could be the Miss Cole (Coale) of Sudley[17] mentioned by Andrews. But the Coales of Sudley were Quakers[18] while Charles Drury's family was Roman Catholic. This raises the question of interfaith marriages in the seventeenth and eighteenth centuries unless there was more than one Cole family in the county. If she is a daughter of William Coale and Hannah as association with Sudley seems to suggest, it is unlikely that her father would approve of such a marriage. William Coale converted sometime in 1657 and became an important Quaker minister throughout the next two decades.[19] Quakers, like Catholics, insisted that their children be brought up and instructed in the faith. This would have created a major conflict between their families.

Moses Adney, deceased husband of Alice who married Charles Drury as her second husband, had to be nearly as old as Charles. At a court in Dec. 1705, Anne Arundel Co., Moses Adney was named Cryer of the Court[20] and would have to have been at least 21 years old at that time to be named to such an office. This places an estimate of his birth as not later than 1684 and probably earlier. He was also Cryer of the Court in 1716 though we don't know if he held this position continuously in the interim. Moses Adney died between 13 Feb 1732 and 18 Oct. 1733 when his wife (since remarried to Charles Drury) administered his estate.[21] Charles Drury (second husband of Alice) died in 1740 when she administered his estate. According to his will[22] she received a life interest in the home plantation "Essex Land" that Charles had purchased in 1736 except for a portion that he had evidently sold. When Alice died, "Essex Land" was to pass to Charles' grandson Edward Boteler, the son of his daughter Sophia.

Five children are mentioned in his will.[23] They are Sarah, Esther, Mary, Charles, and Sophia. Given the fact that Charles and Alice Adney were only married seven years before his death and that Sarah, Esther, Sophia and Mary were all listed as married and that Charles Jr. married in 1739, it can be confidently assumed that these children were by Mary, his first wife. Birth, land, and other records were destroyed in a fire in 1704 but we can estimate from the later records we have that all these children were born probably between about 1700 and 1725.[24] Sarah married Abraham Simmons, Esther was wed to Nathan Selby, Sophia married Charles Boteler, and Mary married someone named Dart. The marriage of Sophia to Charles Boteler establishes the only link to date between the Ann Arundel Drurys and those in St. Mary's County. Sophia's husband Charles was a grandson of Charles Boetler (1635–1686) who patented *Dansbury Hill* in 1665 and lived there the rest of his life. He was both a Surveyer and Assemblyman for St. Mary's County.[25] *Dansbury Hill* was close to *Howard's Mount* where our Drurys lived. He and John Drury (d. 1724) would certainly have known each other.

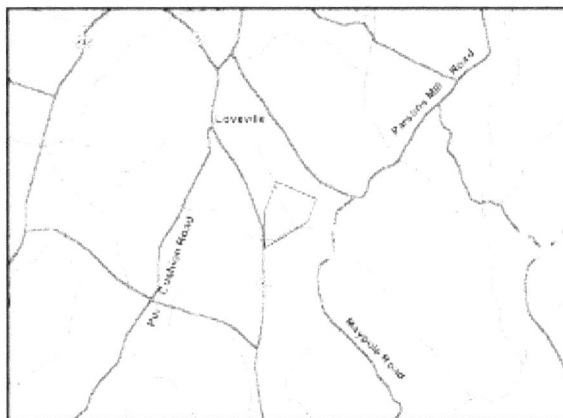

Dansbury Hill[26]

Charles Jr. married twice, first in 1739 to Elizabeth Miles[27] and again in 1749 to Mary. We do not have a surname for Mary though some have speculated that his second wife was Mary Jerningham, daughter of Dr. Henry Jerningham and Catharine. Another possibility suggested by Kathleen Simons, a descendant of this line, is that she could be Mary Childs. There were close associations between the Drury and Childs families for several generations. Charles Jr. accumulated a number of plantations before he died. His will was probated in 1766 mentioning nine children and five separate parcels of land in Prince George, and Anne Arundel Counties.[28] His son William was born in 1750. Another son, Samuel, was born in 1759 but we can assume that the others were born at about two year intervals throughout the 1750s though the order of birth cannot be determined.

Robert Drury

The earliest Drurys we find in St. Mary's County colonial records are Robert Drury, Richard Drury, and William Drury.[31] This reference, while not conclusive, seems to indicate that Robert went first to Virginia before coming to Maryland. William may have been the brother of Robert Drury. Little more is verifiable about William. Robert is listed as immigrating to Maryland. The precise ancestry of Robert Drury who obtained a patent to the plantation in Maryland known as "Dry Docking" is vague, but it is generally conceded that he was the progenitor of most of the Drurys in southern Maryland. There was a John Drury who owned an estate called Dry Docking in England in 1649. John's brother Robert Drury was named administrator of the estate on 4/15/1658 after his brother's death. The two were said to be sons of Robert Drury and Mary Radcliff. However investigation in England in 2000 on this line of Drurys by Tom Stevenson, a Drury researcher, reveals that they are probably not the direct ancestors of our Maryland Drurys. [32]

In an e-mail sent to me on his return he stated:

> "The Docking Drury pedigree chart published by Gerald Hagan in his book, "Dry Docking" and sent in his notes to Drury researchers in the U.S. (some of which are on file in the Ste. Genevieve library in Missouri), has what appears to me to be a key omission. Specifically, all of Robert Drury, Gent. of Docking's sons except one - William – are designated "s. p.", meaning that they died without issue. John, Robert, and Thomas all have this designation. Hagan had copied his chart from the original Docking Parish Register, but did not record these designations.

> Assuming they are shown in the correct sequence on the chart, the youngest son is William, who was born in 1604. It raises additional doubt that any of the older brothers would have traveled to a new world to serve their indenture and receive a land grant as late as 1670. This would lead to the assumption that our Dry Docking Farm Robert is not the son of Robert, Gent. of Docking.

> My wife René [Stevenson] found the Will of Robert Drury, Gent. of Docking from 1624. It mentions wife Mary, sons Thomas and William and several daughters, but has no mention of Robert or John. If they were alive, why were they not mentioned? Based on this will, and the "s. p." designations in the Parish Register alone, I would assume that both Robert and John were dead by the time their father made his will in 1624.

> I have read that Robert Drury, Gent. of Docking's estate was passed to his eldest son John and upon his death in about 1658, to his (John's) brother Robert. I didn't see either mentioned in his will. I don't understand this discrepancy. Are they the sons of Rob't. Drury, gent. or perhaps his nephews?

> I also have read that Robert Drury of Dry Docking Farm in Maryland had a farm of the same name in Norfolk. I did not find a record of it (which doesn't mean much) but the best current historians of the area don't believe that a farm of that name existed. The closest I found was Docking Hall that apparently wasn't owned by Drurys. They did rent land on Docking Manor however."

Donnelly places the birth of Robert Drury, owner of Dry Docking farm in Maryland, as about 1634[33] while Robert Drury, husband of Mary Radcliff, was dead by 1625--nine years before Donnelly's estimate of Robert's birth. In addition, the research in England by Tom Stevenson quoted above indicates that both John and his brother died childless. Tom did find a Robert Drury who had been receiving rents from the village of Docking who could have left when payments were suspended. This scenario is pure conjecture though the dates fit nicely. The problem I have with it is accounting for the children of Robert Drury of "Dry Docking" farm in Maryland. If Robert (immigrant) was transported in 1663 as suggested and since we know that indentured servants were forbidden to marry until their contracts were fulfilled, then how could he have been having children during the decade of the 1660s?

There is another Robert Drury in England that we must consider. He is the Robert Drury who received payments from the Overseers of the poor for the town of Docking in 1659 and 1660. They continued the paying of two shillings to Mr. Robert Drury every week until the said Robert be settled in an Hospital at London as by the aforementioned order of this Court they were bound to do.[34] The entry for 7 May 1663 makes it clear that in future Robert was to receive 40 shillings a year, paid quarterly, so he was still eligible for Poor Law assistance, and his condition was such that payment was to continue for the foreseeable future. Indeed, Robert may by this time have been in a London Hospital. It seems unlikely that a man who was unable to support himself through sickness would embark to Maryland.

Patricia Obrist has suggested the following linkage for St. Mary's County Drurys to the Drurys in England. The only son of Robert Drury and Mary Radcliffe still alive by the mid 1600s was William Drury. She suggests that William was the father of Robert (immigrant) and possibly also the father of Richard and William who were listed by Skordas. We propose the following descendant list but should add that this is entirely speculation. No proof for this linkage exists to our knowledge.

William Drury (b. 1604)
......Richard Drury   b. abt 1630
........William Drury   b: abt. 1632
........Robert Drury   b: abt. 1634 in Norfolk, d: 1702 in St. Mary's Co., MD
.......+ Unknown
.........Robert Drury   b. 1660, d. aft 1727 in St. Mary's Co., MD
..........Margaret Drury b: abt. 1668 in St. Mary's Co., MD, d: bet. 1725 - 1726
...........+John Taunt   b: bef. 1647 in Norfolk, Eng., m: abt. 1684 in St. Mary's Co.,
            d: 1702 in St. Mary's Co., MD
.............James Drury b: abt. 1669, d: aft 1714 in St Mary's Co., MD
............+ Unknown
.............John Drury   b: abt. 1672, d: 1724 in St. Mary's Co., MD
------------+Ann Payne b. bef. 1693, d: bef 1714 in SMC, m: aft 1693 in SMC
.............+Mary Ford b: 1685, d: aft 1724 in SMC, m: bet. 1711 - 1714 in SMC

Another possibility for the identity of Robert (immigrant) arises with the following information: On 24 July 1635 Robert Drury age 16 (which would have made his birth year 1619) was transported to Virginia aboard the "Assurance" sailing from London.[35] This same Robert Drury was reported transported by Robert Freeman though the date (Sep 1638) is different.[36] We presume these entries refer to the same Robert Drury because names of several other transportees appear together with his on both documents. Seven years of indentured servitude was normal payment for passage though this was sometimes negotiable. This would have enabled Robert to pursue his own interests by at least 1642 when he would have been 23 years old, and to have ample time to be married with children by the time he went to Maryland.

On 31 Jan 2003 a website was found on *Rootsweb* tracing the descendants of the Robert Drury transported in 1635.[37] It is apparent from this data that he remained in Virginia and thus is eliminated from our list of candidates. That site traces his ancestry to Robert Drury and Mary Radcliffe in England as well and may have to be modified unless the confusion engendered by Tom Stevenson's discoveries can be resolved.

There were also two men named Robert Drury who were transported by Colonel Edmund Scarborough to Accomack County, Virginia, on the same ship. Scarborough applied for land in 1663 for transporting 29 persons.[38] The two Robert Drurys were among those named in the application. It is unfortunate that no trace has been found of what became of these men in the years between their arrival and 1668 when Robert Drury witnessed the will of George Reynolds. One of them may be our Robert but no evidence has yet been found to document this. Another Robert Drury was listed in "Catholic Records Society Miscellanies -V" as a convicted recusant (one who refused to give up his Catholic faith) in the Village of Salthouse in England about 13 miles from Dry Docking. He would also be a candidate for immigration after his lands were confiscated.[39] No matter which Robert we select, or even if our Robert is none of those mentioned above, we are able to say with certainty that he was in Maryland by January 28, 1669, when he witnessed the will of Robert Joyner. We then see a continuing series of entries in the Provincial records until 1694.[40] These entries partially document his life as a respected friend and neighbor who aided those around him in whatever ways he could.

Skordas tells us Robert immigrated to Maryland in 1670, but he must have been traveling back and forth between Virginia and Maryland on a regular basis and was obviously familiar with the St. Clement's Bay and Breton's Bay areas. His friend Robert Joyner was established in Maryland early. Like many others, Joyner was transported into Maryland as a servant by 1651 at the age of 17.[41] After completing his period of servitude he obtained 100 acres of "Scotland" from the Calverts.[42] This land had previously been the property of Walter Peake but had reverted to the Proprietors after Peake was hanged for murder.[43] Robert Joyner's plantation, Scotland, was only about five miles from the site where Robert Drury established "Dry Docking".

Carr reports that Robert apparently lived near St. Mary's City and was probably a carpenter as well as a farmer. He sold a chest with lock and key to George Bayton in exchange for a pig and some "dutch planke." Bayton was living on Thomas Evans' plantation "Colebrook" that was adjacent to "Dry Docking" and "Dry Docking Addition".

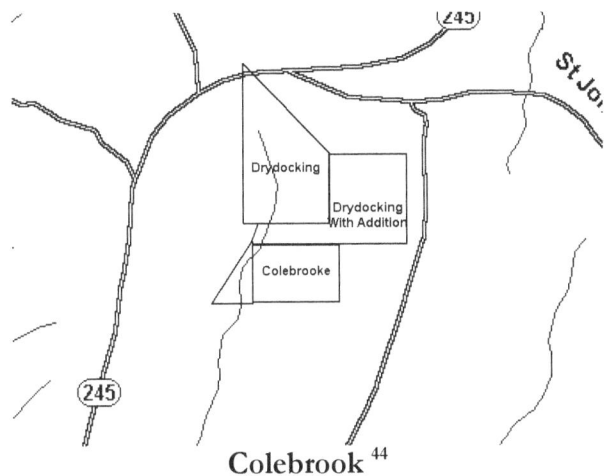

Colebrook [44]

"...He (Bayton) bought a chest of Robert Drury for a sowe shoate and as much "dutch planke" which he borrowed of Evans to make Robert Drury another chest for which planke Bayton promised Evans he could have the chest bought of Drury if he did not repay. Bayton had one sowe and three barrows remaining when he died. Bayton never had a mare that they know of and that when he died he had no cow neither nor never had either cow or calf since the great mortality of cattell. Bayton owed them one HHD of tobacco for his first year's accommodation. For trouble and charge during his sickness one HHD. To Robert Drury for making his coffin £100. To William Meekin for digging his grave £100, to a shroud £100, to expenses at his buryall and three days attendance on the corps by company that while in the house which I believe cost mee 400 lbs. of tobacco – £200. [45]

It is likely that Robert lived on his Dry Docking plantation and occasionally traveled to St. Mary's City for news and supplies. Dry Docking was only about 15 miles north of St. Mary's City near Leonardtown. Even with a family to help him, growing tobacco was a full time job requiring dawn to dusk labor and left little time for him to be exclusively a carpenter. These early settlers had to employ many skills they might not have used in England. There were simply not enough skilled artisans in Maryland, and people had to make do with what they could create on their own.

These Drury families do not appear to be among the colonial elite. Robert (immigrant) was able to vote during the 1600s because of his ownership of "Dry Docking." We have a record of him signing a petition in 1694 opposing the move of the State Capital from St. Mary's city to Annapolis.[46] This appears to have been strictly along religious lines with Catholics voting to retain St. Mary's city and Protestants favoring the move that would place the Capital in a more central location for Protestant citizens. Robert's ownership of land during this period of Catholic influence gave him status though he was not involved with the government. He also acted as a witness for a number of wills for his neighbors. By the time his children had grown, times and their situations had changed. For whatever reason Robert's land had been disposed of and his sons were leasing land from their wealthier neighbors. This does not mean they were without influence. Through marriages and friendship as well as their common religion they were associated with a number of influential families. Robert received personalty in the will of Edward Clarke in 1675[47]

25

that shows some sort of association. Edward had previously been commissioned as County Clerk, an important and influential position. Additional examples could be found, but this illustrates the interconnections of such families whose association with other Catholics permitted them to have access to the centers of power in spite of their relatively modest means.

In spite of his ownership of Dry Docking and his registration of a cattle mark in 1672, Robert's life was not easy. 1667 saw what was called "The Dreadful Hurry Cane." This storm destroyed eighty percent of the tobacco and corn crops and blew down fifteen thousand houses in Maryland and Virginia.[48] There was a "Great Blizzard" in 1673 that killed over half the cattle in the colony.[49] Cattle at this time were not confined but were allowed to roam. They were expected to survive on their own until the owner caught them and brought them in for fattening before slaughter. Most of the cattle in the colony died from exposure and starvation during this extremely harsh winter.

This was undoubtedly the *"great mortality of cattell"* mentioned earlier in Lois Green Carr's notes concerning George Bayton. We have no idea whether or how many cattle Robert lost as well. Tobacco farmers in both Maryland and Virginia suffered not only from the usual weather related problems of farming but also from overproduction and a consequent glut of the market.

Tobacco prices were depressed during most of this entire period. Much of the time it hardly paid to plant a crop. On a typical small farm of the time the average crop would be about one thousand pounds of merchantable tobacco. Out of this, nearly eight hundred pounds went to the landlord for rent leaving only two hundred pounds that the farmer was able to sell for himself. On average this amount would yield about £1 13S 4p to support the family for the entire year. Efforts in Britain and the colonies to remedy the situation only made things worse. Unfortunately laws that were passed mainly benefited the merchants and officials in England often to the detriment of the planters.

The following paragraph though taken from *"An Economic History of Virginia"* applied equally to Maryland. Both Colonies (especially Maryland's Western Shore) could be considered a single economic unit dominated by the Tobacco trade.

> *"In 1682 tobacco was selling at the lowest rates,*
> *and had been selling at those rates for a number*
> *of years, with the result of reducing the people to*
> *extremities. In 1683, a prodigious crop was planted,*
> *and as the production of the previous year had been*
> *so much shortened, tobacco now commanded more*
> *remunerative returns: in consequence of this fact, the*
> *inhabitants of the Colony were, in 1684, contented*
> *and peaceful, the insurrectionary impulse having been*
> *entirely allayed. ..."* [50]

In spite of the above quote, crops were subject to great variations in weather. There was a hurricane in August of 1683 that undoubtedly did much damage to the crops due to be harvested that fall.[51] Calamities such as this happened regularly over the next 150 years causing much localized damage each time.

A question we could ask is, why did Robert settle near Breton Bay? There were probably a number of reasons for his choice. By 1670 available land farther south near St. Mary's City was becoming scarce. Even in the Breton Bay area most of the land along the rivers was taken. A major reason though was the fact that there were a number of other Catholic settlers nearby including his friend Robert Joyner. The presence of a Catholic Chapel on nearby Newtown Neck was an additional factor though there are records indicating that services were also held at "Scotland."[52] Robert and his family would have wanted to be near their church.

Jesuit priests began working in this area from the beginning of settlement and had control of large tracts of land. In 1662 and 1663 two prominent Catholics, Thomas Mathews and Cuthbert Fenwick, conveyed separately three important manors to Henry Warren of St. Inigoes, unquestionably for church purposes as Jesuit holdings, although no reference is made to this in the deeds which were not recorded until 1666. On July 12, 1663, Fenwick conveyed to Warren the manor of St. Inigoes containing 2000 acres and St. George's Island, both lying in St. Mary's County. The deeds were recorded March 22, 1666.[53]

Luke Gardiner on St. Clements Manor was also a prominent Catholic official who had influence and contacts within the Colonial government. A number of other Catholic settlers, people like Edward Clark and John Graves, either were or soon would be, neighbors. These new settlers had to depend on each other to survive. In England kinsmen provided this aid, but for the most part there were none in Maryland. The Church community took the place of these missing relatives.

In speaking of church groups Michael Graham gives us some idea of what these groups were like.

> " An examination of the communities these groups established
> shows how neighbors in early Chesapeake society became
> substitutes for kin networks left behind in England. Moreover
> these communities, grounded in faith, provided their members
> with a strong sense of cohesion and identity that often helped
> to mitigate the hardships of early Chesapeake life." [54]

We don't know if Robert Drury and his family worshipped at the Newtown chapel on Medley's Neck, or if he maintained ties to one farther south at St. Inigoes. Eighteenth century records indicate there were Drurys living near both locations. Peter Drury, a grandson of Robert (immigrant), was in Beaverdam Manor in Newtown Hundred along with his uncle James. His brother John moved to St. Inigoes Hundred. The best we can say at present is that Robert was not listed as a parishioner at Newtown in 1674 when Luke Gardiner died.[55]

Robert Drury was also, in all probability, beginning to think of the future or, at least he would begin to do so within a few years. He would need additional land in order to provide economically viable sized farms to leave to his sons. This area was still open enough in the last half of the seventeenth century to enable him to patent additional land nearby at reasonable cost.

Lorena Walsh states,

> *" ...In families with more than one child, prudent fathers took up
> additional land off the manor for the majority of the children and
> designated the manor tract for one child only. Good undeveloped land
> in St. Mary's County remained a modest investment for anyone with a
> little spare capital or access to credit, and most landowners took up
> undeveloped tracts as an inheritance for their male, and sometimes
> for their female, offspring."* [56]

In the 1680's the Drury family was beginning to prosper. We know Robert patented an additional 100 acres in 1683 that he called Dry Docking Addition.[57] He and others probably were scrambling to obtain additional land before the Proprietor increased the price. Everyone knew that the caution money of 100 pounds of Tobacco per hundred acres was due to be raised in 1684 to 240 pounds.[58] Presumably this land was distributed to his sons. His education stood him in good stead as an appraiser for a number of estates in Southern Maryland. He appraised the estate of Thomas Thomas (August 12, 1671)[59] and gave his oath about Robert Joyner's will the following year that he had witnessed in 1669.[60] He had a cattle mark issued to him in 1671, so he obviously was considering or already engaged in farming. In 1675 he received a legacy from the will of his neighbor Edward Clarke, and in 1680 he received a payment from the estate of Gregory Rouse. The last definite record we find for Robert (immigrant) was a reference dated 13 October 1694 when he signed a petition to keep the capital at St. Mary's city.[61]

By the 1690's the Drury family was becoming influential. Robert was listed as "constable" which was an influential position in the colony. His son, Robert, may have been acting as an emissary for the colonial government even though he did not have the advantage of a formal education. In the documents included below we see that his son had traveled as far as New York, New England and Penobscot in Maine, and was in that area for a long enough time to be familiar with the local Indians.

When on 9 March 1692/3 Robert DRURY made the deposition that he, Robert DRURY, was "aged thirty two years or thereabouts," he was speaking about the identity of a certain French Indian. Robert stated that "he was brought in the sight of the supposed Monsr. CASTEENE [formerly the Gov. of Canada] of Pennobscott beyond Penciquid upon oath taken before me Saith that he is not Monsr. CASTEENE, but some other Person for he the said Robert DRURY, knoweth Mr. CASTEENE very well but never saw this Frenchman before nor any such marks as it was reported to be on his Breast & further saith not.
        Robert DRURY
    Sworn before me the day and date above said. Casparus August HERMAN."
    Robert DRURY of Caecil County was called in and examined...[62](This may be the same Robert Drury, but this is not definite). Due to the testimony of Robert and a Henry

Thompson, the council decided to write to the governors of New York and Virginia, and set in action plans to make three forts to protect themselves from the strange Indians.

No record of a will for Robert (immigrant) has survived, and the first records we have of the properties his presumed sons occupied show that they were near but not the same as his initial patents. How they came to be at those locations and the sequence of transactions concerning members of the family remains a mystery. This seems to be the last real opportunity to purchase additional land by the Drurys. By 1717 land prices had doubled again to 480 pounds of Tobacco per hundred acres effectively putting it out of reach.[63] Robert apparently disposed of his holdings though descendants lived on some of these parcels.

The house he initially built would have been spartan and more primitive than anything he might have been used to in England. It would have been a single room perhaps 10 by 20 feet with a large fireplace either in the center opposite the door or at one end. This fireplace was large enough to hang iron cooking pots inside over the flames. Windows were usually described as "unglazed," which meant an opening in the wall with a solid shutter to close out winter winds.[64]

His household furnishings illustrate vividly the rude simplicity of his life. A pot or pan and a skillet with a large spoon and bowl for serving probably comprised his kitchen utensils. Only ingenuity in using the available natural materials enabled his family to cook and eat in a civilized manner. Dried gourds took the place of cups and glasses; larger varieties served as bowls. Woodenware substituted for plates and platters and, in place of forks, human fingers did the job in a manner medieval peasants would have fully approved. Much of the time meals consisted of a stew containing a few vegetables and whatever meat was available. The floor was plain earth smoothed and tramped flat and, until the family had time to build beds, they slept rolled in blankets on the dirt floor. The roof would have been some type of thatch that was easy to construct. With no light except from the fireplace and occasionally a few candles, activities were pretty much restricted to daylight hours.[65]

Typical Utensils [66]

When improvement became possible he might have constructed a bed frame and tied strips of leather across it to make a support for a straw-stuffed mattress. There were usually no tables or chairs. His house could hold little more than essential furniture if the family was to have room to move around.[67] This existence was a great let down from what the family would have been used to in England, but we cannot be sure just what his circumstances were before coming to America. We can only assume that lack of opportunity and religious persecution at home propelled him into this life-changing move.

If his housing was lacking, however, his diet was not. Within a generation the average colonist was taller and stronger than his counterpart in England. This has generally been ascribed to a more varied and nutritious diet. Food would have been plentiful with the abundance of wild game. White-tailed deer were plentiful. Raccoon, opossum and squirrel, as well as land birds such as quail and turkey, offered a variety of meat over the course of a year. Many species of duck migrated through the area and were also taken when opportunity offered.[68] Most game like this was reserved in England for the Lord of the Manor and would not be available to yeomen. Many colonists could not afford to take the time to hunt. Instead they employed local Indians to hunt for them. This helped both groups. The colonists could concentrate on their crops and the Indians, who were excellent hunters, turned their skills to advantage in cooperating with the settlers. In addition we can assume that our Robert also kept cattle, swine and probably chickens that were referred to as "Dunghill Fowls." He applied for and received a cattle mark in 1672.[69] This would have been typical of the time. English settlers generally preferred domestic meat if enough was available. In addition, cattle and hogs could provide a supplemental source of income if there was a dip in the price of tobacco. Much meat was sold to ship owners and sent to the West Indies.[70] These animals could also fend better for themselves in the unfenced farms of the time. Robert would certainly not have had time to herd them or confine them with fences. There was simply too much work to do building a cabin and outbuildings, clearing the land, and tending the tobacco crop.

Growing tobacco was, and for the most part still is, hard brutal labor-intensive work. The process from beginning to harvest usually took seventeen months. Early colonists cleared the ground and cultivated the crops with hoes. Many, when they cleared the land, often left the tree stumps intact and planted around them. Later, when time permitted, they might dig out the stumps by hand. The growing season started in February or March when the tiny tobacco seeds were planted in a small patch of ground called a seedbed. As the seeds began to grow, they would have to be watched carefully. While the plants grew in seedbeds, the fields were prepared. When the tobacco plants were large enough, they were transplanted into the fields. The plants would take the rest of the summer to grow.

As the tobacco grew in the fields, it would have to be checked quite often. Weeds that grew around the plants had to be pulled, and sometimes plants might have to be watered if there was little rain. Most importantly, farmers had to make sure that tobacco worms did not eat their tobacco plants. These worms fed on the leaves of the tobacco as it grew. The only way that farmers found to get rid of the worms was to go through the fields and pick them off the leaves, one at a time. Plants had to be checked continually until they were ready to be harvested. Late summer or fall was harvest time for the tobacco crop. The entire stalk of each tobacco plant was cut at the bottom and allowed to wilt in the fields for a few hours. Then, a hole was cut in each stalk so that it could be threaded onto a long stick, called a tobacco stake. Perhaps as many as six or eight stalks could be put on each stake. These stakes were then hung in tobacco barns to dry for six to ten weeks. Once they were dry, the plants were taken down and the leaves were stripped from the stalks. Planters made sure to do this on a rainy day so the leaves were not so dry that they would crumble and break. The leaves were bundled into "hands." A hand was a bunch of ten to twenty leaves wrapped together. These hands were packed into large casks called hogsheads and readied for shipping. These hogsheads could hold between 300 and 500 pounds of tobacco, depending on how well they were packed. Once the crop was grown and harvested, it was shipped to England.[71]

An old Tobacco barn on Dry Docking Farm. This may be the oldest surviving tobacco barn in St. Mary's County. It may have been built as early as the 1820s.[72]

Even today almost everything done in growing and harvesting tobacco is handwork. There was no labor-saving machine like the cotton gin for tobacco. Robert would have planted some Indian corn and a few vegetables in a kitchen garden, but this would have been secondary and probably tended by the younger children.

Robert's wife and those of his sons would have lived lives typical of the times. By 1700 most women married at age fifteen or sixteen and one in five was pregnant when they married.[73] We cannot however make judgments about the Drury wives since we don't even know who they were. Nor do we have statistics on the percentage of Catholic girls who were pregnant when they married. Many girls dreaded marriage because they feared the hazards of pregnancy. We can be certain that they were a hardy lot if they survived multiple pregnancies and the diseases prevalent at the time.

Many women had to help their husbands in tending the tobacco crop in addition to caring for their children. A description of a typical colonial housewife can be found in the following quote.

> *"She is a very civil woman and shows nothing of ruggedness or immodesty in her carriage, yet she will carry a gunn in the woods and kill deer, Turkeys and other game, shoot down cattle, catch and tye hoggs, knock down beeves with an axe and perform the most manfull exercises as well as most men in these parts."*[74]

The necessary separation of plantations in seventeenth and eighteenth century St. Mary's County limited social contacts though the situation gradually improved over time. Most people had regular contact only with neighbors living not more than about two and a half miles away--the distance a person could walk conveniently in an hour or so.[75] This remained generally true even into the eighteen hundreds. When help was needed in building or in tending crops, it was expected that one's neighbors would help. In turn, when they needed assistance, that help was reciprocated. Additionally, opportunities for socializing were scarce in the isolation of these plantations. Planters and their families took every opportunity available to get together and visit. Durand of Dauphine, a Huguenot visitor to the Chesapeake area, complained of this stating,

> *"The land is so rich and fertile that when a man has fifty acres of ground, two men servants, a maid, and some cattle, neither he nor his wife do anything but visit among their neighbors."*[75]

Social contacts for wives were even more restricted than for their husbands. Pregnancy and the care of infants and toddlers made travel to neighbors farther than a few miles from home difficult. Husbands had a slightly greater range of contacts but the necessity to tend crops restricted their ability to travel as well. As a consequence everyone made good use of whatever social situations were available. The most regular, of course, was the Sunday church service. Lorena Walsh says,

> *"On Court days, Saturday afternoons and especially on Sundays, neighbors got together for more organized recreations. This usually*

32

meant more smoking and drinking (activities in which, Durand noted, the women were foremost), perhaps singing and dancing, sometimes political discussions, and very often games. Visiting after church was an established practice. Those who lacked either the opportunity or the inclination to attend Sunday services nonetheless met on Sunday for convivial entertainment."[76]

This practice of church services followed by a "Church Social" for lack of a more precise phrase continued even in the nineteenth century after many families had migrated farther west into Kentucky.

Ben Webb tells us:

"Five miles to church was considered exceptionally convenient. All, or nearly all, walked; the women as well as the men plodding along the road with shoeless feet. Some of the former, however, carried in their reticules pairs of coarse cloth slippers, fashioned by themselves, to be put on when they came in sight of the church. Their tiring-room was ordinarily in the shadow of a clump of trees in the vicinity of the chapel, where their simple toilets were made, and whence, with their cotton bonnets pulled closely over their faces, they marched demurely to the church. Under other circumstances, the natural curiosity of the sex would have indicated itself by furtive glances directed toward their neighbors; but here and now, every sentiment that had not reference to the Great King whose earthly tabernacle they were approaching, was smothered in their hearts, and neither turning to the right nor to the left, they entered the chapel with bowed heads and silently took their places. "Service over, and beyond the precincts of the church, absorbed recollection in the minds of these unsophisticated beauties gave place to the mingled feelings that ordinarily prompt human action. They were still modest and sedate, to be sure, but the "return from church" was always for them a pleasant time. Then it was that the family groups found themselves minus the young men of their own households and plus those of their neighbors. Not infrequently on such occasions, and under the eyes of observant and well-pleased parents, words were spoken that bound young hearts together for life."[77]

As Walsh again states,

"For many only the inevitable rituals of birth, marriage, and death provided a justifiable excuse for a break in the daily work routine. All the talking, feasting, drinking, singing, and dancing that strength permitted had to be packed into a few hours or, at most a day or two. With few other outlets available, the resulting celebration or

commiseration doubtless served as an essential emotional outlet for hard working farm families who otherwise had only chance opportunities for gathering together."[78]

We can imagine Robert and his family, on a frigid January Sunday, sailing up St. Clement's Bay, muffled from head to toe to protect themselves from the cold, on their way to Scotland Plantation to worship and visit with their friends after the service. The wind whistles around the sail and mast with perhaps snow flurries or freezing spray from the bay whipping around their cloaks and shawls. Nothing, however, short of a major storm would have kept these devout Catholics from this weekly ritual.

[1] Menard, Russell R., *British Migration* in Colonial Chesapeake Society, Ed. Lois Green Carr, Phillip D. Morgan, and Jean B. Russo pp 106-109

[2] Ibid

[3] Archives of Maryland, *Kent Co. Court Proceedings 1645-1656* Vol. 54, p 13

[4] *Archives of Maryland* Vol. 19 374-375

[5] Skordas, Gustav, *The Early Settlers of Maryland 1633-1680*, Liber 5, Folio 607; Transported 1663

[6] Culver, Francis B., Ed. *Society of Colonial Wars in Maryland* Vol. 2, p 167 Heritage Books 1940 (reprinted 2002)

[7] Christian Merrican's first husband, John Merrican, died in 1663. She patented "Merrican" in 1665. She would not have done this in her own name if she were married. My notes state she married William after a widowhood of several years. Their daughter had to be born after 1665 when she was still a widow. Therefore the daughter had to be not older than 10 or 11 years old when William died.

[8] The daughter Christian died sometime between 22 August 1676 when she received a bequest in her father's will, and 29 June 1679 when her half brother Hugh Merriken petitioned to recover "New Scotland" the property his father John Merriken had patented when he immigrated in 1669.

[9] Archives of Maryland, *Proceedings of the Court of Chancery 1669-1679* Vol. 51, P 3

[10] Archives of Maryland, *Proceedings of the Court of Chancery 1669-1679* Vol. 67, P 407

[11] Greer, George C., *Early Virginia Immigrants, 1623 – 1666*

[12] Ramey, *Immigrant Ancestors of Maryland*

[13] *Prince George's County Land Records 1739-1743* Liber Y, p 18

[14] Andrews, M.P.,*Ter'y History of Maryland Vol I*, p 757; Ramey, *Immigrant Ancestors of Maryland*; Note: This Charles may have fathered a son named Charles born in 1700. The possibility also exists that Charles (b. 1700) and Charles (b. 1675) are the same person with only the birth dates confused. So far no record has been found confirming that Charles (b. 1700) is a separate person. Nor does any record suggest that they are one and the same. If they are different individuals we must refer to Charles (b. 1700) as Charles Jr.

[15] Andrews, M.P.,*Ter'y History of Maryland Vol I*, p 757

[16] *Land Records of Prince George's County, MD*, Liber M Page 450

[17] Sudley is a post village in Anne Arundel County. Post Villages are incorporation communities, population places, rather than cities, towns or census designated areas. Kathi Jones-Hudson, http://www.usgwtombstones.org/

[18] Kelly, *Quakers in the Founding of Anne Arundel County*; In Colonial times "Sudley" aka "Cumberstone" was south of the Old Quaker Burying Ground on Old Sudley Road. It was built before 1683 by Richard Arnold, a Quaker, and it was held by Quakers until sold to Mr. & Mrs. Wm. Kelly in 1942. "Cumberstone" was granted to Capt. John Cumber in 1659. The family that was connected to the Quakers of this area usually spelled their name Coale. William Coale, son of William Coale by 2d wife Hannah, married Elizabeth Sparrow on 30 July 1689. This William Coale had a son William, b. 11 Apr. 1697, who married Sarah White, Samuel, b. 4 Aug. 1701, and Thomas, b. 1705/6. Thomas did not marry till 3 Dec. 1730, so he would probably have not been the father of the wife of Charles Drury. Marriage dates are unavailable for William and Samuel.

[19] Graham, Michael, *Meetinghouse and Chapel* in Colonial Chesapeake Society Ed. Lois Green Carr, Phillip D. Morgan and Jean B. Russo p 254

[20] Roth, Marilyn, *email message of 10/20/2000*

[21] MSA S 1161-1-7 1/4/5/44, inventory of Mr. Moses ADNEY, AA, 13 Feb 1732 & 18 Oct. 1733, by Alice, w/o Chas. DRURY.

[22] *Maryland Calendar of Wills Vol. 8 1738-1743 p 198; Maryland Probate Records, Prerogative Court Abstracts, 1738 – 1744* pp 38, 93

[23] Ibid

[24] Roth, Marilyn, *email message of 10/20/2000*

[25] Dennis Witmer <dawitmer@aol.com> Charles Boteler (1635-1686), was a surveyor and assemblyman, of St. Mary's County

[26] Courtesy of Peter Himmelheber

[27] Maryland Probate Records, Maryland Calendar of Wills Vol. 7 1732-1738, p 138

[28] Maryland Calendar of Wills, pg 103; Anne Arundel County Inventory and Accounts 92.259; Abst. of Inv. of Perogative Court. of MD, 1766-1769, p. 20

[31] Skordas, Gustav, *The Early Settlers of Maryland, 1633-1680*

[32] Stevenson, Thomas, Electronic

[33] Donnelly, Mary Louise, *Colonial Period Tenants and Owners of Beaverdam Manor* 1998, p 95

[34] Norfolk Order book 1657-1668

[35] Hotten , John Camden *The Original Lists of Persons of Quality ... and Others who went from Great Britain to the American Plantations - 1600 - 1700* (London 1874)

[36] Nugent, Nell Marion, *Cavaliers and Pioneers* Bk. 2 p 207

[37] Storey, L. E., (http://worldconnect.rootsweb.com/cgi-bin/igm.cgi?op=DESC&db=lestory.htm)

[38] Nugent, Nell Marion, *Cavaliers and Pioneers,* Bk. 4, p 425

[39] Catholic Record Society, *Miscellanea V* London 1909 p 296

[40] 1668: Witnessed Will of George Reynolds, Cotton, Jane Baldwin, *Maryland Calendar of Wills*, Vol. 1 p 46; 1669: Witnessed Will of Robert Joyner, Cotton, Jane Baldwin, *Maryland Calendar of Wills*, Vol. 1 p 71; 1670: Immigrated to Maryland, Skordas, Gustave, *The Early Settlers of Maryland, 1633-1680*; 1672: Robert Drury obtained Cattle Mark, *Index to Maryland Colonial Judgements*, Liber II 1669 – 1672; 1674: Robt. Drewry signed a bill of 1468 pounds of tobacco to David Norrey, Dorman, John Frederick, "Westmoreland Co. Virginia Deeds, Patents, Etc. 1665-1677 -- Part Two, v.6, p.179a); 1675: Received Personalty from Edward Clark, Cotton, Jane Baldwin, *Maryland Calendar of Wills*, Vol. 1 p 185; 1683: Dry Docking Addition surveyed for Robert Drury, 1704 *Rent Rolls, Chronicles of St. Mary's,* Vol. 21, No. 5; 1694: Robert Drury signed petition to keep Capital at St. Maries City, Archives of Maryland on line: *Assembly Proceedings 20 Sept. – 18 Oct., 1694* Vol. 19 pp 71 – 77

[41] Peden, Henry C. Jr., *Maryland Deponents* Vol. 1 p 109

[42] Land Office, Maryland State Archives, *Land Patents*, Vol. 19 pp 71-77

[43] Thomas, James Walter, *Chronicles of Colonial Maryland*, Google Books p 91 : "Escheats, as they existed in early Maryland, may be defined to be the reversion to the Proprietary, of the land granted, upon the conviction of the tenant of crime, or upon his death without heirs"

[44] Courtesy of Peter Himmelheber, Electronic

[45] Carr, Lois Green, {excerpt from MSA sc54094 0306-3 Lois Green Carr research notes for George Bayton} {TP 13:190-91, 200}

[46] 1694: Archives of Maryland on line: *Assembly Proceedings 20 Sept. – 18 Oct., 1694* Vol. 19 pp 71 – 77 Robert Drury signed petition to keep capital at St. Maries City

[47] Cotton, Jane Baldwin, Maryland Calendar of Wills, Vol. 1 p 185

[48] Bruce, Philip Alexander, *"An Economic History of Virginia"* Macmillan 1896 p 395

[49] Ibid p 372

[50] Ibid p 407,408

[51] Ibid p 345

[52] Maryland Archives Vol. 41, p 522

[53] Proceedings of the Provincial Court of Maryland 1666-1670, Volume LVII Preface 55

[54] Graham, Michael, *Meeting house and Chapel: Religion and Community in 17th Century Maryland*, in Colonial Chesapeake Society, Ed. Lois Green Carr, Phillip D. Morgan, and Jean B. Russo p 243

[55] Ibid

[56] Walsh, Lorena, *Community Networks in the early Chesapeake*, in Colonial Chesapeake Society, Ed. Lois Green Carr, Phillip D. Morgan, and Jean B. Russo p 216

[57] Land Office, Maryland State Archives, *Rent Rolls* (Patents 25:36); *Proceedings of the Council of Maryland 1692 – 1694*, pp. 459-462

[58] Gould, Clarence P., *Economic History of Maryland 1720–1765*, PhD Dissertation Johns Hopkins University 1911 p3

[59] Maryland State Archives Thomas Thomas appraisal 1671

[60] Cotton, Jane Baldwin, *Maryland Calendar of Wills*, Vol. 1 p 71

[61] Archives of Maryland on line: *Assembly Proceedings 20 Sept. – 18 Oct., 1694* Vol. 19 pp 71 – 77

[62] Maryland Archives VIII 460-461,467 book of Depositions , p 55

[63] Gould, Clarence, *Economic History of Maryland 1720 – 1765*, PhD Dissertation Johns Hopkins University 1911 p3

[64] Horn, James, *Adapting to a New World: A comparative study of Local Society in England and Maryland 1650 – 1700*, in Colonial Chesapeake Society, Ed. Lois Green Carr, Phillip D. Morgan, and Jean B. Russo p 152; Land, Aubrey C., *The Planters of Colonial Maryland* in Maryland Historical Magazine Vol. 67 # 1 p 122

[65] Ibid p 166; Main, Gloria, Tobacco Colony, pp 174,175

[66] Hawke, David Freeman, Everyday life in Early America Harper 1988

[67] Ibid p 215

[68] Land, Aubrey C., "*The Planters of Colonial Maryland"*, in *Maryland Historical Magazine* Vol. 67 # 1 p 124

[69] *Index to Maryland Colonial Judgements*, Liber II 1669 – 1672

[70] Hawke, David Freeman, *Everyday life in Early America*, Harper 1988 p 39

[71] *Economic Aspects of Tobacco* URL: http://www.tobacco.org/history/colonialtobacco.html , p 3

[72] Stevenson, Thomas, *The Dry Docking Farm* (Private Pub.) 2001

[73] Carr, Lois Green and Walsh, Lorena, S., "*The Planter's Wife: The experience of white women in Seventeenth Century Maryland*" in *William and Mary Quarterly* 3rd series Vol. 34 # 4 p 564; http://www.jstor.org/stable/2936182

[74] Land, Aubrey C., "*Planters of Colonial Maryland*" in *Maryland Historical magazine* Vol. 67 p 117; original in *Virginia Magazine of History and Biography* Vol. 1, p 21

[75] Walsh, Lorena, S., *Community Networks in the Early Chesapeake*, in Colonial Chesapeake Society, Ed. Lois Green Carr, Phillip D. Morgan, and Jean B. Russo p 225

[75] Ibid. p 233; Original in Durand of Dauphine, *A Huguenot exile in Virginia or, voyage of a Frenchman exiled for his religion*, Editor Chinard, Gilbert, (New York 1934) p 111

[76] Ibid

[77] Webb, Ben, *Centenary of Catholicity in Kentucky* pp 81-83

[78] Op cit p 235

Chapter Three

The Early Years
1700 - 1750

British policy at this time was to make her colonies totally dependent on the mother country. Laws were passed making it illegal to export tobacco to any country except England without first passing through English ports and paying custom duties to England. When planters began avoiding this by exporting to other colonies before shipping to Europe, the law was amended to include duties payable to England for such transfers. It was estimated in 1672 that losses from this illegal trade (especially with Holland) was about £10,000 sterling. Most of these losses were from Maryland and Virginia.[1] This disregard of the law was driven by economics. Dutch ships were much more economically operated and therefore could underbid English merchants and ship owners in carrying the leaf to Europe. The English sought to create a monopoly in order to maximize their profits and the custom revenues to the King. This even went so far as to prohibit growing of tobacco in England itself. Rogers tells us "Tobacco was produced in large quantities in Gloucester, Devon, Somerset, and Oxford shires and its quality is represented to have been so fine, that it was frequently sold as coming from Spanish provinces."[2] Spain at that time had some of the finest quality available. This continued until as late as 1677 in spite of attempts by constables and even the militia to enforce laws prohibiting its production in Britain.

For over a decade the greediness of British merchants and ship owners kept the planters in the colonies almost in poverty. Some were even forced to sell some of their land in order to pay their bills in England. It was not until 1684 as mentioned in Chapter Two that tobacco prices rebounded due to the poor crop in 1682 that reduced the amount available for shipment. Several times in the previous decades proposals were advanced to reduce or suspend production but they were never implemented. Various objections were raised but the underlying motive was always the fact that too many people would lose the huge amounts of money being made from the trade.

In the following years however new obstacles were placed in the path of prosperity. England went to war with France in 1689 and again in 1702, and hostilities created new problems in getting essential goods from Europe and in exporting the tobacco to pay for them. Much of the Maryland tobacco was sold to France. During the American Revolutionary War, tobacco helped finance the revolution by serving as collateral for loans the Americans borrowed from France.[3]

The wars created additional hardship for the colonists because they were forced to defend themselves against Indian raids encouraged by the Canadian French. To the physical danger of being attacked was also added economic distress. The Calverts refused to contribute any money for the defense of the colony. In consequence the people were forced to support efforts to defend themselves in addition to maintaining payments to the proprietor.

This was not the only hardship suffered by the Drurys. As we know, the family was Roman Catholic. Under the Catholic Calverts they were freer to worship as they wished than would have been the case in Anglican England. France was also a Roman Catholic country. This fact produced a great deal of suspicion about English Catholics and revived Protestant prejudices that had never completely disappeared. There is no evidence that any Drury was involved with the French or their Indian allies. In fact, Robert Drury, who we think was John's brother and a son of Robert (immigrant), was actively involved as an emissary of Maryland to Albany, New York and New England to coordinate resistance efforts between the colonies against the French and the Indians.[4] Some of the Protestant factions increased suspicions by spreading rumors that Catholic colonists were secretly helping the French and provoking Indian attacks. A few influential Protestant colonists including Josias Fendall and John Coode, wishing to replace the Calverts and create a Protestant Royal Colony, were behind most of these efforts.

Many French Canadians, especially from Nova Scotia, were allowed to immigrate to America after the English took over Canada. Maryland was one of the few places that would accept them. Even so prejudice made things so difficult that many of them moved on to Louisiana where they later became known as Cajuns. By the middle of the century there were even prominent Marylanders like Henry Jerningham who helped by investigating the possibility of relocating them into the Louisiana Territory.[5] Not until the 1760s were Catholics even allowed to build churches.

Nonetheless, suspicion against Catholics remained and attempts at persuasion had little effect. This was particularly true since Protestants, once they assumed power under the Royal Governor, now had charge of the government. Many of the freedoms permitted under the Calverts were rescinded. Office holders had to take an oath of allegiance to the king upon being sworn that Catholics, in good conscience, could not ascribe to. Public worship was again forbidden, baptisms had to be recorded in the Anglican Church in order for the child to be able to inherit property, Catholic religious education was forbidden, and special reports were commissioned to count the number of Catholics in the Colony, the number of priests, places of worship and so on. By 1715 at the end of Queen Ann's war, Protestants were firmly in control of the government. Laws were passed to deprive Catholics of the right to vote, to hold office, to build churches, and even to hold services. Repression was as bad as it had ever been in England. This continued throughout much of the eighteenth century. It was not until almost the time of the Revolutionary War that Catholics again enjoyed complete freedom of religion. This situation necessitated a furtive practicing of their faith, even forcing priests to travel by night and hold clandestine services in order to avoid arrest. This, along with the disastrous courthouse fires of 1704 in Ann Arundle County and 1831 in St. Mary's County, provides much of the reason why so little is known about the Drurys and their genealogy. What we can deduce about the lives of this family is mainly conjecture with little to support it. We have only a few firm dates on which to base our reconstruction of their lives.

Charles Drury

The Drury families of Ann Arundle County were much wealthier than those of St. Mary's County. In his will of 1766 Charles Drury Jr. lists five separate plantations in Prince George and Ann Arundle counties.[6] As descendants of the Hawstead Drurys, the family owned considerable land in England as well. These Drurys also developed close familial connections with prominent and politically powerful families like the Hills, Lloyds, and Darnalls.[7]

Charles and his four sisters were all married by the time his father died in 1740.[8] We have no documented record of their birth, but we can estimate that they were all born between about 1700 and 1725 assuming that the girls did not marry before they were at least 15 years old, and Charles Jr. was at least 21 years old in 1739 when he married Elizabeth Miles.[9] She evidently died before 1749 when he married a second time to Mary whose maiden name is not known though some have speculated that she was Mary Jerningham, daughter of Henry Jerningham and Catharine.

The sisters were Sarah who married Abraham Simmons Jr.; Sophia who married Charles Boetler, the son of Charles Boetler and Alice about 1738;[10] Esther who married Nathan Selby, the son of Samuel Selby and Sarah Smith;[11] and Mary who is named as Mary Dart in the will of 1740. This connection to the Botelers provides the only direct link we have between the Drurys of Ann Arundle County and those in St. Mary's County. Charles Boteler, the grandfather of the Charles who married Sophia Drury, lived in St. Mary's County on a plantation called "Dansbury Hill" that was situated near present day route 5 just south of Loveland. This property was also near to "Hopewell" and to "Howard's Mount" that was leased by John Drury (son of Robert who had Dry Docking). Given the proximity between "Howard's Mount" and "Dansbury Hill" it is probable that the two families knew each other but there is nothing to show any links or association between them.

Robert Drury (immigrant)

Most children of immigrants were not formally educated though, if the family was wealthy enough, the sons might be sent to Europe to be educated. For Catholics the preferred education was at the Jesuit school at St. Omers in Holland. However much he might have wished it, the immigrant Robert Drury, from what we can gather, lacked resources for any such plan. This tells us a good deal about the hardship endured in those times when a father could not pass on his education to his sons. We have no record showing that his sons learned any of the carpentry skills demonstrated by their father in the construction of chests and coffins as mentioned in Dr. Lois Green Carr's notes, nor do we find carpentry tools specifically listed among John Drury's effects in the inventory of 1724.[12] We also have no record that his sons were taught any but the most basic skills needed to construct and maintain a dwelling house and the farm buildings needed on the plantation. John was apparently a farmer assisting his father until he married sometime in the late 1690s. His brothers probably had a similar life.

Birth and marriage dates are difficult to find before 1750. Most of the existing records for St. Mary's County were destroyed in the earlier mentioned courthouse fire in 1831. Much of our information is extrapolated from known facts included in wills, administrative accounts, land records, and other surviving official documents. The immigrant Robert married but his wife is unknown.

They had the following children:

Robert Drury Jr.

Robert Drury Jr. is an enigma within a mystery. The only records we have of his existence are the two depositions cited in Chapter Two and references in the Maryland Archives that he was sent as a representative of the Colony to meet with other colonies to consider common defense against Indian tribes during the 1690s. We have assumed he was a possible son of Robert (immigrant) only because his birth would place it in the range of dates possible for a son and that few other Drurys were in southern Maryland at that time. We also have no reliable record of his immigration unless he was one of the two Robert Drurys transported by Edmund Scarborough by 1663.

Another puzzle arises in explaining how Robert arrived in Northern Maryland by 1790. He obviously had traveled quite a bit as information from his deposition of 1690 assumes he had been to Albany, New York, possibly on colonial business. Casparus Hermann was a prominent planter in Northern Maryland and would not have traveled to St. Mary's County to take a deposition concerning Indians in his own neighborhood.

Robert Drury was a son of Robert (immigrant) inferred by Patricia Obrist, a Drury researcher, who tells us that "Robert Drury, age 32, was deposed in 1692 concerning Indians at the head of the (Chesapeake) Bay."[13] If his age were 32, this Robert Drury would have been born about 1660. This leads us to believe that Robert Drury, immigrant, had a son Robert Drury Jr. This birth could have been in Virginia. We do have a report in Maryland Archives of a 1726 dispute in a tavern that was reported to the legislature in which a Drury (reported to be an old man) was present.[14] It is most likely this Robert Drury who was mentioned. This would eliminate him as being Robert (immigrant) who, even if we assume he was born as late as 1634, would most likely be deceased before 1726.

It seems evident from entries in the Archives preceding the above deposition that this Robert Drury was well regarded in Maryland and had probably been among the volunteers who went to the aid of the settlers in Schenectady and Albany, New York, during the French and Indian raids in that area in 1690. This could undoubtedly be one of the places where he would have come into contact with the Frenchman Mr. Casteen mentioned in the deposition. This Frenchman had to have been Baron de Castin who led a number of Indian raids against the New England colonists. Robert actually traveled as far as Penobscot in what is now the state of Maine where he met Baron Saint-Castin. Robert described the encounter saying that in a single day he saw Saint-Castin both in Indian habit and in scarlet, the traditional dress of aristocrats.[15] A close examination of these and other associated documents in the Archives leads to the conclusion that this Robert Drury may have remained in the area of Northern Maryland.

1.)   The deposition referenced above was taken by Casparus Augustus Herman who was an influential land owner in northern Maryland.

2.)   The Indians who were the subjects of the deposition were said to be "at the head of the bay" (most likely Chesapeake Bay), again north of St. Mary's County, Maryland.

3.)   The 1726 deposition concerning the discussion in the Ordinary (what we would call an inn or a tavern) mentions the "old man called Drury." This would not have been Robert s/o John who married in St. Mary's County in 1725. The mention that the Robert of Cecil County was old suggests that he was the possible brother of John rather than his son.

A quote from this deposition will enlighten us not only as to the temper of the times, but also the temperament of Drury males in those times. Without other examples we can only assume that this was typical. We should understand that this deposition was a report of the happenings that night by a third party.

The discussion concerned a "Tobacco Law" which we can assume was one proposing a tax payable to the Proprietor on tobacco shipped to Europe and that was to regulate the quality of the shipped product. Even though this discussion was taking place in 1726, similar discussions had taken place and laws enacted for at least the previous fifty years. At this time however the plantation owners on the Eastern Shore of Maryland began shifting production from tobacco to wheat and other grains that they were shipping to Philadelphia. Since no duty was imposed at the time on grain shipments, farmers on the Western shore felt unfairly taxed to support the entire colony. You will notice that the discussion concerned certain members of the Assembly from the Eastern Shore, according to the participants, were unduly influencing the creation of bills favorable to Eastern shore planters.

"This Deponant [Edward Harris] saith to the best of his knowledge on Tuesday night the 15th of this Instant October he was going through George Nelsons middle Room where they sometimes dress Victuals and U. H. J. there was a Company of about ten or Dozen men sitting in said Passage amongst which there was one man had a Sword by his Side (who as this deponent) was inform'd was Major Samuel Perrie who upon sight of this Deponent damn'd him and [asked] him several times if he was for a Tobacco Law or not. If he was he should have some Punch if he was not he should have none and that his Room was very good Company this deponent also saith that an Old man that lost some money at dice that night they call Drury swore that Mr Perrie or himself should fight him either with a Sword or without it. This deponent further saith that it instantly came into his mind of Mobs that constrains Persons either to Agree with their Sentiments or to be knocked down. The Consequence that might happen he did not know, however, answered 'em as followeth, first that if he wanted any Punch he could have it without being obliged to them, Secondly that his declaring himself for or against a Tobacco Law wou'd be of no Service to the Country because he had no vote in the House of Assembly but as he had a Family to maintain shou'd be very glad of a Tobacco Law provided 'twas a good one, Thirdly he further saith he told 'em that if he had disobliged any of the Company he should think it his duty to ask Pardon but inasmuch as he knew he had given no Offence he made use of this extravagant Expression viz, that he would as soon be darnn'd to a Truffle as submit and be bullied by them notwithstanding there was so many of 'em and had a Sword upon which this Deponent saith three or four of the Company rose of their chairs and very much importuned him to sit down with 'em. He also saith that he directly called for a Bowl of Punch and sat down with 'em and after some discourse they told this Deponent that several people had been peeping in and listening to their discourse had made Remarks and Spoke of severall things that was said amongst 'em and that they thought Mr. Peter Taylor to be one that took notice of what they said and this deponent for another however in a short time Mr. PERRY begun to curse the Eastern Shore Burgesses prodigiously because they was against a Tobacco Law but particularly James Holliday Esqr. & that he said Holliday was not fit to be in the House. This deponent saith that he asked said Mr Perrie why and said Perrie answered that Mr. Carroll bullied and Scared Mr Holliday some time ago about a Tobacco Law and that said Holliday was influenced by Esqr. Bennet likewise from making a Tobacco Law. This Deponent also saith that he told Mr. Perrie that he never took Mr. Holliday to be such a man neither did he believe that Esqr. Bennet ever concern'd himself so much in State affairs as to endeavour to sway or rule the Government. Said Perry swore directly by his God it was true & that he would justify it to their Faces & that he knew Esqr. U. H. J. Bennet would give a Thousand pound to subvert the Government & that there should not be a Tobacco Law. Abundance of more Words happened amongst which this deponent saith to the best of his Knowledge said Samuel Perrie one Bigger Head & a Young Fellow they call Wilson and the aforesaid Drury that lost money at Dice did say and swear they wou'd have a hundred Prince Georges County men upon the State House Hill either that week or the next to face the Assembly in order to Obtain a Tobacco Law."[16]

John Drury

John Drury who died by 1724 is the one about whom we know the most among these early Drurys. He did not have the benefit of an education and died a poor man. The inventory and account administered by his wife Mary after his death states that much of his equipment and furniture was in very poor condition and the total value of the estate, after a lifetime of farming, was only £56.[17] The only thing of real value was his land and that was leased. We can assume he married for the first time sometime between 1695 and 1700. We can infer this as his children John, Peter, Robert, Ann, and probably Thomas were all born by 1715 if his son Robert was of age and married by 1725. We know John married a second time to Mary Ford Seale, a daughter of Robert Ford and Lydia and widow of Jonathon Seale, who died by 1714.[18]

Little is known about John Drury's early years or those of his brothers James and Robert. We can only assume they grew up assisting their father in farming. We can also assume that their formal education was minimal as they would not have had educational opportunities possibly available to their father. There is no proof that they could read or write though we can be fairly confident that their father was educated.

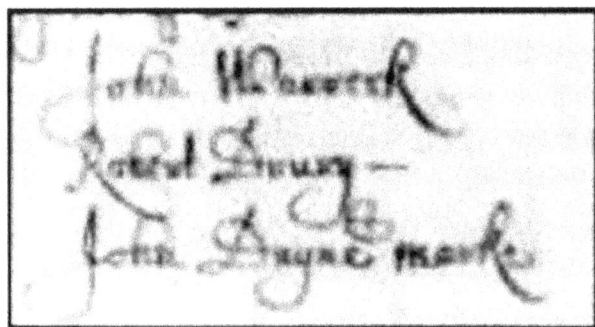

19

John Drury (d. by 1724) was a son of Robert (immigrant) and the only one for which we have any documentary proof linking the two. Donnelly cites the inventory of Thomas Payne (39C: 187) where John Drury is referred to as the son of Robert Drury and is named next of kin.[20] He could not be a son of the Robert cited above in the deposition. Robert Drury of the deposition was 32 years old in 1692. The John Drury who died by 1724 was most likely married and having children by 1700.

Mary Louise Donnelly in her book on Beaverdam Manor owners and families lists John's first wife as Rachel Payne and assumes that Rachel was Charles Payne's sister.[21] Unfortunately there is confusion about this assertion. According to Norma Thompson, a knowledgeable researcher, and others, there are two Payne families at this time in St. Mary's County, Maryland. John Drury was associated with the family of Henry Payne through his residence on part of "Howard's Mount." It is possible that Donnelly misread the name of Henry's son Ezchiel as Rachel, or possibly accepted someone else's misinterpretation of the name. The other Payne family was that of Thomas Payne and his wife Jane Smallpiece. Rachel was the only surviving daughter of Thomas Payne and the wife of Arthur Kerse before he died in 1700.[22] So far as can be determined the two Payne families were not linked. I believe that most of John's children would have been by his first wife whoever she may have been.[23]

Henry Payne and Mary Assiter did have a daughter Ann Payne who is mentioned in her grandmother's will.[24] If we assume that it was Ann Payne who he married first, then it had to be after 1693 because Ann was mentioned in the will of her grandmother and was still unmarried at that time. His being named next of kin by her brother Thomas would then make more sense. The fact that John was living on land patented by this family gives us additional plausibility. This, of course, is not the only possible kinship link. We have no record of the name of his mother. If she was either a sister or cousin of Henry Payne, or an Assiter, he would also be kin to both Charles and Thomas Payne.

John's second wife, Mary Ford, was a widow when they married probably between 1714 and 1717. Mary Drury was listed as administrator for his admin accounts dated 2 June 1724. The account mentions a Robert Drury who I assume was a son of John though there is nothing to support this assumption. He would have to have been of age at the time to be listed as next of kin. This would have placed his birth somewhere around 1703 or before. A second possibility for Robert would be John's brother mentioned above.[25]

In 1717 John and his unknown wife (possibly Ann Payne) were living on "Howard's Gift" a 75 acre farm in north central St. Mary's County part of a larger tract called "Howard's Mount," Charles Payne's will in 1717 bequeaths this farm to his son Peter stating that this is "where John Drury now lives."[26] It seems reasonable here to assume that John Drury was "of age" when he married though there is no documentary proof at present.

Assuming this to be true would place his birth date somewhere around 1662. It is also logical to assume that since he probably married after 1693 many of his children were born in the period between then and 1717.

John and his family lived a simple life tending their livestock and their crops. John's inventory in 1724 lists horses, cattle, sheep, and hogs. The horses obviously provided transportation and muscle power for farming. He no doubt got dairy products from the cattle, wool from the sheep, and meat from the rest. He grew flax as well because the inventory mentions linen, and they made cloth from both the flax and the wool.

John fathered seven children before he died. We calculate that he had five by Ann Payne and probably the last two by Mary Ford. Estimates of their births are: Thomas (abt 1700), Robert (abt 1704/5), John Jr. (abt 1711), Ann (abt 1713), Peter (abt 1715), Jane (abt 1718) and Tecla (abt 1720). Thomas married Mary, widow of James Duff, before 1751 (this was probably a second marriage); Robert married Mary in 1725; John Jr. married Susanna Hayden 12/10/1734; Ann married Francis Hayden, Susanna's brother, about 1731; Peter married Jane Bailey about 1735; Tecla possibly married Enoch Joy by 1735 though others have suggested with equal plausibility that his marriage was to Tecla Thompson the widow of Thomas Payne. We have no data on any marriage for Jane.

James Drury

James Drury is a third inferred son of Robert (immigrant) born about 1669 in St. Mary's County, Maryland. This inference is based on generational averages and the age data we have for his children and grandchildren. James Drury leased lot # 34 in Beaverdam Manor called "Terra Collium" in the names of his granddaughters Eleanor and Mary Chamberlain in 1714 when the girls were eight and one years old respectively. This property was later renamed "Fertilitas." This lease also appears in the 1768 Rent Rolls with his grandchildren Eleanor and Mary Chamberlain listed as in residence.

It is possible that he was also living on this plantation at[27] that time. Beaverdam Manor in the eighteenth century was part of Newtown Hundred. For James to have an eight-year-old granddaughter by this date, and assuming his daughter Mary, the girl's mother, married by at least age seventeen, then James would have to be at least forty five to fifty years old by 1714. Calculating backward gives us a birth date for him in the late 1660s, right in the same range as Robert's other children. There is no available record of who he married but we know he had at least two children, Mary Ann, who married Charles Chamberlain in 1705, and James Junior.

Charles died in 1750/1 in Virginia but made his will in Maryland since he had property in both colonies.[28] We know Charles was Anglican. He stated his "desire to be buried in a Christian manner, according to the rules of the Church of England" in his will of 1750. This fact apparently made little difference to Mary whose family was presumably Catholic as were the rest of her kinsmen. By the time he died Charles was fairly well-to-do. He left 11 slaves, an 800 acre tract of land on the south side of the McHerring River in Brunswick County, Virginia, to his wife Ann Chamberlin. Executors were George Graves of St. Mary's County, Maryland; Sampson Limare of Brunswick County, Virginia; and his wife. Witnesses to the will were James Drury, Jr., Mary Ann's brother Joseph Drury, her first cousin one time removed; and Robert Drury who is possibly her cousin Robert Drury, a son of John Drury and Ann Payne. It is possible that Joseph is another of Mary's brothers or an unnamed son. In any case he had to be a close relative.

Charles and Mary had three known children, Eleanor (1706), Mary (1714), and Thomas (probably about 1708). As we mentioned above, in 1768 the girls were living on lot # 34 in Beaverdam Manor. It was called "Terra Collium" and later "Fertilitas."[29] Thomas married first Elizabeth Clark the daughter of John Clark who died in 1727,[30] and second in 1737 to Catherine the widow of John Bullock who had died the year before.[31] [32]

James Drury Jr., James' other known child, married Sarah before 1767 when his eldest son Stephen was born. We do not have a birth date for him but he died on 19 Mar 1779 in St. Mary's County, Maryland.[33] He was at least 21 years old in 1766 when he witnessed the will of Richard Cooper written 11/27/1766, probated 12/17/1766. Sarah Drury purchased 163 acres of "Chatham" where they had been living. The plantation was part of Beaverdam Manor in 1786 when this land was sold as confiscated British property. It is possible, though not proved, that Sarah was a Thompson.[34] James and Sarah had four known children, Stephen (1767), James (1771),[35] Thomas (1774),[36] and Richard whose birth date is unknown. They were all mentioned as legatees in their father's will. Stephen and James were to receive the land after their mother died. Thomas and Richard were to divide the personal property between them. James must have been having an uneasy relationship with a tenant on part of the property. He specifically states in his will that "It is also my will and desire that if Monica Dogen shall make any Trespass on my Land whereon she now lives, by cutting any wood except Dog Wood, or any old, or if she should make any disturbance in the family, that then my Executors may turn her off at their discretion." She was the recent widow of Thomas Dogen.

The eldest son Stephen was in Freeport, Armstrong Co, PA, in the 1850 census. He said he was age 83, born 1767 in Maryland. He had some education and training as a watchmaker. He had his own business in 1850 in Freeport. He also had a brother or relative named James. They both bought land in 1794 in Huntingdon borough, of Huntingdon Co, PA. Stephen married there (wife's name unknown) before 1795. His oldest son, James D. Drury, was born in 1796 in Huntingdon, PA. Stephen was on the 1790, 1800, and 1820 census.[37]

Margaret Drury

Mary Louise Donnelly tells us that Margaret Drury married John Tant (also spelled Taunt). At the time of their marriage John Tant received a tract of land from Robert Drury. John Tant also received two patents in his own name for a total of 200 additional acres of land on 14 Dec 1683 (patents 25:35 and 25:44). Whether the land he received from Robert Drury was "Dry Docking" or "Dry Docking Addition" is not clear from Donnelly's text. She calls it "Dry Docking" which was the tract patented to Robert Drury on 12 Aug 1672 (patent 12:571), but the date and patent number she cites are those for "Dry Docking Addition" 20 Oct 1683 patent (25:36). In any case this would not have happened if Margaret were not Robert's daughter. This land was probably her dowry with Robert filing a patent almost immediately for a second 100 acre tract. We can see this from the consecutive patent numbers for John Tant (25:35) and Robert Drury (25:36).

Other researchers disagree with this assessment citing the fact that land was usually devised to sons and Robert had at least one and possibly three. They say it is more likely that Margaret Tant's maiden name was Bloomfield. This is based on the facts that first, John Tant (and after his death his widow Margaret Tant) owned portions of "Revelle" which was formerly owned by Luke Barber and Elizabeth Young and which came into the Bloomfield family through Elizabeth's second marriage to John Bloomfield; second, that John Tant's will in 1702 left bequests to Jaffel and Maryann Bloomfield (children of John Bloomfield and Elizabeth Young) who would have been his nephew and niece by marriage; and third, that he possibly named his son Mark after the child's uncle Mark Bloomfield.

The key here may be the ownership of "Revelle" verses the ownership of "Dry Docking." This confusion leaves us with several possibilities. Perhaps John Tant married twice, first to Margaret Bloomfield and second to Margaret Drury. Perhaps, as we originally surmised, he married only to Margaret Drury, or third, and perhaps most disturbing, there never was a Margaret Drury at all. Donnelly's reference to Margaret Drury is the only place I have ever seen her mentioned and the estimation of her birth is derived solely from her estimated marriage date with John Tant.

No matter how this controversy is resolved it seems clear that there was some association between the Drury and Tant families. John Tant did receive Dry Docking around 1683 whether by marriage or purchase and the other lands owned by John Tant were in the same vicinity as Dry Docking and Dry Docking Addition. All were near Leonardtown in what was known as Newtown Hundred.

Reproduced with permission of the St. Mary's County Historical Society.

St. Mary's County – 1707[38]

The following description of land transfers may help to serve to illuminate some of the above discussion.

REVELLE - This 300 acre tract was originally surveyed for Randall Revelle on 14 December 1641 and eventually came into the possession of Luke Barber. Luke Barber and his wife Elizabeth, sold to William Tattershall in November 1665.[39] Maryland Chancery records show – "12/20/1714: Commission to examine the bounds of Revelle on Breton Bay formerly conveyed by Luke Barber and his wife Elizabeth to William Tattershall and now in the possession of James Tant. Luke Barber and Margaret Tant were in possession of the residue of the said tract.

James Tant came into possession of all of William Tattershall's land through his wife Mary, who, after the death of her brother Lawrence Tattershall in 1701/2, was sole heir to the estate of her father William Tattershall.[40] According to Maryland Land Office rent rolls, Luke Barber was in possession of 180 acres, Widow (Margaret) Tant was in possession of 70 acres, and James Tant was in possession of 50 acres. James Tant's will

47

bequeathed this land to his wife, Mary, and at her death to their son Matthew Tant.[41] By 1729 this land was in the possession of James' daughter Ann, as rent rolls show the following transfers: George Medley and wife (James' daughter Ann and her first husband) to Robert Ford on 24 January 1729. William Williams and Ann (James Tant's daughter and her second husband) to Robert Ford on 9 March 1732, and 150 Acres from Robert Ford to John Manning on 19 April 1738, 151 Acres from Robert Ford to John Manning on 18 November 1741.[42]

(UNKNOWN NAME) later known as **NO NAME**
100 acres SE side of Breton's Bay on south side of Nevill's Creek. This land was probably located just north of Revelle. Luke Barber and his wife, Elizabeth, sold this tract to William Tattershall in November 1665 at the same time they sold Revelle. It was bequeathed to Lawrence Tattershall by his father's will with statement that the tract was between the land of Dr. Luke Barber and land of John Greenwell. This land was in James Tant's possession after Lawrence's death. James' will bequeathed this land to his son John Tant.[43] By 1797, 77 acres of this land again is in possession of the Drury family. John Drury, great Grandson of Robert (immigrant) purchased the tract from Ignatius & Mary Medcalf [Medley].[44] This was transferred to Francis Desales Drury, John's son by 1801.[45] After Francis' death it was willed to his children and in 1846 his grand daughter Celestia Beetly sold this property to James Thompson Yates.[46]

Dry Docking

100 acres located inland just northeast of Breton Bay in Newtown Hundred. Originally surveyed for Robert Drury in 1672, it came into the possession of John Tant and was given to John's son James upon his marriage. James Tant's will bequeathed this land to Matthew Tant who apparently died young with no heirs. The land later came into the possession of James' daughter Ann and through her to her first husband George Medley. When George died he willed it to his son Bennett with the provision that his wife Ann was to remain in possession for the rest of her life. When she remarried to William Williams they lived there.[47]

John and Margaret Tant had nine children before he died in 1702.[48] To produce this many children they would have to have been married eighteen to twenty years. It seems reasonable therefore that they married sometime around the time John obtained his patents for the 200 acres in 1683. Margaret was probably at least sixteen or seventeen years old when they married. That would put her birth date about 1665, a few years before her father can be definitely placed in Maryland. This all assumes that she was, in fact, Margaret Drury.

Her husband John Tant (also spelled Taunt) was transported into the province of Maryland in 1672 (Patent 17:612) His service was very short for in 1675 he witnessed the will of William Cain in St. Mary's County. On 14 Dec 1683 he obtained 2 patents (25:44, 35). One was 40 acres of "Taunton Dean" William Tattershall's land, and the other was 160 acres of "Taunt's Mark." At the estimated time of his marriage he received the tract "Dry Docking" near St. Lawrence creek, which had been patented to Robert Drury on 20 Oct 1683 (25:36). In 1694 John Tant administered the estate of John Blumfield.[49]

Raphael and Maryann Blumfield and Eleanor Deakins were probably the children of John Blumfield who received legacy in John Tant's will. John Tant wrote his will on 10/17/1702 and it was probated on 11/12/1702 (11:274). In his will he left "Dry Docking," given to him at his marriage, to son James and heirs, and personalty to son Mark at 18 years of age, and the residue of his lands. If Mark died without issue the land was to pass to his daughters Mary, Ann, Jane, Elizabeth, Winifred, Margaret, and an unborn child (not named in the inventory with the other children). He left personalty to Raphael and Maryann Blumfield and Elinor Deakins (no relationship shown for these three). His wife Margaret received personalty and was to act as his executrix. When his estate was appraised by Edward Cole and Henry Spink on 12/9/1702, all his children were named and mention was made of an orphan Mary Welsh.[50]

In 1707 Margaret Tant was in possession of 50 acres of "Noble's Victor" (which had been patented to John Noble), 70 acres of "Revelle," 100 acres of "Revelle's backside," and the lands owned by her husband (40 acres of "Taunton Dean" and 160 acres of "Taunt's Mark"). "Dry Docking" had become the property of her son James Tant. Margaret Tant, the widow of John Tant, wrote her will on 24 Dec 1725 and it was probated on 2/1/1726. To her grandson, Mark Lampton, she left 15 pounds Sterling and personalty at the age of 21. To her grandson William Thompson she left 15 pounds Sterling at the age of 21 and if he died during minority, the legacy was to pass to his brother Henry Thompson. She left 40 pounds Sterling to Rev. Francis Lloyd (a Jesuit priest). To her grandson John Manning she left personalty and if he died during minority it was to pass to two grandsons Joseph and Vitus Herbert and their heirs. She left personalty to her grandsons Walter Pye, Joseph Herbert, and daughters Margaret Pye, Jane Thompson, and Winifred Herbert. Her son-in-law Richard Thompson administered her estate on 26 Apr 1726 and it was valued at 209 pounds eleven shillings Eleven pence. The next of kin on her inventory were Winifred Herbert and Jane Thompson (11:497)

---

[1] Bruce, Philip Alexander, An Economic History of Virginia, Macmillan 1896, p 350, 351

[2] Rogers, *History of Agriculture and Prices in England*, Vol. V, p 64

[3] History of Tobacco, Boston University Medical Center, http://academic.udayton.edu/health/syllabi/tobacco/history.htm#industry

[4] *Maryland Archives*, viii, 460-461, 487 book of depositions, page 55

[5] Conrad, Glenn R. *Some Maryland Germans who settled in Louisiana* http://www.angelfire.com/la/oryfamily/settlers.html

[6] Maryland Probate Records, CALENDAR OF WILLS, VOL 13, 1764-1767, p. 103

[7] Ibid; This Drury family must have been closely associated with the Hills and also with Henry Darnall since two of the tracts listed for Abell Hill are now listed for Charles in this will, and in an inventory of 1741 a payment is listed for Henry Darnall (of Portland Manor).

[8] Maryland Calendar of Wills, Vol. 8. 1738-1743, p. 198

[9] Charles II's marriage to Elizabeth Miles is proved by probate records where she administered Samuel Roberts estate. Maryland Probate Records, PEROGATIVE COURT ABSTRACTS, 1733-1738. p. 103

[10] Sophia's son Edward received a portion of the dwelling plantation "Essex Land" in her father's Will

[11] There is a Nathan Selby mentioned in Maryland Probate records, Perogative court Abstracts, 1738-17744 p. 38 along with Charles Bottelin who I assume is Charles Boteler, husband of Ester's sister Sophia. Esther is also named in her father's will as Esther Selby

[12] Prerogative Ct. (Test. Proceedings), 27 (MdHR 983), p. 38 Film 3299, Pt. 2, Liber IX, Folio 451, 452, 453; Abstracts of the Administration Accounts of the Prerogative Court of Maryland" Libers 6-10, 1724-1731 by V. L. Skinner, Jr. Page 48

[13] *Maryland Archives*, viii, 460-461, 467 book of depositions, page 55

[14] Ibid

[15] Michigan State University, French Colonial History Vol. 5 (2004) pp 43-61, Stanwood, Owen, The Baron of Saint-Castin and the Transformation of the Northeastern Borderlands

[16] Gould, Clarence P., *Economic History of Maryland 1720 – 1765*, PhD Dissertation, Johns Hopkins University 1911 p 46

[17] Prerogative Ct. (Test. Proceedings), 27 (MdHR 983), p. 38 Film 3299, Pt. 2, Liber IX, Folio 451, 452, 453.; V. L. Skinner, Jr., Abstracts of the Administration Accounts of the Prerogative Court of Maryland, 1724-1731 Libers 6-10, Folio 48

[18] Skinner, V. L. Jr., Abstracts of the Inventories and Accounts of the Perogative Court of Maryland 1674-1718, Liber 32b, Folio 149

[19] Signature courtesy of Robert Dora, 7th great grandson of Robert Drury

[20] Donnelly, Mary Louise, *Colonial Period Tenants and Owners of Beaverdam Manor*, 1998 pp 187, 188

[21] Ibid p 96

[22] Reno, Linda, electronic, msg of 8/13/2010, "Rachel Payne married Arthur Kerse based on this record: Admin. accts. of Arthur Kerse (Planter), SMC, 9/11/1700; payments to Gilbert Turberville for Mr. Cheseldine and Rachel Kerse; Admr., Isaac Payne (Skinner). Rachel Payne, a daughter of Thomas Payne and Jane Smallpiece based on this record: Admin. accts. of Arthur Kerse (Planter), SMC, 9/11/1700; payments to Gilbert Turberville for Mr. Cheseldine and Rachel Kerse; Admr., Isaac Payne (Skinner)."

[23] Op Cit. p 97,98

[24] Will of Ann Assiter, SMC 11/4/1693-3/20/1693-4.; Note by Linda Reno concerning this will – "Maryland Calendar of Wills says it is Henry Assiter. I called and had the will pulled at the (St. Mary's County) courthouse to verify the name. It is the will of Ann Assiter. I should have gone further and gotten a copy of the will. That needs to happen. If the transcriber messed up the name of the testator, other things may have also been missed, specifically the mention of Ann Paine". : Carr, Lois Green, card file sc4040 - 1166 ,1695: Ann Assiter, widow of William. Inventory, personal estate. Ann willed 200 ac. to her daughter Mary and male grandchildren to split equally. To Ann Paine: 1 cow, 1 calf, at the age of 21 or marriage.

[25] Reno, Linda, *Electronic* <lreno@comcast.net>

[26] Abstracts of the Administrative Accounts of the Perogative Courts of Maryland 1715-1718, p 68 (on CD 206)

[27] Brumbaugh, G.M. *Maryland Records---Vol. II, State of His Lordship's Manor*, Genealogical Publ. Co., Baltimore, Md, 1985 p. 65

[28] Maryland Probate Records, CALENDAR OF WILLS, VOL 10, 1748 1753, p. 154, FTM CD 206

[29] Linda Reno, Email message of 3/24/98. "I have only found two Chamberlains in St. Mary's County Records. They are sisters -- Eleanor b. 1706 and Mary b. 1714 were living in 1768. (Brumbaugh).

[30] Will of John Clark s/o Thomas Clark & Ann Barber and father of Luke Clark: bequests to Thomas Clark s/o Luke Clark -- 5 pounds current money and to Thomas Chamberlain h/o Elizabeth Clark "My gray suit of cloth, one pair of wooden heeled shoes, a pair of stockings, and one blue riding coat"

[31] John Bullock 22.322 SM £32.9.6 Apr 9 1737 Jun 8 1737, Appraisers: John Bond, Simon Reeder. Creditors: Robert Pilbrough. Next of kin: John Bullock, Margaret Bullock. Administratrix/Executrix: Katherine Bullock.

[32] Family Tree Maker CD 206, Maryland Probate Rercords, Prerogative court Abstracts 1737 - 1744 (Libers 16 - 20). John Bullock 17.105 A SM #32.9.6 #10.12. 2 Apr. 20, 1739, Sureties: John Graves, Sr., William Biggs Received from: John Bond Payments to: Mr. John Cartwright Executrix: Catherine Chamberlain, wife of Thomas Chamberlain

[33] St. Mary's County Wills Liber JJ No. 1 p 91

[34] Note 1/29/2013 from John Dobricky <john.dobricky@gmail.com> "I am extrapolating Sarah _____ Drury as a Thompson because there has to have been some reason that Benjamin Thompson was the godfather of both children. There had to have been some kind of close familial relationship."

[35] O'Rourke, Timothy, Colonial Source Records: Southern Maryland Catholic Families

[36] Ibid

[37] Helen Austin <AustinART@aol.com> 118 Ryan Crest Lane Decatur, AL 35603-3716, electronic

[38] Menard, Russell R., *1705 Tract Map of St. Mary's County,* **in** Chronicles of St. Mary's, Vol. 21 # 5 (May 1973)

[39] *Maryland. Archives* Vol. 49 p 588

[40] Cotton, Jane Baldwin, *The Maryland Calendar Of Wills* Volume I; Family Line Publications Westminster, Maryland 1988, p. 54

[41] Ibid vol. 2 p 251

[42] Deed Williams to Ford 1732

[43] Cotton, Jane Baldwin, *Maryland Calendar of Wills*, Vol. 2 p 251

[44] 25 Feb 1797: Deed: (DA:TH25:046) No Name, 77-acres from Ignatius & Mary Medcalf [Medley] to John Drury

[45] 1801Tax Assessment (MSA:CM900): Francis D. Drury. No Name 76-acres in Lower Newtowne Hundred.

[46] 5 Aug 1846 Deed: Robert T and Celestia Beetly(sp) of Baltimore to James Thompson Yates. **St Anns** and **No name** 187-acres. Celestia was the daughter of Caroline Drury Sanner, the daughter of Francis Desales Drury.

[47] Cotton, Jane Baldwin, *Maryland Calendar of Wills*, Vol. 2 p 251

[48] Taunt, John, Will Abstract, 17th Oct., 1702; 12th Nov., 1702. liber 22 p 94
[49] Inv 13A:192
[50] Inv 22:94

Chapter Four
Children of John Drury (d. by 1724)

It is when we come to Robert's grandchildren that we begin to enter that furtive period when Catholics had to be careful not to display their religious preferences too openly. This secretiveness makes it difficult to correctly identify their children. We are not even sure we have identified all the children of this generation. However we do, in all probability, have most of John's children. The two most completely researched of John's children are John Jr. and Peter who are identified in the 1741 lease of "Drury's Venture" that we will discuss in more detail later. Two daughters, Ann and Tecla, are also documented by their marriages in 1734 though the marriage of Tecla has been disputed. Two more children, Thomas and Jane, are the least known. Thomas married, probably for a second or subsequent time in 1751, and Jane is only known because Tecla lists Jane as a sister in her will. John's son Robert is mentioned in John's administrative accounts in 1724 but it is not clear exactly who that Robert is.[1]

Robert Drury

There is a Robert Drury who received payment from John's estate in 1724. Robert Barnes in *Maryland Marriages* lists a marriage of a Robert Drury to Mary in Ann Arundle County in 1725. It is unlikely this would be "the old man named Drury" mentioned in the 1727 deposition. It is possible that this was the Robert who we assume was a son of John and received payment from John's estate as mentioned above, but if so no one knows what he was doing in Ann Arundle County. Later records show a Robert Drury in southern Maryland. We do not know if these were the same person. Records of the debt rolls for St. Mary's County show Robert Drury listed as leasing "Part of Howard's Mount" in Beaverdam Manor between 1754 and 1758.[2] Such movement apparently was not uncommon. We have a documented later example of a similar situation. A century later in 1825 Thomas Theodore Drury married Martha Ann Lydaman in Ann Arundle County.[3] All subsequent records for this couple show them living in southern St. Mary's County near the town of Ridge. In addition, Martha's parents also lived in the area near Ridge. Why they chose to marry in Ann Arundle County is unknown.

John Drury Jr.

We also have no will for John Drury Jr. or for his wife Susanna Hayden. We can deduce some of their life from other records. We believe he was born before 1711 in St. Mary's County, Maryland.[4] We know he married Susanna Hayden, daughter of William Hayden and Elizabeth Thomas, on 10 Dec 1734 in St. Mary's County, Maryland. Susanna was born in 1711 in St. Mary's County, Maryland.[5] We have no record of her death but the will of Elizabeth Hayden (her mother) lists her as a legatee in 1760 so she was still alive at that time.[6] By 1741 they had at least three children, Frances (b.1735), William (b.1737), and John (1739 - 1797). There is no definite proof that John (1739-1797) was a son of John Jr. but a preponderance of evidence leads us to a strong supposition that this was the case. John Jr.'s brother Peter obtained a lease for a tract he named "Drury's Venture" on 6 August 1741 and included William (b.1737) and two of his own children as lessees on the land.[9]

In the ensuing years John and Susanna had at least three more children. Francis married Mary Ann Carpenter, daughter of John Carpenter and Elizabeth, before 1776 in St. Mary's County, Maryland.[10] Monica married Nicholas Moore Jr. about 1770 in St. Mary's County, Maryland. Nicholas was born in 1748 in St. Mary's County, Maryland. He died on 1 Sep 1827 in Perry County, Missouri. Mary Drury, their next child born about 1746, married Richard Basil Knott.

Two additional children of John Jr. and Susanna Hayden are assumed here also on the basis that they were living in St. George's Hundred in the late 1700s and were congregants at St. Inigoes along with the rest of the family. They were Elizabeth Drury who married Jeremy Gatton,[11] and Jeremiah Drury (b. 1750).[12] We know he married and had 4 children by 1800.[13]

Finally there is Joseph Drury (b. abt.1751) who we believe went to Virginia and became a Baptist minister. He apparently became estranged from the family when he converted and had little to do with them thereafter.

By 1769 John and his family had moved to St. Inigoes Manor farther south near St. Mary's City and was leasing land in St. George's Hundred and probably on St. George's Island from the Jesuits.[14]

St. Inigoes Manor *(Chronicles of St. Mary's,* Vol. 8, No. 3)

It was granted to Ferdinand Pulton in 1639, [{01:040}] and repatented to include St. George's Island by Cuthbert Fenwick in 1641 [{01:115}]. At this time Fenwick was an agent for the Jesuits. In 1662 and 1663 two prominent Catholics, Thomas Mathews and Cuthbert Fenwick, conveyed separately three important manors to Henry Warren of St. Inigoes, unquestionably for church purposes and probably as Jesuit holdings, although no reference is made to this in the deeds which were not recorded until 1666. On July 12, 1663, Fenwick conveyed to Warren the manor of St. Inigoes containing 2000 acres and St. George's Island, both lying in St. Mary's County. The deeds were recorded March 22, 1666.[15]

John seems to have remained there throughout the duration of the Revolutionary War. During the War he and his relatives were providing provisions for the Continental Army in Virginia. In 1776 he petitioned for reparations for property destroyed by the British during the raid by Lord Dunmore on St. George Island.[16]

Dunmore raid – Revolutionary War

John Murray, Earl of Dunmore and former royal governor of Virginia, assembled a flotilla of about 80 vessels, mostly armed merchant ships, schooners and sloops backed up by a few British warships. They began raiding along the lower Chesapeake Bay and put Norfolk to the torch.

Lord Dunmore's early successes turned to disaster and by the winter of 1775 his so-called army, with many loyalist families who had sought his protection, embarked for Gwynn's Island. By the following spring people were dying of smallpox and other diseases and, when patriot forces began bombarding the island on July 9, 1776, Dunmore loaded his remaining supporters aboard the vessels of his flotilla and sailed to St. George Island, a two square mile piece of low-lying marshland at the mouth of the St. Mary's River.

The loyalist force built a breastwork there and spent most of that month raiding the countryside for food and water. At one point about a hundred Maryland militiamen waded across to the island where they destroyed water casks and filled up a well. Cannons from the British warship *Fowey* finally drove them off. Conditions among the British worsened and in August, Dunmore and his followers set sail for England.

Islands of the lower bay, particularly St. George, continued to serve as shelters and bases for loyalist activity, most particularly raids against shipping on the Potomac and Chesapeake Bay. To put these Tories out of action, in May 1781 the Maryland General Assembly ordered the evacuation of all islands below Hooper strait. Islanders had to leave their boats that the state would sell, but could take with them whatever else they owned. Nothing could be left behind that would aid the Tory raiders.[17] We have no idea when John Jr. or his wife died, but he could have been alive as late as 1781 when a John Drury was paid for supplies furnished to the Continental Army.[18] It is not clear which John Drury this was. John (m. 1734) would have been more than 70 years old at this time. It seems clear however that his son John remained on this property until his death in 1797.

Peter Drury

We do know a bit more about Peter Drury due to the facts provided by his will of 1770 and the 1741 lease for Drury's Venture. There are undocumented references to two marriages but the only one mentioned in corroborating documents is the one to Jane in the lease. We have references to five of his sons between the two documents; Peter and Nicholas in the lease and Peter, Robert, Philip, and Michael in the will. The remaining children were placed with Peter because of baptismal associations with children of the documented sons. It is possible however that some of them could be children of John and Susanna Hayden.

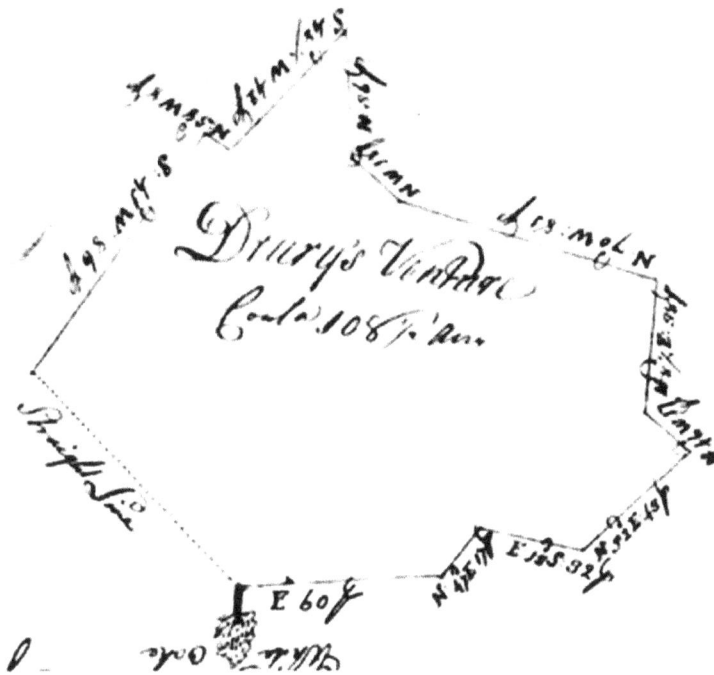

Surveyd for Peter Drury of Saint Mary's County a parcel of land lying in the said County on his Lordship's Mannor of Beaverdam it being that parcel of land heretofore surveyd for John Drury the father of the said Peter for fifty five acres to which I have now added fifty three acres and an half of vacant land the whole being now called Drury's Venture

Bounded as follows Beginning at a white oake standing on the east side of Accuponkin branch it being a Tree originally bounded for the Beginning bounder the said land and running thence East 60 perches, then north 47 deg east 17 perches , then East 16 deg South 32 perches, then North 32 deg East 43 perches, then North 46 deg West 17 perches, then North 8', deg East 38 perches, then North 70 deg West 81 perches, then North west 18 perches, then North 36 perches, then South 484 deg West 42 perches, then North 58 deg West 8 perches, then South 41 deg West 86 perches, then by a Straight line to the first beginning containing 108.5 acres

Note: The term "Perch" is a an archaic measure of distance equaling approximately 16 and a half feet

Survey'd the 6th day of August Anne Dom 1741

The Lives to be inserted in the Lease are Nicholas and Peter Drury the sons of Peter Drury and Jane his wife and William Drury son of John Drury and Susanne his wife.[19]

Though the warrant and description of "Drury's Venture" is clear, the land "formerly owned by Peter's father John Drury" is not. John Drury (d. 1724) is known to have been on "Part of Howard's Mount" at Charles Payne's death. This cannot be the land specified in the "Drury's Venture" warrant. In 1754 "Part of Howard's Mount" is in possession of John's son Robert Drury and the other 75 acres of that parcel was willed to Charles' son. This leaves the question open as to the identity of the 53 acre parcel to which was added the 55 acres to make up "Drury's Venture." In addition, since the land is described as "formerly owned," it begs the question of who is the current owner is if it is not Peter Drury or John Drury.

From the wording of the warrant the two sections had to have contiguous boundaries and I assume without proof that Peter was living on the land resurveyed as "formerly owned by John Drury the father of Peter". If this were not the case a resurvey would not have been necessary. He could have simply applied for a survey.

The following description explains this procedure.

> "....if it [the land] was contiguous to land already
> held by the applicant the procedure had to be varied
> so as to permit the officers to collect an extra
> patent to cover the value of any improvements that
> there might happen to be. In this case the applicant
> came at once to the judges of the land office and
> petitioned for a warrant to resurvey his own land
> with leave to include the contiguous tract.[20]

Peter Drury has references for two wives but neither marriage date is documented. The wife named Jane mentioned in the lease for "Drury's Delight" in 1741 is reported to have married Peter in 1725. Jane is assumed to have died before Peter made his will on 3/12/1770 as it makes no mention of her. Mary Louise Donnelly states that Ann Bailey d/o William Bailey and Ann Morgan married Peter Drury.[21] Unfortunately there are no references to support this statement but I believe that Jane was also a Bailey and possibly a sister of a different Ann Bailey.

Peter Drury leased a tract called "Part of The Bottom" between 1754 and 1758.[22] We can only assume that this was Peter (the father) because he willed "Drury's Venture" to his son Michael in the will of 1770. This property had been in the Bailey family for 75 years. "The Bottom" was a one hundred acre plantation originally surveyed for John Bailey in 1683 and in his possession in 1707. In his will of 1712, he left one fifty acre portion to granddaughter Mary Bailey, daughter of his son William and Ann Chessum. This granddaughter Mary married James Medley. He left a second fifty acres to his granddaughter Susanna Shanks, daughter of Mary Bailey and Robert Shanks.[23]

Mary Medley sold her 50A tract to Thomas Reeder in 1764. The other 50A tract, or portion thereof, is the one that falls into the hands of Peter Drury. The 1717 rent rolls show James Bailey on one tract and Robert Shanks on the other. James is occupying the tract belonging to Mary Medley. The 1740 rent rolls show John Mills occupying one of these tracts. John Mills, I believe, married Susanna Shanks, daughter of Mary Bailey and Robert Shanks.[24]

The 1740 roll shows John Mills as having 50 acres.[25] He must have added another 50 acres to that received by his wife from her grandfather because at this time John Mills transfers 50 acres to Mark Bailey and 50 acres to the "sisters of Mark Bailey." These sisters are not named but one of them had to be Elizabeth Bailey since she sold 25 acres to Thomas Reeder in 1758.[26] The other sister had to be either Ann Bailey or one of the unnamed sisters.

Since Mary Medley sold her 50A tract to Thomas Reeder in 1764, it was the other 50 acres, or a part thereof, that somehow came into the possession of Peter Drury. In 1752/3 Mark Bailey sold 50 acres to Thomas Reeder. We already know that Mary Medley still has her share.

Of the two unnamed sisters we know that one of them married William Frees. She could not have been the one who received property in 1740 because she died before her husband, and he died by 1734.[27] Therefore it had to be the other unnamed sister who received the final 25 acres.

William Bailey (son of John Bailey above) married Ann Chessum and fathered these children. But Ann Chessum Bailey had at least two sisters. They were named Jane and Mary.[28] It would not be unusual for her to name two of her daughters after her sisters. We see above that she did name one that we know (Mary) after one sister, so it would be logical to assume that one of the two unnamed daughters would be named Jane after the other.

Additionally, Peter's father John Drury was living on part of "Howard's Mount"[29] that was only a short distance from The Bottom.[30] This proximity makes it additionally likely that Peter could have courted Jane Bailey without having to travel too far from home.

Howard's Mount, Hopewell, and the Bottom

No current references other than the 1741 lease and the will of 1770 have been found to assign Peter's children to either wife.

Tecla Drury

Tecla Drury was born probably between 1715 and 1720 in St. Mary's County, Maryland. She is said to have married Enoch Joy, son of Peter Joy and Ann Stone, by 1735 in St. Mary's County, Maryland, but this has never been confirmed. One objection to a marriage is that if she was born by 1720 she would be too young to marry by 1735. Early marriages in eighteenth century colonial Maryland were possible because women occasionally married as young as age 15. If she did not marry Enoch we have no idea who her husband was.

There is other evidence, also not conclusive, that Enoch married Tecla Thompson Payne as her second husband after the death of Thomas Payne in 1731. Neither can be considered fact. Enoch was born in 1689 in St. Mary's County, Maryland. He died by 1746 in St. Mary's County, Maryland.[31] No matter who Enoch Joy married, we do know that Tecla Drury Joy lived until sometime between March 1796 when she wrote her will, and May of 1796 when it was probated.[32] We know that Tecla Joy's maiden name was Drury because she names Jane Drury as sister in her will.

Enoch had six children before he died: Ann Joy was born in 1735 in St. Mary's County, Maryland. Ann married Ignatius Joy Jr., son of Ignatius Joy and Joan, before 1767 in St. Mary's County, Maryland. Their son Enoch Jr. was born in 1742 in St. Mary's County, Maryland. Ignatius, their third child, was born before 1768 in St. Mary's County, Maryland. He died on 29 Mar 1827. He married Dorothy Booth, daughter of George Booth and Winifred Clarke, before 1788 in St. Mary's County. Dorothy was born before 1773 and died in 1829. Charles Joy died in 1783/1784 in St. Mary's County, Maryland.[33] Charles married Elizabeth French, daughter of John French Sr. and Brown. Elizabeth was born before 1749 in St. Mary's County, Maryland. She died after 1787 in St. Mary's County, Maryland.[34] Linda continues, "There is no other information in this deed so it doesn't tell me the relationship between Elizabeth Joy and Ignatius Medcalf, but I have to assume mother and son. Perhaps Charles Joy didn't name Ignatius in his will because he knew that Ignatius had already gotten land." Finally we have Athanatius Joy and Peter Joy.

Ann Drury

Ann Drury was born about 1713 in St. Mary's County, Maryland. She married Francis Hayden, son of William Hayden and Elizabeth Thomas, in 1731 in St. Mary's County, Maryland. Francis was born in 1709 in St. Mary's County, Maryland. He died in 1748 in St. Mary's County, Maryland.[35]

Sebastian and Elizabeth Thompson administered the estate of Francis Hayden on 4 April 1749. There is no record of what happened to Ann Hayden Drury. Some have speculated that the Elizabeth w/o Sebastian Thompson was really Ann Hayden who remarried after Francis died. This is where the attribution of Elizabeth as another name of Ann comes from. It seems likely but more proof would be desirable.

Francis and Ann had the following children: Ann Hayden was born on 20 Dec 1735. Francis Hayden was born about 1737 in St. Mary's County, Maryland.[36] George Hayden was born about 1738 in St. Mary's County, Maryland.[37] Elizabeth Hayden was born on 17 Jan 1741, and James Hayden was born on 9 Feb 1746. He died before 28 Nov 1846.

Thomas Drury

Little is known about Thomas. We do have a marriage in 1751 to Mary Duff who was listed as next of kin on William Holland's inventory of 1733. From this we have assumed that she was a widow because she would have been of age in 1733 to be listed on that document. This would have made her birth about 1712 and her marriage to Thomas at age 39, much too old for a first marriage. From these facts we also assume Thomas was born about the same time as Mary or a bit earlier. This would make him a brother of Peter and John Jr. It is possible that he was instead their cousin and an undocumented son of James and brother of Mary who married Charles Chamberlain. The only conjecture we can make with certainty is that he was of the same generation as John Jr. and Peter. The only additional record we have that could possibly be this Thomas Drury is of a Thomas Drury in the 1769 census of St. Inigoes hundred.

Jane Drury

Nothing is known of Jane except her being mentioned as a sister by Tecla Joy in Tecla's will in 1796.

[1] *Administration Accounts of the Prerogative Court of Maryland*, Liber 7 Folio 333, Willow Bend Books.

[2] Reno, Linda Davis, *Debt Books of St. Mary's County Maryland (1753-1758)* St. Mary's County Historical Society 1995 pp 18, 56, 94, 133, 173, 215

[3] [Marriage notice: DRURY Thomas T. -LYDAMAN Martha A 26 Nov 1846 On the 26th inst., by Rev. R. M. LIPSCOMB, Thos. T. DRURY to Martha A. LYDAMAN, all of St. Mary's county, MD. 28 Nov 1846 Baltimore Sun; Thomas Drury Will, Burger, Judith A., Register of Wills, St. Mary's County, Maryland. JTMR 1 287-288; Georgeanna Drury Will, Burger, Judith A., Register of Wills, St. Mary's County, Maryland. JBA 1 194-195, Note: The surname of the son-in-law Forwell, may be Foxwell, but if so the x is not crossed

[4] birth date calculated from marriage in 1734 and assumes he was probably a few years older than his spouse

[5] Cotton, Jane Baldwin, *Maryland Calendar of Wills 1685-1777, Vol. 2* p 152

[6] Keddie, Neil, *St. Mary's County Wills* Liber TA1 folio 412

[9] St. Mary's County *Land Office*, Unpatented Certificate of Survey, #141

[10] Carpenters and Drurys were living close by each other in St. George's Hundred and also appear to be associated in Missouri.

[11] Robert BARNES' *Maryland Marriages*: Jeremy Gatten, 14 Feb. 1773, Rev. Jas. Walton, SJ, Newtown, SM, Eliz. Drury Woodstock Archives 6.3; published in "Newtown Hundred," *MD Historical Magazine*, Je. 1956, 125 - 139.)

[12] American Genealogical-Biographical Index (AGBI) Jeremiah Drury, Born 1750 Birthplace: Maryland

[13] 1800 Census St. Mary's County Maryland Series: M32 Roll: 12 Page: 17

[14] Himmelheber, Peter, Electronic, msg of 4/9/2007, "Re: Drury Lands"

[15] *Proceedings of the Provincial Court of Maryland 1666-1670*, Volume LVII Preface 55

[16] *Archives of Maryland*, Volume 78, p. 266

[17] *The disappearing Islands of the Potomac* pp 128-129,William B. Cronin JHU press, 2005

[18] Abercrombie, Janice L. and Richard Slatten, *Virginia Revolutionary Publick Claims*, Iberian Pub. Co., Athens, GA, 1992, p. 329

[19] St. Mary's County *Land Office*, Unpatented Certificate of Survey, #141

[20] Gould, Clarence, "Economic History of Maryland 1720 – 1765", John Hopkins University, PhD Dissertation, 1911, pp 12, 13

[21] Donnelly, Mary Louise, "Colonial Settler's St. Clement's Bay 1634-1780" p. 33

[22] Reno, Linda Davis, *Debt Books of St. Mary's County Maryland (1753-1758)* St. Mary's County Historical Society 1995 pp 52, 90, 128, 168, 210

[23] Burger, Judith A. Will of John Bailey d. 1712 Register of Wills, St. Mary's County, Maryland, Liber P. C. No. 1, p. 191-192

[24] Marriage of Susanna before 1727: She had to be born by 1712 when she is mentioned in her grandfather's will. Girls usually did not marry before at least 15 years of age, therefore she probably did not marry before 1727 at the earliest.

[25] From Peter Himmelheber: *Rent Rolls,* 7&8:041a

[26] Land Office (Rent Rolls), Maryland State Archives, Annapolis, Md., MSA No.: S18-54. Liber 43, page 29a

[27] Skinner, Jr., V. L. *Abstracts of the Inventories of the Prerogative Court*; Libers 18-23 1733-1738; Family Line Publications, Westminster, Maryland; November 1990, p. 5

[28] Maryland Calendar of Wills, *Will of William Chisum*, SMC 10/21/1697 (no probate date). Three daughters: Jane, Mary, and Ann at age 16 personal estate. Wife: Ann (Exec.) residuary legatee of estate, real and personal. Wit: Arthur Keane and William Gibson.

[29] Donnelly,Mary Louise, *Colonial Settlers St. Clement's Bay 1634-1780,* p 188

[30] Himmelheber, Peter, Electronic 12/5/2010, *map of "Hopewell" and "The Bottom"*

[31] Inventories & Accounts 33.321 (8/20/1746 – 10/7/1746)

[32] St. Mary's County Will books 1791-1805 Vol JJ2: 161,162

[33] See Will Bk. JJ#1:249-50

[34] Courtesy Linda Reno and Pete Himmelheber in msg of 12/31/2008: 3/3/1787 Deed from Elizabeth Joy and Ignatius Medcalf to Jeremiah Milburn for "Fibney", 84 1/2 Ac. (At: 005/CSM:27:02:015)

[35] Family group record LDS files (AFN 10jz-qnl)

[36] Family group record LDS files (AFN 1q21-p6q)

[37] Family group record LDS files (AFN 1q21-p5j)

Chapter Five

Charles Drury

Charles Drury (second husband of Alice) died in 1740 when she administered his estate.[1] According to his will she received a life interest in the home plantation *Essex Land* that Charles had purchased in 1736. When Alice died *Essex Land* was to pass to his grandson Edward Boetler, the son of his daughter Sophia.

Five children are mentioned in his will. They are Sarah, Esther, Mary, Charles, and Sophia. Given the fact that Charles and Alice Adney were only married seven years before his death and that Sarah, Esther, Sophia and Mary were all listed as married and that Charles Jr. married in 1739, it can be confidently assumed that these children were by Mary, his first wife. Birth, land and other records were destroyed in a fire in 1704 but we can estimate from the later records we have that all these children were born between about 1700 and 1725.[2] Sarah married Abraham Simmons, Esther was wed to Nathan Selby, Sophia as we can infer, married Charles Boetler, and Mary married someone named Dart.

This marriage to Charles Boetler gives us a definite connection to St. Mary's County and our other Drury families. Sophia's husband Charles was a grandson of Charles Boetler (1635–1686) who patented *Dansbury Hill* in 1665 and lived there until at least 1707. He was both a surveyor and assemblyman for St. Mary's County.[3] *Dansbury Hill* was in the same vicinity to both *The Bottom* and *Howard's Mount* where our Drurys lived.

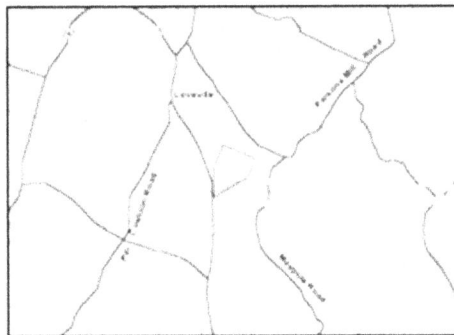

Dansbury Hill, St. Mary's County[4]

Charles Drury Jr.

His son, Charles Jr. married first in 1739 to Elizabeth Miles[5] and again in 1749 to Mary. We do not have a surname for Mary though some have speculated that Mary Jerningham, daughter of Dr. Henry Jerningham and Catharine was his second wife. His will was probated in 1766 and mentions nine children and five separate parcels of land in Prince George, and Anne Arundel Counties. These were *Birkenhead's Chance*, *Gullock's Polly* (or possibly *Folly*), *Vale of Pleasure*, *Talbott Search*, and *Portland Manor*. *Portland Manor* seemed to be his home plantation. It was located in western Ann Arundel County and contained the Drury post village that is still marked on maps today. It is just east of the town of Upper Marlboro. [6]

"Birkhead's Parcel," another Drury holding, sits in Lothian, Maryland, today on a working tobacco farm of nearly 50 acres. The land has been in owner Susanne Smith's family since 1799 when her ancestor, Jerningham Drury, acquired it. Susanne and her husband Gordon have lived in the area all their lives. When they laid the foundation for their new home in 1994, they built in the style of home that both grew up in. "And it went with the barn," says Smith.

"Outside, you'll follow a green meadow up a long driveway to the eight-room, two-bathroom home. Screened porch and kitchen are telescoping wings to either side of the central structure with its four symmetrical windows, two on either side of the entrance door. Inside, the home is furnished in part in family antiques. It's all on a scale that feels cozy and lived in. Cross through the orchard in the back, and you'll find neighboring Some Day Farm, that also belonged to the Drury family until 1952. Next to Some Day Farm's circular drive, Smith's relatives rest under a dozen 19th-century tombstones...."[7]

Children of Charles Jr.

Charles' son William was born in 1750. Samuel was born in 1759. His sons Charles III, William and Samuel had to be the ones who supported the revolution and forfeited property in England. They were the only ones alive and "of age" in 1778.[8]

William, the eldest was born in 1750 and married Elizabeth Ijams in 1768 at age 18.[9] She was a daughter of Plummer Ijams Sr. and Ruth Childs.[10] They had three known children, Elizabeth who married John Green, Henry Childs Drury (of William) whose wife is unknown at present, and William Jr. who married Maria Smith.

William's brother Charles, who married Margaret Childs in 1774, took the Oath of Allegiance to Maryland in 1778[11] and enlisted in the West River Battalion of Militia in Ann Arundel County as 1st lieutenant in William Simmons Company[12]. Charles and Margaret had a total of seven children. They were Jerningham who married Sarah Hill, Charles, Joseph, Henry Childs, Samuel, Mary who married Van Simmons,[13] and an unnamed daughter who married a Mr. Welch.[14]

Charles Jr.'s remaining five children were all girls; Sarah born in 1753 married Hercules Courtenay;[15] Elizabeth married to Mathew Cooley in 1774;[16] Margaret married John Pindell by 1770;[17] Ann married Zebedee Wood in September 10, 1776[18] and Easter (or Hester) who apparently remained unmarried. There is evidence that Hester was either mentally unstable or (as they said at the time) feeble minded.[19]

Samuel (1759 – 1850) married William's sister-in-law, Ann Ijams born July 2, 1759.[20] In their 66 year marriage, they had eleven children. We have birth dates for all but two: Marydell who married Richard Hill and William who married an Evans. One of them was probably the first born but we cannot tell which one. This youngest brother, Samuel Drury, is also a recognized patriot and was commissioned Ensign in the same company as his brother.[21] He is listed in several publications and is the ancestor that several family members have proven their lineage to, in order to qualify for membership in the Daughters of the American Revolution.[22]

Samuel and Ann Ijams had the following children in addition to Marydell and William mentioned above: Elizabeth (1781- bef. 1842) who married Samuel Ward November 23, 1798, (and possibly a Mr. Lyles as a second husband); Ruth (1783 - ?) who married Benjamin Welch in 1804; Ann (abt 1785 - ?) who married George Gardiner May 12, 1826; Mary (abt. 1787 - ?) who married William Smith (and possibly a Mr. Humphrys as a second husband); Margaret (abt. 1789 - ?) who married William Hopkins; Plummer Ijams Drury (abt. 1791 – aft. 1868) who married Margaret Cannon; Samuel Drury Jr. (1792 – 1867) who married Mary Nolan; Henry Childs Drury (1795 – 1873) who married Mary Ann Owens in 1823; and John Ijams Drury (1797-). All these children plus some grandchildren were mentioned in the will of Samuel Drury written in 1848.[23]

The War of 1812

By the beginning of the nineteenth century the new country was still having problems gaining respect from European countries. Problems continued with both Britain and France over U.S. expansion in the Northwest Territory and in the west. Neither European superpower respected the neutrality of the United States in the conflict between them. Instead, both tried to prevent U.S. ships from carrying goods to their enemy. Both Britain and France imposed blockades to limit American merchants.

In response to this denial of American sovereignty, President Jefferson and his secretary of state James Madison crafted an imaginative, but fundamentally flawed, policy of economic coercion. Their Embargo of 1807 prevented U.S. ships from any trade with Europe in the belief that dependence on American goods would soon force France and England to honor American neutrality. The plan backfired, however, as the Republican leaders failed to understand how deeply committed the superpowers were to carrying on their war despite its high costs.

The most hated practice however was the forced removal of Americans from United States merchant vessels known as impressment. Between 1793 and 1812, the British impressed more than 15,000 U.S. sailors to supplement their fleet during their Napoleonic Wars with France. By 1812 the United States government had had enough. On 18 June, the United States declared war on Great Britain, citing, in part, impressments.

Maryland was in the center of the conflict because of it's proximity to Washington D.C., our capital, and the ease of transportation up Chesapeake Bay. As in the Revolutionary war, Drurys supported the cause enthusiastically. The British victory at the Battle of Bladensburg in August 1814 allowed them to capture and burn Washington, D.C. American victory in September 1814 repulsed the British invasion in Baltimore. The Battle of Baltimore in 1814 (which inspired the lyrics of the American national anthem, "The Star-Spangled Banner") produced a sense of euphoria over a "second war of independence" against Britain.

Plummer Drury volunteered as a private in the first regiment in the District of Columbia Militia and was probably among those in that brigade under Brigadier General Walter Smith who marched up from Long Old Fields. Plummer's cousins Jerningham and Henry C. volunteered as privates in the second regiment Maryland Militia and were also most likely among the defenders. On 20 August Brigadier General Tobias Stansbury moved from Baltimore to Bladensburg[24] and was to "...take the best position in advance of Bladensburg... and should he be attacked, to resist as long as possible." Although Smith's brigade was strongly posted behind a creek, Smith had not conferred with Stansbury before deploying his brigade, so there was a gap of a mile between them, and Smith's men could not support Stansbury. Also, if Stansbury was overcome, Smith's left flank would be open to attack.

Another relative, William Tillard lost considerable property at a place called Tracey's Landing due to a skirmish with British troops. In 1836 and 1837 depositions were taken documenting the loss, and by 1844 his descendants had submitted a petition to Congress for a "Bill of relief" to compensate them.[25]

A PARTIAL TEXT OF THESE DEPOSITIONS IS INCLUDED HERE.

"...that the militia that were called out for the defense of the neighborhood at the time the inspection warehouse was burnt by the British at Tracey's Landing were two companies: Jacob Franklin was captain of one, Thomas Sullivan was lieutenant, and William Wiem ensign; William S. Tillard was captain of the other, Thomas Tongue, jr. was lieutenant, and John H. Tillard ensign—all of whom are now dead."

A second deposition taken in 1836 states, "Personally appeared before the subscriber, a justice of the peace for the county and State aforesaid, Samuel Gover, who, being sworn on the Holy Evangels of Almighty God, doth depose and declare: That he acted as commissary to the Maryland militia, who were called out to defend that part of the shores of the Chesapeake bay from Fishing creek to Tracey's Landing during the year 1814; doth depose and declare that Commodore Barney took possession of the large tobacco inspection warehouse located at Tracey's Landing some time in the spring of 1814, and kept possession of the same until some time in the summer of the same year; and that the said tobacco inspection warehouse was used as a place of depot for the stores belonging to the United States flotilla, consisting of provisions, ammunition, spare sails, and other munitions of war, which were carried by land to Patuxent river, where said flotilla lay a considerable time, over which said stores and munitions of war a detachment of men and some officers were placed; and the said deponent further states and says, that a few days before the British burned down the said inspection warehouse, and, while the British were lying off in the Chesapeake bay, the militia, under the command of Captain Jacob Franklin, (the same officer, now dead,) *rolled out a quantity of tobacco from the said tobacco inspection warehouse, and made a breastwork or fortification by standing the hogsheads of tobacco endwise,* as a protection for the militia to fight under. The deponent doth further state, on oath, that a few days after this, the British landed from their ships and took possession of the said tobacco inspection warehouse at Tracey's Landing, burned and destroyed the same, together with all the fixtures there belonging, and together with a quantity of tobacco."

The Civil War

During the Civil War in the 1860s Drurys again took up arms though in this case it was often cousin against cousin or brother against brother. In Washington DC, Henry Drury a son of Plummer Ijams Drury and Margaret Gannon and his second cousin John Henry Drury both volunteered in the Union Army. In the meantime some of their cousins in southern Maryland and in the west joined the confederate cause. Sympathies generally followed those of their region. Southern Maryland was still primarily agricultural with tobacco being the main cash crop while the area around the Monocacy valley and Washington D.C. had a more diverse economy. This meant that areas like St. Mary's County relied more heavily on slave labor though this was not entirely the case. Maryland, as a border state, had difficulties during the war. Union troops took over the city of Baltimore causing riots that resulted in numbers of troops and civilians being killed and injured. The sympathies of many Marylanders especially in the south were with the Confederacy.

In the last quarter of the century descendants of Charles Drury of Ann Arundel County flourished in Northern Maryland. Census reports and city directories list Drurys as butchers, merchants, hucksters (salesmen), teachers, carters (delivering ice and coal), magistrates, Justices of the peace, farmers, tax collectors, and other gainful occupations.[26][27] By the beginning of the twentieth century they began holding positions in government and publishing as well.

Twentieth Century

One example is James Washington Sheahan, husband of Mary Elizabeth Ann Drury the daughter of Samuel Drury and Mary Nolan. He was widely known in the West, both from his intimate association with Judge Steven A. Douglas and his long connection with the newspapers of Chicago. He was born in Baltimore, Maryland, February 22nd, 1824, and died after a protracted illness at the age of 60 on 17 June 1883.

This is a brief excerpt from his extensive obituary. "Mr. James W. Sheahan died at his home, No. 355 Superior Street, at 5 o'clock yesterday morning, only members of his family being present at the time of his death. Shortly after midnight, he sank into a troubled sleep, which gradually became more peaceful, and in this condition passed away, the sorrowing family by his bedside scarcely knowing the moment of final dissolution."

His parents were natives of Ireland. Not long after his birth, his parents removed to Washington, where he resided until their death. Mr. Sheahan got his first education in the schools of that city, and completed it at the Jesuit school in Frederick, Md. After he had finished his course of study, he read law and in 1845 was admitted to the bar, but never practiced his profession.

The accidental absence from duty of a newspaperman with whom he was acquainted led to his taking up that business. It didn't take him long to acquire great proficiency in his new profession, and for several years he continued reporting the Congressional proceedings for the press of the District and the New York Associated Press.

In 1847 he made his first visit to the West; he came for the purpose of making the report of the proceedings of the Illinois Constitutional Convention which was held at Springfield during that and the following year. This gave him a chance to become acquainted with the persons among whom his future lot in life was to be cast. He became very popular among the many Illinoisans whom he met during the convention, and when he retuned to the State a few years later they met him with a cordial welcome. While thus employed he became acquainted with Judge Steven A. Douglas, the most powerful Democrat of his time. At his insistence Sheahan came to Chicago to publish a Democratic newspaper in 1854. Sheahan started the Chicago Times in August that year.

In July 1860, after having firmly established the Times, he sold it to Mr. McCormick who renamed it The Chicago Tribune, and in the following December, with his former staff of writers, began the publication of the Post, which, in turn, he sold to the Republican Company in April 1865. He remained as Editor during the administration of Mr. Dane, and when that gentleman left the paper in 1866, Mr. Sheahan accepted an editorial position on The Tribune, where he remained up to the time of his death.[28]

Another who rose to prominence is Louis Mason Drury, a Washington, D.C. native, who was the son of John Samuel Drury and Alice Mason Drury. He was born 19 January 1910 and died in 2004. He was a direct descendent through his mother of George Mason (December 11, 1725 – October 7, 1792) an American Patriot, statesman and a delegate from Virginia to the U.S. Constitutional Convention. Louis began working for the Department of State in 1931, and was graduated that same year from the National University Law School in Washington, D.C. He entered the Foreign Service in 1954, where he was posted in Mexico City to serve as executive officer of the consular section of the U.S. Embassy. He was later appointed Consul General of the United States in Ciudad Juarez and in 1959, sent to Caracas, Venezuela as first secretary in charge of consular affairs at the U.S. Embassy there.[29]

This was an especially critical time in our relations with Venezuela. Dictator Pérez Jiménez was overthrown in 1958, and the exiled Romulo Betancourt returned to Venezuela, made peace with other democratic elements, and was elected president. Harassed by pro-Cuban communists on one side and frightened conservatives on the other, he steered a middle course, passing an agrarian law to expropriate large estates, initiating an ambitious program of public works, and fostering industrial development to prevent complete dependence on petroleum revenues. Several attempts had been made in the United States legislature during the mid 1950s to limit the import of foreign oil and protect domestic oil producers. By 1958, global oil prices had slumped and the pressure from domestic producers on the legislature grew stronger.

By March 1958 Vice President Nixon had added Venezuela to his planned tour of South America, noting the 'rather shaky and inexperienced' provisional government, and that an official visit by the United States government could offer them encouragement and a 'well done' for restoring democratic rule. In reality, Nixon could have hardly have picked a worse time to visit the country; Anti-Americanism was rampant, and his visit to Caracas in May 1958 provided a visceral demonstration of how the tacit support for dictatorships and inflexible insistence upon free trade had alienated the US from its supposed allies. On May 13th 1958 his reception at Caracas provided a climactic and violent demonstration of the deep resentment towards US foreign policy. Descending from the Vice-Presidential plane, Richard Nixon, his wife Pat Nixon and his accompanying advisors (including Assistant Secretary of State Richard Rubottom) were met with a storm of abuse and spit from two hundred Venezuelan student demonstrators. Abandoning the customary speeches, Nixon's party and the Venezuelan foreign minister Oscar Garcia Velutini made straight for Caracas. On the highway and within the city limits, their motorcade was repeatedly ambushed by protesters, smashing the car's windows with rocks and steel pipes and at one point nearly turning Nixon's limousine over, with their Venezuelan police escorts unwilling and unable to contain the crowds. With several injured by broken glass, Nixon and Velutini included, the motorcade escaped the highway and made straight for the American Embassy.[30] As we can see his job was far from routine.

During World War II, Drury was a lieutenant commander with the United States Coast Guard. In 1945 he was assigned by the Department of State to General Eisenhower's staff at Supreme Headquarters of the Allied Expeditionary Forces. While serving on the General's staff, he worked in London, Paris and Frankfurt.[31] Since the General was now President, it makes us wonder if he remembered the Lieutenant Commander who had served him during the war and had some involvement in the appointment.

---

[1] Maryland Calendar of Wills Vol 8 1738-1743 p 198; Maryland Probate Records, perogative Court Abstracts 1738-1744 pp 38,93

[2] Roth, Marilyn, Email msg of 10/20/2000

[3] From Dennis Witmer,<dawitmer@aol.com> Charles Boteler 1635-1686 was a surveyer and assemblyman of St. Mary's County

[4] Courtesy of Pete Himmelheber

[5] Maryland Probate Records, perogative court abstracts 1733-1738 p 103

[6] Maryland Calendar of Wills p 103; Anne Arundel County Inventory and accounts 92.259; Abstract of inventory of the perogative Court of Maryland 1766-1769 p 20

[7] Dodd, Darcy, http://www.bayweekly.com/year00/issue8_18/life8_18.html, Inside Southern Anne Arundel's Stately Homes

[8] Peden, *Revolutionary Patriots of Anne Arundel County*

[9] Md. State Archives: Maryland indexes; marriage references; msa s 1527: William; 17 Nov, 1768, Elizabeth Ijams ("marriage register of Rev. David Love", discovered by Peter Wilson Coldham in the Public Record Office, London (PRO:AO 13/61(II)/ 420 ff) Provincial Court

[10] Newman, Harry Wright, Anne Arundel Gentry Vol. I, 1970 pp 300,301,313,319

[11] Peden, Henry C. Jr., Revolutionary Patriots of Anne Arundel County, Maryland, Oath of Allegiance before Hon. Samuel Lane, on 1 March 1778

[12] Liber C. B. No. 24 p.78

[13] St. James Parish, AA CO, Md; Mary DRURY married VAN SIMMONS May 5, 1774

[14] these children were all named on his will of 1809

[15] Peden, Henry C. Jr., Revolutionary Patriots of Baltimore Town and Baltimore County Maryland 1775-1783 Family Line Publications, Silver Spring, Maryland, 1988: COURTENAY HERCULES. (October 15, 1736, Newry, Ireland - August 21, 1816, Baltimore County, Maryland) Married Sarah DRURY (1753-1788) in 1774

[16] Married in St. James Parish, Ann Arundel County, Md

[17] Maryland Indexes; Marriage References; MSA S 1527: "PINDELL ... John, m. by 1770, Margaret Drury (Hodges cites St. James' Parish Register at MHS).

[18] Kitty Crowley, lookup volunteer: St. James Church Records sent on 24 Jul 2000, Zebedee Wood and Ann Drury m. 10 Sep 1776.

[19] Maryland State Archives; Maryland Indexes; (Chancery Papers, Index); 1713-1787; MSA S 1432: CHANCERY COURT (Chancery Papers) 1786/04/07 1571: Charles Drury vs. Hester Drury. AA. Appointment of trustee for Hester Drury. Accession No: 17,898-1571. MSA S512-1640   1/36/1/; Drury, Charles vs. Hester Drury a Lunatic, Anne Arundel County, 1786 Petition... not recorded' Anne Arundel County, 25 March 1786...Petitioner's sister, Hester Drury, is frequently in a state of Insanity

[20] Family Archive #224 Marriage Index: Maryland, 1655-1850 Married: May 29, 1779 in Anne Arundel Co., MD. ; Anne Arundel Gentry, Vol. 1, Ijams Family; Page number: 301: "Ann Iiams, born July 2, 1759, married Samuel Drury

[21] Per Lois Selby, email message 12-27-1998: Samuel was an Ensign in Captain William Simmon's Co. in the West River Battalion, 1778

[22] DAR ID Number: 70926; Born in Washington, D. C.; Wife of Louis Cassidy; Descendant of Samuel Drury; Daughter of John Samuel Drury (b. 1861) and Alice Mason (b. 1865), his wife, m. 1883. Granddaughter of Charles W. Drury (b. 1835) and Virginia Poore (b. 1842), his wife, m. 1859. Great-granddaughter of Samuel Drury, Jr. (1792-1867), and Mary Nolan (1794-1867), his wife, m. 1814. Great-Gr-granddaughter of Samuel Drury and Ann Ijams, his wife

[23] Per Gary O'Neill, e-mail to me 01 Mar 2001: "In the name of God, Amen. I Samuel Drury of Anne Arundel County and State of Maryland being infirm from age and weak of body but of sound and disposing mind memory and understanding considering the certainty of death and the uncertainty of the time thereof and being desirous to settle my worldly affairs and thereby be the better prepared to leave this world when it shall please God to call me home, do

therefore make and publish this my last will and testament in manner and form following that is to say , ...? and principally I commend my soul into the hands of Almighty God and my body to the earth to be decently buried at the discretion of my Executors herein after named and after my funeral charges are paid I devise and bequeath as follows: Item. I give and devise unto my beloved wife during her natural life should she survive me and not otherwise all my real estate with the use of all my servants , farm stock, farming utensils to carry on and work said estate solely for her use and benefit, also all my crops of every description on hand and growing at my death, the Real and personal property and my estate therefore should she not consent to receive the same instead of or in lieu of her dower. I hereby annul all the devises and gifts and here in her favor just as if she was not named in this will or instrument at all at the death of my beloved wife. Should she survive me and stand to this will , it is my will and desire that the whole of my Estate shall be divided as follows: Item - I give and bequeath to my two Grandsons George H Lyles and Plummer I Lyles, sons of my deceased daughter Elizabeth the sum of three hundred and fifty dollars each and no more but with this promise nevertheless that in case either of them or any one by their auth only shall set up a claim to any other part of my estate under my plea whatever that my executors shall not be bound to pay either of them or their heirs the aforementioned legacies. Item, I give and bequeath to my Grandson, John W? Gardner, my Negro boy Zachariah about fourteen years of age now in his Father's possession and when John shall arrive at the age of twenty one years a legacy of fifty dollars also. Item, it is my will and desire that the residue of my personal estate including what is left to my beloved wife during her life shall be divided into nine parts or shares and ...over in the following manner - my daughter Ruth Welch and her heirs to have and receive one part or ninth share. My daughter Anne Gardner and her heirs to have and receive one part or ninth share. My daughter Mary Humphreys to have and receive one part or ninth share during her live only and after her death to be equally divided amongst her present children and their heirs under this express promise nevertheless that my executors shall not be compelled to pay into the hands of her husband anything herein willed to my said daughter Mary Humphreys but that the same shall remain and continue in the hands of my Executors of such person or persons and she shall appoint during the life of her husband and that during his life the profits thereof shall be paid to my said daughter Mary and that any receipt of writing witnessing the payment of any part thereof to the said Mary Humphreys and signed by her through caveat shall be sufficient to discharge to my Executors or person or person by her appointed as aforesaid, Levins (Lewis?) Gardner to have and receive one part or ninth share in trust nevertheless that the sum shall be exclusively for the use and benefit of my daughter Margaret Hill(last name?) during her life and at their death the balance (if any) shall be equally divided among her heirs to have and receive one part or ninth share. My Son Samuel and his heirs to have and receive one part or ninth share. My granddaughter, Louisa B. Jones and her heirs to have and receive one ninth share with this promise nevertheless that the debt her husband owes me is to come out of her share or proportion if not paid at my death as part or parcel of her said share. My son, Henry C and his heirs to have and receive two parts or two ninths shares, my Negro man Moses to be included in his share as part and parcel thereof at his appraisement. Item, I give and bequeath to my son John I, the feather bed stead and furniture now used by him and a home in my dwelling house in case said house on the division of my land shall fall to my son Henry but in case it does not my Executors is to build him, John I, a comfortable house on the land that falls to my son Henry not to cost over three hundred and fifty dollars the cost of which my son Henry is to pay one half of and my sons, Samuel and Plummer I the other half. Item. I give and bequeath to my son Plummer I, one fourth part of my real estate after the death of his mother to him and his heirs forever. Item. I give and bequeath to my son Samuel and his heirs one fourth part of my real estate after the death of his mother. Item, I give and bequeath to my son Henry C. after the death of his mother, and his heirs, one half of my real estate the same to be laid off adjoining his farm and in consideration of having left my son Henry C more property than any other child it is my will and desire that he pay towards my son John I, and his heirs legally begotten of his body reasonable support the sum of one hundred and fifty dollars annually while my son, John I and his said heirs shall live but in case my son, John I. or his heirs as aforesaid survive my son Henry C, it is my will and desire that one half the land herein bequeathed to my son Henry C shall revert back to my son John I or his heirs as aforesaid unless my son Henry C, heirs Executors or administrators shall pay him or them the sum of sixteen hundred dollars as a consideration for the same - but in case my son Henry C. survives, John I or his heirs as aforesaid all the property herein bequeathed to Henry C. is to be his and his heirs in fee simple forever. Item, I hereby will and direct that my Executors shall soon after my death enclose my family graveyard under a good and substantial rail or ...? fence the cost of which is to be paid out of my estate before final division of the same the cost thereof to be considered a part of my funeral expenses and lastly, I do hereby constitute and appoint my sons Samuel and Henry C executors of this my last will and testament revoking and annulling all others by me made ....? and confirming this and none other to be my last will and testament in testimony whereof I have hereunto set my hand and seal this 28th day of January Eighteen hundred and forty two if not paid at my death being interlined on the third page also in the same page and that signed seal published and declared by Samuel Drury the above named testators as and for his last will and testament in presence of us who at his request in his presence and in the presence of each other have subscribed and name as witnesses thereto Benjamin C Neff (or Ness), Thomas Armiger Chas. (Charles) Hodges. Whereas I Samuel Drury of Anne Arundel county have made and duly executed my last will and testament in writing bearing date the 28th Day of January Eighteen Hundred and forty two which said last will and testament and every clause bequest and devise therein contained I do hereby ratify and confirm (saving and excepting such clauses bequests and devises therein mentioned as are by me herein revoked and made void and being desirous to alter some parts thereof and of making........... Gary noted here that he still has to obtain codicils to this will

[24] http://en.wikipedia.org/wiki/Battle_of_Bladensburg#cite_note-Elting206-9

[25] PETITION FOR BILL OF RELIEF – 1844 FOR MATILDA DRURY AND OTHER LEGAL REPRESENTATIVES OF CAPTAIN WILLIAM S. TILLARD, LATE, OF MARYLAND.

[26] 1864 Washington D.C. Directory: Charles Drury, waggoner, h 174 22d west**, Colbert Drury, huckster, h 96 D south, L. M. Drury, clerk Pension office, Samuel Drury, magistrate, h 133 I north**, Samuel T. Drury, lawyer, 363 L north, h same, T. Drury, wood and coal, 165 Pa av, h 399 K north, W. C. Drury, huckster, 17 & 18 Centre market, William P. Drury, h 433 11th west, Drury & Mullins (Richard Drury & Wm. C. Mullins, provisioners), 175 Northern & 140 Centre markets

[27] Washington, D.C. City Directory, 1890:Charles S Drury clerk 1528 6th northwest District of Columbia DC 1890, Charles W Drury watchman 923 N H avenue northwest   District of Columbia, 1890

[28] The Chicago Daily Tribune, June 18, 1883, page 2

[29] United States Department of State Washington, D.C. August 13, 2002

[30] www.e-ir.info/2011/10/30/The Dreamboat that ran aground - U.S. policy towards Venezuela 1955-1960

[31] Katherine E. Simons, Obituary of Louis Mason Drury 1910-2004

Chapter Six

Descendants of John Drury (1710 - _____)

John Drury married Susanna Hayden in 1734.[1] He was born about 1710 in St. Mary's County the son of John Drury (d. 1724) and Ann Payne. Susanna was born about 1711 to William Hayden and Elizabeth Thompson. John undoubtedly took the oath of allegiance along with his cousins Nicholas and Peter though there is no record of them doing so. He probably fought with the rebels and supplied them with food and feed for their horses. By the time the revolution started in 1776 he and his family had moved to St. George's Hundred near the St. Mary's river that also included St. George's Island.

Frances Anna was their first child born in 1735. She married Joseph Tucker in 1744. Nine of the ten children born to the Tuckers were born in Maryland. Joseph took the oath of allegiance and fought in the revolution though his children were too young.[2]

Their next child was a son, William Drury, born in 1737. He was listed along with his cousins Nicholas and Peter Jr. as a lessee on Drury's Venture that his uncle Peter patented in 1741. William is still living there as late as 1768 when he is listed along with his cousins on what is then listed as Sandy Ground. He married Mary Ann Wooten, a daughter of neighbors Thomas Wooten and Mary Shircliffe, about 1759. They had two sons in Maryland, Clement in 1759 and Raphael in 1764.

By the time of the revolution in 1776 John's family had moved to St. George's hundred and was leasing land from the Jesuits. William, his father, and his brother John, furnished supplies to the Continental army.[3] It was probably shortly after he was paid that William and his family decided to leave Maryland.[4]

John Drury (1739 – 1797) is assumed to be another son of John and Susanna. We do not have a record of his birth or christening, but everything we know about him fits with this conclusion.[5] John married twice but all the children mentioned in his will of 1797 had to be by his first wife. Ann Jarboe, almost certainly a widow when they wed, married him in 1795 only two years before he died.[6] [7]His nine children were Ignatius – 1760, John Chrysostom - between 1760 and 1765, Susanna – 1765, Francis Desales- 1768, Anastasia – 1770, William – 1777, Mary - before 1780, Monica - between 1780 and 1786, and Joseph – 1786.[8]

Jeremiah Drury is a possible son of John and Susanna born about 1750.[9] In 1800 he is living in St. George's Hundred and in 1810 his same neighbors are living next to John C. Drury and Mary Drury. He sponsored the baptism of Eleanor Davis, daughter of Joseph and Mima, 19 Apr 1778.[10] By 1790 he was married with a daughter though his wife is unknown.[11] In 1794 he was listed on the muster roll for St. Mary's County.[12] By 1800 he added two boys and another daughter to his family.[13] It is likely he remained in St. Mary's County.

Monica Drury was born in February of 1751. She married Nicholas Moore Jr., a son of Nicholas Moore and Diana Gentle, in St. Mary's County about 1770. They had three children: Isadore (1771), Bede (1773), and James (1775).[14] The Moores, along with everyone else living in St. George's hundred, suffered much destruction of their crops and livestock due to British raids during the war. They, along with their neighbors, applied for reparations after the war in 1781.[15] They probably left for Kentucky by 1788 where Nicholas bought fifty acres in Nelson County, Kentucky.[16]

Mary Drury was born in St. Mary's County about 1746. She married Basil Knott before 1767. Their children were James (1767-1817), Elizabeth (1769-1817), Susanna (1771-1817), Mary (1772-1852), Nancy (1774) and Clement (1780-1847).[17] By 1800 the couple was in Nelson County, Kentucky. Her husband died there in 1817.

Elizabeth Drury is the final girl assumed to be a child of John and Susanna. She is also living in St. George hundred and was listed as a congregant at St. Inigoes. She married Jeremy Gatton in 1773[18] and is assumed to be the Elizabeth listed along with others as congregants at St. Inigoes. Other names in this reference are assumed to be children or other relatives.[19] Nothing more is verifiable about her life or her connection to this family.

Francis Drury is the eighth child we presume is a possible son of John Drury and Susanna Hayden. He was born sometime after 1755. There was a Francis D. Drury mentioned but they could not be the same person because he was too young to sign the oath of allegiance in 1776. Richard Fenwick left one cow and calf each to several Drury members including Francis. See also notes for John (d. 1797).[20] Drurys, Moores, and Carpenters were all living in St. George's Hundred during the last quarter of the 18th century. He married Mary Ann Carpenter in 1778 and later was in Perry County, Missouri.

Finally there was Joseph Drury who went to Virginia and was estranged from the family because he converted to Baptist. Some people dispute this connection, but there is a fair amount of evidence connecting them that will be discussed in Chapter Twelve.

Descendants of Peter Drury (1700 – 1770)

Peter Drury was one of the grandchildren of the immigrant Robert Drury who patented Dry Docking in 1672. He was probably born sometime between 1700 and 1715. His father, John Drury, died before 1724 when his second wife Mary Ford Drury administered John's estate.[21] Peter Drury had at least five and probably ten children between the birth of his son Nicholas in 1738 and Peter's death in 1770. We know he had sons Nicholas and Peter Jr. because they were named in the lease for "Drury's Venture" in 1741. We also can be confident that he had sons Michael, Richard, and Philip because Michael was named as executor and Richard, and Philip were named as next of kin in his will of 1770.[22] The remaining five children, John Baptist, Ignatius, Mildred, Enoch, and Catherine are presumed children of Peter because of connections between them and the various families into which they married. If we assume that Peter was married twice then the only children we can positively ascribe to Jane would be Nicholas and Peter Jr. since they are named in the lease along with Jane who would still be alive at that point. The rest are in limbo so far as identifying a mother.

Nicholas Drury

Peter's first son Nicholas was born in 1738. At the age of 3 his father named him as a lessee of "Drury's Venture" along with his brother Peter and his cousin William. Nicholas married Monica _____ sometime before 1759 when his oldest son Leonard was born.[23] We can assume that he had at least three more children than we know of because the next child we positively can place with him was Bennett christened 17 April 1768.[24] Nine years between children was unthinkable in the eighteenth century. Most couples conceived children fairly regularly every two years. The next children we show for Nicholas after Bennett is a set of twins, Joseph and Mary, christened 2 September 1770.[25] Finally we have a daughter Monica christened 4 October 1772.[26] He possibly had more children after 1772. Nicholas wrote his will on 2 May 1789 and died in July of that same year. He was 51 years of age.[27]

Peter Drury Jr.

Peter Jr., born about 1740, was living with his brother on "Sandy Ground (Lot #28)" in 1768.[29] We know that this was Peter Jr. and not his father as his age was listed as 28 at that time. This places his birth as 1740 when his father patented Drury's Venture and designated Peter and his brother Nicholas as two of the three patentees. He married Eleanor _____ before 1771. She was born before 1756 and died sometime after her husband. They had a son Jesse christened 22 September 1776. Peter executed the will of his brother Nicholas in 1789 and died some time after that.

Michael Drury

Michael, the third son, was born about 1743 and married Ann Yates, the daughter of Thomas Yates and Mary French, 3 November 1770 only a few months after the death of his father.[30] The bequest of "Drury's Venture" in his father's will would have given him the means to assure his in-laws that he was able to provide comfortably for his new bride. Michael did quite well over the years raising a large family. During the Revolution he served as a Private in the Corps of Invalids in Continental Troops.[31] There are also stories about Michael and his neighbors hiding on his farms to avoid British troops on raiding expeditions during the War of 1812. He did not die until 14 February 1825 when he was in his 80s and was reported to be blind.[32]

Michael Drury lived one and a half miles from Joseph Leonard Johnson, who had married his daughter Mary Ann and was managing his farm. He owned "Drury's Delight," "Hard Times," and "Males" farms.[33] Two Johnson boys married Drury girls (Joseph L. to Mary Ann and John to Sarah Marthalina), and one Johnson girl married a Drury boy (Michael Jr. to Catherine). Michael Drury died 2/14/1825 when in his 80s and blind. "Males" farm was not listed in George Fenwick's survey of Beaverdam Manor. This was a misspelling of "Wales" farm (Lot 32) that was listed in 1790 as purchased or possessed by William Fenwick. The three farms mentioned above had contiguous boundaries in 1790 and had a combined total of approximately 230 acres.[34]

Michael changed his will shortly before he died, leaving his estate to his two daughters Dorothy Joy and Catherine Drury. This caused considerable consternation among the rest of his children. On 3 June 1828 a petition was filed objecting to probate of the will of Michael Drury by his daughter Marthaney Drury, now the wife of John Johnson of Leonard; Thomas Drury; Dorothy, Julian and Elizabeth Drury, heirs and children of his son Edward Drury; Rose Ann Emeline Drury, Edward Drury and Eleanor (by Joseph Johnson their next friend) children of his son Michael Drury; William Johnson; John Johnson, Joseph Johnson, Ann Johnson, and Michael (by Joseph Johnson their next friend) children of Mary Ann Johnson, formerly Mary Ann Drury. In July 1829 a hearing was held to determine if Michael Drury was of sound mind when he made his will. [35]

Beaverdam Manor 1790[36]

We can see from this map how most of Peter's children and relatives all had plantations close to him and to each other. We had Peter Sr. on part of "The Bottom" only a few miles north until 1760, Michael on "Drury's Delight" and Wales," Enoch's wife Tabitha Wimsatt on "Hard Times," Philip on "Flower of the Forrest" (formerly part of Wimsatt's Delight) just to the southwest, and his cousin James Jr's wife Sarah on "Chatham" after James Jr. died. All of these plantations surrounded or were near "Swamp Island" that was owned by George Fenwick who we think employed William and Clement Drury, sons of Philip.[37]

John Baptist Drury

John Baptist Drury's estimated birth is about 1744. His first recorded wife was Elizabeth who he married sometime before 1766 when their son John Drury was born. Most eighteenth century men did not marry before the age of 20. Assuming they were married at least a year before his son's birth would make John Baptist's birth about 1744 to 1746. A second assumption for John Baptist is that Elizabeth probably died in childbirth or shortly thereafter and he remarried Mary Margaret in 1767 in order to have a wife to care for his infant son. He had two daughters with his second wife. They were Mary born in 1768 and Elizabeth born in 1770. We have no documented data for the death of either John Baptist or Mary Margaret. There are unsubstantiated reports of a John Baptist Drury visiting Drury relatives in Baltimore. We don't know if this was the same man but up to now he is the only John Baptist Drury known to be in Maryland at this time.[38]

Ignatius Drury

The fourth Son, Ignatius, born about 1748, married Anastasia French 11 December 1769.[39] She was a daughter of John French and Monica _____. There is confusion about whether this was his only marriage. A descendant, William Rodman, wrote the following letter to his brother in 1914 and it was reprinted in "A History of The Roman Catholic Diocese of Owensboro Kentucky." In it he speaks of a previously unreported marriage with another son being born.

Dear Brother:
> Ignatius Drury and Charles Drury were grandmothers' brothers. She (grandmother) named her first-born Ignatius. Zachariah Drury was an older half-brother of grandmother. As to Mary M. Drury and Anna S. Drury - these were probably full sisters of Zachariah or his wife and the wife of Ignatius, Charles and Elizabeth possibly husband and wife. I am under the impression our great grandmother Drury was a widow when she left Maryland. She had a stepson, Zack, I know and maybe a step-daughter, but I think not. This great-grandmother Drury's name was Alice Anastasia (French) Drury. She had six children, Ignatius, Charles, Dolly or Dorothea Payne, Elizabeth or Betsy Jarboe, Martha or Moccie Warren, Eleanor or Nellie Hogan. Our Grandmother was the youngest child of the family. Mother's grandfather's name was either Ignatius or Zachary Drury. His

wife, (mother's grandmother) was Anastasia French. (She was Grandfather Drury's second wife.) The name of his first wife is not known.[40]

This assertion gives us a problem in reconciling all the relevant dates. Most males in the eighteenth century did not marry before majority (twenty one years of age). If Ignatius was born in 1748 and married Anastasia at age 21 in 1769, then this was most probably his first marriage. If this was a second marriage as suggested then it is most likely that his birth is in error by at least four or five years, and Zachariah (treated in unplaced Drurys) had to be born before 1768 at the latest.

Six children of Ignatius and Anastasia were mentioned in the letter. We have seven listed here in order of birth; Dorothy (1771) who married John (Jackie) Payne, Ignatius (1773) who married Deborah Thorne and died in Kentucky, Charles (1776) who married Ann Thorne (possibly a sister of Deborah) and second Elizabeth Leach, Elizabeth (1780) who married Charles Burkham Jarboe, Monica (aft 1780) who married Charles Warren, Ann (1790) who married James E. Bowling, and Mary Ellen (after 1790) who married William Hogan. The one not confirmed by the letter is Ann. She is assumed to be a daughter because of the family associations listed in her death notice.[41] The only reference in the death notice that is not accounted for is the reference to a sister, Mary. There could easily be another daughter in the decade between 1780 and 1790 since only one child's birth is listed there at present. One great grand child, George Montgomery, (grandson of his son Charles) distinguished himself in the hierarchy of the Catholic Church becoming Archbishop of California.

Mildred Drury

Mildred was born sometime between 1748 and 1755. She married Ignatius Russell between May 19, 1771 and September 1772. She was listed as Mildred Drury at the baptism of her cousin Philip Joy in 1771 and as Mildred Russell in 1772 when she sponsored her niece, Thecla Drury. Her first child Eleanor was born May 22, 1773 so she had to marry at least nine months before that. Her connection as a child of Peter Drury is supplied by her presence as godmother for these children.[43]

Ignatius Russell was born March 10 1748/9 a son of William Russell and Ann _____.
The 1800 census lists the following data:
1M under 10 (b aft 1790)
1M 10-16 (b. 1784-1790)
3M 16-26 (b. 1774-1784) (Philip 25, Charles 17, 1 other, probably around 20)
1M over 45 (Ignatius 52 yrs old)
1F 10-16 (b. 1784-1790) (Allusia 16) ??
1F 16-26 (b. 1774-1784) (Eleanor 26)
1F over 45 (Mildred 47 to 50)
0 slaves.[44]

76

The only discrepancy here is the birth date of Allusia Russell. Her birth was listed as 24 December 1777. Such a specific date must have a reference somewhere though I cannot cite it at present. If true this would place her along with her sister in the 16-26 category in the 1800 Census. If, on the other hand, the census data is correct then she could not have been born earlier than 1784. More research is needed here.

It is unfortunate that we have no information as yet about the other three boys. We can only speculate that one was a child, the second a teenager, and the third a young adult. Charles is the only one about which we have additional information and he is not positively identified with this family. In a note to Linda Reno sent 9/30/2007 I wrote:

Dear Linda,

John Dobricky and I have been working on trying to determine who the Jane Drury was who married John Radford Jr. and then his ancestor John B. Raley. We're trying to find out who were the parents of Charles Russell 1783-1816 who married Monica French 8/10/1812. I've been in contact with Dolores Bohn in Louisville Ky. She has given me a great deal of Russell data but most of it is for descendants of Charles Russell 1759-1813 who went to Kentucky in the 1780's. His father William Russell according to her data had five sons: John by a first wife Catherine Leake about 1730, and four by his second wife. They were William Jr., Ignatius, James, and Charles.

I've been trying to narrow down the possibilities. Given the mortality rates at the time I've discounted John as being born too early to father a son in 1783. Charles was in Kentucky at least by 1788 when he married Jane Mattingly. He would have been 29 at that time. This could have been a second marriage but I have found no evidence of any earlier marriage.

William Jr. could have been Charles' father. He married in 1774 and the two children I show for him were born one earlier and one later than Charles. I'm also sure Ignatius Russell had more than three children. In 1783 he would have been 34 years old. I have no additional data on either him or Mildred Drury but it certainly would have been possible for them to be his parents.

I know absolutely nothing about James other than his birth in 1755. I did find mention of a James Russell in Port Tobacco in the 1790 Census but could not find the name on the image that was presented for that reference so I don't know what happened there.

I've been going on the theory that there may have been close connections between the French, Russell, and Drury families around that time. Ignatius Drury married Anastasia French, Charles Russell married Monica daughter of Anastasia's brother Bennett French and Ignatius Russell married Ignatius Drury's sister Mildred. Given the above data I've concluded that Charles' father most likely could have been William Jr., Ignatius, or James.

Her response follows here:
Hi Don,

I think the most likely candidate for the father of Charles Russell who married Monica French was Ignatius Russell who married Mildred Drury. At the time of the 1800 census, he had 5 sons. Charles wasn't the son of James Russell and Maria Graves. He could have been the son of William Russell, Jr., but I just don't think so.

Linda

This placement is speculation based on probability. More proof is needed but it is the best we have to go on at present.

Richard Drury

Richard's birth date is unclear but is accepted to be sometime around 1749 or 1750. We know very little about him or his wife Elizabeth. They married before 1770 because a child, Peter, was christened 7 Nov 1771.[45] We can assume they had more children than Peter and Richard Jr. who are listed here. Birth control was non existent and children tended to come at two year intervals unless the husband died or was forced to be away for an extended period. Richard, like his father and brothers, took the oath of allegiance to Maryland as required in 1777 and he probably enlisted in the revolutionary army or the local Maryland Militia when it became clear that war was inevitable. Richard Jr., the other child we have documented for him was born sometime before 1786.[46] There is no record of how Richard made his living but his son Peter and a grandson Benedict were apparently shoemakers. Peter taught Benedict the craft and took several apprentices over the years. Benedict bought a shoemaker's shop at what was known as Clifton Factory near the present town of Great Mills. He married Susan Fowler, a widowed textile worker, in 1823 and lived until sometime in the 1830's.[47]

Enoch Drury

Enoch was born about 1749.[48] He married Tabitha Wimsatt a daughter of James Wimsatt and Elizabeth Cissell, before 1770.[49] He was living in Beaverdam Manor on Lot 34 called Terra Collium alias Fertilitas from 1768 until at least 1781 and probably until his death in 1784.[50] He served as a private in the Maryland Militia during the Revolutionary War.

[1] Beitzel, Edwin Warfield, History of the Jesuit missions of St. Mary's County, p 67

[2] O'Rourke, Timothy, Catholic Families of Southern Maryland, p 82

[3] "Virginia Revolutionary Publick Claims," Abercrombie, Janice L. and Richard Slatten., Iberian Pub. Co., Athens, GA, 1992, p. 329

[4] Message from Bob Dora 4/25/2001: Joe (Dora – a Drury researcher) says, "The Drury and McNabb families appear to have come to Illinois together, they may have stopped for a while in Kentucky. Raphael Drury married Elizabeth

McNabb. The Hughes family was probably part of the same group. The Beitzel family was from the area of Pennsylvania north of St. Mary." This next contribution from Joe, supports Don's (Drury – another researcher) idea that William was still in Maryland during the revolution: Archibald McNabb was a witness to the will of William Elder who lived in the Mt. St. Mary's area of Frederick County Maryland. This seals it: (maybe) 1780- The Frederick County Docket Books list: Luke Mudd vs. Wm. Druroy. Luke Mudd was a constable in an area about 11 miles southwest of Mt. St. Mary's College. I conclude that William most likely came down the Ohio in 1781. They were in Illinois by June of 1782 and the Ohio was difficult then, as now in the spring. I do not believe that they would go down it on a raft in April or May, much less in winter. They therefore must have done so in the previous summer - 1781

[5] A.) John (d. 1797) must have been born by 1740 at the latest in order to be married and have a child by 1760. John (his father) and Susanna were married in 1734. I have their daughter Frances born in 1735 and a son William in 1737. Assuming a 2 year span in births that puts John (d. 1797) born in 1739. ; B.) Birth dates for the children of John (d. 1797) follow. I've estimated those I do not have documented records to support: Ignatius – 1760, John Chrysostom - between 1760 and 1765, Susanna – 1765, Francis Desales- 1768, Anastasia – 1770, William – 1777, Mary - before 1780, Monica - between 1780 and 1786, Joseph – 1786. At the time of the oath of allegiance in 1776 neither John C. nor Francis would have been old enough to sign such a document. C.) In 1765 (when Susanna Drury was born) Susanna Hayden would have been too old to be still having children. D.) If the Francis Drury named as legatee in Richard Fenwick's Will was Francis Desales Drury he would still have been a minor and the will would probably have specified that he receive his legacy on attaining majority. We can assume from this that Francis was some other Francis Drury. This supports the suggestion that the Francis of the Will was another child of John and Susanna. E.) The only other John Drury I know of in the period from 1730 to 1790 was John Drury s/o John Baptist Drury and Elizabeth but he was born in 1766 and so would be to young to figure in our discussion. (Christened 2/2/1767 – Catholic Families of Southern Maryland p 2) (John Baptist was referred to as John B. in records.) F.) Mary d/o John & Susanna (b. 1753) married Richard Basil Knott bef 1771 and was in Missouri by 1797 while Mary d/o John (d. 1797) married (probably Matthew) Mandley bef 1797. G.) William s/o John & Susanna (b. 1737) married Mary Ann Wootten and was in Missouri by 1798 while William s/o John (d. 1797) married Elizabeth Edwards and died in Kentucky in 1851.

[6] MARYLAND RECORDS VOL I, Gaius Marcus Brumbaugh, 1993, Genealogical Pub. Co.,Baltimore, p. 333 "1795 April 21   Drury, John and Ann Jarbo."

[7] Ann Jarboe is listed as head of household in 1790 census for St. Mary's County Maryland, No Ann Jarboe listed in 1800 but Ann Drury listed in 1800 for St Mary's County.

[8] John Drewry - his last will.

   In the name of God amen, I John Drewroy (Drury) of Saint Mary's County in the State of Maryland being sick & weak of body but of sound & disposing mind memory & understanding. Considering the certainty of death & the uncertainty of the time thereof, and being desirous to settle my worldly affairs,& thereby be the better prepared to leave this world when it shall please God to call me home, do therefore make & publish this my last will & testament in manner from following that is to say..first and princepally I commit my soul into the hands of almighty God, & my body to the Earth to be decently buried at the discretion of my Executor herein after named and after my just debts are paid I devise and bequeath as follows...Item, I give and bequeath unto my beloved wife Ann Drury (Drury) one third part of my real estate during her natural life and likewise one part of my household furniture and stock to her their heirs forever.... It is forth my will that my wife shall have her choice of my stock and furniture to the amount of her thirds...Item I give and bequeath to beloved sons Francis Decalus (Desales) Drury, Joseph Drury & William Drury seven pounds ten shillings current money each to them & their heirs forever..Item I give and bequeath unto my beloved daughter Monica Drewry (Drury) one cow to her and her heirs forever...Item I give and bequeath unto my beloved children Annastania Vepells (Vessels) Susanna Raliy (Raley) Mary Mandley Monica Drewry (Drury) John Christophor (Christopher) Drewry (Drury) Francis Decalus (Desales) Drury Ignatius Drewry (Drury) Joseph Drewry (Drury) & William Drewry (Drury) all the residual & remaining part of my estate both real and personal to be equally divided between my children before mentioned to them & their heirs..Lastly I do hereby nominate & appoint my son Francis Decalus (Desales) Drewry to be whole & sole executor of this my last will & testament disannulling any written wills by me heretofor made ratifying & confirming this and no other to my last & testament in testimony whereof I have hereto affixed my hand and seal this 17th day June 1797
Signed sealed and declared to be the last will & testament of the named testator in the presents of us
her mark   His mark
Aloweser Greenwell Eleanor (X) Stone   John (X) Drewry (Drury)
John Greenwell jun.
     On the back of the foregoing. Was the following, court.
Saint Mary's County, Court, the 29th day of June 1797. Then came John Decalus (Desales) Drewry (Drury) and made on the holy angels of the almighty god. That the written instrument of writing, is the true & whole will & testament of John Drury late of Saint Mary's County deceased, that hath come to his hands and possession & that he doth not know of any other.   Certified per. Jeremiah Jordan Reg. Of Wills For Saint Mary's County
[9] American Genealogical-Biographical Index (AGBI) Jeremiah Drury Birth Date: 1750 Birthplace: Maryland
[10] O'Rourke, Timothy, Catholic Families of Southern Maryland p 19

[11] 1790 Census St. Mary's County Maryland Series: M637 Roll: 3 Page: 333

[12] O'Rourke, Timothy, Catholic Families of Southern Maryland p 85

[13] 1800 Census St. Mary's County Maryland Series: M32 Roll: 12 Page: 17

[14] O'Rourke, Timothy, Maryland Catholics on the Frontier, Brefney Press, 1981

[15] Archives of Maryland, Vol. 78 p 266

[16] Nelson County Deed book bk. 2, p 12 & 115

[17] Obrist, Patricia, Dora, Robert and Drury, Donald, Remember the Drury Family Vol. II pp 194-197

[18] Robert BARNES' Maryland Marriages: Jeremy GATTEN, 14 Feb. 1773, Rev. Jas. WALTON, SJ, Newtown, SM, Eliz. DRURY; Woodstock Archives 6.3; published in "Newtown Hundred," MD Historical Magazine, Je. 1956, 125 - 139

[19] O'Rourke, Timothy, Catholic Families of Southern Maryland p 99

[20] St. Mary's County Wills Liber JJ 1 page 54 Linda Reno

[21] *Prerogative Ct. (Testementary Proceedings),* 27 (MdHR 983), p. 38 Film 3299, Pt. 2, Liber. IX, Folio 451, 452, 453 (Kindness Joann April from Tim O'Rourke); also Skinner, V. L. Jr. *Abstracts of the Administration Accounts of the Prerogative Court of Maryland* Libers 6-10, 1724-1731 Page 48

[22] Burger, Judith A. *Will of Peter Drury d. 1770 Register of Wills, St. Mary's County, Maryland,*, Liber T. A. No.1., Page 633

[23] Reno, Linda, *electronic* – "Monica was probably either a Ford or a Thompson. The 1790 Census lists a Monica as Head of Household indicating she was widowed by that time and not remarried. Don't know for sure if this was the same Monica or not.": (dd), Statement that Monica was either a Ford or a Thompson I think was based on the fact that a number of Thompsons and Fords were sponsors when their children were christened

[24] O'Rourke, Timothy, *Catholic Families of Southern Maryland* - p. 4

[25] O'Rourke, Timothy, *Catholic Families of Southern Maryland* - p. 7

[26] O'Rourke, Timothy, *Catholic Families of Southern Maryland* - p. 11

[27] Burger, Judith A. *Will of Nicholas Drury d. 1789 Register of Wills, St. Mary's County, Maryland*, Liber. J. J. No, 1 p. 481

[29] Brumbaugh, G.M. *Maryland Records---Vol. II, State of His Lordship's Manor,* Genealogical Publ. Co., Baltimore, MD, 1985 p. 65

[30] Barnes, Robert, *MARYLAND MARRIAGES, 1634-1777*, Genealogical Publ Co. Baltimore, MD, 1976, p.54; also Diary of Rev. James Walton, S. J. while at Newtown, St. Mary's County, Maryland, p 135

[31] White, Virgil D., *Index to Revolutionary War Service Records Volume I: A-D*, The National Historical Pub. Co., Waynesboro, TN., 1995, pp. 799, 801

[32] Will of Michael Drury, *Register of Wills, St. Mary's County, Maryland*, Liber E.J.M. 1, p.36, and Liber EJM 1, pp 100 thru 111

[33] Drury's Delight by Patent; Hard Times by deed from George Fenwick; and "Males" (Wales) by deed from William Fenwick; *St. Mary's County Land Records,* Liber I. H. Folio 30, 31 dated 9/11/1813

[34] Cryer, Leona, *Some Johnsons of Southern Maryland* -- Gateway Press, Baltimore Md. 1991 P. 14 & 15

[35] Liber EJM 1 p 36

[36] Fenwick, Laverne M., *The confiscation of British Property in Maryland* in Chronicles of St. Mary's V.5 # 7 (July 1957) *Resurveyed map of Beaverdam Manor*

[37] Maryland State Archives, Georgetown University Special Collections, *Letters from William and Clement Drury to George Fenwick*, Box 39 Folder 10

[38] From Linda Lawson Ransom, Typed papers outlining family tradition mention a Baptist Drury, who would visit them in Baltimore who was a cousin

[39] Barnes, Robert *Maryland Marriages 1634-1777,* Genealogical Publ Co. Baltimore, MD, 1976, p. 54

[40] Turner Publishing Company, *A History of The Roman Catholic Diocese of Owensboro* p 229

[41] Bowling, Ann 68 on 31st ult wid/o James Bowling & m/o 5 ch. Gettysburg &Leonardtown copy, 2 Jan 1858 (*Departed This Life, Death Notices from the (Baltimore) Sun 1851-1853* v. 1.) - Her presumed father's name is Ignatius Drury, her sisters are Mary and Elizabeth and her Grandmother is Jane. Also, Family oral records show Annie's name as Anne Mary Jane Drury. Her Uncle is named Phillip Drury, her grandfather is John French, her uncle is William Drury and her husband is James Bowling

[43] O'Rourke, Timothy, *Catholic Families of Southern Maryland*, May 19, 1771 Baptism of Philip of Athan. & Dian. Joy, Sp: Bennet Thompson & Mildred Drury, p. 119; Listed as Mildred Russell when sponsoring the baptism of Thecla Drury (daughter of her brother Philip) 12/20/1772, card file, St. Mary's County Historical Society

[44] United States Census, St. Mary's County, Maryland 1800

[45] O'Rourke, Timothy, *Catholic Families of Southern Maryland* Genealogical Publishing Co. Baltimore Md. 1985 p. 9; Sponsors: Michael and Elizabeth Drury

[46] O'Rourke, Timothy, *Catholic Families of Southern Maryland* Genealogical Publishing Co. Baltimore Md. 1985 p. 9; Sponsors: Michael and Elizabeth Drury

[47] Maryland Historical Magazine, Vol. 80 # 1 (Spring 1985) pp 58, 59

[48] O'Rourke, Timothy J., Catholic Families of Souhern Maryland Genealogical pub. Co., Baltimore 1985 pp 8,11,14

[49] Note: This date is estimated from children's christenings. Alathair is thought to be the oldest child and had to be born at least by 1770

[50] Brumbaugh, G.M. *Maryland Records---Vol. II, State of His Lordship's Manor*, Genealogical Publ. Co., Baltimore, MD, 1985 p. 65; Burger, Judith A., *Will of Enoch Drury Sr.* from a photocopy of the original court Document obtained from Norma I. Dawson, Registrar of Wills, Saint Mary's County, Maryland: JJ3 154-155

Chapter Seven

Children of John Drury (1739 – 1797)

John Drury, a son of John Drury and Susanna Hayden,[1] was born about 1739 and died between 17 June and 29 June 1797.[2] He married first an unknown wife before 1760. She, whoever she was, was probably at least seventeen years old when they married. We can estimate from this that she was born sometime around 1742. John's youngest child, Joseph, was born in 1786 so she must have died sometime between then and, assuming a normal interval of mourning for John, 1793. A second possibility, given the state of medicine in colonial Maryland, is that at age 44 she died in childbirth with this last child. He had nine children by her between 1760 and 1786. John married a second time to Ann Jarboe on 21 April 1795.[3] It is likely she was a widow at the time.[4] After John died she was listed as Ann Drury in the 1800 Census.[5]

Ignatius Drury

John's first child was Ignatius Drury born in 1760 in St. Mary's County.[6] As an adult Ignatius is recorded renting a 228 acre farm in St. Inigoes Hundred that is owned by William Bennett.[7] This is near the area where the rest of John's (1739 – 1797) family was living.

John Chrysostom Drury

John Chrysostom Drury, known variously as John, John C., John Christopher, or Christopher was born in St. Mary's County sometime between 1760 and 1765. He married sometime in the 1780's and had at least four children. There is little direct information about John but we can infer a fair amount. John and his family were still in St. Mary's County in 1790 when the first census was taken[8] but he was gone by 1800. No direct evidence exists detailing his movements, but a deed from 1870 in Kentucky provides insight. This document records a sale by Charles J. Peck and his wife Nancy of Mead County, Kentucky, to George H. Vessels of Hardin County of a parcel originally owned by her father Elias Drury deceased, who is described as a son of Christopher Drury deceased.[9]

Elias married Ann _____ on 3 January 1804 in Kentucky.[10] John's family moved there probably before 1800 when John disappeared from the Maryland records. Elias' birth can be estimated to a certain extent from his marriage date. Assuming he was 18 years old in 1804 he had to be born in 1786. Unfortunately we have no way to determine John's death except to say it was probably either in or on the way to Kentucky. By 1810 Elias' family had increased.[11] He married a second time to Anastasia Cain on 3 February 1834. She was the widow of Thomas Mattingly.[12] Elias Drury is buried in the St Patrick Catholic Cemetery on Fort Knox.[13]

Susanna Drury

Susanna was John's eldest daughter born before 1767. She married Bennett Riley in 1784.[13] He was a veteran of the Revolutionary War in a Continental Army artillery battalion. They had five children by 1790.[14] Then they disappear from St. Mary's County records. Presumably by this time, he's moved his family to Alexandria, Virginia.[15] By 1803, Susanna Drury has died and Bennett remarries to Frances Frazier in Alexandria, Virginia.[16] Bennett Riley, husband of Susanna Drury and Frances Frazier shows up in 1810 in Baltimore.[17] He died in Baltimore in 1811 at the age of 47.

The Bible record referenced in note 15 was most likely altered by Bennett's second wife in order to attempt to qualify for a Revolutionary War widow's pension. The following paragraph signed by the clerk explains the situation.

Frances Haley (widow of Bennett Riley who was a private in the Maryland Artillery in the War of the Revolution). She applied to me in 1841 to obtain for her a pension stating without proof that she was married to Bennet Riley in 1789. She having been married twice since the death of Riley, and the amendment declaring that a marriage again would not be a bar not having at that time been passed, I told her that she could not get a pension. As soon, however, as the barrier about the second marriage was removed (in August 1842) I informed her thereof, and was about to make application for her under the Act of July 7, 1838 and August 23, 1842, when on examination as to the date of her marriage to Bennett Riley, I found that it took place on or after September 18, 1799 instead of 1789. I then informed her that she could not obtain a pension until Congress shall extend the law to widows whose marriages took place at or after the date of hers (1799). She has, however, succeeded in obtaining a pension without my knowledge and, as I believe, fraudulently. Signed by Alex Yeadley.

Bennet Riley and Susanna Drury were the parents of General Bennet Riley, for whom Ft. Riley, Kansas is named.

The Beginnings of San Francisco

Illustration 44
BRIGADIER-GENERAL BENNET RILEY
From a painting in the office of the commandant at Fort Riley, Kansas.

Source: Eldredge, Zoeth Skinner. *The Beginnings of San Francisco.* 1912. San Francisco.

General Riley Obituary - 6/11/1853

Brevet Major-General Bennet Riley, U.S.A., died at Buffalo on Thursday evening, at the advanced age of 66 years. Gen. Riley has filled a prominent niche in the history of the Military heroes of the century. Born in 1790 in St. Mary's County, Md., he entered the Army at an early age. On the 19th of January, 1813, he was appointed Ensign in the Rifles; in March, 1813 in he was rated as Third Lieutenant; in April 1814, became Second Lieutenant in the First Rifles; and was promoted in the First Lieutenancy in March, 1817. In August, 1818, he reached a Captaincy in the Fifth Infantry; and in 1821 was transferred to the Sixth Infantry. He distinguished himself in an engagement under Col. Leavenworth, with the Arickarco Indians in August, 1823; and was made Brevet Major for ten years' faithful service, on the 6th of August, 1828. Passing through the grades of Major in the Fourth Infantry, in 1837, and Lieutenant-Colonel. Second Infantry (December, 1839) he was finally promoted as Brevet-Colonel in February, 1844 to rank from the day (June 2, 1840) on which was fought the battle of Chokachatta, in Florida. In this action, Col. Riley was particularly distinguished for his bravery and good conduct. His commission at this time bore ample testimony to his merits and gallant services. Col. Riley was in command of the Second Infantry, under Gen. Scott, and in the Valley of Mexico during the Mexican War, he commanded the Second Brigade of Twiggs's Division consisting of the Fourth Artillery and the Second and Seventh Infantry. For his share in the hotly contested battle of Cerro Gordo, on the 18th April, 1847, Col. Riley was made Brevet Brigadier-General in the month of August, 1848. He received his title of Brevet Major-General in the Army in March, 1851 as the reward of gallant conduct during the action at Contreras on the 20th August, 1847. In the years 1849 and 1850, Gen. Riley was in command of the Military Department in Upper California and so exercised the functions of Provincial Governor. In this position, he fully sustained his character for probity, humanity, and energy. At the close of his administration on the Pacific, he was ordered to take command of a regiment on the Rio Grande, but ill-health compelled him relinquish further active service, and he returned to his residence in Buffalo. The hardships of campaign life undoubtedly produced an unfavorable effect on his constitution, and the disease which finally proved fatal to him was an aggravated form of cancer. He leaves a wife and five children. [18]

The Rileys had a strong military tradition. Susanna's husband, as we said, served in the revolution. His son, General Bennett Riley, served in every major conflict during his career. The General's son Bennett born in 1835 was a midshipman aboard the sloop of war *Albany* and was lost at sea about 1854. Another son, Edward Bishop Dudley Riley, was born May 8, 1834 in Indian Territory and died on Feb. 28, 1918 in Buffalo, New York. Edward also graduated from West Point, but when the Confederate states seceded from the Union he resigned his commission and joined the confederacy. He became a member of the staff of General Robert E. Lee.

Their daughter Ann[19] married William Bliss in 1812 and later Benjamin Lawson as her second husband in Baltimore. The other children are only names and dates in the Bennett Riley Bible.

Francis Desales Drury

John's third son, Francis, was born about 1768 in St. Mary's County. We know he grew up during the Revolutionary War but was too young to register or fight. As the eldest son still at home Francis was named executor of his father's will in 1797. Ignatius was on his own, John C. and William were about to leave for Kentucky and Joseph at eleven years old was too young. John Sr. bought a plantation near Leonardtown in 1797 that everyone now refers to as "No Name." It is designated as "D" on the map below. Other properties designated "A" (John Baptist Drury), "B" (Enoch Drury), "C" (Michael Drury), and "E" (Heirs of Philip Drury who died in 1795) are other nearby Drury Plantations. He then transferred this property to his son before he died.[20] Francis married Ann Yates, a daughter of Edward Yates and Mary, on 15 October 1799.[21] In 1803 he purchased an adjoining 100 acre plantation "Nevitt's St. Ann" from Thomas Caddeen.[22] He retained these properties until his death in 1809. Two daughters were born to Francis and Ann. They were Mary Ellen and Ann Caroline. Exact birth dates are unknown but they had to be born before 1807. On 11 November 1807 Francis married a second time to Winifred Lowe Greenwell, the widow of Joseph Greenwell who had died in 1803.[23] [24] Mary Ellen did not marry,[25] and Ann Caroline married John Sanner 25 January 1825.[26]

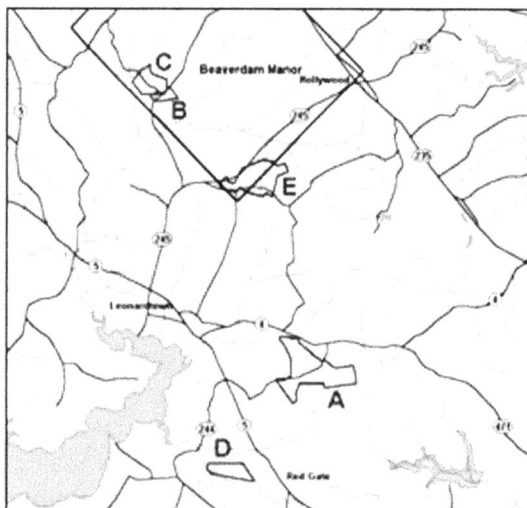

Some Drury Farms 1800 – 1809[27]

William Drury (1777 – 1851)

William Drury was born about 1777. We have no direct proof that he was a son of John Drury who died in 1797. John did have a son William named as a legatee in his will,[28] but no other evidence proves that this William and the one of the will was the same person. William's birth in 1777 fits well into the sequence of children we have for John though he could have been a son of other less-documented Drury families at the time. This placement is the most likely given what we know about all the Drury families in St. Mary's County.

William's marriage or marriages is another puzzle. Researchers agree that his wife's given name was Elizabeth. Research by some descendants says she was Elizabeth Edwards (or Evans) born in Pennsylvania. Others list her as Elizabeth Langford born in Maryland. The Elizabeth from Maryland would make more sense since William was also born there. It is entirely possible that there were two marriages. The marriage to Elizabeth Langford is listed as 1799 in Dorchester County, Maryland[29] and the marriage to Elizabeth Edwards is recorded as 9 January 1819. There were Elizabeth Edwards' in St. Mary's County, but none of them were married to William Drury or had associations with the Drury family.

It is also possible that the Elizabeth Drury who died in Mercer County, Kentucky, in 1850 was neither of these women. The William Drura married in 1799 in Dorchester County is assumed to be William Drury with a misspelled surname. However there was another William L. Drura who married Janetta Robinson on 5 Sep 1833 also in Dorchester County. This William could have possibly been William Langford Drura and thus a son of the William who married in 1799. This suggests that there was a Drura family in Dorchester County and that the 1799 marriage was not William Drury (son of John Drury). There was also a marriage of a William Drury to Elizabeth Evans in

Baltimore County. This might be a possibility but we should remember that there were numerous Drury families in North Central Maryland who were not closely related to those in St. Mary's County.

No matter who she was, William had to be married before his first son John was born about 1811 or 1812. There may have been other children before Joshua, the next recorded child we have was born about 1817 as calculated from the 1860 census.[30] This period from 1812 to 1817 was the time when the War of 1812 was in progress. William, like other citizens, was in the Militia and may not have been at home as much. Three more children were born in the early 1820s. They were Mary, Indiana, and Harvey. He married Martha Inman shortly before their first child was born in 1844.[31] Harvey would have been about 20 and his bride about 17.

Anastasia Drury

Anastasia was born in 1768 and married Charles Vessells in 1788.[32] The couple had at least three children, Eleanor (3/23/1788), Mary (3/14/1790) and Anna (3/3/1793).[33] She died sometime after 1797 when she was listed in her father's will as Anastasia Vessells.[34]

Mary Drury

Mary, though we have no firm date, was probably born sometime in the late 1750s and married Mathew Mandly sometime before 1763. The 1790 census lists 5 Males Under 16, 2 Males - 16 and over, and 2 Females.[35] Of the 2 males over 16, one had to be Matthew Mandly. The other was probably a son born at the latest in 1773 (1790 minus 17 years). Assuming a marriage when Mary was 17 gives us a birth date for her of 1756. If the other person over 16 was another relative then we have 5 and possibly 6 children. This gives us a minimum of 12 years of marriage. This puts their marriage in 1778 or 1780 and again, assuming a marriage when Mary was 17, gives us a birth date for her of 1761 or 1763.

Monica Drury

Monica Drury had to be born in the late 1770's in order to be old enough to sponsor her niece at christening.[36] She was still alive when her father died in 1797.[37]

---

[1] John (d. 1797) must have been born by 1740 at the latest in order to be married and have a child by 1760. John (his father) and Susanna were married in 1734. A daughter Frances was born in 1735 and a son William in 1737. Assuming a 2 year span in births places John's (d. 1797) birth in 1739. Birth dates for the children of John (d. 1797) are below. I've estimated those I do not have documented records to support.

       Ignatius – 1760 [12/14/1760: Ignatius Drury was baptized at St. Joseph's RCC. Joseph Mosley. GP: James and Sarah Hamilton (Catholic Families of So. Md. by O'Rourke).]
       Mary - 1758
       John Chrysostom - between 1760 and 1765
       Susanna – 1765 [Jesuit Missions/Father's will/Fresco.]
       Anastasia - 1768
       Francis Desales- 1770
       William - 1777
       Monica - between 1780 and 1786
       Joseph - 1786

At the time of the oath of allegiance in 1776 neither John C. nor Francis would have been old enough to sign such a document. In 1765 (when Susanna Drury was born) Susanna Hayden would have been too old to be still having children. If the Francis Drury named as legatee in Richard Fenwick's Will was Francis Desales Drury he would still have been a minor and the will would probably have specified that he receive his legacy on attaining majority. We can assume from this that Francis was some other Francis Drury that supports the suggestion that the Francis of the Will was another child of John and Susanna. The only other John Drury I know of in the period from 1730 to 1790 was John Drury s/o John Baptist Drury and Elizabeth, but he was born in 1766 and so would be to young to figure in our discussion. [Christened 2/2/1767 – O'Rourke, Timothy, Catholic Families of Southern Maryland p 2] John Baptist was referred to as John B. in records. Mary d/o John & Susanna (b. 1753) married Richard Basil Knott before 1771 and was in Missouri by 1797 while Mary d/o John (d. 1797) married (probably Matthew) Mandley before 1797. William s/o John & Susanna (b. 1737) married Mary Ann Wootten and was in Missouri by 1798. All of these differences cannot be easily dismissed as coincidence.

[2] John Drewry - his last will.   In the name of God amen, I John Drewroy (Drury) of Saint Mary's County in the State of Maryland being sick & weak of body but of sound & disposing mind memory & understanding. Considering the certainty of death & the uncertainty of the time thereof, and being desirous to settle my worldly affairs,& thereby be the better prepared to leave this world when it shall please God to call me home, do therefore make & publish this my last will & testament in manner from following that is to say..first and princepally I commit my soul into the hands of almighty God, & my body to the Earth to be decently buried at the discretion of my Executor herein after named and after my just debts are paid I devise and bequeath as follows...Item, I give and bequeath unto my beloved wife Ann Drury (Drury) one third part of my real estate during her natural life and likewise one part of my household furniture and stock to her their heirs forever.... It is forth my will that my wife shall have her choice of my stock and furniture to the amount of her thirds...Item I give and bequeath to beloved sons Francis Decalus (Desales) Drury, Joseph Drury & William Drury seven pounds ten shillings current money each to them & their heirs forever..Item I give and bequeath unto my beloved daughter Monica Drewry (Drury) one cow to her and her heirs forever...Item I give and bequeath unto my beloved children Annastania Vepells (Vessels) Susanna Raliy (Raley) Mary Mandley Monica Drewry (Drury) John Christophor (Christopher) Drewry (Drury) Francis Decalus (Desales) Drury Ignatius Drewry (Drury) Joseph Drewry (Drury) & William Drewry (Drury) all the residual & remaining part of my estate both real and personal to be equally divided between my children before mentioned to them & their heirs..Lastly I do hereby nominate & appoint my son Francis Decalus (Desales) Drewry to be whole & sole executor of this my last will & testament disannulling any written wills by me heretofor made ratifying & confirming this and no other to my last & testament in testimony whereof I have hereto affixed my hand and seal this 17th day June 1797. John (X) Drewry (Drury)
Signed sealed and declared to be the last will & testament of the named testator in the presents of us
her mark   His mark
Aloweser Greenwell   Eleanor (X) Stone   John Greenwell jun.

[3] Brumbaugh, , Gaius Marcus, Maryland Records Vol. I 1993, Genealogical Pub. Co., Baltimore, p. 333 (marriages) "1795 April 21 Drury, John and Ann Jarbo."

[4] Ann Jarboe listed as head of household in 1790 census for St. Mary's County Maryland

[5] No Ann Jarboe listed in 1800 but Ann Drury listed in 1800 for St Mary's County.

[6] O'Rourke, Timothy, Catholic families of Southern Maryland, 12/14/1760: Ignatius Drury was baptized at St. Joseph's RCC. Joseph Mosley. GP: James and Sarah Hamilton

[7] Shuhart, Wanda M., Federal Direct Tax of 1798 St. Mary's County, Maryland, St. Mary's County Historical Society, Leonardtown, Maryland, 1998 p 181

[8] [1790 census]

[9] Hardin County Court, deed book 2, page 229, DEED

Charles J. Peck
            to
George H. Vessels

This indenture made this sixth day of September 1870 between Charles J. Peck and his wife Nancy A. Peck of the first part of Mead County Kentucky and George H. Vessels of Hardin County Kentucky witnessth that the parties of the first part for and in the consideration of $40.00 in hand to them paid by the said George H. Vessels the receipt whereof is hereby acknowledged have sold and due hereby convey to the said George H. Vessels all the rights, title and interest the said parties of the first part have or may have in and to a tract of land lying on Rude Creek in Hardin County Kentucky containing three hundred forty six acres being the same conveyed by John S. Helm to Elias Drury dec. (deceased) and by Charles Helm to Elias Drury by joint deed recorded on page 229 of deed book 2 in the office of the clerk of the Hardin County Court. This conveyance embracing the interest of said Nancy A. Peck, late, Drury in the real and personal estate of her father the said Elias Drury, dec. and her mothers interest in the real and personal estate of the said decedant and the interest of the said Nancy A. Peck in and to the estate of her deceased sister Rebecca Drury dec. and the estate of Elias Drury dec. son of Christopher Drury dec. the interest hereby conveyed being the present interest and whatever interest the parties of the first part may have in and to the various estates mentioned.

The parties of the first part hereby bind themselves to the warrant and defend unto the said George H. Vessels his heirs and assigns forever the title the various interest and property herein conveyed against the claim of any person whatsoever.

Witnessed the hand and sealed of the said Charles J. Peck and his wife Nancy A. Peck the day above written.

	his mark
Witnessed	Charles J.(X) Peck
H.G. V. Wintersmith	Nancy A. Peck

State of Kentucky
Hardin County   Sct.

I, Virgil Hewitt clerk of County court for County aforesaid, certify that on 6 September 1870 the foregoing deed was dually acknowledged before me by Charles J. Peck and Nancy A. Peck his wife, parties thereto to be there act and deed and was lodged for record, being dually stamped.

Whereupon I have truly recorded the same together with this certificate in my office this 12th day of November 1870.

Virgil Hewitt, clerk

[10] "Hardin Co, KY marriages (1793 to 1850)" compiled by Mary Josephine Jones for the Ancestral Trails Historical Society and it lists; Elias Drury and Nancy Thomas. bond 1 Jan 1804 surety Samuel Humphries married 3 Jan 1804 by J Smith book A3 and A17.

[11] In the 1810 Hardin Co, KY census Elias Drury is listed with 3 males under 10, 1 male 10/16, 1 male 16/26 and 1male 26/45, 2 females under 10 and 1 female 26/45.

[12] Married first to Thomas (Bernard?) Mattingly (d. before 1834) in Breckinridge County KY on 3 Feb 1817 (LDS Film #1903981)

[13] St. Patrick Catholic Church History and Records, Stithton, Hardin County, Kentucky, 1831-1920, Mary M. Olson, 1999, McDowell Publishing Company, Utica, Kentucky, P. 210 (age 53) and 214 (states dead in 1864)

[13] *"Muster Rolls and other Records of Maryland Troops in the American Revolution 1775-1783"* Volume XVIII pp. 579, 582, 584

[14] 1790: Bennett Raily: 2M over 16; 2M under 16; 3F; 0 slaves.

[15] Bennet Raley -his bible "born to bennet raley and his wife Susanna- John Raley B. June 1 ,1785; Bennet Raley,2d-November 27 1787; Nancy Raley- September 18, 1789; wife Frances Frazier Raley- b. Joseph Raley-January 25, 1796; Elizabeth Raley-b. October 16, 1801

[16] Marriage Index: District of Columbia, Delaware, Maryland and Virginia, 1740-1920, FTM CD #399

[17] 8th Ward, Baltimore: Bennett Ryly: 1M 16-25; 7M over 45; 1F under 10; 3F 16-25; 1F 26-44; 0 slaves.

[18] New York Daily Times, 6/11/1853

[19] Fresco, Jesuit Missions, GP: Francis Drury and Margaret Williams

[20] Tax assessment: Francis L? Drury. No Name 76-acres in Lower Newtowne Hundred. MSA:CM900

[21] St. Mary's County Wills, Bk. JJ3, p 213-4

[22] 18 Oct 1803 Deed: Thomas Caddeen to Francis D Drury. Nevitts St Anns, 100-a DA:TH25:381

[23] 15 Nov 1809 Admin Acct: Of Francis D Drury by Peter Gough. AA:JJ03:271

[24] 11/1809: Winifred Drury and Peter Gough, administrators of Francis D. Drury were authorized to sell as much of his personal estate as necessary for payment of debts (Orphan Ct. Rec., Fenwick)

[25] Mary Ellen Drury, Nun-cuperative Will, Stated: February 23, 1845, Liber G.C. No. 2 p.153, On the 23rd of February 1845 it being the day preceding the one on which my Sister Mary Ellen Drury died she called me to her bedside and told me she should die. That she wished her old negro woman Sarah to be set free. That after all her Just debts were paid she wished her niece Ann Celestia Sanner to have her bureau her bed and bedstead her work stand and all the rest of her things. /s/ Caroline Sanner

[26] Fresco: John Dunbar Sanner, b. 11/29/1802, s/o Johnathon Biscoe Sanner and Frances Dunbar, m 1/25/1825 Ann Caroline Drury - Sanner Family of the U.S.A.

[27] courtesy of Pete Himmelheber

[28] See note 2 above

[29] Barnes, Maryland Marriages 1655-1850, Elizabeth Langford, Female, 4 Feb 1799, William Drura, William Drura, Dorchester County

[30] 1860; Census, District 1, Washington County, Kentucky; Roll: M653_399; Page: 202; Image: 198; Family History Library Film: 803399

[31] marriage date/ place per Margaret Morris Green on Drury Family Genealogy Forum: http:genforum.genealogy.com/drury/messages/810.html

[32] "Taken from Aunt Nellie Sheehan's Bible", from hand written notes of Mary Martina Zerbee read after her death in 1999.

[33] Ibid

[34] See Note 32 above

[35] 1790; Census Place: Unknown Township, St. Mary's, Maryland; Series: M637; Roll: 3; Page: 341; Image: 573; Family History Library Film: 0568143.

[36] O'Rourke, Timothy, 3/24/1794, Mary Drury of John and ___, Catholic Families of Southern Maryland, p. 29

[37] See Note 32 above

Chapter Eight

The Revolution

The end of the French and Indian War in 1763 did not bring peace. The conflict merely shifted from the military to the economic front. For years the colonists had been protesting the refusal of the Proprietor to contribute to the defense of the Colony against their Indian enemies. But now, with the enactment of the tax on sugar and the stamp tax, it brought opposition to Parliament in England as well.

These events had little immediate effect on the Drury families. Though they were now able to vote with the repeal of the discriminatory laws of the early 1700s, they did not meet the wealth and property requirements to be eligible to run for elective office. In order to vote for elected officials colonists had to own at least 50 acres of land or be able to prove assets of £40 in cash or equivalent. These restrictions were continued even after the revolution, but the asset requirement was decreased to £30 cash or its equivalent.[1][2] In order to be eligible to run for elected office they had to have property worth at least 1000 pounds of tobacco (the current unit of exchange at that time). The only elective offices were those of Sheriff and members of the lower house of the Assembly.[3] Drury families were still mostly the owners or lessees of small farms, or they were overseeing larger tracts for wealthier neighbors.

By the 1770s the Drurys had migrated into two general areas. John Jr. and his descendants moved to southern St. Mary's County in what was known as St. George and St. Inigoes Hundreds. The Jesuits owned this land. It gave John opportunity to support the Church as well as to make a living. They were probably living in Newtown Hundred as late as 1767.[4] They probably moved because Nicholas, Peter Jr. and his son William were living on Drury's Venture that included the land his father had farmed. This left no ancestral land for John in that area. Peter and his descendants remained in Newtown Hundred clustered mostly in Beaverdam Manor near Leonardtown. James Drury Jr. also leased land in Newtown Hundred though his sister Mary Drury, who married Charles Chamberlain, moved with Charles to Virginia where she remained until his death sometime after 1750.

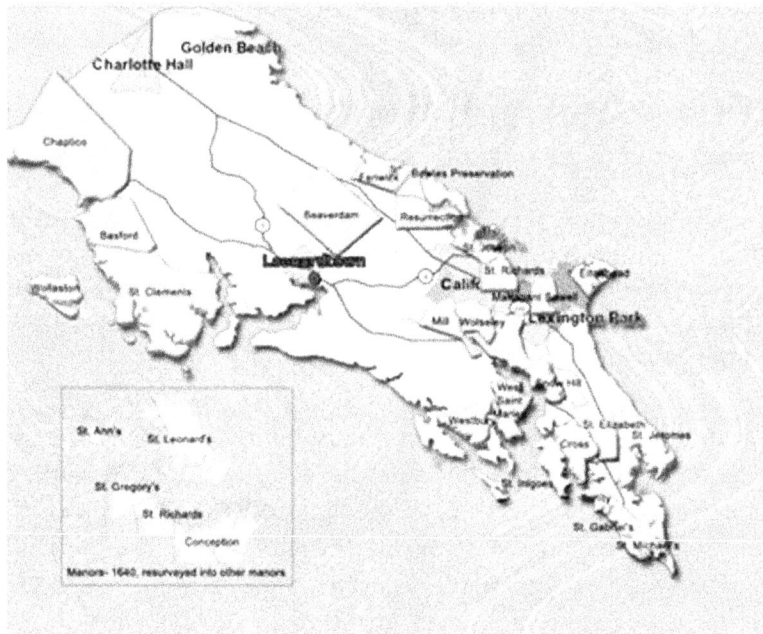

St. Mary's County Manors[5]

By the 1770s sentiment was growing for Maryland to secede from Britain and become an independent country even though Governor Robert Eden was well liked and generally respected in the Colony. As was usual these opinions divided, for the most part, along religious lines. Catholics under the urging of the Jesuits were strongly for becoming independent. Anglicans on the other hand were less enthusiastic and many, when the break finally came, left and returned to England.

Drury families numbered about a dozen by this time and all supported the revolution or at the very least did not openly oppose it. In 1777 the Maryland legislature passed a resolution requiring all adult males to take an oath of allegiance to Maryland. This was in response to increasing resistance sparked by attempts to organize a loyalist Militia on Maryland's eastern shore. This was a drastic step for most inhabitants because it constituted an act of treason against Britain that carried the death penalty. On the other hand those not taking this oath were to be taxed at three times the regular rate, lose all civil rights, and be disbarred from practicing any profession or trade.

Drurys were still farming at the time so not practicing a trade would not have affected them, but a triple tax rate was a real incentive for folks such as the Drurys who lived on smaller farms of from about 50 to a couple of hundred acres.

The text of this oath is reproduced below and was administered by the Justices of each district.

"I do swear, that I do not hold myself bound to yield any
allegiance or obedience to the King of Great Britain, his heirs or
successors, and that I will be true and faithful to the State of
Maryland, and will, to the best of my power, support, maintain,
and defend the freedom and independence thereof, and the government
now established, against all open enemies, and secret and traitorous
conspiracies, and will use my utmost endeavors to disclose and make
known to the Governor or someone of the judges or justices thereof,
All treason and traitorous conspiracies, attempts, or combinations
against this state or the government thereof, which may come to
my knowledge. So help me God."[6]

This was a serious business for these people. An Oath was the same as a legal document or written contract today. In addition, because they ended the oath, as we do today, with the phrase "So help me God," it added a moral imperative. Renouncing or disregarding this promise would send them to Hell when they died. In the eighteenth century when most people could neither read nor write and lawyers were an expensive luxury for all but the wealthy, a man's word was his bond. Promises were not made lightly because everyone knew that once made it was a promise not only to your neighbor or your country, but also to God. The only modern counterparts that have survived are the oath taken when testifying in a Court of Law and those taken by elected officials and members of the military services. Even these now tend to become formalities.

Drury men we can identify who took the oath in 1777 were Robert Drury, Enoch Drury, Ignatius Drury, John Baptist Drury, Michael Drury, and Philip Drury who were sons of Peter Drury and Jane Bailey, James Drury Jr. who married Sarah (possibly Thompson) and was a son of James Drury, William Drury a son of the John who married Susanna Hayden, and Thomas Drury. Exactly who this Thomas Drury was is unclear. He could be Thomas who married Mary Duff in 1751. We assumed previously that he was a son of John Sr. and brother of Peter and John but this is only speculation and has not been verified. He could also be an unidentified son of one of the Drury families of this generation. James Junior had a son Thomas by his wife Sarah but he would have been too young to register.

Other Drurys such as Leonard, oldest son of Nicholas and Monica, or John the son of John and Susanna Hayden would also have registered even though the above names are all that have survived.[7] Leonard was one of the earliest Drurys to volunteer. He relates that he volunteered after Harvest time in 1777 for nine months. By this time hostilities had been going on for more than a year and British raids in the area were constant. John Drury and members of his family were directly affected by a series of raids on St. George Island by Lord Dunmore starting in July of 1776. Much property was destroyed, but stubborn resistance by the Militia convinced the British to leave after some time. They confiscated property, destroyed crops, knocked down fences, carried off and butchered livestock and created general destruction on the Island. In addition, the inhabitants filled up their wells to prevent the British from using them. Once they returned they had to rebuild what had been destroyed.

Leonard stated in his pension application in 1832 that when he enlisted he was living near "Ye Coole Springs." The springs are near present day Charlotte Hall, Maryland, and are still quite well known. His unit apparently moved around quite a bit but saw no action. According to his description he spent the first six months of his enlistment near Leonardtown most likely in training. He was then sent down to Point Lookout probably on sentry duty watching for British ships in the bay. Following that he went to Bladensburg for a "short time" and then down to the Potomac again.[8] Though no connection has ever been established, I wonder if he and the Joseph Drury who married Sibyl Wiggenton in Port Tobacco were related? Since Leonard was only 17 when he volunteered I am assuming that his family was also living near the springs and therefore close to Charles County. Joseph was too old to be a brother but could have been an uncle or older cousin. Joseph's disconnect from the family could have been because he married outside the faith (the Wiggentons were Anglican) and then converted when he moved to Virginia. It is also possible, of course that he was originally from one of the Virginia Drury families and not connected at all. The riddle of his origin has not yet been solved.

Records of five other Drury men from St. Mary's County who served in the Army have survived in the Archives. It is unfortunate that they cannot be positively connected to any of our Maryland Drury families though it is almost certain they are somehow related. They were Joseph and Robert B. Drury of the second regiment Maryland Line, Thomas and John Drury in the third regiment Maryland Line, and John B. who would possibly be the same as John. He was listed as simply Continental Army.

Joseph Drury and Robert Barton Drury enlisted together in the 2nd regiment in July of 1778 and served until the following April. Because they enlisted and served together during their period of service I am speculating that they were brothers or perhaps first cousins. Their records indicate that Robert became sick and was in a hospital on 9 July 1778, but both were at White Plains on July 26th and again on Aug 12th. Joseph was in a hospital on 16 Sep 1778, but both were apparently recovered enough to be at Fishkill by October 5th. At the end of the year they were posted to Camp Middlebrook.[9]

Thomas Drury enlisted as a private in the 3rd regiment 3rd Battalion of the Maryland Line commanded by Mordecai Gist on 10 Dec 1776 and served until 1 June 1779. I have not been able to connect him to any of the Drury families in St. Mary's County. I think the Thomas who married before 1751 would have been too old to serve. From the date of his enlistment and the mention that Mordecai Gist commanded, I am suggesting that he was one of the replacements for men killed at the battle of Brooklyn. There is also a John Drury, again without connection to any of my Drury families, who enlisted in the same regiment about a year after Thomas. He may have been killed or taken prisoner at some time. He was listed as missing in action.[10]

The St. Mary's County Drurys have one additional known connection to the revolution. That was through Bennett Riley who married Susanna Drury after the war. She was a daughter of John Drury who died in 1797. Bennett was a Matross in the Second and Third companies of the Maryland Artillery Battalion.[11] The Matross was the person who loaded the charge and shot in the cannon and then swabbed the inside of the barrel after firing to make sure no sparks or embers remained before loading the next charge.

Financing the war had become a huge problem during its five year duration. Maryland did have a large amount of money on deposit in the Bank of England but those sums naturally became unavailable while the Colonies were fighting England. Instead the state issued paper money[12] and backed it with the sums on deposit and, if they were not returned, would be backed up with land held by British subjects in the Colony. If the bank funds were not forthcoming the land would be confiscated. Eventually this is what was done and the land was sold to repay the State's war debt.

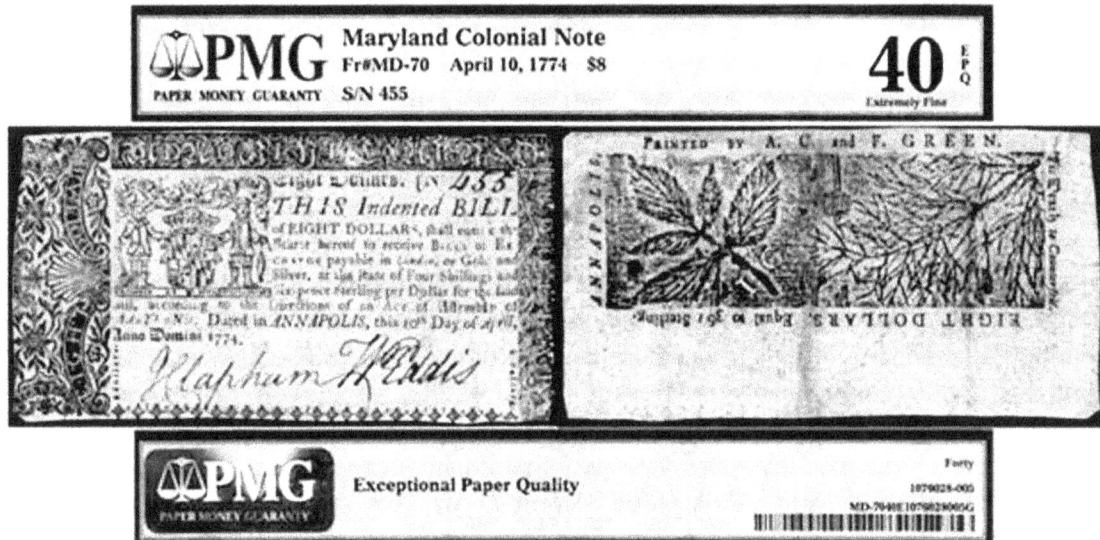

Eight Dollar Maryland Colonial Note

Obverse   **Reverse**

Chalmers Shilling 1783

By the end of the war in the1780s times had become difficult for many of the residents of southern Maryland. Continual British raids had destroyed many farms and much livestock in the area. Those that were left went untended while their owners were away fighting in the war.

These years after the war were difficult for the Drurys as well as most of the other families in Maryland. There were a few wealthy and powerfully connected people like Charles Carroll and Samuel Chase who profited from the war. Most, however, were having difficulty making a living. After the war Maryland wanted to retire its debt as quickly as possible and proposed redeeming the certificates issued during the fighting. Some, especially the wealthy speculators who held many of these, lobbied the legislature to redeem them at face value. This group became known as the creditor faction. Unfortunately this would remove a great deal of hard currency from circulation. Those who lost their livelihood because of the British blockades and raids on the colony were agitating for redeeming the certificates at much less than face value. They were known as the debtor faction.

Many had been leasing farms from George Calvert, the proprietor of the Colony. In 1780 and again in 1790 Proprietary lands including Beaverdam Manor were resurveyed and sold to individuals. The first "law" for the sale was in 1780 when we were under Articles of Confederation. It appears hardly anybody paid for their lands in 1781 and the surveys contained many errors. Once we came under the Constitution, another law for sale was passed in 1786. Beaverdam Manor was then resurveyed by George Fenwick.[13] Almost all of the other proprietary manors were also resurveyed.

Some Drurys chose to remain and buy the farms they had been living on for generations from the State. These families were given first option to buy their land. Drury families who remained on their original farms were Enoch Drury on "Hard Times" a 30 and three quarter acre farm, Michael Drury who lived on a 85 and three quarter acre portion of "Drury's Venture since renamed "Drurys Delight," and Sarah Drury whose husband James had died in 1779, who bought the 163 acre "Chatham" in the name of her two sons Stephen and James. Others chose to move and take up grants of land in Western Virginia (which later became Kentucky) that they obtained as payment for their service during the war.

[1] Crowl, Philip D., *The revolution and after: 1774-1789* p 43 in The Old Line State: A History of Maryland, Morris L. Radoff, Ed., Hall of Records Commission State of Maryland, Annapolis 1971

[2] Risjold, Norman K., Chesapeake Politics 1781 – 1800, Columbia University Press 1978, p 73

[3] Ibid

[4] From Jan Creek E-mail msg 11/6/98 There is an entry in the jesuit records dated July 12, 1767, for the baptism of Joseph Wellemores of Robert & Elizabeth Wellemores. His godparents are: John Drury and his daughter Monica Drury.

[5] Fenwick, Laverne M., *The confiscation of British Property in Maryland* in Chronicles of St. Mary's V.5 # 7 (July 1957) *Resurveyed map of Beaverdam Manor*

[6] [O'Rourke, Timothy, *Catholic Families of Southern Maryland* reprinted Genealogical Publishing Company 1985]

[7] O'Rourke, Timothy, *Catholic Families of Southern Maryland* pages 71-82, reprinted 1985, Genealogical Publishing Company.

[8] Leonard Drury Pension Application # 15035 dated 10/10/1832 issued in Jackson Twp., Stark County, Ohio; see also NSDAR Genealogical Abstracts of Revolutionary War Pension files Vol. 1 P 1029

[9] NARA catalog ID 570910; Beitzel, Edwin, Calendar of events St. Mary's County in the American Revolution, St. Mary's County Bicentennial Commission, pp 60-61

[10] Beitzel, Edwin, Calendar of events St. Mary's County in the American Revolution, St. Mary's County Bicentennial Commission, pp 60-61

[11] "*Muster Rolls and other Records of Maryland Troops in the American Revolution 1775-1783*" Volume XVIII pp. 579, 582, 584

[12] Risjord, Norman K., Chesapeake politics 1784-1800, Columbia University Press, 1978 p. 99

[13] Ben Tippett's Journal book A in 1790

Chapter Nine

Children of Peter Drury

Nicholas Drury

Nicholas Drury was born in 1738 in St. Mary's County, Maryland. He is documented as a son of Peter Drury by being listed as lessee in the lease of Drury's Venture in 1741.[1] Nicholas wrote his will on 2 May 1789 and died in July of that same year. He was 51 years of age.[2]

Nicholas married Monica.[3] We have five children documented from the records though there were almost certainly more.

Their first child, Leonard Drury, was born 17 June 1759 in St. Mary's County, Maryland. He served in the Revolutionary War with a nine months enlistment. He relates that he volunteered after Harvest time in 1777 when he was 18 years old. By this time hostilities had been going on for more than a year and British raids in the area were constant. Leonard stated in his pension application in 1832 that when he enlisted he was living near "Ye Coole Springs". They are located in Charlotte Hall, Maryland directly across from the gates to Charlotte Hall School (now the Veteran's Home). Charlotte Hall is less than a mile from Charles County.[4] His unit apparently moved around quite a bit but saw no action. According to his description he spent the first six months of his enlistment near Leonardtown most likely either in training or guarding British prisoners. He was then sent south to point Lookout probably on sentry duty watching for British ships in the bay. Following that he went to Bladensburg for a "short time" and then down to the Potomac again. After the war he lived at Port Tobacco, Maryland for about 4 or 5 years, then moved to near Fredricktown, Maryland. Then he moved to Leesburg, Virginia, then to the warm springs near Martinsburg, Virginia. After that he moved to near Hagerstown, Maryland, then to Franklin County, Pennsylvania and finally to Stark County, Ohio where he applied for his pension.[5]

The next child, Bennett Drury, was christened on 17 Apr 1768 in St. Mary's County, Maryland. No additional records have been found to tell us more about his life. Two years later on 2 September 1770 twins Mary and Joseph were christened.[6] Finally Monica Drury was christened 4 October 1772. She married Joseph Herbert, son of Matthew Herbert and Mary, on 9 Feb 1795.[7] Joseph Drury married and had at least two children, Joanna who was christened on 7 Feb 1787 and Joseph Jr. who was christened on 5 Apr 1789. Joseph Jr. married Mary Ann Dixon on 22 Jul 1823 in St. Mary's County Maryland. Mary died before 1840 in St. Mary's County Maryland. He died in 1859.[8]

Joseph Jr. and Mary Ann had a son named Robert Barton Drury born in 1825 in St. Mary's County. He married Mary Ann Long March 01, 1848 in Saint Mary's County, Maryland. She was born 1825 in St. Mary's County, Maryland. Also living with them was Mocky (probably Monica) Long, Mary Ann's younger sister.[9] There is some confusion about their birth dates. The 1850 census lists their ages as 25 years but the 1860 census gives their ages as 38 and 28. That would make his birth in 1821 and hers in 1831. Their Children were Emily (1849), Joseph Levi (1851), Sabra Ann (1853), Catherine (1855), and Robert Barton Jr. (1858). [10] By 1880 Mary Ann had died and Robert's children were married and on their own. We find him living as a laborer in the household of Richard Bucklie in northern St. Mary's County.[11]

Joseph Levi Drury, Robert's oldest son, was born in Feb 1851 in St. Mary's County Maryland. He married Mary Jane Hill May 20, 1872 in St. Mary's County Maryland. She was a daughter of James H. and Elizabeth E. Hill. They had a daughter Mamie Elizabeth Drury, born 1873.She married Charles Joseph Wood December 31, 1895 in Mechanicsville RCC, St. Mary's County, Maryland. He was born 1871.

Sabra Ann Drury was their third child born in 1852 in St. Mary's County Maryland. She had a son Francis Eugene Drury born on 17 Feb 1885[12] in St. Mary's County Maryland. His father is unknown and he was reported to be illegitimate.[13] In 1900 he was living with his mother in Chaptico, St. Mary's County. After his marriage he moved with his bride to Mechanicsville.[14] He died after 1933 in St. Mary's County Maryland. Francis married Elizabeth Cecelia Long a daughter of George Henry Long and Georgeanna Lacey about 1915 in St. Mary's County Maryland. Elizabeth was born in 1897.[15]

Michael Drury

Michael Drury was born about 1736 in, St. Mary's County, Maryland.[16] He died about 1826 in St. Mary's County, Maryland.[17] Michael married Ann Yates,[18] daughter of Thomas Yates and Mary French, on 3 Nov 1770 in St. Mary's, County Maryland. Ann was born between 1743 and 1755. Michael Drury lived one and a half miles from Leonard Johnson who managed his properties for a time.[19] Michael inherited "Drury's Venture" from his father.[20] Michael purchased a small part of "Hard Times" from George Fenwick and also added "Males" farm to his holdings.[21] "Males" farm was not listed in the 1790 survey of Beaverdam Manor. This is most probably a misspelling of "Wales" farm (Lot 32) which was listed as purchased or possessed by William Fenwick and mentioned in Michael Drury's Will as having been purchased from William Fenwick in 1813.[22] Drury's Delight", "Hard Times", and "Wales" farms had contiguous boundaries with a combined total of approximately 230 acres.

Michael served as a Private in the Corps of Invalids in Continental Troops during the Revolutionary War[23] along with his brothers Nicholas, Peter, Ignatius, Philip, and his cousin John.[24]

Michael Drury died 14 Feb 1825 when in his 80's and blind. He changed his will shortly before he died[25] leaving his estate to two daughters as named. In July 1829 a hearing was held to determine if Michael Drury was of sound mind when he made his last will.[26] A number of Leonard Johnson's children testified at this hearing.

By 1790 when the first federal Census of St. Mary's County was recorded, five children had been born to Michael and his wife.[27] Their second child, Joshua, christened in 1774 died before the census was taken. There were 1 Free white male under 16 (Michael Jr. born 1785), 2 Free White Males of 16 years and upwards including head of household (Michael's eldest son Edward (1771-1819) and Michael himself) and 3 Free White Females including heads of household (his wife Ann and daughters Dorothy (1775-after 1860) and Mary Ann (1785-aft 1825)). His last three children were all born in the next decade. Birth dates for them are uncertain but they probably were born between 1795 and 1800. They were Catherine, Sarah Marthalina, and George.

Edward "Neddy" Drury was born 1771 in St. Mary's Co., MD, and died Bet. 1819-1820. We don't know who he married but it had to be by about 1794 or 1795. His oldest child, a son, John Thomas Drury, was born in 1796. John married first Susanna Greenwell 19 January 1824. Susanna died sometime after their fifth child was born in 1834.[28] John then married Ann Priscilla Joy.

John William Drury (1834-1955) [29]

John William Drury, eldest son of John Thomas, was born on 8 Oct 1834 in St. Mary's County. He died on 5 Dec 1922 in Clements, St. Mary's County. He was buried on 7 Dec 1922 in St. Josephs. John married Mary Burch. Mary was born in 1837 in Maryland. Their children were Martha, born in 1857, John H. Drury, born in 1860, and James Enoch Drury, born on 17 Sep 1861. He died on 19 Apr 1907.

James Enoch Drury (1861-1907) [30]

Richard Ignatius Drury, their next child, was born in 1863 in St. Mary's County. He married Gussie (Augusta?) Roenicker and died after 1939 in Baltimore. William Drury his fifth child and fourth son, was born in 1867 in St. Mary's Co. Philip C. Drury was born on 2 Jun 1869. He died on 23 Nov 1939. He married Mary Lucinda "Lucy" Bailey daughter of William Thomas Bailey on 19 Jan 1897 at St. Joseph's, Morganza, Md. Mary was born on 14 Jul 1876. She died on 14 Jan 1962.

Philip C. Drury (1869-1939) [31]

Their children were Catherine Elizabeth Drury, born on 10 Nov 1897. She married Mattingly Gibbons Johnson on 30 Nov 1922 and died on 15 May 1956. Her husband died on 10 Nov 1973; William Albert Drury, born on 3 Apr 1899. He died on 23 Jan 1966. William married Mary Thelma Graves. She was born in 1897 and died on 22 Nov 1988; Philip Maguire Drury, born on 15 Jun 1901. He died 28 Jul 1951; Mary Lucinda Drury, born 5 Aug 1903. She died on 25 Nov 1909; Agnes Mabel Drury, born 25 Nov 1906. She died on 29 Mar 1995 in Nazareth, Ky.; James Philip Drury, born 5 Jan 1908 and died 20 Jan 1973. He married Catherine; Cecilia Jeanette Drury, born 19 Apr 1909. She married William Carlton Hicks and died 7 May 1991 and Thomas Harry Drury born 14 Dec 1911. He died on 5 May 1966. Thomas married Mary Veronica Brehany on 7 Nov 1937. Mary was born 12 Nov 1912.

Mary Veronica Brehany (1912-2002) [32]

Robert V. Drury was born in 1870. He died in 1929. Finally there was Daniel Maguire Drury, born on 18 Jul 1875. [33]

Edward's daughter, Elizabeth, was born before 1800 but we don't know exactly when. It could have been in 1798 but no one has found a record of her birth so far. All we know about her is that she lived until sometime after 1828. Dorothy Drury, his next child was born about 1799/1800 in St. Mary's County, Maryland. She died sometime after 1860. She married Joseph Pilkington on 24 May 1841 in St. Mary's County, Maryland. He was born about 1780 in St. Mary's County and died between 1850 and 1860. This was his third marriage and probably a second or third marriage for her as well. She was about 40 years old and he was 20 years older. They had no children together.[34]

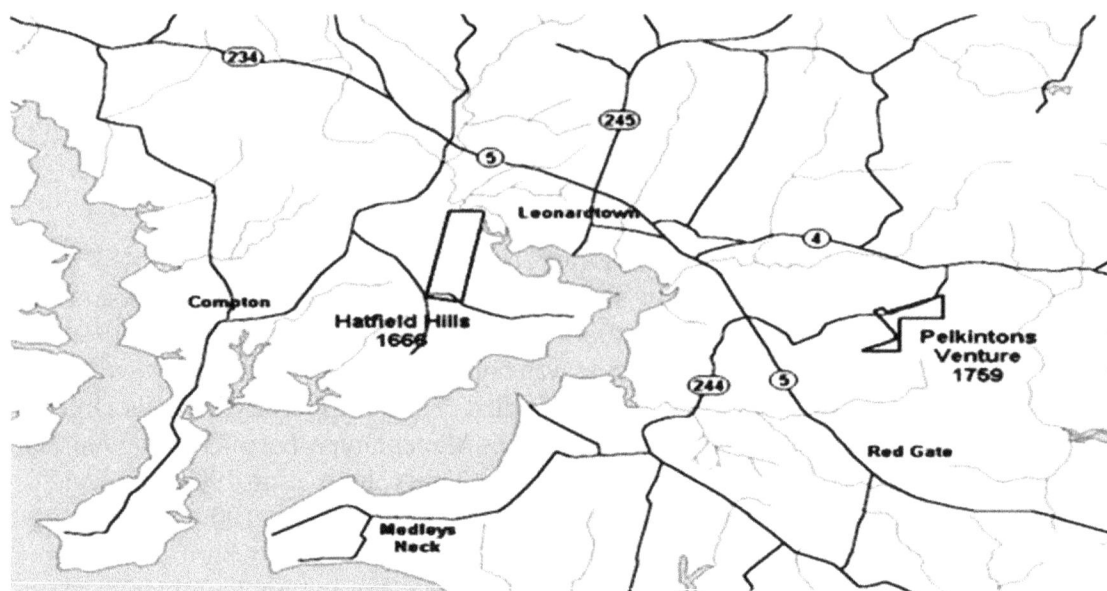

Pilkington's Venture [35]

Julia Ann Drury, the last child we have recorded for Edward, was born in1801 and died 07 June 1885 in St. Mary's County, Maryland. She married Bennett Greenwell, 23 Apr 1838.[36] He was born in1786 and died 27 Jan 1863. Bennett served two tours in the war of 1812. One initially from 24 June 1812 at the beginning of the war until 5 July 1814 under Captain John Briscoe, and a second short stint under Captain Walker from 14 July 1814 to 26 July 1814. These earned the couple two pension awards – one for each period of service.

Dorothy was Michael's next child to live to adulthood. "Dolly" as she was called was born in 1775 in St. Mary's County, Maryland. She was christened[37] on 29 Dec 1776 and died after 1860 in St. Mary's County, Maryland. She married Ignatius Joy Jr., a son of

Ignatius Joy and Eleanor Adams, on 11 Jan 1807 in St. Mary's County, Maryland. Ignatius was born in 1761/1763 in St. Mary's County. He died 16 Mar 1838. We have three known children for the couple. Ignatius Summerfield Joy was born on 20 May 1812 in St. Mary's County, Maryland. He died on 4 Aug 1887. He married Mary Edley Morgan on 1 Feb 1853. Mary was born in 1837 in St. Mary's County and died in 1912. Next was Elizabeth Joy born in 1813 in St. Mary's County, Maryland. She died between 1850 and 1860. She married Henry Hilton Jr. on 7 Aug 1841. Henry was born in 1806 in St. Mary's County and also died between 1850 and 1860. Dorothy's third child, John Michael Joy, was born in 1821 in St. Mary's County. He died in Aug 1883. John married Eleanor Johnson on 18 Jan 1853 in St. Mary's County. Eleanor was born in 1830 in St. Mary's County and died between 1860 and 1870. On 10 Jan 1870 John married Amanda Ann Mattingly. Amanda was born on 29 Jul 1838 in St. Mary's County and died on 21 Jun 1897.

Mary Ann Drury, Michael's second daughter, lived from 1785 to about 1825 in St. Mary's County, Maryland. She married first Rhodolphus Gibson[38] probably between 1800 and 1805.[39] He died sometime before her second marriage to Joseph Leonard Johnson on 22 September, 1812. He was a son of their neighbor Leonard Johnson and his wife Ann Howard. Joseph was born in 1775 and died in 1833.[40] Leonard and his family lived one and a half miles from Drury's Delight and the families were close. Two Johnson boys married Drury girls (Joseph L. to Mary Ann and John to Sarah Marthalina) and one Johnson girl married a Drury boy (Catherine to Michael Jr.). Joseph Johnson owned 10 slaves in 1820. In 1822, he lived on, and managed, Michael Drury's farms. At the Caveat hearing[41] he was best friend of the children of his wife Mary Ann and the children of his sister Catherine, wife of Michael Drury Jr. Ignatius Joy, another son-in-law, was managing the farms at the time of Michael Drury's death. This couple had six recorded children. William Peter Johnson was born on 29 Jun 1813 in St. Mary's County, Maryland. He died on 16 Dec 1892 in Lewisport, Hancock County, Kentucky. He was buried in St. Columba Cemetery, Lewisport, Hancock County, Kentucky. Sources vary on his death date. One has him dying at age 80 in 1892. Others have his death as 26 Dec 1897 at age 95. He married Lucretia A. Jarboe. Ann Johnson was born about 1815; John Lewis Johnson was born on 17 Apr 1817. He died on 6 Jan 1890. He married Elizabeth Dorothy Payne on 21 Nov 1843. Joseph Leonard Johnson Jr. born on 22 Feb 1819 who died on 16 Mar 1901. He married Martha Ann Payne on 12 Jan 1847; Michael Hilary Johnson was born about 1822; Richard B. Johnson was born in 1825.

Michael Drury Jr. or "Miley" was born in 1785 in St. Mary's County, Maryland. He died before 1823 in St. Mary's County, Maryland. The birth dates of Michael Drury Sr. and Michael Drury Jr. are recorded in an old Catholic prayer book which, at the time of writing, was in the possession of Mrs. Lillie Hamner, a granddaughter of Michael Drury Jr. Mrs. Hamner, whose maiden name was Hall, was a daughter of Michael Drury Jr's daughter Rose Anna and Alfred Hall. The dates listed there were December 1723 for Michael Sr. and December 13, 1783 for Michael Jr. The date for Michael Sr. is improbable since he would have been over 100 years old at the time of his death. The date for Michael Jr. is close enough to other dates given for him that they could be a misreading of the handwriting in the original document.[42] Michael married Catherine Johnson, daughter of Leonard Johnson and Mary Howard, on 30 Aug 1813 in St. Mary's

County, Maryland. Catherine was born in 1791 in St. Mary's County, Maryland. She died in St. Mary's County, Maryland. Their children were Edward Drury, born in 1814 in St. Mary's County, Maryland;[43] Rose Anna Drury, born on 5 Apr 1815 and died on 5 Oct 1885;[44] and Eleanor Drury, born in 1817 in St. Mary's County, Maryland.[45]

Sarah Marthalina Drury, mentioned above, was born in 1799. She married John Johnson, a son of Leonard Johnson and Mary Howard, on 9 Jan 1819. John was born in 1784. He died in 1860.[46] John Johnson served in the War of 1812 as a Leonardtown volunteer under Capt. Floyd Millard Williams. He later served as Private Richard Johnson's substitute in the 45th regiment in Capt. J.F. Sothern's Company. On 15 July 1829, on application of John Johnson of Leonardtown, it was ordered that his name and that of his wife's children be discontinued on the docket as caveators to the Will of Michael Drury, they being entered there without his consent or knowledge.[47] John Johnson's will in 1860[48] gave the 88 and a half acre farm known as "Part Grange," located in the third district, to son Joseph Stephen, with all the rest of his estate to be equally divided between his other children. At the time of his death he owned one farm occupied by son in-law Enoch R. Evans and his wife Mary Priscilla, one occupied by his son Joseph Stephen, and one containing two dwelling houses occupied by sons Hillery and William. These children were also listed in the 1850 federal census for the 3rd district St. Mary's County, Maryland.[49]

Their children were Mary Priscilla Johnson, born on 27 Dec 1819 who married Enoch R. Evans; and Uriah Johnson, born 25 Mar 1821 who married Clarissa "Clara" Eleona Shircliffe, daughter of John Shircliffe and Maria Tennison, on 13 Jan 1847. Clarissa was born on 14 Jan 1828. She died on 17 Nov 1895. She was buried in Old St. Joseph Roman Catholic Cemetery. Uriah died on 23 Apr 1896. Next came Joseph Stephen Johnson born 26 Dec 1825, Thomas Johnson born about 1827, Eleanor Johnson born in 1829/1830, Hillery E. Johnson born on 22 Apr 1832, William Edward Johnson born in Apr 1836, Martha Johnson born in 1837/1838, and John T. Johnson, born in 1839.

John Johnson is also listed in the muster rolls as having been in Capt. William Floyd's company of the 12th Regiment, St. Mary's County, stationed at Leonard Town to St. Inigoes in St. Mary's County July 14 to August 4, 1813. This would have been about the time the British were probing up the Potomac. Johnson is shown as having served for 5 days. Richard Johnson, though, is listed as having served 22 days in the period July 16 to August 17, 1814 under Capt. John H. Briscoe of the 45th Regiment, and this company included men transferred from Sothoron's company. Some of those days were possibly served by John Johnson.[50] John Johnson of Leonard claimed to have served as a private under Captains Floyd, Millard and Williams and applied 13 February 1851 for bounty land. He was listed as a resident of St. Mary's County, volunteered at Leonard Town, and afterwards served as a substitute for Richard Johnson as a private in Captain J. F. Sothoron's company in the 45th Regiment. At the time of the 1851 claim, Johnson was listed as age 65 years. He applied again 7 April 1855 and was again listed as a resident of St. Mary's Co. Apparently both claims were rejected. Witnesses listed were William T. Perry and Samuel E. Abell, also of St. Mary's Co.[51]

One account of the British raid on Leonardtown 19 July 1814 stated "...every housekeeper was plundered except one - to the Court House they did great injury; not a sash of glass but what they destroyed; much of the inside work cut to pieces, all the tobacco about 70 hogshead carried off."[52]

A second account states, "Mrs. Thompson and Miss Eliza Key were reputed to have been instrumental in saving the courthouse from being burned by claiming it was sometimes used as a place for divine worship. The Key family, related to Francis Scott Key, lived at Tudor Hall in the late eighteenth century, which is now the St. Mary's County Historical Society Library. Brigadier General Philip Steuart with about 250 militia was in the neighborhood but did not think himself capable of dislodging the enemy."

Ignatius Drury

Ignatius Drury was born in 1745 in St. Mary's County. He was a son of Peter Drury and (probably) Jane Bailey. He died after 1800 in Nelson County, Kentucky. Ignatius married Anastasia French, daughter of John French and Monica, on 11 Dec 1769 at St. Francis Xavier, St. Mary's County, Maryland. Anastasia was born on 29 Jul 1750 in St. Mary's County, Maryland.

Dorothy Drury

Their first daughter, Dorothy Drury, was born in 1771 and married John H. Payne on 20 October 1794 in St. Mary's County, Maryland. She died in Kentucky about 1850. John was born 14 Feb 1769 in St. Mary's County, Maryland. He died on 24 Mar 1846 in Daviss County, Kentucky. They both are buried in St. Lawrence Cemetery, Daviss County, Kentucky.

John and Dorothy had the following children: John Payne, born on 30 May 1799 in Prince George's County, Maryland. He was christened on 30 Jun 1799 in Prince George's County, Maryland; [53] Ignatius Payne, born on 27 Aug 1801 in Prince George's County, Maryland. He was christened on 20 Sep 1801 in Prince George's County, Maryland.[54] Cornelius Payne, born on 28 Aug 1803 and died on 3 Feb 1835; Dennis Henry Payne and Charles Payne who was born in 1809 in Prince George's County, Maryland and was christened on 2 Mar 1809.

Ignatius Drury Jr.

It was thought that Ignatius who married Harriet Redding on 5 Dec 1799 in Georgetown, Montgomery County, Maryland[55] and Ignatius who appears in Kentucky by 1810 married to Deborah Thorne[56] were the same person. Researchers cite the fact that he had a daughter, Mary Ann Drury, born on 2 Nov 1801[57] and that her baptismal sponsors were relatives from St. Mary's County. There is no doubt that he is connected somehow to the St. Mary's County Drurys, but he is not the Ignatius Drury reported in Frederick County census in 1800.[58] Ignatius who appears in Kentucky by 1810 married to Deborah Thorne was a son of Ignatius and Anastasia French[59] as was his brother Charles who went with him to Kentucky. At least three children were born after arriving in Kentucky. These children born with Deborah Thorne were William born in 1817,[60] Milburn,[61] and George Francis Drury.[62] We can infer from the will that Ignatius sired at least three more children, but we have not identified but who were still alive when he died.

Charles Drury

Charles Drury, their next child, was born 7 Feb 1776 and died in 1852. He married first Emily Thorne, born in 1783. Charles married a second time to Elizabeth Leach,[63] daughter of James Leach and Elizabeth.[64] Elizabeth was born in 1782 in St. Mary's County, Maryland. Charles and his family were devout Roman Catholics. He bought land and built a large brick house on the Bardstown Road overlooking the site to which the *Sisters of Charity at Nazareth* Community moved in June 1822. The house was still standing in 1983. Mr. Drury paid 45 (cents) an acre for the property.

He had eleven children. Catherine Drury SCN was born on 31 Mar 1805. She died on 16 Aug 1890. Catherine entered the convent of the Sisters of Charity at Nazareth and was known as Sister Martha[65] [66] Catherine's sister, Anastasia, known as Sister Isabella, entered the convent two years later in 1824. She was born in 1812 and died in 1875. [67]

During the Civil War Sister Martha nursed the soldiers at Paducah, Ky. In 1883 she became the first SCN to observe her 60th anniversary of vows. SCN Mary Agnita Speake's great-grandmother was a sister of Sisters Martha and Isabel Drury. Sister Mary Ethel O'Bryan was in the same relationship to the Drury sisters. Her great grandmother was either Mary or Matilda Drury. Her parents are listed in the Nazareth archives as M. L. O'Bryan and Mary Frances Blinco.

Mother Columba Carroll exhibited both great compassion and administrative skills for the Convent and Academy during the Civil War. Leaders from both the Union and Confederate sides honored her. Bishop Martin Spalding of the Louisville Catholic Diocese responded to the needs of Civil War casualties. He wrote Archbishop John B. Purcell of Cincinnati about the acute need for chaplains and nurses at the Louisville hospitals. Spalding issued a call for the Sisters of Charity at Nazareth, Kentucky to serve as nurses. In Paducah Union surgeon Dr. Hewit urged General Smith to obtain the Sisters' help in the fall of 1861. So Sister Martha Drury set up facilities in the old courthouse and enlisted several of her colleagues to help, including Sisters Mary Lucy Dosh, Sophia, Justine, Beatrice, and Jane Frances. Doctors Fry, Kay, and Austin were very pleased with their work. Paducah received many hundreds of casualties from such battles as Shiloh, Fort Donaldson, Fort Henry, and Belmont. The President of the United States also honored the Nazareth order. Abraham Lincoln sent a personal thank-you card to Mothers Columbia Carroll and Frances Gardener. In 1865 he issued an order that read, "Let no depredation be committed upon the property of the Sisters of Charity of Nazareth, near Bardstown, Kentucky." This document is still contained in the archives at Nazareth.[68]

Other children were James T. born in 1823,[69] George who married Elizabeth McClain, Robert who married Rose Carrico, Pius who married Mary Blandford, Mary who married Stephan Theodore O'Bryan (1801- aft 1860) s/o Lewis O'Bryan (1757 – 1835) and Mary Ann Blandford (1748 –1846), Matilda who married Martin O'Bryan (1810 - 1839) also a son of Lewis O'Bryan (1757 – 1835) and Mary Ann Blandford (1748 - 1846), Martha who married another brother John Robert O'Bryan (1811 - aft 1880), and Susan who was born in 1816. She died in 1841 in Nelson County, Kentucky from pulmonary consumption that today we call Tuberculosis.[70] Finally there was Mahala Drury about whom we know nothing else.

Monica Drury

Monica Drury, our fourth recorded child of Ignatius and Anastasia French, was born about 1785 in St. Mary's County, Maryland and died 12 June 1866 in Nelson County, Kentucky. She married Charles Warren. Charles was born on 27 Sep 1782 in St. Mary's County and died 4 April 1868. They had a daughter Harriet who married Pius Montgomery. Their grandson, George Montgomery entered the priesthood in 1879 eventually becoming the first Anglo Bishop of Los Angeles and later Archbishop of San Francisco.[71]

Archbishop George Montgomery [72]

Mary Ellen Drury

Mary Ellen Drury was born 19 June 1787 in St. Mary's County and died 2 February 1858 in Washington County Kentucky. She married William Hogan (1788 – 1854) in Nelson County, Kentucky, on New Year's Day 1814. The Hogans came originally from Ireland.[73] Their children were Ignatius Hogan born about 1815,[74] Mary who married John H. Rodman s/o Hugh Rodman (born 1788) in 1836, and Ann, William, Christine, Helen, Elizabeth, and Matilda Hogan. The following letter from William Rodman to his brother

Hugh Rodman M.D. details his recollections of his ancestry.[75]

Her grandson Hugh Rodman M.D. was born on 22 May 1842 in Jefferson County, Kentucky.[76] He is listed in the 1882 Nelson County Atlas practicing medicine in New Haven. New Haven is located about twelve miles south of Bardstown on Highway 31E.[77] He is also listed in the "Minutes of the Board of Trustees of Bardstown, 04/07/1827 to 1966: October 18, 1912 - sidewalks to be installed on the south edge of Market, from Court Square to South 5th Street. One of the property owners listed is H.D. Rodman. Market is now Stephen Foster Avenue. The house would therefore have been located between the Court House and St. Joseph's Cathedral. He died in 1922, and is buried in St Joseph Cemetery... [78]

DRURY, FAMILY (Taken from William Rodman's letter to Dr. H.D. Rodman, dated March 12, 1914)

Dear Brother:

Ignatius Drury and Charles Drury were grandmothers's brothers. She (grandmother) named her first-born Ignatius. Zachariah Drury was an older half-brother of grandmother. As to Mary M. Drury and Anna S. Drury - these were probably full sisters of Zachariah or his wife and the wife of Ignatius, Charles and Elizabeth possibly husband and wife. I am under the impression our great grandmother Drury was a widow when she left Maryland. She had a stepson, Zack, I know and maybe a step-daughter, but I think not. This great-grandmother Drury's name was Alice Anastasia (French) Drury. She had six children, Ignatius, Charles, Dolly or Dorothea Payne, Elizabeth or Betsy Jarboe, Martha or Moccie Warren, Eleanor or Nellie Hogan. Our Grandmother was the youngest child of the family.

Billy.

To Ignatius or Zachary Drury and Anastasia French were born the following children: one son, Charles Drury; and four daughters, namely, Dorothy called Dolly; Elizabeth called Betsy; Martha or Monica called Moccie; and Ellen or Eleanor or Helen, called Nellie. Dorothy or Dolly Drury married John, called Jackie, Payne. From this union sprung all the Paynes in Knottsville, Daviess County, including Ignatius Payne of West Louisville. Elizabeth or Betsy Drury married a Mr. Jarboe. From this union came Ignatius Jarboe, formerly of Knottsville, KY, also "Algie" Jarboe of Knottsville. There were probably other descendants but they are not known.

Martha, or Moccie, Drury married _____ Warren. From the union came the Warrens of Hardin County and Archbishop Montgomery. Ellen, Helen or Eleanor Drury known as Nellie, married William Hogan of Fredericksburg, Washington County, KY. From this union came William and Ignatius Hogan and several daughters. Bishop Montgomery's grandmother was daughter of Charles and Moccie Warren.[79]

Elizabeth Drury

Elizabeth was born in Maryland in 1782. She married Charles Burkham Jarboe in 1805. The couple subsequently moved to Kentucky where they both died in 1866. Charles was a son of Charles Jarboe Junior and Alice and was born in 1785.[80]

Ann Drury

Ann was a daughter of Ignatius Drury and Anastasia French born in St. Mary's County in 1789. Ann married James E. Bowling on 7 Mar 1818 in Baltimore, Maryland.[81] James was born in 1792 in Fauquier County, Virginia. It appears that there were two James Bowlings born in Fauquier County, Virginia about 1790-1792. One married Annie Drury and was probably born in 1792. The other married Margaret Jones and moved to Illinois. However there was a Charles Bowlin in St. Mary's County who had a son the right age to be James[82] so it is still unclear who the James Bowling that married Ann Drury was. James died on 22 Oct 1848 in Baltimore, Maryland.[83] Additional support for Ann being a daughter of Ignatius and Anastasia is provided by the following references from her family and in Ann's obituary in 1858.[84] Her husband James was a carter (teamster or truck driver in today's parlance) and later a watchman.[85] She was buried in St. Patrick's Cemetery, Philadelphia Road, Baltimore, MD.

Their children were John Lewis Bowling born 1820 in Baltimore, MD; Mary Jane Elizabeth Bowling born 1 Jun 1823 in Baltimore, MD; William James Bowling born 1826 in Baltimore, MD; James Philip Bowling born 6 Jun 1829 in Baltimore, MD; and William Ignatius Bowling born 13 Feb 1827 in Baltimore, MD.

Peter Drury Junior

Peter Drury Junior was born about 1740 in St. Mary's County Maryland. He was named as a lessee on the survey for Drury's Venture in 1741. In 1768 he was living on "Sandy Ground" with his wife, his brother Nicholas, and his cousin William.[86] He married Eleanor _____ though we have no maiden name for her, and had at least two children. Jesse was christened 22 September 1776 and Wilfred on 24 January 1779.[87] Wilfred married Nellie Bailey on 9 May 1799 and was awarded a bonus for gallantry during the War of 1812.

Enoch Drury

Enoch Drury is a son of Peter Drury born about 1749.[88] He died in 1784 when his brother Peter Jr. administered his estate. He married Tabitha Wimsatt, a daughter of James Wimsatt and Elizabeth Cissell, sometime before 1768 or 1769.[89] She was mentioned in her father's estate distribution in 1820 as Tabitha Drury.[90] He was living in Beaverdam Manor on Lot 34 called Terra Collium, alias Fertilitas, from 1768 until at least 1781 and probably until his death in 1784.[91] He served as a private in the Maryland Militia during the Revolutionary War.

The couple had at least six and possibly nine children. One was Alathair who died in 1807.[92] In her will she leaves her entire estate to her mother for life, then to be equally divided between her sisters and brother. The others were Aloysia (1771),[93] Elizabeth (1772),[94] Eleanor (1774),[95] James (1776),[96] Winifred (1777),[97] Frances, Mary, and Enoch Jr.

Marriage information for the children is incomplete. We have marriages for only three of the children. Eleanor was christened on 6 February 1774.[98] There is not definitive proof that she is a daughter of Enoch and Tabitha, but it is likely. She married Philip Abell, a son of Philip Abell and Ann Dryden, on Christmas Eve 1796. She died three years later in 1799, and Philip remarried to Helena Peake in 1806, and third to Julia Ann Greenwell in 1810. Both Philip and Eleanor are buried in grave 147 at St. Nicholas Church on the Patuxent River Naval Air Station.[99]

Winifred Drury is another daughter of Enoch and Tabitha Wimsatt. She was born April 1, 1777 and died 17 February 1856. She married James Thompson, the son of John Basil Thompson and his wife Sarah, on December 23 1805. James was born in the early 1770's and died on 14 March 1846. They had at least three children, Maria (1806/1810 – 1845/1850) who married John B. Raley, a son of Zachariah Raley and Ann Wilkinson, on 28 February 1828; John B. (1813 – after 1850) who married Mary Louise Tarleton, a daughter of Rhodolph Tarleton and Sarah Coombs, November 11, 1839. Mary died in 1844, and he remarried the following year to Ann Marie Bean (1820 – after 1852). Winifred's third child, a daughter, was Elizabeth (1816 – after 1860).

Enoch's only son, Enoch Jr., was probably born in the 1770's. He died November 4th 1817. He married Mary Brewer, a daughter of Thomas Brewer and Catherine Aud, on 27 November 1807.[100] The Elizabeth Drury (1818 – after 1850) who married Joseph Thompson (1809 – after 1850), a son of John Basil Thompson Jr. (1809 – after 1850) and his second wife Anastasia Wathen, may have been Enoch's daughter though no definitive proof can be cited.

Mildred Drury

Mildred was born sometime between 1748 and 1755. She married Ignatius Russell between May 19, 1771 and September 1772. She was listed as Mildred Drury at the baptism of her cousin Philip Joy in 1771 and as Mildred Russell in 1772 when she sponsored her niece, Thecla Drury. Her first child, Eleanor, was born May 22, 1773 so she had to marry at least nine months before that. Her connection as a child of Peter Drury is supplied by her presence as godmother for these children.[101]

Ignatius and Mildred had the following children:[102] Eleanor born 26 May 1773, Phillp born on 15 Sep 1775, Allusia born on 24 Dec 1777, and Charles born in 1783. Charles died in 1816 in St. Mary's County, Maryland. He married Monica French, daughter of Bennett French and Susanna Mills, on 10 Aug 1812 in St. Mary's County, Maryland. Monica was born in 1796 in St. Mary's County, Maryland. She died in 1850 in St. Mary's County, Maryland.

The only discrepancy in the census is the birth date of Allusia Russell. Her birth was listed as 24 December 1777. Such a specific date must have a reference somewhere though I cannot cite it at present. If true this would place her along with her sister in the 16-26 category in the 1800 census. If, on the other hand, the census data is correct then she could not have been born earlier than 1784. More research is needed here.

It is unfortunate that we have no information about the other three boys. We can only speculate that one was a child, the second a teenager, and the third a young adult. Charles is the only one about which we have additional information, and he is not positively identified with this family. His grandfather William Russell had five sons: John by a first wife Catherine Leake about 1730, and four by his second wife. They were William Jr., Ignatius, James, and Charles. Given the mortality rates at the time we can eliminate John as being born too early to father a son in 1783. William's son Charles was in Kentucky at least by 1788 when he married Jane Mattingly. He would have been 29 at that time. This could have been a second marriage but no evidence of any earlier marriage has been found.

William Jr. could have been Charles' father. He married in 1774 and his two children were born one earlier and one later than Charles. Ignatius Russell most likely had more than three children. In 1783 he would have been 34 years old. It certainly would have been possible for Mildred and Ignatius to be his parents. James Russell was born in 1755. He was living in Port Tobacco in the 1790 Census.

There may have been close connections between the French, Russell, and Drury families around that time. Ignatius Drury married Anastasia French; Charles Russell married Monica, the daughter of Anastasia's brother Bennett French; and Ignatius Russell married Ignatius Drury's sister, Mildred.

Linda Reno, a respected St. Mary's County genealogist, says,

> *"I think the most likely candidate for the father of Charles Russell who married Monica French was Ignatius Russell who married Mildred Drury. At the time of the 1800 census, he had 5 sons. Charles wasn't the son of James Russell and*

Maria Graves. He could have been the son of William Russell, Jr., but I just don't think so."

This placement is speculation based on probability. More proof is needed but it is the best we have to go on at present.

Robert Drury

Robert Drury is a possible son of Peter Drury who lived on a part of Dry Docking. He married a girl named Mary Margaret sometime before 1770 when the first child we have documented was christened on 9 May 1770.[103] A second child, Ann, was christened on 5 April, 1772.[104] Nothing else is known at present.

---

[1] Land Office Unpatented Certificate of Survey, SM #141; MSA 51228, MdHR 40,042, 1-26-1-59

[2] Burger, Judith A. Will of Nicholas Drury d. 1789 Register of Wills, St. Mary's County,Maryland, Liber. J. J. No, 1 p. 481

[3] According to Linda Reno Monica was probably either a Ford or a Thompson 1790 Census lists a Monica as Head of Household indicating she was widowed by that time and not remarried. We don't know for sure if this was the same Monica or not.

[4] Linda Reno – electronic

[5] *Leonard Drury Pension Application # 15035* dated 10/10/1832 issued in Jackson Twp., Stark County, Ohio; see also NSDAR *Genealogical Abstracts of Revolutionary War Pension files* Vol. 1 P 1029

[6] Baptism: September 02, 1770, St. Francis Xavier, St. Mary's County, Maryland, Sponsors Michael Drury, Ann Thompson, Michael and Ann Ford Twin: Of Mary Drury

[7] www.Stmary'sfamilies.com; court records

[8] Joseph Drury Oct 28 1850 Image # 17 Age: 69,Estimated Birth Year: 1780, Birth Place: St Mary's Co, Gender: Male, Home in 1850, District 5, St Mary's, Maryland Page: 347, Roll: M432 p. 296 dwellings 1586 1523, Joseph Drury, 69 M W Farmer, $1000, born St. Mary's County, Robert B. Drury, 25 M W Farmer, born St. Mary's County, Mary A. 25 F W born St. Mary's County, Joseph L. 1 M W born St. Mary's County, Mocky Long, 13 F W born St. Mary's County

[9] 1850 US Census St. Mary's County, Maryland.

[10] 1860 United States Federal Census, R Barton Drury District 5, St. Marys, MD age 38 est. birth 1821 Male, Mary Drury age 28 est. birth 1831 Female, Emily Drury age 11 est. birth 1848 Female Joseph Drury age 9 est. birth 1850 Male, Sabra A Drury age 7 est. birth 1852 Female, Catharine Drury age 5 est. birth 1854 Female, R B Drury age 2 est. birth 1857 Male

[11] Family History Library Film 1254514 NA Film Number T9-0514 Page Number 91B

[12] Francis Eugene Drury, SR. World War I Draft Registration Cards, 1917-1918

[13] Linda Reno electronic

[14] Ancestry.com, 1900 Census St. Mary's County, Maryland Ed: 113 page B10

[15] Ibid

[16] Will of Peter Drury, 4/10/1771 - Perogative court Records pg. 72, Peter Drury, 106.3805m L41.6.11

[17] Will of Michael Drury 2/14/1825-2'6/1828 Liber EJM No. 1 p. 36

[18] Timothy J. O'Rourke, Colonial Source Records - Southern Maryland Catholic Families; Barnes, Robert, Maryland Marriages 1664 - 1777 p. 54

[19] Some Johnsons of Southern Maryland -- Leona Cryer Gateway Press, Baltimore Md. 1991 P. 14 & 15

[20] Will of Peter Drury, 4/10/1771 - Perogative court Records pg. 72, Peter Drury, 106.3805m L41.6.11

[21] Will of Michael Drury 2/14/1825-2'6/1828 Liber EJM No. 1 p. 36

[22] Signed: February 14, 1825 Proved: February 13 1828 Liber E.J.M. No. 1 p. 36

[23] INDEX TO REVOLUTIONARY WAR SERVICE RECORDS VOLUME I: A-D, transcribed by Virgil D. White, The National Historical Publishing Co., Waynesboro, TN., 1995, pp. 799, 801

[24] Boles, David, Barth-Hickey Ancestry p 152 (references Clements and Wright 1987)

[25] Liber E.J.M. 1, p. 36

[26] Liber EJM 1, pp 100 thru 111

[27] Census of St. Mary's County, 1790 P 107

[28] 1850 Census-Source Information: Dodd, Jordan, Liahona Research, comp.. Maryland Marriages, 1655-1850 [database on-line]. Provo, UT, USA: Ancestry.com Operations Inc, 2004

[29] courtesy of Jim Gangler <ganglerj@yahoo.com>

[30] courtesy of Jim Gangler <ganglerj@yahoo.com>

[31] courtesy of Jim Gangler <ganglerj@yahoo.com>

[32] courtesy of Jim Gangler <ganglerj@yahoo.com>

[33] Children except Daniel listed in 1870 Census M 593 roll 594 pg 661 and 662

[34] Source Citation: Year: 1860; Census Place: District 6, St Marys, Maryland; Roll: M653_479; Page: 215; Image: 515; Family History Library Film: 803479

[35] courtesy of Peter Himmelheber

[36] Dodd, Jordan, Liahona Research, comp.. Maryland Marriages, 1655-1850 [database on-line]. Provo, UT, USA: Ancestry.com Operations Inc, 2004

[37] Timothy J. O'Rourke, Colonial Source Records Southern Maryland Catholic Families

[38] Marriage: Rhody GIBSON bef 1812

[39] Typical marriages occurred between ages 15 and 20

[40] Cryer, Leona, Some Johnsons of Southern Maryland -- Gateway Press, Baltimore Md., 1991 P. 16

[41] In July 1829 a hearing was held to determine if Michael Drury was of sound mind when he made his last will, Liber EJM 1, pp 100 thru 111

[42] History of Union County, Kentucky, p. 687

[43] Mentioned in Michael Drury Sr's Will in 1823 per Linda Reno <lreno@erols.com> e-mail messages of 5/21 and 5/22/2000

[44] Ibid

[45] Ibid

[46] Some Johnsons of Southern Maryland -- Leona Cryer Gateway Press, Baltimore Md. 1991 P. 16/17

[47] Liber E.J.M. 1, p 100

[48] Liber J.T.M.R. 1, p 190

[49] *1850; Census District 3, St Mary's, Maryland; Roll: M432_296; Page: 265B; Image: 289*

[50] Wright, Maryland Militia War of 1812, Volume 5, St. Mary's & Charles Counties." p. 20

[51] Ibid p. 74, 55-rej-98108

[52] Report for August 14, 1814, republished in Chronicles of St. Mary's.

[53] June 30, 1799 - Baptized John Paine, born May 30, 1799 of John and Dorothea Paine, living in Prince George's County. GodMother, in proxey-Anastatia Druery for Elizabeth Druery

[54] Sept. 20, 1801 - Baptized Ignatius Paine born August 22, 1801 of John and Dorothy Paine living in Prince George County, Godmother, Elizabeth Druery.

[55] Trinity Church-Georgetown DAR - vol.. 47 Trinity Church Marriage & Baptism Records 1795-1805 - December 5, 1799 - With license married Ignatius Drury and Harriett Redding of Montgomery Cty. before the underwritten witnesses; Charles Drury, Elizabeth Drury, Haney Drury, Gabriel Newton, Ignatius Newton.

[56] Perrin, W. H.,Kentucky Biographical Sketches Vol V p 249

[57] Trinity Church-Georgetown DAR - vol.. 47 Trinity Church Marriage & Baptism Records 1795-1805, December 25, 1801 - Baptized Mary Ann Druery Born Nov. 2, 1801 of Ignatius and Hariot Druery living in the District of Columbia. Sponsors, Ignatius Druery, Elizabeth Druery, Elionor Druery.

[58] Boles, David, Barth-Hickey Ancestry, p 150

[59] Perrin, W.H., Kentucky Biographical Sketches Vol. 5

[60] DRURY, William (age 16) d. 20 Nov.1833, son of Ignatius & Debary DRURY. Nelson Co., KY Cemeteries," p. 93.

[61] Mary Lou Nash Email msg of 8/21/99

[62] Nelson County Kentucky, Will of Ignatius Drewery 6/30/1833

[63] CENSUS YR: 1850 STATE: Kentucky COUNTY: Nelson DIVISION: District 1 REEL NO: M432-215 SHEET NO: 285B REFERENCE: Enumerated on 7th August 1850 by G Balbott (Page 569): 34 136 136 Drury, Charles, 75 M farmer, 4,500, Md.; 35 136 136 Drury, E. 68 F Md. 36 136 136 Drury, J.T. 27 M farmer Ky.

[64] Jennings, Tom <Consettct@aol.com>, Descendants of James Leach, James Leach - 1785 d: Aft. 1785 +Elizabeth Leach Unknown - 1785 d: Aft. 1785, John Leach - 1785 d: Aft. 1785, Sarah Leach - 1785 d: Aft. 1785, Elizabeth Leach - 1785 d: Aft. 1785. Refs: Will of William Leach 7/12/1785; 9/19/1785 St. Marys Co. Son: James Leach 1 shilling, Dau. Priscilla Hunt one shilling, Grandchildren of James & Elizabeth Leach: John & Ann. Granddaughter, Sarah Leach, Dau-in-law Elizabeth Leach, Execx. Stephen Penn of Charles Co. witn. Leonard Branson & Ann Penn.

[65] Courtesy of Sr. Bridgid Clifford, SCN, Archivist the Sisters of Charity of Nazareth Archival Center, P.O. Box 3000, Nazareth, KY 40048; Sister Martha Drury, Catherine Drury B. 3/31/1805 in MD. Entrance 7/25/1822, Habit Dec. 18, 1822, Vows Dec. 18, 1823 D. 8/16/1890, Louisville Nazareth Cemetery: South Section, Row-M, grace-2

[66] 1850 Census Nelson County: Roll: M432_215 Township: District 1 Page: 302 Image: 58 C. Drury 45 F W born KY Nazareth Female Academy

[67] Webb, Ben J.,Centenary of Catholicity in Kentucky, p. 63, p.431.

[68] Courtesy of SCN Archives

[69] CENSUS 1850 STATE: Kentucky, COUNTY: Nelson, DIVISION: District 1, REEL: M432-215, SHEET 285B

[70] Obit in Catholic Advocate V.6 #7 20 March 1841 Died in Bardstown, on Tuesday morning, last, the 16th inst., of pulmonary consumption, Mrs. Susan E. Wehlan, wife of Mr. James Wehlan, and daughter of Mr. Charles Drury of Nelson County, aged 25 years. Requiest in Pacem.

[71] Hierarchia Catholica Medii et Recentioris Aevi, Volume 8, Page 136, and Page 276; Hierarchia Catholica Medii et Recentioris Aevi, Volume 8, Page 392, and Page 550

[72] Courtesy of Dorothy Payne Krumpleman

[73] Perrin, W. H., Kentucky Biographical Sketches Vol V p 249

[74] History of the Roman Catholic Diocese of Owensboro, p 229, Named as first born in letter of William Rodman to his brother in 1914

[75] History of the Roman Catholic Diocese of Owensboro" p. 229

[76] Perrin, Kentucky Biographical Sketches Vol 5, 249.

[77] Smith, Sarah B., Historic Nelson County, Its Homes and People, 1982 P. 255, NEW HAVEN, KY.

[78] History of the Roman Catholic Diocese of Owensboro" p. 325

[79] History of Daviess County, Kentucky

[80] 1860, Daviess Co., KY: J. Jarboe, 46, farmer, b. KY; Martina Jarboe, 43, domestic duties, b. KY; Henry Jarboe, 18, farm hand, b. KY; Victoria Jarboe, 16, domestic duties, b. KY; Albert Jarboe, 14, b. KY; Ben J. Jarboe, 12, b. KY; Josephine Jarboe, 8, b. KY; James E. Jarboe, 5, b. KY; Charles Jarboe, 75, b. MD; Elizabeth Jarboe, 78, domestic lady, b. MD.

[81] Index to Marriages and Deaths in the (Baltimore) Sun 1837-1850, p. 10/26/46-2

[82] 1800 Census, St. Mary's MD M20957, p. 391

[83] Burial: 24 Oct 1846 St. Patrick's Cemetery, Philadelphia Rd, Balto.,MD

[84] Bowling, Ann 68 on 31st ult wid/o James Bowling & m/o 5 ch Gettysburg & Leonardtown copy 2 Jan 1858 (Departed This Life Death Notices from the (Baltimore) Sun 1851-1853 v. 1.)] [Her presumed father's name is Ignatius Drury Her sisters are Mary and Elizabeth and her Grandmother is Jane. Also, Family oral records show Annie's name as Anne Mary Jane Drury. Her Uncle is named Phillip Drury and her husband is James Bowling. Her grandfather is John French, her uncle is William Drury and her husband is James Bowling

[85] 1821 Petition for job of watchman in Fells Pt, Eastern Dist.; 1845 185 Wolfe St., carter (Wm. Lamdin, 162 Wolfe St.)

[86] Brumbaugh, G.M. *Maryland Records---Vol. II, State of His Lordship's Manor,* Genealogical Publ. Co., Baltimore, MD, 1985 p. 65

[87] Timothy J. O'Rourke, Colonial Source Records - Southern Maryland Catholic Families

[88] O'Rourke, Timothy J., Catholic Families of Souhern Maryland Genealogical pub. Co., Baltimore 1985 pp 8,11,14

[89] marriage date estimated from birth dates of their children

[90] Saint Mary's County Balances and Distributions - 1/16/1790: Admin. accts. of James Wimsatt, SMC. Widow, 1/3. 6 children, equally: Tabitha Drury, Jamima Davis, Eleanor Wimsatt, James Wimsatt, Francis (sic) Ward. NOTE: Only 5 children named. Admin.: Elizabeth Wimsatt.

[91] Brumbaugh, G.M. *Maryland Records---Vol. II, State of His Lordship's Manor,* Genealogical Publ. Co., Baltimore, MD, 1985 p. 65

[92] St. Mary's County wills: JJ3 p. 154-155

[93] O'Rourke, Timothy J. Colonial Source Records - Southern Maryland Catholic Families p. 8

[94] Ibid

[95] Ibid p. 14

[96] Ibid

[97] Ibid

[98] Ibid

[99] St. Nicholas Church Burials Patuxent River Naval Air Station St. Mary's County, MD, NAS project E38; Linda Reno-County Court Records

[100] Maryland Militia, War of 1812, Vol. 5, St. Mary's and Charles Counties by F. Edward Wright, 1983. 1/16/1851: Pension application of Mary Hooper, 65, a resident of St. Mary's County, widow of Enoch Drury

[101] O'Rourke, Timothy, *Catholic Families of Southern Maryland,* May 19, 1771 Baptism of Philip of Athan. & Dian. Joy, Sp: Bennet Thompson & Mildred Drury, p. 119; Listed as Mildred Russell when sponsoring the baptism of Thecla Drury (daughter of her brother Philip) 12/20/1772, card file, St. Mary's County Historical Society

[102] 1800 Census for St. Mary's County, Maryland per Linda Reno in post of 9/30/2007. 1M under 10 (unknown son b aft 1790) 1M 10-16 (1 unknown son b. 1784-1790) 3M 16-26 (Philip (1775), Charles (1783), 1 unknown son (b. 1774-1784)) 1M over 45 (Ignatius) 1F 10-16 (b. 1784-1790) 1F 16-26 (Allusia) (b. 1777) 1F over 45 (Mildred)

[103] O'Rourke, Timothy, *Catholic Families of Southern Maryland*

[104] Ibid

Chapter 10

Philip and Richard Drury

Philip Drury was born in St. Mary's County, Maryland about 1750. His father was Peter Drury.[1] His mother's identity is not certain but she was probably either Jane or Ann Bailey. Both parents were dead by the time he married in 1770.[2] Nothing is known of his childhood but he grew up on his father's plantation called "Part of The Bottom". He married Emerentia Bibianna Newton, the daughter of Clement Newton (d. 1760), on September 4, 1770. Philip always referred to her as Ann.[3] We should not confuse this Clement Newton with several others in this same general time period. His parents were Thomas Newton (1702 –1741) and Katherine. Clement had a son and a nephew with the same given name, but this Clement's wife was named Elizabeth.

This time of year was evidently a good time for weddings. Philip married in September, his brother Michael married two months later in November, and another brother Ignatius married at the end of the previous year. By this time harvests were in for the most part, and there was time for thoughts of other things.

This era in which Philip lived was turbulent. The end of the French and Indian War in 1763 did not bring peace. Even though the Treaty of Paris that ended the war gave the British undisputed claim to the area west of the Appalachian Mountains, they discouraged colonists from settling there. Indians living along the Ohio River were harassing the settlers even into the 1770s and 1780s, and funds to combat them continued to drain both Maryland and Virginia.[4]

There was also conflict on the economic front. For years the colonists had been protesting the refusal of the Proprietor to contribute to the defense of the Colony against their Indian enemies.[5] They considered his efforts to be an attempt to get as much money from the colony as possible without regard for the welfare of those providing his income. Alienation fees provided much of the cause for grumbling among the colonists. These were a tax to be paid whenever any land was transferred from one owner to another. Colonists developed a number of schemes to avoid payment such as leasing to the new owner (which avoided payment of the fine) and then executing a so called "release" that released the lessee of all obligation to return the land to the original owner. As early as 1754 Governor Sharpe had suggested a stamp tax on all legal documents as a way to insure collection of these fees, but this idea was never implemented.[6] Now in the 1770s with the enactment by the British Parliament of the stamp tax and the tax on sugar, there was greater opposition to the mother country as well.

By the 1770s sentiment was growing for Maryland to secede from Britain and become an independent country even though Governor Robert Eden was well liked and generally respected in the Colony. As was usual these opinions divided, for the most part, along religious lines. Catholics under the urging of the Jesuits were strongly for becoming independent. Anglicans on the other hand were less enthusiastic and many, when the break finally came, left and returned to England.[7]

Historians estimate that only one-third of the population supported the movement for Independence, while the remaining two-thirds either openly opposed the war or attempted to remain neutral.[8] Drury families numbered about a dozen by this time and all supported the revolution or at the very least did not openly oppose it. In 1777 the Maryland legislature passed a resolution requiring all adult males to take an oath of allegiance to Maryland. This was a response to increasing resistance to the independence movement and was sparked by attempts to organize an armed loyalist militia on Maryland's strongly Anglican eastern shore. Taking this oath was a drastic step for most inhabitants because it constituted an act of treason against Britain that carried the death penalty. On the other hand those not taking this oath were to be taxed at three times the regular rate, lose all civil rights, and be disbarred from practicing any profession or trade. Philip, as well as his brothers and other relatives, took the oath and cast their lot with the rebels.

The text of this oath is reproduced below and was administered by the Justices of each district.

> " I do swear, that I do not hold myself bound to yield any
> allegiance or obedience to the King of Great Britain, his heirs or
> successors, and that I will be true and faithful to the State of
> Maryland, and will, to the best of my power, support, maintain,
> and defend the freedom and independence thereof, and the government
> now established, against all open enemies, and secret and traitorous
> conspiracies, and will use my utmost endeavors to disclose and make
> known to the Governor or someone of the judges or justices thereof,
> all treason and traitorous conspiracies, attempts, or combinations
> against this state or the government thereof, which may come to
> my knowledge. So help me God."[9]

This was a serious business for these people. An Oath in the eighteenth century was similar to a legal document or written contract today. In addition, because they ended the oath, as we do today, with the phrase "So help me God", it added a moral imperative. Renouncing or disregarding this promise would send them to Hell when they died. Many people could neither read nor write in the 18th Century and lawyers were an expensive luxury for all but the wealthy. A man's word was his bond. Promises were not made lightly because everyone knew that once made it was a promise not only to your neighbor or your country, but also to God. The only modern counterparts that have survived are the oath taken when testifying in a Court of Law and those taken by elected officials and members of the military services. Even these now tend to become formalities.

These events had little immediate effect on the Drury families. Though they were now able to vote with the repeal of the discriminatory laws of the early 1700's, they did not meet the wealth and property requirements to be eligible to run for elective office. In order to vote for elected officials colonists had to own at least 50 acres of land or be able to prove assets of 40 £ in cash or equivalent. These restrictions were continued even after the revolution but the real asset requirement was decreased to 30£ cash or its equivalent.[10] In order to be eligible to run for elected office they had to have property worth at least 1000 pounds of Tobacco (the current unit of exchange at that time). The only elective offices were those of Sheriff and members of the lower house of the Assembly.[11] Drury families were still mostly the owners or lessees of small farms, or they were overseeing larger tracts for wealthier neighbors. Only a few owned slaves even though slaves had been brought to Maryland since the turn of the century.

Philip lived through the Revolutionary War and through the confusion and turmoil that ensued afterward while the new United States was trying to form its own government. In addition folks in Maryland experienced a severe depression starting in 1784 that was made worse by attempts to quickly retire the state's war debt. This reduced the available supply of money to dangerously low levels. Then in 1786 tobacco prices collapsed and further depressed the economy.[12] Financing the war became a huge problem during and after the five years of fighting. Maryland had large amounts of money on deposit in the Bank of England, but those sums naturally became unavailable while the Colonies were fighting the mother country. Instead the state issued paper money and guaranteed it with the sums on deposit. If the bank funds were not returned, then land held by British subjects in the Colony would be confiscated, sold, and the money used to redeem the paper notes. Eventually this is what was done and the land was sold to repay the State's war debt. Even so the State scrambled to find monies to keep fighting. Many families donated their silver dishes, utensils and other valuables to aid the effort. Most were also donating or selling supplies to the Army on credit with hopes of repayment when the war was over.

By the end of the war in the 1780s times had become difficult for many of the residents of southern Maryland. Continual British raids had destroyed many farms and much livestock in the area. The farms and stock that were left went untended while their owners were away fighting in the war. In addition the traditional markets for tobacco, Maryland's staple crop, were unavailable during the war and merchants in Europe were forced to seek other sources of supply. After the war many of them remained with these alternate suppliers.

Most Marylanders had been leasing their farms from Cecil Calvert, the proprietor of the Colony. In 1780 and again in 1790 Proprietary lands, including Beaverdam Manor where Philip and his relatives lived, were resurveyed and sold to individuals. The first "law" for the sale of confiscated property was in 1780 when the new country was operating under the "Articles of Confederation." It appears that hardly anybody eventually paid for the farms they bought in 1781 and the surveys for the lands contained many errors. Once the United States Constitution had been adopted, another bill directing the sale of these lands was passed in 1786. George Fenwick resurveyed Beaverdam Manor in 1790 at the direction of the Maryland legislature.[13] Almost all of the other proprietary manors were also resurveyed.

Drury Lands - 1790 [14]

Many, including some Drurys, chose to remain and buy the farms they had been living on for generations. These families were given first option to buy their land. Drury families who remained on their original resurveyed farms were Enoch Drury on "Hard Times" a 30 and three quarter acre farm, Michael Drury who lived on "Drurys Delight" consisting of a resurveyed 85 and three quarter acres, and Sarah Drury whose husband James had died in 1779, who bought the 163 acre "Chatham" in the name of her two sons Stephen and James. Others chose to move and take up grants of land in Western Virginia (which later became Kentucky) that they obtained as payment for their service during the war.

The following quote describes typical conditions immediately following the war.

> Beginning about 1785 there was a considerable
> migration of County people, particularly from the
> St. Inigoes area, to Kentucky. British depredations
> along the waterfront had ruined many of the planters.
> Their sons had been killed in battle, their unworked
> fields had grown up, many of their slaves and much
> of their stock was gone and homes and farm buildings
> had been burned. Many decided to try a new frontier. [15]

118

The war and the hard times had taken their toll. In 1785 Philip, at age 35, was not well and would only live another ten years. This was no doubt why he elected to stay and continue to lease from the new owner George Spalding, who had renamed the plantation "Flower of the Forest." In the remaining years he lived he was able to acquire the plantation to leave to his family.

We have no information on what happened to Ann Newton Drury. She was still alive in 1795 when she was named co-executor for her husband's will. Given the customs of the times she probably lived with her eldest son Bernard and his family after Philip's death. There is no record that she ever made the trip to Kentucky so she probably died sometime before 1810. Bernard would have become head of the family by default but most of his brothers and sisters were married and in their own homes by the time he left. The only ones there are no records for are Emerentia and John. If they didn't wish to make the trip they could have stayed with one of their brothers or sisters.

Philip fathered nine children in his twenty five year marriage.[16] We have positively identified seven of them with possibilities for the other two. Bernard, the eldest, was born in 1771 a year after Philip was married. A daughter Tecla came the following year. A possible third child, Benedict, was born in 1773 but his connection to Philip is only circumstantial[17] because of his sale of "Dryarkins Addition," which we think is a misspelling of "Drydocking Addition." This property was very near to Philip's plantation "Flower of the Forest" that was called "Wimsatt's Frolic" prior to 1790.[18] Others have suggested that the child possibly born in 1773 was Zachariah Drury who we document elsewhere. Benedict seems more likely since he has proved connections with Dry Docking Addition and he remained in Maryland.

The next three children, Samuel (1775), Emerentia (1777), and Joan (possibly Jane) (1779), are documented by baptismal records.[19] A son, Clement (most probably born about 1784), states he received his one-ninth part of the ancestral plantation "Flower of the Forest" from his father Philip Drury.[20] He is probably the Clement Drury who was building a house for George Fenwick in the summer of 1811.[21] Another possible son of Philip was William Drury who was also corresponding with George Fenwick in August 1811 concerning management of Fenwick's "Swamp Island" plantation.[22] We do not know the outcome of this negotiation as George Fenwick died in Georgetown two and a half months later in October 1811.[23] Finally we have John Drury mentioned in Philip's will of 1795 but not listed in the 1790 census of St. Mary's County.[24]

Bernard Drury

Bernard at 24 was "of age" when his father died in 1795. He was named executor of the will along with his mother. He married Catherine Wimsatt eighteen months later on 7 November 1796.[25] Catherine was a daughter of Robert Wimsatt and Dorothy Abell. Their courtship seemed a natural thing since they lived on nearby plantations[26] and were members of the same congregation. The couple remained in St. Mary's County until sometime between 1810 when they register a final time for the St. Mary's County census[27] and 1813 when Bernard appears on the Militia lists in Washington County, Kentucky.[28] There are reports he was declared absent without leave from the Maryland Militia. This, no doubt, was during the time he was moving his family to Kentucky. No one can say with certainty exactly why Bernard decided to move, but it probably had a lot to do with the devastation wreaked upon the St. Mary's County population by British raids during the Revolution and the War of 1812, and by the fact that many of the men were away fighting in the war and could not take care of their farms.

By 1800 the couple had two small children.[29] In the next ten years they added six more children- three boys and three girls.[30] Three more were born in Kentucky. Bernard settled in the Rolling Fork community in Washington County that is known today as Calvary in Marion County and died in 1819 at age 48.[31] His widow Catherine remarried in 1823. Her second husband John Greenwell died in 1834.[32] Catherine lived another 4 years and died in Union County, Kentucky in 1838. She and Bernard are buried at old Holy Name of Mary Cemetery in Calvary.

Their children were Robert (not proved) born about 1798, Maria born in 1801, Benedict born 28 Jan 1802, Sarah born in the fall of 1802, James born 9 May 1803, Catherine born 1804, Ignatius born 28 Oct 1806, Elizabeth born in 1810, William born about 1814, Ann Clare about 1815, and Joseph born 3 June 1816. Three of the girls, Maria (Sr. Francisca), Sarah (Sr. Susan), and Elizabeth (Sr. Marcelline), entered the Sisters of Charity of Nazareth Convent at Loretto.[33] Three sons, Benedict, James, and Ignatius, married and raised large families in Kentucky. James moved his family to Missouri about 1835,[34] but the others remained in Kentucky.

On 22 November 1824, Bernard's daughter Catherine married Clement Molohon, the brother of Mary Jane who had married Zachariah Drury.[35] She died three years later and left no children.

William married twice, first to Elizabeth Hardesty, a daughter of Charles Hardesty and Ann Riney, in 1835 and then to her sister Mary on 20 December 1863 eight months after Elizabeth's death. William and Elizabeth had eight children together.

Ann Clare married Joseph Clements in 1850. This may have been a second marriage though no earlier marriage has been documented to date. She was born in 1815[36] and age 35 was unusually late for a girl's first marriage in the 1800s. In 1827 after her mother had remarried, the 12 year old Ann Clare requested that her brother-in-law Clement Molohon be appointed her guardian to secure her estate.[37] By 1850 she was listed in the household of Ignatius A. Spalding and in 1880 she was living with her brother Ignatius Drury.

Joseph, born a year later, was unlucky in love. He married three times and outlived all but the last wife. He may have buried her as well, but we don't know when she died other than it had to be after the birth of the last child we show for him in 1867.[38]

Tecla Drury

Tecla Drury, Philip's second child, was born in the fall of 1772.[39] She is reported to have married Allen Norris on 7 January, 1811 in St. Mary's County. This would have been about the time her brother Bernard was preparing to leave for Kentucky.

Benedict Drury

Benedict Drury, the assumed third child of Philip and Bibianna Drury, married Mary Simms (possibly Semmes) 5 March 1810. She was a daughter of Anthony and Mary Simms.[40] The couple had at least three children before Benedict's death in 1819. Their known children were Elizabeth, Mary Ann, and William all born by about 1817.[41] In 1818 Benedict was appointed one of the Tobacco inspectors for St. Mary's County. These men were charged with insuring that tobacco that was shipped was of good quality and not mixed with broken stems and sweepings from the floors of the barns.

Samuel Drury

Samuel Drury was born during the winter of 1774-75. He was christened 2 February 1775 probably at St. Francis Xavier.[42] He married Eleanor Jarboe (b. 11/2/1768) on 21 October 1799 two years after the marriage of his brother Bernard.[43] Eleanor was a daughter of Joshua Jarboe and Jane who lived on an adjacent plantation called "Satisfaction". As was the case with Bernard, proximity led to marriage.

Emerentia Drury

Emerentia Drury was christened December 27, 1777.[44]

Joan or Jane Drury

Joan was christened in 1779 according to an entry in the Hodges Card file at the Maryland Historical Society. Nothing more is known about her at present. Some researchers claim this entry was an abbreviation of Joannes, the latin form of John, making the child a boy instead of a girl. One additional possibility can be added. There is a Jane Drury whose parents are unknown. She married Zachariah Peacock in St. Mary's County in 1804 and died by 1811. Her birth date calculated from census records is 1779. This is the same year as Joan Drury from the Hodges card file of baptisms. The two names are close enough in pronunciation and spelling for mistakes to easily be made. It would also not be unusual for Philip to name a daughter after his mother Jane Bailey. In addition the Drurys and the Peacocks all lived close by each other. These facts support the notion that Jane who married Zachariah Peacock might be the same person as Joan Drury, daughter of Philip Drury. We should make it clear that if true this Jane Drury is not the Jane Drury cited elsewhere as a sister of Tecla Drury Joy nor is she the Jane Drury who married John Radford Jr. in 1750.

Clement Drury

Clement Drury was born sometime between 1780 and 1784. His parents are proved by an entry for a deed of sale to Edmund Key in 1805 transferring one ninth portion of "Flower of the Forest" that he received "from his father Philip Drury."[45] In order to sell his interest in the plantation he would have to be at least 21 years old. This makes his birth not later than 1784. He married Ann Cissell on 29 January 1803. She died by 1811. He then married Dorothy Boyd on 6 June 1811, probably to have a wife to care for the infant son listed in the 1810 census.[46] This would have been particularly important to him since he was away from home building a house for George Fenwick.[47]

William Drury

There is a possibility that this William Drury is one of the other males born to Philip and Ann Newton in the 1780s. No direct proof exists at present but a possible connection can be inferred because William is corresponding in August of 1811 with George Fenwick who lived in Washington D.C. concerning a contract to manage Fenwick's "Swamp Island" plantation in St. Mary's County. "Swamp Island" was in Beaverdam Manor and was adjacent to both "Dry Docking" and to "Flower of the Forest" where we assume William would have grown up. In addition it seems probable from the text of the letter that William had previously managed the plantation.[48] This shows us that William was a trusted and responsible individual. An absentee owner was not apt to put several hundred pounds worth of slaves, implements and land in charge of any but competent and reliable men. The overseer or manager was the owner's personal representative on the plantation.[49]

At this time in 1811 the letter makes it evident that William is married with two small children. He says in his letter, "Such a place as yours would suit me better than for me to give a hogshead of tobacco rent for what little land I am able to tend myself." This gives us some idea of what life was like in this era.

John Drury

We know nothing about this youngest son of Philip. He is mentioned in Philip's will in 1795 but does not appear on the 1790 census of St. Mary's County. This establishes his birth as between 1790 and 1795 but nothing else is known at present.

Richard Drury

Richard Drury is an assumed son of Peter Drury (1715 – 1770). This assumption is questionable unless a birth date for Richard can be found in the 1750s. Other possibilities would be that he was a younger brother of James Jr. or a son of Thomas by an unknown wife before 1750. We know of no source to date substantiating any of these possibilities. His wife's name was Elizabeth but we have no surname for her. Because Peter, the earliest son we know of, was christened in 1771 they must have married before then.

Richard had two sons that have been identified: Peter and Richard Jr. We can assume there were additional children because there could be as much as 13 years between the two. It is even possible that Peter was not the first child born to this couple.

Peter Drury was christened as a son of Richard Drury and Eleanor on November 7 1771.[50] His parents must have been married before 1771. He was a shoemaker who probably learned the trade from his father. The only other way to learn a trade in the eighteenth century was by being an apprentice. There is no record of such an arrangement for Peter.

He first married in 1793 at the age of 22. We don't know the name of this first wife but she bore him nine children before 1816 when Peter married Ann Hayden, the daughter of Ignatius Hayden and Mary.[51] They were Benedict (1794), Susan (1797), Mary (1799), Cornelius (1801), William (1804), Bennett (1806), Elizabeth (1808), Ann (1810), and Rebecca (1812). He needed a wife to care for the 4 children still under 12 years old. Any children born of this second marriage have not been identified but we can be sure there were some before Ann died. The only thing we can be sure of is that he married for a third time to Mary Cox on 29 December 1828.

His father-in-law Ignatius Hayden died less than three months after Peter and Ann were married. Four years later Peter administered Ignatius' estate and was involved for the next five years with its settlement.[52]

By 1801 Peter was apparently doing well as a shoemaker. He accepted six year old Adam Adams as an apprentice.[53] The following year he added seventeen year old Ignatius Newton[54] and in 1804 sixteen year old Charles Alvey.[55] Taking an apprentice was not a simple matter. By doing so Peter was promising to treat them almost as his own children until they were 21 years old. He was obligated to teach them his trade "to find them during their servitude sufficient cloathing, meat, drink, mending and making, washing and lodging, to give them six months schooling and at the end of their servitude to give them a suit of freedom clothes such as is usually given to apprentices." All of this was under Court order and he would be fined if he failed to live up to the agreement.

Benedict's life was probably that of most small children in the eighteenth century. This supposition is reinforced by the fact that his father, when he found the need for additional help, agreed to take apprentices between 1800 and 1804 rather than train his own son. When Benedict was old enough, probably after 1804 when Benedict was 10, he did train him in his craft. Benedict is listed in 1823 as a shoemaker at Clifton Factory near the present town of Great Mills.

The Great Mill factory was a failed business attempted late in the 1700s to early 1800s. Sometime in the early 1800s the factory was sold and renamed The Clifton Factory. Clifton Factory was a textile mill that was one of a handful of St. Mary's manufacturing industries in the early 1800s. They also manufactured flour and meat in the basement level of the building. By 1828 there was a tavern with 11 boarding rooms as well as the support infrastructure associated with a bustling town.[56]

Clifton Factory [57]

The main occupation of workers at the factory was as textile workers. Most of them were widows and their daughters. Susan Fowler and her daughter Jane were two of these workers. They managed to live with a rent of $12 per year. On November 24th 1823 Susan married Benedict Drury. Their combined income apparently enabled them to rent a shoe shop and a better home.[58] Susan was born about 1795.[59] Benedict died sometime in the 1830s, but Susan was still living in Clifton after 1840.[60] The 1850 census lists William H. Drury (b. 1825) who was a farmer, Susan Drury (b. 1795), Peter M. Drury (b. 1827), Nicholas Combs (b 1840), and, James H. Norriss, a Sailor (b 1822).[61] This is consistent with our other known data about this couple.

Peter's second child, Susan E. Drury, was born about 1798 in St. Mary's County, Maryland.[62] She died on 7 Nov 1834 in St. Mary's County, Maryland. Susan married John Walter Bevan, son of Walter Bevan and Charity Simpson, on 27 Feb 1821 in St. Mary's County, Maryland. John was born in 1797. After Susan died he married secondly Margaret Susan Coombs (b.1820, d 1/15/1890). Their marriage record stated he was from

Charles County. John Walter Beavan died age 74 on 10/17/1872 at Medley Neck "of old age."[63]

Their children were Rebecca Bevan, born about 1821 in St. Mary's County, Maryland and died as an infant; Sophia Bevan born in 1824 in St. Mary's County, Maryland; Mary Elizabeth Bevan "Sedellia" born on 10 Apr 1825 in St. Mary's County, Maryland and died on 9 Sep 1887; Mary Savilla Bevan born in 1826 in St. Mary's County, Maryland and died on 23 Nov 1884; and Susan Bevan born May 1831 in St. Mary's County, Maryland. She was christened on 14 Aug 1831 in St. Mary's County, Maryland.

Peter's third child was another daughter Mary Pollie Drury born on 20 Jan 1799 in St. Mary's County, Maryland. Mary married Marcellas Simpson on 2 Jul 1821.

The fourth child born to Peter was Cornelius Drury in 1801. Cornelius also followed his father's trade as a shoemaker. He married three times but both he and his third wife Sarah Dorsey were dead before 1860. St. Mary's County Levy Court records indicate he was still alive but very sick with Tuberculosis in 1856.[64] His first wife was Mary Ann Dunbar who he married on 25 Oct 1828 in St. Mary's County, Maryland. They had two daughters, Ann Catherine born in 1829 and Margaret in 1830. Ann Catherine[65] married William James Jarboe, December 23, 1846.[66] They were living in the first election district in 1850 and he was listed as a blacksmith.[67] We have no death date for Mary Ann but she must have died before 1838 when Cornelius married Elizabeth Smith. Cornelius had three more children with Elizabeth. A son, William C. Drury, was born in 1839, a daughter Ann in 1841 and another son, Charles, in 1843. Both William and Charles were listed as musicians in the Confederate Army during the Civil War.[68] By 1850 Elizabeth had died, and Cornelius had married Sarah Dorsey.[69] By 1860 both Cornelius and Sarah are dead and the children are living in other households.[70] It appears from the above data that Cornelius apparently died sometime between 1856 and 1860. The children are now on their own and making a living for themselves. Charles apparently continued the tradition of his ancestors by being the fourth generation of shoemaker.[71]

William Drury, Peter's next son, was born on 15 April 1804. He married Julianna Thompson on 8 February 1831 and by 1840 was living in northern St. Mary's County.[72] In following years he gradually moved north perhaps following opportunities for employment. By1850 he was in Ann Arundle County and remained there the rest of his life.[73] His daughter Laura married Joseph Smith (a plasterer born in England) about 1757 and William and Julianna were living with them.[74] By 1880 both William and his wife were listed as destitute and were on the poor list for the State.[75]

We have few details about Peter's last four children, Bennett (1806), Elizabeth (1808), Ann (1810), and Rebecca (1812). Elizabeth married William S. L. Abell, son of Philip Abell and Eleanor Drury, on 9 Feb 1831 in St. Mary's County, Maryland.[76] According to some accounts William was born in 1805 in St. Mary's County, Maryland. Other accounts list his birth as 1811.[77] He died in 1859 in St. Mary's County, Maryland.

William's mother may possibly not have been Eleanor Drury, Philip Abell's first wife. Her date of death is not certain and William's birth date is also unclear and may overlap between her death and his father's marriage to Helena Peake in 1806. Ann, the daughter born on 12 Mar 1810 in St. Mary's County, Maryland, married John Beatty. Peter's youngest daughter Rebecca married Samuel Wise on 7 Jan 1832 in St. Mary's County, Maryland. Samuel was born in 1803. He died after 1860. They had five recorded children. They were William born in 1833 who married Mary E. Joy 27 Jan 1862; John born in 1840 and died on 25 Sep 1883; James born in 1847; Ann Marie born in Jun 1849. Ann married James H. Stone, son of Dr. Joseph Stone and Mary Jane Leigh, on 12 Jun 1865. James Stone was born in Aug 1841; and Francis born in 1850.

Richard Drury Jr., the second documented son of Richard, was born before 1786. He died after 1827. He married Jane Blair on 9 Jan 1806. Jane was born before 1791. She died after 1827 in St. Mary's County. Richard and Jane Blair are also listed as having two children named William Henry and Peter W. Drury. Confusion arises because both Richard Jr. and Benedict had sons named William and sons named Peter who were born in 1825 and 1827 respectively. William Henry is the one who married Martha E. Dyer and is listed in the 1860 census as William H of R.[78]

James Drury, William Henry's great grandson tells us that William married Mary Ellen Coombs before 1824. James has at least three children listed for them and tells us that his grandfather was Ben Drury who ran Drury and Sanders General Store in Leonardtown.[79] They were George H. Drury born 17 October 1824, William Henry Drury born on 28 Dec 1825. He died on 12 Mar 1862 and Peter U. Drury born about 1827. He died on 29 Jul 1885 in St. Mary's County. Peter was buried at Our Lady RCC in Medley's Neck. The 1880 census listed him as a farmer in St. Mary's County third election district.

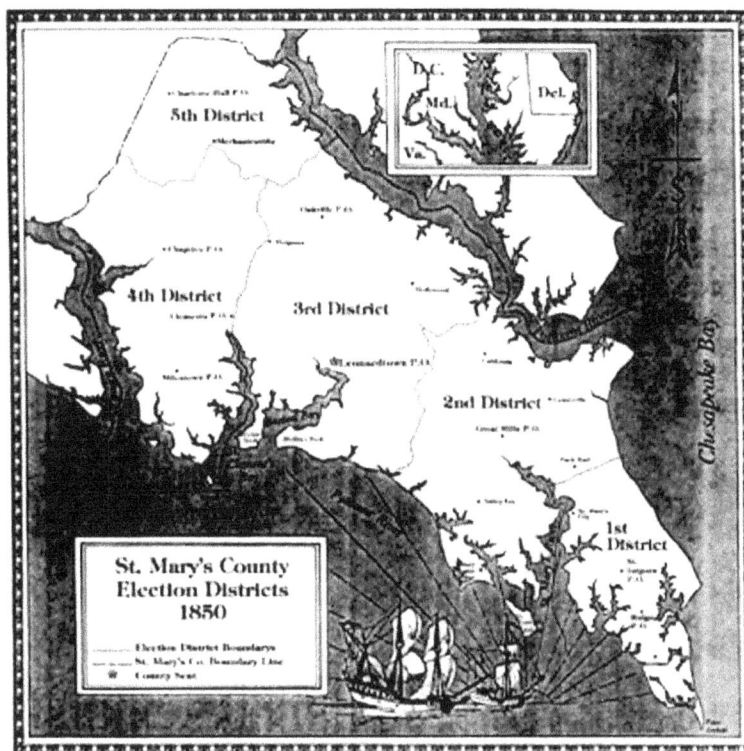

St. Mary's County Election Districts

William married Martha Ellen Dyer, daughter of William S. Dyer and Mary E. Coombs, on 12 Apr 1851.[80] Martha was born in 1836 in St. Mary's County, Maryland. She died in 1867 in St. Mary's County, Maryland.

They had the following children: Mary Drury was born on 3 Nov 1853. Mary married William Hugh Longmore in 1871 in St. Mary's County, Maryland. William was born in 1847. Then came Susanna born in 1854, and Martha Joanna born in 1856 who married John Van Reswick. Joseph Benedict Drury Sr. was their first son born on 7 Jul 1857. A sister Margaret was born on 11 Sep 1859. She died in 1897 and finally another son William A. Drury born on 30 Nov 1860. He died in 1881 in St. Mary's County, Maryland, and apparently never married.

Joseph Benedict Drury Sr. was born on 7 Jul 1857 and died on 3 Jan 1952[81] in Leonardtown where he and his brother-in-law Joseph Albert Saunders operated Drury and Saunders General Store for 37 years.[82] Everyone knew them as Ben and Al. Ben married Mary Lillie Maude Saunders, a daughter of James Saunders and Mary E. Wise, by 1894. Mary (Lillie) was born in 1872. They started a family soon after and had six children at two to three year intervals. Their children were Mary Lillian Drury born in 1895, William E. (Elbert?) Drury born in 1899, Estelle Drury born in 1901, Joseph Benedict Drury Jr. born in 1905, Thomas F. (Foley?) Drury born in 1910, and Miriam E. Drury born in 1912.[83]

127

Drury & Saunders General Store
Leonardtown, Maryland about 1950 [84]

Joseph and his family led comfortable lives. He owned half of the business, owned property in town, and at least one farm a few miles from Leonardtown. In October 1912 Joseph and his wife donated a quarter acre parcel of land in California, Maryland, to the Archdiocese of Baltimore for a church designated on the deed as California Church lot, Saint Mary's County. It was a portion of a larger tract known as "Benecia or part of California" facing on three Notch Road. It is described in the deed as being a part of a parcel Joseph bought from Walter F. Jarboe on 7 July 1912 as recorded in Liber EBA 9, folio 401. [85]

[1] Burger, Judith A. *Will of Peter Drury d. 1770 Register of Wills, St. Mary's County, Maryland,*, Liber T. A. No.1., P 633

[2] See notes and comments on Jane in the previous chapter

[3] Beitzel, Edwin, *History of the Jesuit Missions of St. Mary's County*, p 88; see also Barnes, Robert, *Maryland Marriages, 1634-1777*, Genealogical Publishing Co., Inc., Baltimore, 1976, p. 54; and Burger, Judith A., *Will of Clement Newton d. 1760 Register of Wills, St. Mary's County, Maryland*, Libra: *T.A.I.*, pp 399-400

[4] *A Transcription from Crumrine's History,* http://www.chartiers.com/pages/articles/dunmore.html

[5] Schlesinger, Arthur M., *Maryland's share in the last Inter Colonial War*, Maryland Historical Magazine, Vol. 7 pp 119-149 and 243-257

[6] Gould, Clarence P, *Economic History of Maryland 1720 – 1765*, pp 32, 35

[7] Radoff, Morris L., Ed. *The Old Line State- A History of Maryland*, Baltimore 1971 p 39

[8] Keddie, Neil, *Maryland in the revolution*, posted on Ancestry.com, 2000

[9] Beitzel, Edwin, *Calendar of Events, St. Mary's County Maryland in the American Revolution,* St. Mary's County Bicentennial Commission, 1975 p 131

[10] Crowl, Philip D., *The revolution and after: 1774-1789* p 43 in The Old Line State: A History of Maryland, Morris L. Radoff, Ed., Hall of Records Commission State of Maryland, Annapolis 1971

[11] Ibid

[12] Ibid p. 45

[13] Ben Tippett's Journal book A - 1790

[14] Brumbaugh, G.M. *Maryland Records---Vol. II, State of His Lordship's Manor*, Genealogical Publ. Co., Baltimore, MD, 1985 p. 65

[15] Beitzel. Edwin, Calendar of Events St. Mary's County in the American Revolution, St. Mary's County Bicentennial Commission 1975 p 124; see also Webb, Ben, The Centenary of Catholicity in Kentucky; Beitzell, Edwin, The Jesuit Missions of St. Mary's County; and McSherry's History of Maryland

[16] Burger, Judith A., *Will of Philip Drury*, St. Mary's County, Md., Will Book JJ 2, pp. 122, 123

[17] Benedict Drury, sale of Dryarkins addition and other properties to John Raley (of Gabriel) 3/3/1814 in *Chronicles of St. Mary's Vol. 7 p 171*

[18] Himmelheber, Peter, *electronic msg.of10/02/2010 to Linda Reno concerning survey of Wimsatt's Frolic –"* by ca 1790 both Williams Good Luck and Wimsatts Frolic had been resurveyed into three tracks called Peace & Quietness, 129-acre for Robert Wimsatt {UC:336}; Satisfaction, 191-acres, for Josuhua Jarbo {PC:572} and Flower of the Forrest, 95-acres for George Spalding {UC:161}"

[19] O'Rourke, Timothy, *Catholic Families of Southern Maryland* - p. 13, 18; see also Hodges card file, Maryland State Archives

[20] Clement Drury sale of one ninth part of Flower of the Forest to Edmund Key 11/1/1805 in *Chronicles of St. Mary's* Vol. 7 p 171; Himmelheber, Peter, *electronic msg. of 7/23/2010 to Linda Reno* "Got THE answer from the deed abstract {TH25:466} which states "...yadda yadda.... undivided ninth part of...being in Beaverdam Manor...called Flower of the Forrest..which land was devised to me by my father Philip Drury...

[21] Maryland State Archives, Georgetown University Special Collections, *Letter from Clement Drury to George Fenwick*, Box 39 Folder 10

[22] Maryland State Archives, Georgetown University Special Collections, *Letter from William Drury to George Fenwick*, Box 39 Folder 10

[23] King, Jackie, *Transcription of will of George Fenwick*, Electronic

[24] *St. Mary's County, Maryland, census* 1790; Burger, Judith A., *Will of Philip Drury*, St. Mary's County, Maryland, Will Book JJ 2, pp. 122, 123

[25] *Maryland Genealogical Bulletin* Vol. 2 Pg 5 Jan 1931; see also Brumbaugh, Gaius Marcus M.S., M.D., *Maryland Records Colonial, Revolutionary, County and Church from original sources, Vol I*, Genealogical Pub. Co. Inc. 1993, Baltimore, p. 333

[26] Bernard on Flower of the Forest and Catherine on Peace and Quietness

[27] St. Mary's County, Maryland, *1810 Census p 166*

[28] Cook, Michael L. & Bette Ann, *A Pioneer History of Washington County, Kentucky*, p 273, McDowell Publishing Co., Utica Kentucky

[29] St. Mary's County Maryland *1800 Census Roll: M32_12* p 14 Image 16

[30] St. Mary's County, Maryland, *1810 Census p 166*

[31] *Early Catholic Cemetery Listings of Washington, Nelson, and Marion Counties, Kentucky*, West Central Kentucky Family Research Association, McDowell Pub., 1984, p. 37, 38

[32] Revolutionary War Record of John Greenwell, Green Co., Ky. Sept. 11, 1834 Age 74, John Greenwell enlisted in 1781 in St. Mary's Co., Md. under Capt. Sam Jniper for 3 mos., and in 1781 in St. Mary's Co., Md. substituted himself for a man by the name of George Combs for four months under Corp. Richard Barnes. They marched under Capt. John Mills from Leonardtown to Annapolis and came under the command of Capt. Mainger in the 3rd. Maryland Regiment. Born in St. Mary's Co., Md. Oct. 2, 1760, removed to Ky. 36 yrs. ago. He resided in Green Co., Ky. for the past 32 yrs.

[33] Clifford, Sr. Bridgid, SCN Archivist, Sisters of Charity of Nazareth Archival Center P.O. Box 3000, Nazareth Kentucky, 40048, *Record Card of Sr. Mary Brendan Bradddock*

[34] Leo Bowls & wife Deed to Jas. Drury (40 acres in St. Charles Co. Mo.) courtesy Connie Riley (criley@ghg.net) post of 3/9/2000; and James W. DRURY St. Charles Co., MO Tax List (1836), having 40 acres. *(MO Gen. Rec. & Abst., Eddlemon, Vol 1, p. 16.)*

[35] Thompson, Gerald, *Early Kentucky Catholic Pioneers - The Rolling Fork Settlement* Book I, p. 236, Marriage bond 11-22-1824, Teste. Johnathan W. Drury

[36] *1850 Census, Union County, Kentucky, Roll: M432_220 Township: District 2* p 513 Image: 271 lists C. A. Drury, 35 F, born MD living in household of Ignatius A. Spalding

[37] *Washington County, Kentucky Court Order Bk.* "D", p. 62

[38] 1880 Census *LDS Census Place* Hitesville, Union County, Kentucky Family History Library Film 1254444 NA Film Number T9-0444 p 693B

[39] O'Rourke, Timothy, *Catholic Families of Southern Maryland* - p. 11 Christened 12/20/1772

[40] Fresco, Margaret. K., Marriages & Death in St. Mary's Co., Md. 1634-1900 -Supplement, p. 499; *Will of Anthony Simms*, dated December 31, 1823. Probated April 6, 1821, mentions daughter Mary Drury

[41] *St. Mary's County Deeds*, JH 12, 557, 10/11/1842: Deed from Mary D. Drury, William H. Drury, and Mary Ann Drury of SMC to Elizabeth D. Combs, wife of John C. Combs "Green Hills", 389 ac. they own in the right of their father, Benedict Drury

[42] O'Rourke, Timothy, *Catholic Families of Southern Maryland,* p. 15 Christened 2/2/1775

[43] Donnelly, Mary Louise, *Colonial Settlers – St. Clement's Bay 1634 – 1780 St. Mary's County, Maryland*, Privately Published 1996 p 139; see also Fresco, Margaret, *Marriages, Births, and Deaths in St. Mary's County*

[44] O'Rourke, Timothy, *Catholic Families of Southern Maryland,* Genealogical Publishing Co. Baltimore 1985 p. 18 "Emerentia of Philip and Ena"

[45] *Chronicles of St. Mary's* Vol. 7, p 171; *deed abstract* TH25: 466

[46] Barnes, Robert, *Maryland Marriages, 1655-1850 Saint Mary's County, Maryland* Clement Drury Marriage: 29 Jan 1803 to Ann Cissell. Clement Drury Marriage: 6 Jun 1811 to Dorothy Boyd; *1810 Census*, St. Mary's County, Maryland

[47] Maryland State Archives, Georgetown University Special Collections, *Letter from Clement Drury to George Fenwick*, Box 39 Folder 10

[48] Maryland State Archives, Georgetown University Special Collections, *Letter from William Drury to George Fenwick*, Box 39 Folder 10

[49] Gould, Clarence P, *Economic History of Maryland 1720 – 1765*, p 94

[50] O'Rourke, Timothy J, Catholic Families of Southern Maryland, p 9

[51] Ignatius Hayden (JJ3-431) 17 May 1815-9 Apr 1816 St Mary's County, MD To 3 grandchildren Jane Hayden, Ignatius Hayden & Edward Hayden all my estate except for $1 to daughter Ann Drury wife of Peter Drury, after death of wife Mary Hayden, whereas property hath been acquired by intermarriage, etc. Appoint Edward Hayden my kinsman exec now living in Kentucky & Uncle to my said grandchildren & if he will not accept exec then appoint Bennet Hopewell of St Mary's County. Witnesses: Ethelbert Cecil, Eleanor Vessels

[52] PROCEEDINGS OF THE ORPHAN'S COURT OF ST. MARY'S COUNTY, MARYLAND, BOOK III, 1809-1826, Claude G. Blackwell,1996, St. Mary's County, Historical Society, Leonardtown, Maryland, p. 81 Hayden, Ign' Oct 1820 Page 181 The Court authorise the Reg' Wills to grant Peter Drury letters of adm' W. A. on the estate of Ign' Hayden.; Hayden, Ign' Feb 1821 Page 188 The Court order Peter Drury adm' Ign' Hayden decd' to sell at public sale - all the decd's personal property upon a credit of six months where the amt' exceeds 10$ all under cash.; Hayden, Ign' Feb 1822 Page 201 Jere' Russell the security for Peter Drury adm' Ign' Hayden petitions the Court for a subpoena to issue ag' him to compel him to appear & give counter security.; Hayden, Ignatius Oct 1825 Page 252 On application of Tho' Woodward. The Court authorise the Reg' to grant him letters of adm' D.B.N. on the Estate of Ignatius Hayden deceased.

[53] PROCEEDINGS OF THE ORPHAN'S COURT OF ST. MARY'S COUNTY, MARYLAND, BOOK II, 1801-1809, Claude G. Blackwell, no date, St. Mary's County, Historical Society, Leonardtown, Maryland p. 3 Adams, Adam May 1801 Page 7 The court binds Adam Adams (son of Nancy Adams) she being present in court agrees thereto, to Peter Drury to serve him, the said Drury until he arrives to the age of twenty one, his being six years old last August. In consideration of such service, the said Peter Drury doth oblige himself to find the said Adam during the time of such servitude, sufficient accommodations and clothing and at the expiration of his servitude give him a good suit of clothes under the penalty of 20L current money

[54] PROCEEDINGS OF THE ORPHAN'S COURT OF ST. MARY'S COUNTY, MARYLAND, BOOK II, 1801-1809, Claude G. Blackwell, no date, St. Mary's County, Historical Society, Leonardtown, Maryland p. 69 Newton, Ignatius Apr 1802 Page 15 The court bind Ignatius Newton (with the consent of his mother Sarah Newton) to Peter Drury to learn the trade of a shoemaker, to serve him the said Peter Drury until he the said Ignatius shall arrive to the age of twenty one years, he being seventeen years old, the twenty sixth day of March next. In consideration of which service the said Peter Drury doth hereby oblige himself to do his endeavour to learn the said Ignatius Newton the art and history of a shoemaker, to find him during his servitude sufficient cloathing, meat, drink, mending and making, washing and lodging, to give him six months schooling and at the end of his servitude to give him a suit of freedom clothes such as is usually given to apprentices under the penalty of 50L current money.

[55] PROCEEDINGS OF THE ORPHAN'S COURT OF ST. MARY'S COUNTY, MARYLAND, BOOK II, 1801-1809, Claude G. Blackwell, no date, St. Mary's County, Historical Society, Leonardtown, Maryland p. 4 Alvey, Charles Jun 1804 Page 81The court bind Charles Alvey, son of Elizabeth Alvey to Peter Drury to learn the mystery and business of a shoe and boot maker, to serve him the said Peter Drury until he arrives to the age of twenty one years, he being not about sixteen years old. In consideration of which servitude the said Peter Drury doeth hereby bind and oblige himself to give the said Charles Alvey six months schooling and to do his best endeavor to learn the said apprentice the art and occupation of a shoemaker and at the expiration of his servitude to give him the customary freedom dues. Under the penalty of 30L current money.

[56] Southern Maryland – this is living, Jackie Zimmer, An Industrial revolution in St. Mary's County, p 2

[57] Ibid p.1

[58] Maryland Historical Magazine Vol. 1 No. 80 (Spring 1985) p. 58,59

[59] This is based on the supposition that her daughter Jane was at least 12 years old and that Susan's first marriage was at about age 17

[60] Op. Cit. p 59

[61] 1850; Census District 3, St Mary's, Maryland; Roll: M432_296; P 282A; Image 322

[62] Linda Reno <lreno@erols.com> Tuesday, September 07, 1999 "I have her as SUSAN E. Drury, b. 1798 and died 11/7/1834. She married John Walter Beaven, b. 1797/1798 and died 10/17/1872. He's buried at Our Lady RCC, Medley's Neck, St. Mary's Co. They were married 2/27/1821 at St. Francis Xavier RCC, Newtown."

[63] September 13, 1999, <Barba94144@aol.com> electronic

[64] St. Mary's County Levy Court Records 1829 – 1877 1856--Cornelius Drury. Has had consumption for the past two years. Persons supporting his application: A. H. Bean, Francis Smith, John A. Crane, J. M. Biscoe, John T. Moore, Robert Ford, Walter L, Biscoe, William H. Ford, James C. Bean, John A. Dunbar.

[65] Linda Reno - I have placed her in this family because she was living next door to Cornelius Drury in 1850

[66] Fresco, marriage/1850, 1st Dist.

[67] 1850 United States Federal Census Name: Wm J Jarboe Age: 59 Estimated birth year: abt 1791 Birth Place: St Mary's Co Gender: Male Occupation: blacksmith Home in 1850: District 1, St Mary's, Maryland Family Number: 886 Household Members: Name Age Wm J Jarboe 59 Catharine Jarboe 21 Martha J Jarboe 18

[68] William C. Drury, Private, Co. B, 1st MD Battery, CSA (Chr. of SM, August 1961). Civil war soldiers website - NARA - Private, Co. B 2nd Battalion, Maryland Infantry - Musician.; 1862-1865, Possibly the Charles F Drury listed in Civil War Soldiers website (NARA) as musician Co. B 2nd Battalion Maryland Infantry.

[69] 1850 Census St. Mary's County 1st district Cornelius Drury, 49 Shoemaker, Sarah 47, Margaret 19, William C. 11, Ann M. 9, Charles L. 7, Mary E. Greenwell 16

[70] 1860 Census St. Mary's County 1st district Margaret Drury 28, Seamstress, 1st Dist., home of Eliza (Dunbar) Jones, her first cousin., Anna Drury 18, Housekeeper, 1st Dist., home of Ann (Langley) Biscoe. Charles Drury 16 Farmhand for Savilla Wise

[71] 1880, 3rd Dist., mends shoes.

[72] 1840, 4th dist., St. Mary's co.:1M 20-30 (?); 1M 30-40 (William); 1F 5-10 (Mary); 1F 5-10 (Laura); 1F 30-40 (Julia Thompson Drury).

[73] 1850, Anne Arundel Co.: William Drury 50, laborer Juliana Drury 37 Mary M Drury 14 Laura E Drury 12 Wilhelmena Drury 9 Joseph L. Drury 2

[74] 1860, Catonsville, Baltimore Co.: William Drewery 80, laborer Julia Drewery 44 Laura Drewery 22 Ann Drewery 20 Joseph Drewery 14; 1870, Howard, Anne Arundel Co.: William Drewery 70, works on farm Julia Drewery 60 Joseph Smith 33, plasterer, b. England Laura Smith 31 Rose Ann Smith 12 John T Smith 7 Mary E Smith 4 Joseph Smith 1

[75] 1880, Howard, Anne Arundel Co.: Wm. Drury 80, on poor list, Md/Germany/Germany Julia Drury 70, wife, on poor list, MD

[76] Maryland Records, Colonial, Revolutionary, County, and Church" Vol. 1 by Gaius Marcus Brumbaugh St. Mary's County Marriage Licenses from A to D 1794 to 1864 p. 313

[77] Calculated birth date from 1850 Census is 1811. Other sources (Pat Place database on U.S. Genweb based on the "Abell Index") list birth as 1805.

[78] 1860 Census District 3, St. Mary's Maryland; Roll M653_479' p 78, image 378

[79] Aleck Loker, A Most Convenient Place - Leonardtown Maryland 1650 - 1950, p 180.

[80] MARYLAND RECORDS, Colonial Revolutionary County Church, Vol I, Gaius Marcus Brumbaugh, Reprint 1993, Genealogical Publishing Co., Baltimore, MD p. 337 St. Mary's County; Maryland Marriages 1851, April 12 Drury, William H. and Martha E. Dyer

[81] St. Mary's Beacon, Leonardtown Maryland, Obituary Friday January 11, 1952

[82] Aleck Loker, A Most Convenient Place – Leonardtown Maryland 1650 1950, p 180.

[83] Ibid

[84] Loker, Aleck, A Most Convenient Place - Leonardtown Maryland 1650 - 1950, p 168

[85] Maryland Provincial Archives box 36 folder 6 in Georgetown University Special Collections.

Chapter Eleven

Drurys and the War of 1812

Before the revolution Colonists in Maryland were continually arguing with the Calverts in the House of Delegates. After the Revolution local interests became the basis for political alignments. Regions with fertile soil, cheap transportation, and proximity to urban markets usually elected delegates who were fiscally conservative. These groups became known as creditor factions and in general were more prosperous. On the other hand, folks with poorer soil who were not close to markets and lacked easy transportation usually elected delegates who became known as debtor minded. They often voted to postpone taxes, delay debt collection, and inflate the money supply.[1]

As was mentioned in Chapter Eight, the redemption of paper certificates along with the collapse of tobacco prices resulted in great hardship in Maryland. A mob in Charles County caused a riot in 1786 protesting a lawyer's attempt to collect British debts.[2] Even some merchants were caught in the squeeze. The largest mercantile house in the state pleaded with Captain Charles Ridgely,

"We do sincerely assure you that we are at present highly distressed for cash. This little sum (£ 120) will be as nothing to your immense funds but will be of great consequence to ours."[3]

This caused a revival of the demand to issue more paper and the two sides campaigned vigorously over the issue. Delegates on the western shore including those from St. Mary's County were evenly split over the issue though debtor delegates in the entire state voted 17 to nothing for the issue.[4]

Our alliance with France during the Revolutionary War was also causing problems at the turn of the century. France aided us during the Revolution by furnishing troops and ships. Now that she was directly at war with Great Britain she expected us to reciprocate. Edmund Genét was a French aristocrat who managed to secure a post as emissary to the United States under Napoleon Bonaparte. He arrived in 1793 with instructions to secure the aid of America in the War between France and Britain. We, on the other hand, were determined to remain neutral even though many Americans were sympathetic and wished to support France.[5] These mixed feelings resulted in confusion and misunderstandings. When Genét arrived in Charlestown South Carolina the people there welcomed him with open arms. Their warm welcome and the banquets given in his honor gave him false ideas about the intentions of our government. Because of this Genét commissioned privateers in Charlestown to prey on the British. President Washington revoked these commissions when he learned what Genét had done.[6]

When Genét finally arrived in Philadelphia he learned of the attitude of the government and decided to bypass it and appeal directly to the people.[7] There had been correspondence between George Rogers Clark and the French government concerning the possibility of Clark mounting an expedition against the Spanish at New Orleans. Clark was angry at the national government as well as Virginia because neither had rewarded him with money or land grants for his outstanding efforts during the war. In addition settlers in the western states were unhappy because they had no access to the Spanish controlled Port of New Orleans. The French promised Clark money for supplies and recruits. They also promised him land from Spanish territory if he was successful. Genét made contact with him and began preparations. When the President found out he was furious, calling Genét a spy and threatening to expel him. He realized such actions would have embroiled America in the war on the side of France. But the government in France had changed in the meantime. All arrangements from France were cancelled and Genét was declared a traitor and sentenced to death. Because of this he was granted asylum and allowed to remain in America where he died in 1834.

These European wars presented a major challenge to the new country. The Napoleonic Wars (1802-1815) were a continuation of the conflict begun in the 1790s when Great Britain led a coalition of European powers against Revolutionary France. Neither European superpower respected the neutrality of the United States. Instead, both tried to prevent U.S. ships from carrying goods to their enemy. Both Britain and France imposed blockades though the dominant British navy was clearly more successful. American merchant vessels were a common target. Between 1793 and 1812, the British seized more than 250 ships and impressed more than 15,000 U.S. sailors to supplement their fleet. The French were equally guilty taking over 315 ships in the Caribbean.[8]

In response to this disrespect of American sovereignty, President Jefferson and his secretary of state James Madison crafted an imaginative, but fundamentally flawed, policy of economic coercion. Their Embargo of 1807 prohibited U.S. ships from trading with Europe in the belief that dependence on American goods would soon force France and England to honor American neutrality. The Act forbade all international trade to and from American ports. Jefferson hoped this would persuade France and Britain to honor America's neutral position. The Embargo not only failed diplomatically, but also caused enormous domestic dissent. Many shippers, who were primarily concentrated in Federalist New England, dodged the law and many more were left with little income and useless ships. Merchants looked on the Act as an attempt to deny them a livelihood and resistance approached the point of rebellion. Its toll was clearly marked in the sharp decline of American imports from 108 million dollars worth of goods in 1806 to just 22 million in 1808. This unsuccessful diplomatic strategy that mostly punished Americans helped to spur a Federalist revival in the elections of 1808 and 1812. The plan backfired, however, as the Republican leaders failed to understand how deeply committed the superpowers were to carrying on their war despite its high costs. American protests were disregarded and finally we had had enough. On 18 June, 1812 we declared war with Britain for the second time in thirty years citing, in part, impressment.

Drurys in central and southern Maryland were mostly farmers and the four decades between 1780 and 1820 were generally difficult for them.[9] The paper certificates printed by the State government to finance the war[10] were now being redeemed. Unfortunately this caused a severe shortage of money to conduct ordinary business. Much of the

Maryland tobacco crop was traditionally sold to France and Britain considered any sales to her enemy as war aid. On the other hand, the French were intercepting ships sailing between Britain and America. Maryland and the other colonies were forced to import practically all their manufactured materials from Britain during the Colonial period. The new country had not yet developed a robust manufacturing industry. It did not take long for hostilities to affect the citizens of Maryland. Raids by Britain were routine both in the Potomac and in Chesapeake Bay.

One raid is recounted by the British commander Rear Admiral Sir George Cockburn:

> "I proceeded on the morning of the 18th with the Ships named in the margin (Albion, Loire, Regulus, Troop ship Melpomene, Troop ship Thistle) up the Potomac for the purpose of commencing by an attack on Leonards Town, the capital of St. Mary's County where I understood the 30th American Regiment to be stationed and much Stores &c. to be deposited...I proceeded at Midnight up the Creek...At the dawn of day the Marines were put on shore at some distance from the Town, and I directed Major Lewis to march round and attack it from the Land side whilst the Boats pulled up to it in front; the Enemy however on discovering us withdrew whatever armed Force he had in the place and permitted us to take quiet Possession of it. I found here a quantity of Stores belonging to the 30th Regiment and a number of Arms of different descriptions all of which were destroyed; a quantity of Tobacco, Flour, Provisions, and other articles likewise found in the Town I caused to be shipped and brought away in the Boats and a Schooner which we took laying off it - This occupied us the most of the day during the whole of which not a musquet [sic] was fired at us nor indeed a single armed American discovered, in consequence of which conduct on part of the Enemy I deemed it prudent to spare the Town, which we quitted in the Evening and returned to the Squadron without having sustained accident of any kind." [11]

Here is an American account of this same raid:

> Leonardtown (Breton Bay, off Potomac River, St. Mary's County). Site of raid by about 1,500 British (July 19, 1814); the British divided up into three forces, some landed near Newtown and marched inland to attack the town from the right, another to the left and a third under Rear Admiral Cockburn landed at the Leonardtown waterfront itself. Though several of the British troops were seriously injured during a boating accident on the return to the fleet, the British took a small schooner, 70 hogsheads of tobacco, 20 barrels of flour, and 40 stands of arms "which the enemy left behind they flying into the woods."

Another American account differs:

> "They [the British] behaved with great politeness to the ladies, respected private property wherever the proprietors remained at home, destroyed about 100 bbls of supplies belonging to Col. Carberry's regt. the whole of Mr. Haislip's store,

and the furniture, clothing and bedding of captains Forrest and Millard, all of whom left town. They got possession of some muskets belonging to the state, which they broke to pieces, saying they were only fit to stick frogs with." [12]

Other raids were not so benign. They paint a more aggressive and harsh picture of British military operations. During the summer of 1813 and 1814 marauding expeditions made frequent inroads among the farmers of St. Mary's County. The British organized small raiding parties who committed all kinds of depredations along the shores of the Potomac and Patuxent rivers. They plundered anything and everything, robbing even the women and children of their clothes and destroying such articles as it didn't suit them to carry away. The countryside was in pitiable condition, farms were neglected and pillaged, slaves run off to the enemy, and unsanitary living conditions brought a wave of illness. [13] Such actions caused many families, including some Drurys, to move west and avoid these troubles.

The formation of the "Maryland League" in 1789 probably was an early expression of such plans though others have attributed religious motives to its formation. In reality it was probably both. [14] The league was organized by a number of catholic families, mainly from St. Mary's County that had the largest concentration of Catholics in the entire state, who agreed to move in groups and in stages to Western Virginia that later became Kentucky in order that they would be able to attract Priests and form congregations after the move. This exodus continued sporadically through the end of the war in 1816 and afterward.

William Drury, son of John Drury and Susanna Hayden, was in Prairie du Roche in Illinois following the revolution. His son Raphael Drury, born in 1763, married Elizabeth McNabb. The Drury and McNabb families lived in St. George's Hundred in the same area and appear to have come to Illinois together. They appear in Fredrick County north of Washington D.C. by 1780. Her father, Archibald McNabb, was a witness to the will of William Elder who lived in the Mount St. Mary's area of Frederick County, Maryland. Luke Mudd, a constable in Fredrick County, brought an action there against William Drury in 1780. [15] A descendant Bob Dora wrote,

"William and his party most likely came down the Ohio in 1781. They were in Illinois by June of 1782 and the Ohio was difficult then, as now in the spring. I do not believe that they would go down it on a raft in April or May, much less in winter." [16]

Zachariah Drury, whose parentage is unclear, was in Kentucky by 1791 [17] where he married Mary Jane Molohon. Zachariah's birth in 1773 was calculated from his stated age in the 1850 census for Marion County Kentucky. [18] One place he would fit is as a son of Philip Drury and Emerentia "Ann" Drury as their unknown third child. But, as we saw in Chapter Ten, there was also Benedict Drury born that same year, who remained in Maryland and was connected to Dry Docking addition. [19] No additional corroboration has surfaced to date so either one or possibly neither really belongs there.

William Rodman, a grandson of Mary Ellen Drury, in a letter to his brother in 1914[20] claims that Zachariah was an older half brother of his grandmother. This assertion also has its problems. If Zachariah was her half brother then he had to have a different mother. We know that Ignatius married Anastasia French in 1769.[21] Zachariah would have had to be born before then and that would make him several years older than the 1850 census indicates. In addition we have found no record of an earlier marriage for his purported father Ignatius. If, on the other hand, Zachariah was born in 1773 as the census suggests then there is additional confusion because Ignatius Jr. was also born in 1773. There is no evidence that Ignatius Jr. and Zachariah were twins though it is possible that they were born in the same year. But in that case Zachariah would not be a half brother. More research is needed here, but at present we cannot comfortably place him with any of our ancestors though he obviously belongs there somewhere.

Mary Jane Molohon was also born in Maryland about 1768.[22] She came to Kentucky with her parents and at least one brother, Clement.

By 1810 we have at least four more Drury families who had left Maryland. Two were Ignatius and Charles Drury, sons of Ignatius Drury and Anastasia French.

Though no record has been found, Charles and Ignatius must also have been members of the local militia. Like other residents they were concerned about the possibility of being caught in a war. Charles Drury was in Washington D.C. in 1800 to witness the marriage of his brother Ignatius to Harriet Redding.[23] Other witnesses from St. Mary's County were his sister Elizabeth, Gabriel Newton, a brother of Ann Newton the wife of his uncle Philip Drury, and Gabriel's brother Ignatius.

By 1805 Charles had moved to Kentucky where his daughter Catherine was born on March 31st 1805. We are assuming that Ignatius went with him, but this leaves us with the question of what happened to Harriet and the child born in 1801. The Ignatius in Kentucky married (or remarried) sometime before 1817 when his son William was born.[24] Unfortunately there is no clear link between Ignatius the son of Ignatius and Anastasia French and the Ignatius who died in Kentucky in 1833. All we have are plausible assumptions. We need more documentation to be certain.

A third was Mary Drury, born Mary Magdalen Goldsborough, the widow of the Ignatius Drury who died about 1803,[25] She went to Kentucky in 1811/1812.[26]

This Ignatius is a mystery. The only information we have about his parents comes from Susan Elliot, a descendant, who cites a diary of Father A. A. Aud.[27] She reports that entries in this diary identify his parents as Bernard and Ann Drury. In order to marry in 1793 Ignatius would probably not be born later than 1773 and therefore his father Bernard would be born sometime in the 1740's or early 1750's. When Mary left after Ignatius died she thought there would be better opportunity in Kentucky to acquire land and raise her family. Her husband was not a farmer and she had no ties to land in Maryland. Leaving also made sense because by 1808 it was becoming obvious that war with Britain was about to break out. The area around Washington D.C. where they lived would be a prime target for attacks.

Bernard Drury, eldest son of Philip Drury and Bibianna (Ann) Newton,[28] brought his family to Kentucky sometime between 1810[29] and 1813.[30] There are family stories that he was reported absent from muster for the militia in St. Mary's county. This was undoubtedly while he was enroute to Kentucky. When he and his family left he was living about a mile from Leonardtown[31] and was undoubtedly thinking of the danger to his family as he recalled British raids during the revolution.

Those who remained in Maryland found themselves facing a major British blockade both in Chesapeake Bay and in the Potomac. Militia members in St. Mary's County were in general too poorly equipped to effectively oppose British regulars. Their main job was to harass the British and keep them from mounting a concerted campaign. Militia Commanders pleaded with the state government for better weapons but this did not usually happen. Militiamen ordinarily were expected to furnish their own weapons. A typical action was one reported in a congressional act to compensate soldiers that involved military action and bravery. One of those mentioned was Wilfred Drury.[32]

It stated:

"Be it enacted by the senate and House of Representatives of the United States of America in congress assembled, that the Secretary of the treasury be, and he is hereby authorized and required, to pay out of any money in the treasury not otherwise appropriated, the sum of five hundred dollars, in equal proportions, to Matthew Guy and John Woodward, of Prince William county in Virginia and Samuel Tennison and Wilfred Drury of St. Mary's county in Maryland or to their heirs; which sum of five hundred dollars, is paid to them as evidence of the sense entertained by the congress, of their valor and good conduct, in capturing a boat, belonging to the enemy, in St. Clement's Bay, in Potomac River, in the month of December last; making prisoners of the crew, consisting of a midshipman and four seamen, with their arms, consisting of four muskets and two sabres; and also as a compensation for the prisoners so taken."

Wilfred was a son of Peter Drury Jr. and Eleanor _____. He was christened 24 January 1779 and married Nellie Bailey on 9 May 1799. By 1815 when the bill was passed his family had increased to 6 family members and 4 slaves.[33]

Another Drury relative who served in the War of 1812 was John Johnson, husband of Sarah Marthalina (Michael Drury's daughter) and a son of Leonard Johnson and Mary Howard. He is listed in the muster rolls as having been in Capt. William Floyd's company of the 12th Regiment, St. Mary's County, stationed at Leonard Town to St. Inigoes in St. Mary's County July 14 to August 4 1813. This would have been about the time the British were probing up the Potomac and when the raid by Admiral Cockburn took place. Johnson is shown as having served for 5 days. We cannot find a record in Wright for him having served in 1814 but that record may be missing. Richard Johnson though is listed as having served 22 days in the period July 16 to August 17, 1814 under Captain John H. Briscoe of the 45th Regiment, and this company included men transferred from Sothoron's company. It is possible that some of those days were served by John Johnson.[34]

Many years later John applied to the congress for bounty land for his service but there seemed to be much confusion about when he served and the application was rejected.

Among the bounty land claims, apparently rejected (55-rej-98108) is one for John Johnson of Leonard, who claimed to have served as a private under Captains Floyd, Millard and Williams and who applied 13 February 1851, listed as a resident of St. Mary's County, volunteered at Leonard Town, afterwards served as a substitute for Richard Johnson, private in Captain J. F. Sothoron's company in the 45th Regt. At the time of the 1851 claim, Johnson was listed as age 65 years. He applied again after being rejected and was again listed as a resident of St. Mary's Co. Witnesses listed were William T. Perry and Samuel E. Abell, also of St. Mary's Co.[35]

Other Drurys who served during the war were Ignatius Drury in the Tenth Regiment from Washington County and William C. Drury who was almost certainly related to Ignatius. Ignatius was Captain of his regiment and William was one of his Ensigns. Ignatius later served as a state legislator.

[1] Risjord, Norman K., Chesapeake Politics 1784-1800, Columbia University Press, 1978, p 37

[2] Maryland Gazette, Baltimore, June 20 and July 21 1786

[3] Wallace, Johnson and Muir to Ridgely, September 30 1786, Ridgely family papers, Maryland Historical Society

[4] Risjord, Norman K., Chesapeake Politics 1784-1800, Columbia University Press, 1978, table 6.5, p 172

[5] Risjord, Norman K., Chesapeake Politics 1784-1800, Columbia University Press, 1978, p 425

[6] Risjord, Norman K., Chesapeake Politics 1784-1800, Columbia University Press, 1978, p 426

[7] Risjord, Norman K., Chesapeake Politics 1784-1800, Columbia University Press, 1978, p 427

[8] Risjord, Norman K., Chesapeake Politics 1784-1800, Columbia University Press, 1978

[9] Risjord, Norman K., Chesapeake Politics 1784-1800, Columbia University Press, 1978, pp 105-109

[10] Ibid, p 97

[11] Rear Adm. George Cockburn to Vice Adm. Sir Alexander Cochrane, July 19, 1814

[12] Letter entitled "Movements of the Enemy," Maryland Gazette, August 4, 1814

[13] Klapthor, Margaret Brown, Southern Maryland in the War of 1812 in "The Record" April 1965, Charles County Historical Society, p 2

[14] Webb, Ben, Centenary of Catholicity in Kentucky

[15] Frederick County Docket Books, 1780, Luke Mudd vs. Wm. Druroy

[16] Dora, Robert, Electronic, 4/25/2001

[17] TAXLIST: Nelson County Tithes 1785-1791, Nelson Co., KY Gabriel Cox --------1791 Daniel McFawls Co north central Nelson Co. Drury Zachariah 1 15 1791

[18] 1850 Census, Marion County Kentucky, image 61

[19] Benedict Drury, sale of Dryarkins addition and other properties to John Raley (of Gabriel) 3/3/1814 in *Chronicles of St. Mary's Vol. 7 p 171*

[20] William Rodman's letter to Dr. H.D. Rodman, dated March 12, 1914 in "History of the Roman Catholic Diocese of Owensboro" page 229

[21] O'Rourke, Timothy, Colonial Source Records, Southern Maryland catholic Families, p 33; Beitzel, Edwin, The Jesuit Missions of St. Mary's County Maryland, St. Mary's County Historical Society, p 135

[22] 1850 Census, Marion County, Kentucky, Image # 61, Jenny (Jane) (w) " Mollihan" Molohon b: Abt. 1769 in Maryland m: January 12, 1797 in Washington County, Kentucky Burial: 1850 Census, Marion County, Kentucky, Image # 61 Father: James Molohon, (1) Mother: Unknown

[23] Trinity Church-Georgetown DAR - vol.. 47 Trinity Church Marriage & Baptism Records 1795-1805

[24] "Nelson Co., KY Cemeteries," p. 93. DRURY, William (16) d. 20 Nov. 1833, son of Ignatius & Debary DRURY

[25] Mary Magdalen Goldsborough, b. 1761, married Ignatious Drury in Frederick County, Maryland in 1793

[26] 6/1809: Mary Drury was granted letters of admin. on the estate of Ignatius Drury (Orphans Ct. Rec., Fenwick). 6/1811: Mary Drury, admx. of Ignatius Drury to sell his vessel and other property for the payment of debts (Orphan Ct. Rec., Fenwick)

[27] Susan Elliot, 1999, electronic

[28] O'Rourke, Timothy J., "Colonial Source records - Southern Maryland Catholic families"; also Cited in Will of Philip Drury Will Bk. JJ2 pgs 122 & 123 (1795) as son and joint executor along with mother "Ann" Newton Drury

[29] 1810 Census County/State: St. Mary's Co., MD, Page #: 166

[30] "Record of the County Malitia" Washington County, Kentucky 3/26/1813, Bernard Drury of the 4th. Regiment Kentucky Militia pleaded "inability"; Also in Pioneer History of Washington County, Kentucky Edited and indexed by Michael L. Cook and Bettie Ann Cook (McDowell Publications, Utica Kentucky); page 273: "Bernard Drury same company (Captain Spalding's Company) plead inability to the court, after investigation ordered that he be continued on the list."

[31] From G.L. Drury letter of 4/10/1936 to Luke Scheer forwarded by Judy Burger. "Cabin for Bernard was about a mile from Leonard town." George Lucian Drury states that he has stood on the spot where the old cabin stood.

[32] A Century of Lawmaking for a New Nation: U.S. Congressional Documents and Debates, 1774-1875. Bills and Resolutions, House of Representatives, 13th Congress, 3rd Session. (Library of Congress). A Bill (No. 50) Concerning Matthew Guy, John Woodward, Samuel Tennison, and Wilfred Drury

[33] 1810; Census, Saint Mary's County, Maryland; Roll: 16; Page: 180; Image: 0193669; Family History Library Film: 00101.

[34] Wright, "Maryland Militia War of 1812, St. Mary's & Charles Counties." Vol. 5, p. 20

[35] Ibid, Vol. 5 p. 74

Chapter Twelve

Joseph Drury of Virginia

Joseph Drury was born on 5 January 1750/1.[1] Some researchers claim he was a son of John Drury and Susanna Hayden, a Roman Catholic family from St. Ignatius parish in St. Mary's county. They believe that John went to Virginia after Susanna died. Others think that John Drury (born before 1710), the husband of Susanna Hayden, later married Ann Jarboe in 1795 and then moved to Virginia. They claim he filed a will in both Virginia and Maryland.

I believe the marriage of John (born before 1710) to Ann Jarboe is incorrect. If this marriage was between John (b. before 1710) and Ann, he would be more than 80 years old when they married. Though not impossible it is unlikely that Ann would marry a man more than 30 years older than she was. This assumption confuses him with John (died 1797). For the purpose of this discussion we will call them John I and John II. The will of John II[2] provides a number of facts that help us resolve the confusion. John II did have a son named Joseph[3] but John II would not have been old enough to be married and father a child in 1751. Joseph (born 1751) and Joseph of the will were clearly different people and Joseph's birth in 1751 would be consistent with his being a son of John I and Susanna Hayden. Both John I and John II had daughters named Mary but they are also different people. Mary, daughter of John I and Susanna Hayden, married Richard Knott, was in Montgomery County Maryland by 1777 and in Kentucky by 1811[4] while Mary, daughter of John II, is mentioned in the will as Mary Mandley and is still in Maryland.[5] Some researchers have misinterpreted Mandley as Medley. But current research in Leonardtown Maryland has confirmed that it was indeed Mandley.[6] We assume here that Mary Drury Mandley was the wife of Matthew Mandley who also lived in this same area.

Another discrepancy concerns Susanna Drury who married Benedict Riley before 1784.[7] Assuming she was at least 17 when they married, her birth would have been in the late 1760's. By this time Susanna Hayden[8] would have been about 50 years old and well past childbearing age.

In addition, William, son of John I and Susanna Hayden, was in Missouri by 1782.[9] The family would know he was not in Maryland so why mention him in the will of 1797. These points convince us that John I and John II are different individuals. The will of John II was also filed in York County Virginia but this only proves that John II also had either relatives or dealings in Virginia.

It is possible that John I, husband of Susanna, did move to Virginia after her death but this would probably have been during or shortly after the end of the Revolutionary war. He was actively supporting the revolution in Virginia.[10] John II was living on land leased from the Jesuits in St. George's hundred. He also purchased land near Leonardtown by 1797[11] He was still in Maryland until his death. The John Drury who married Ann Jarboe was John II.[12] She also remained in Maryland.[13]

We don't know when or why Joseph was convinced to convert to Baptist but this probably caused him to be estranged from his family. He apparently had little to do with them from then on. There are two possible causes for his conversion. Steve Driver, a descendant, claims that it was because of the influence of Jeremiah Hatcher, a devout and wealthy Baptist preacher who was prominent in developing the Baptist church in Virginia. One church he started in Chesterfield County was called the Tomahawk Church.[14] The young idealistic Joseph, still in his teens, was evidently impressed by the charismatic evangelist. He joined Jeremiah and was supported by him as the two of them traveled together throughout northern Virginia starting Churches and helping other already established congregations.

REV. JEREMIAH HATCHER   15

The Broad Run Baptist church was founded in 1762 by David Thomas an eminent and very successful minister who probably did more than any other man at the time to extend the Baptist faith. He was born in Pennsylvania and made a number of trips to Virginia before settling there in 1760.[16] In 1766 Chappwansick church was constituted from Broad Run.[17] By 1770 there were several more. We estimate Joseph was married by about 1770 or 1771, was baptized into the Broad Run Baptist church in 1772 and had a daughter (Mary born September 1772) baptized in 1773.[18] A second daughter, Elizabeth was born 23 February 1775 and baptized the following year. His first wife must have died soon after the birth of Elizabeth because Isaac, Joseph's first child with Sybil Wigginton, was born in 1777. He would have needed a wife to care for his infant daughter. The two daughters may have lived with the Wiggintons as they grew up but Joseph possibly made other arrangements for their upbringing. Two Baptists in an Anglican home would have caused problems. Given his admiration of and association with Jeremiah Hatcher, Joseph may have sent them to live there. Little mention is made of them in the records. Mary later married William Farmer and Elizabeth married Thomas Boudaurant.

Joseph left Broad Run Church in 1785 to go to Bedford County to help Hatcher. They founded a church on Hatcher's plantation in Bedford County called Hatcher's Meeting House. It later became the Otter Creek Church and they both preached there.[19] He represented the new congregation at the Goose Creek Baptist conference in 1787.[20] A second possibility is the fact that Sybil Metcalf, the aunt of his future wife, was a member of the Broad Run Baptist church until she moved to Loudoun County Virginia in 1764.[21] Her membership may have influenced Joseph. She may even have introduced him to Jeremiah Hatcher though all of this is speculation.

One error should be corrected here. There have been numerous postings in email messages, on *Ancestry.com*, and in other places that state that Sybil Wigginton and Joseph Drury were married in Maryland. These postings cite Robert Barnes' "Maryland Marriages" as the source. Steve Driver, a Drury researcher, said that he spoke personally with Robert Barnes who told him that the citation is not correct, and that he never saw such a record.

It is not clear what Joseph's association with the Wigginton family was before his marriage, but he was closely associated with them for the last 30 years of his life. This may have been through the church where both Sybil Metcalf and Sarah Wigginton were members though most of the Wigginton family was Anglican. Joseph and the Wiggintons both moved to Stafford County from Prince William County by 1779. He posted surety for the marriage of Sybil's brothers John III to Margaret McGeorge and George to Sisly Reynolds in 1788.[22] He became guardian for John and Thomas Childress in 1789 and 1790.[23] They were nephews, the children of his sister-in-law Elizabeth Wigginton Childress. He posted bond in 1794 for the marriage of another younger sister-in-law Nancy Wigginton.[24] She married Joseph's ward, Thomas Childress who was just 21.

The map below shows the Brent Town tract as it was in 1737, but little had changed for the Wiggintons between then and the 1770's when Joseph Drury lived there. Sybil's grandfather, John Wigginton, was living on the same property (number 24 on the map) occupied by his son in 1770.[25] Joseph and the Wiggintons were neighbors in the Brent Town settlement. The Broad Run Church, also known as the Slate Run Church, was located at the intersection of Slate Run and old Church road. It was situated on Slate Run about 100 yards upstream from where it enters Cedar Run and was less than half a mile from where the Wiggintons lived.[26]

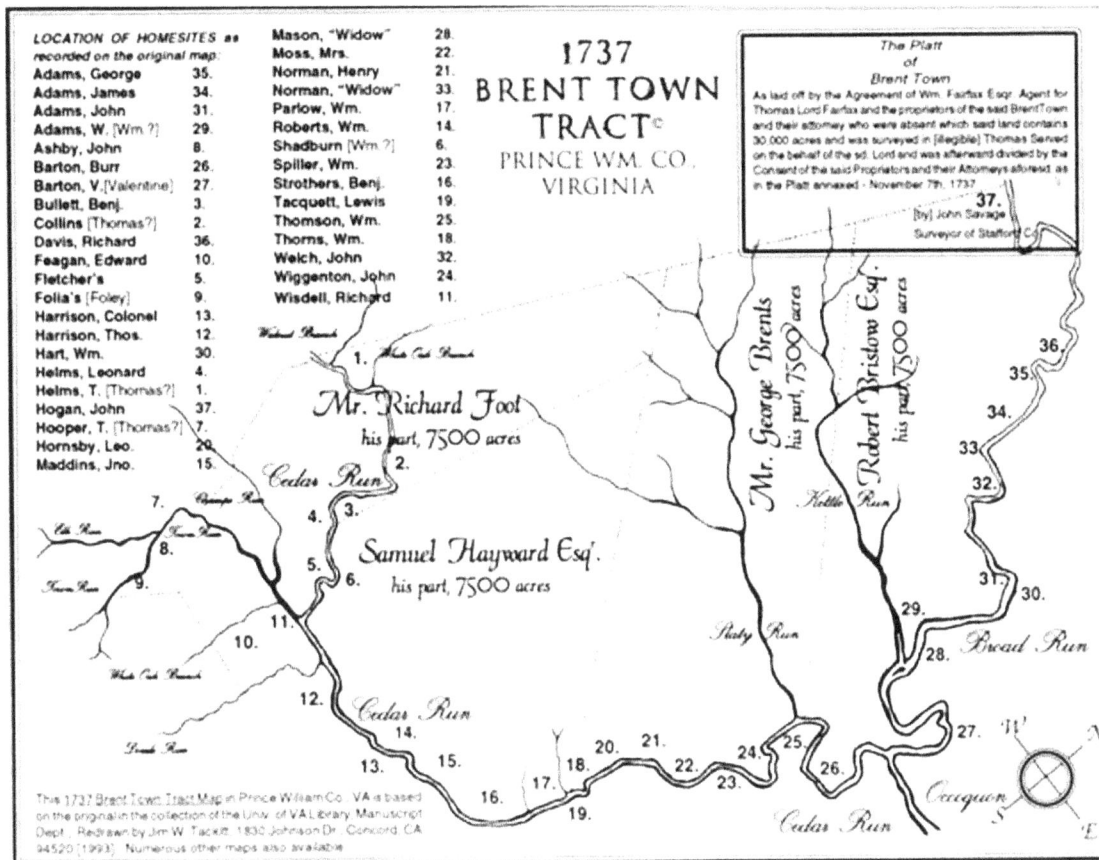

Apparently not all members of the Wigginton family were Baptist. As we mentioned, Sybil Metcalf was a member of the Broad Run church. There was also a Sary (Sarah) Wigginton who was also listed in the church records. She was probably Sybil's Great Aunt Sarah O'Neal Wiggginton. Other Wiggintons, including Joseph's wife, followed the family tradition and remained staunchly Anglican. Sybil's insistence on retaining her Anglican beliefs caused much friction in the family. After years of attempted persuasion, Joseph lost patience and tried to force his wife to agree to be baptized in the Church by whipping her severely. The church censured him for this. The Church Minutes state:

> Monthly meeting June 24th 1785 Joseph Drury was deeply
> censored for whipping his wife. An action we overly esteem,
> not a little scandalous. For a husband to beat his wife we judge
> to be a practice contrary both to scripture & reason, to the law
> & the gospel. – and, as such, not to be once named among christians.
> Not to be tollerated in the church of Christ, on any pretence whatever. [28]

Joseph apparently repented and made amends because he was released from the censure about six months later,[29] but Sybil remained faithful to her Anglican upbringing and raised all her children as Anglicans.

Her resistance to Joseph's pressure was not the only cause of dissention. Religious converts tend to be much more serious about their religion than those raised from childhood in a faith. According to family lore, Joseph spent most of his time away from the family traveling with Jeremiah Hatcher. Descendants said that Sybil and the children were cared for mostly by her brother George while Joseph remained away evangelizing. Hatcher was licensed to perform marriages in 1785.[30] Joseph became a minister and was licensed to perform marriages five years later.[31] One of the first marriages he performed was that of Henry Adams to Rebecca Chaffin on 22 December 1791.[32] Despite his failings Joseph was respected in his community. Steve Driver stated, " I have never thought much of Joseph but I have to accept he had some standing in the community as he was given guardianship of children, served as justice of the peace, and married over 100 couples."[33]

Even with their disagreements family life did not seem to suffer. Sybil was probably in her early twenties when they married in 1776. Joseph and Sybil had eleven children before he died. Sybil had to be pregnant almost continuously in order to have this many children by 1796 when Lucy, the youngest, was born.

Isaac

Their first six children were born in Prince William County while they were living at the Brent Town settlement. By the time the children were of marriageable age the family had moved to Tennessee. As we stated, Isaac the eldest was born about 1777[34] a year after Joseph and Sybil were married. Isaac married Sarah Dowdy in 1833.

Rebecca

Their first daughter Rebecca was born September 11, 1779.[35] She married Sanders Brown in 1817 and died in 1855. She had three children between 1817 and 1820. They were Patricia or Patsy born 17 November 1817, a son, Samuel, born 12 December 1818, and Polly born 12 January 1820. Polly married Robert Hankins in 1845 and died in 1912.

Sarah

Their next child was also a girl, Sarah (or Sallie) who was born in 1782 and married Elijah Russell April 5, 1813.

John

36

The fourth child was a boy, John, born in 1781 who married Rachel Dorris in 1810. He was probably born in Prince William County. The family moved to Bedford County about 1786. He served as a private in the West Tennessee Militia in the campaign against the Creek Indians during the War of 1812. He lived until 1858 and fathered nine children. John and Rachel are buried in the Drury family cemetery on the farm purchased by John Drury on Drury's Ridge in 1837. He was the only child of Joseph and Sybil to remain in Tennessee.

John's children were Polly born on 4 July 1811, William who was born 18 July 1813 and married Caroline Johnson before 1836, Elizabeth in 1817, Lucinda in 1819, Delila in 1821, Stephen in 1823, George in 1827, Francis in 1828, and finally Martha born in 1834. Two of his sons, George and Francis, followed in their grandfather's footsteps becoming Baptist Ministers as did one of George's sons to continue the tradition.

George

Joseph's next children were George born in 1783 and Elizabeth (Betsy) in 1785.

James

Another son, James followed in 1787 but it is not clear if this was before or after the move to Bedford County when Joseph joined Jeremiah Hatcher to start a new congregation. James, like most of his brothers and sisters, married later in life. He was 39 years old when he married the 20 year old Willa Stith in 1826. In the years following the move Joseph and Sybil had four more girls.

Nancy

Nancy was born in 1789 and married David Foster.

Frances

Frances was born in 1791. She married Fieldin Hankins about 1809 and had eight children. They were Deborah born in 1811 who married John Hayes, Jane (1816) who married Morris Merrick, Davis (abt. 1818) who married first to Abigail Elmore and then to Julia Ann Henderson, Wesley (1818), Emily (1823) who married Jonathan Hayes, Andrew (1824) who married Lydia Ann Pennington in 1845, and finally William and Nimrod about whom we know very little.

Martha

Wade Hampton Davis and Martha Drury [37]

Martha was born in 1794 and died in 1888. By the time she was 19 Martha had become famous as a beauty and an equestrian. Her father said it was a pleasure for her to break horses to ride or drive, that she was not afraid of any of them and could tame the wildest ones. She frequently rode in races of the countryside. She married Wade Hampton Davis in 1813. In the 64 years of their marriage they had seven children.

Their first child was William born in 1814. He married Sarah Barnes in 1837. Next was Nancy (1817 – 1831). Then came Smithen Hamilton Davis in 1819. He married Rhoda Jane Moreman in 1836. Elizabeth, who probably was born in 1820, married Thomas Groves and died in 1848.

Hiram Davis born in 1821 had an adventurous spirit. At age 22 he joined the United States Army and fought during the Mexican War. According to Marie Davis "He was a member of that intrepid young Missourians who not only offered their lives to their country, but furnished their own mounts, and the pride of each of them was his famous horse."[38] He married Mary Jane Broyles and died in 1895. Martha Jane Davis was born in 1828. She married Elijah Johnson and after he died was wed to George Washington Long. Finally James Wade Davis was born in 1830. He married Martha Simpson Faulkner and later Martha Ann Robinson.

Lucy

Lucy Drury Dorris and Josiah Dorris
[39]

Lucy was born in 1796 as we mentioned above. She married Rachel's brother Josiah Dorris in 1816. They had ten children.

Their oldest child, Hiram Cassidy Dorris, was born in 1818 in Smith County Tennessee. He married Elizabeth Fulkerson in 1841 in Missouri and died on the way to California in 1847. According to Miriam Leideke, his great granddaughter, his wife, his father-in-law, and their family split from the rest of the party and entered the Willamette Valley on their way west. The last hazard on the trip was Laurel Hill on the west side of Mt. Hood. Wagons had to be let down on ropes. Hiram died there but no one has been able to find out where he was buried.

The next child was Wiley Howell Dorris. He was born in 1820 and died in 1843.

Presley Alexander Dorris, their third son, was born in 1822 and died in 1901. He and his younger brother Cyrus served in the Mexican War and were stationed at Fort Leavenworth and Fort Kearney about 1848. In the mid 1850's the brothers went to California but returned to Missouri to escort the rest of the family to the west coast where they remained from then on.

Another son, Carlos Jefferson Dorris, was born in 1824 and died in 1907.

Sarah Catherine Dorris, fifth child and first daughter of Josiah and Lucy, was born in 1826 in Smith County Tennessee. She married John Porter in 1844. By this time her family had moved to Missouri and in 1855 moved on to Lane County, Oregon Territory where she died in 1894. Her husband John was born in Missouri and also served in the Mexican War.

The next daughter, Letha Parlee Dorris, (1829 – 1854) was living with her parents in Missouri in 1850. It is unclear whether she died in California or while they were traveling west.

Child number seven for the couple was a son, Cyrus Grundy Dorris (1831 – 1903). He married Elizabeth Barnes (1844) in 1860 after he and his brother Presley had returned from the Mexican War. In 1870 he was living next to his parents and his brother in Benicia in Solana County California.

Parthena Dorris (1833 – 1912) married Francis Payne in 1855. The couple lived their adult lives in California.

Columbus Dorris (1837 – 1875) was the youngest of their sons. He married Rachel Cyrus, daughter of William Cyrus, in Linn County Oregon in 1864. Delbert Cantrall of Medford Oregon writes,

> " Columbus was a young boy when the Josiah Dorris family
> crossed the plains by the Lassen trail and settled on a ranch
> in Benecia, California. When he was a young man he helped
> his brothers Carlos and Presley drive sheep to the mines in
> Oregon and Idaho. After he married he moved to Dorris
> Bridge and homesteaded land with his uncles, his brothers,
> and his parents. He also had an interest in a ranch near Dorris
> that was known as the D Ranch. He is considered the founder
> of Alturas, California that was originally called Dorris Bridge."

The youngest child of Lucy and Josiah was Amanda Melvina Dorris (1838 – 1854). She apparently died on the way west and is buried at Humbolt Sink.

Joseph died in 1805 when Sybil left with the family for Kentucky and then Tennessee. She would not have traveled alone. Her brother George and sisters Winifred Wigginton Dalton and Nancy Wigginton Childress were all moving to the same places at the same general time. They probably traveled together or in quick succession.

There is confusion concerning the designation of Joseph's plantation as "Drewry's Bluff". There is a place called Drewry's Bluff located about eight miles below Richmond on the James River. Some researchers say that this is where Joseph lived. However, this spot is in Chesterfield County Virginia, not in either Prince William or Bedford counties where we know Joseph lived. If Joseph had a place he called Drewry's Bluff, it had to be his farm in the Brent Town settlement, or the farm he settled on when he moved to Bedford County.

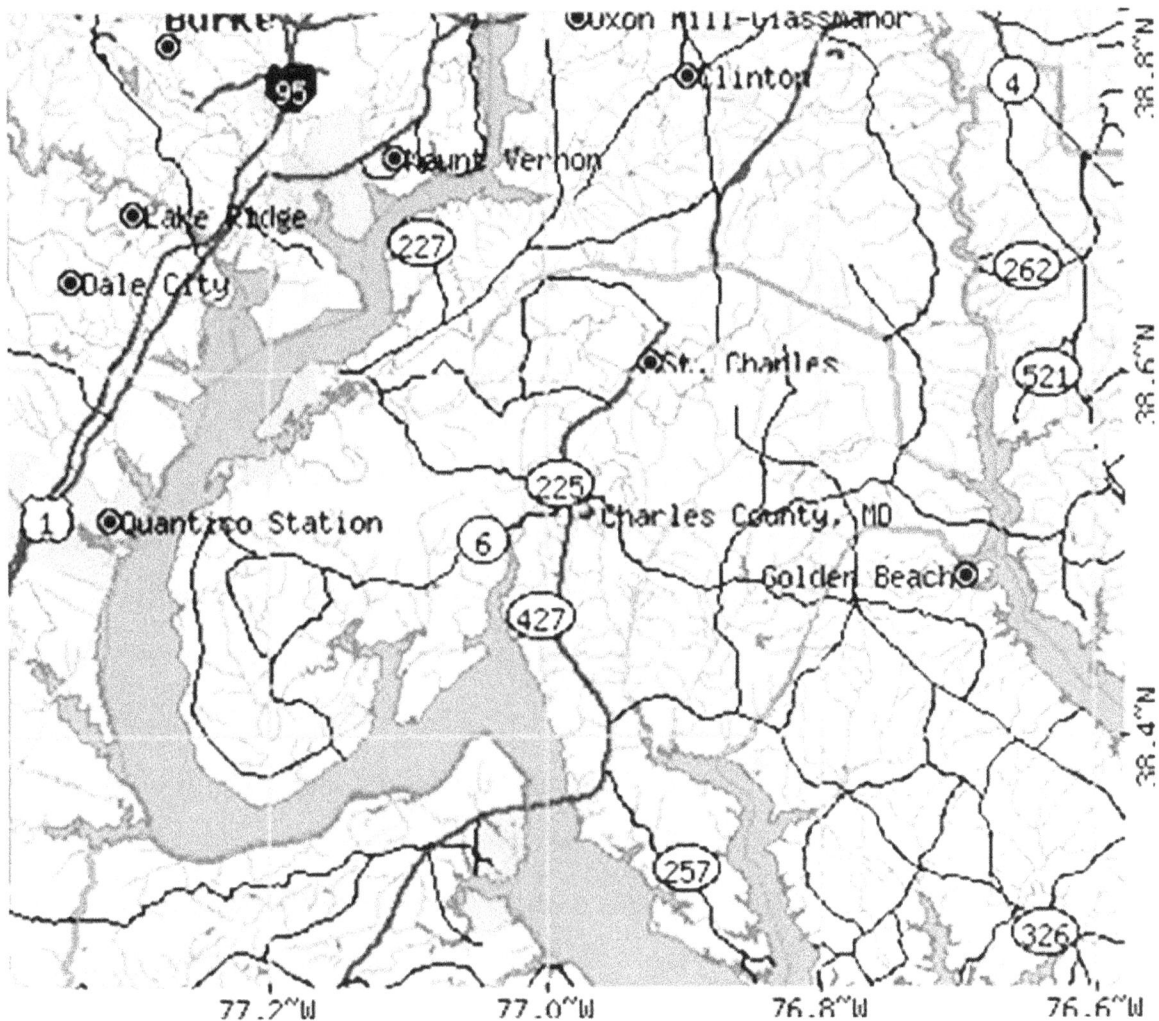

Western Charles County and Eastern Stafford County

In 1776 Joseph was listed in the census for lower William and Mary Hundred in southern Charles County.[40] This area is located on the peninsula about where Route 427 crosses the Potomac to Virginia. The area north of Fredericksburg in Virginia is where Stafford County starts. As we go north from there we get into Prince William County. Joseph took the Oath of Allegiance in 1779 in Charles County but paid taxes in Stafford County Virginia that same year.

As we have seen, most of Joseph Drury's life and interests were in Prince William, Stafford, and Bedford Counties in northern Virginia. Therefore it is curious that his association with the Revolutionary War was in Maryland. At the beginning of this chapter we assumed that Joseph was originally from St. Mary's county in Maryland. There is a fair amount of material supporting this theory. He was supposedly a member of St. Inigoes Parish in St. Mary's County in 1769. He is missing on the Oath of allegiance for St. Mary's County in 1778, but he did take the oath in Charles County and served in a Continental Army regiment from there.[41] If his family came from St. Mary's county why

149

would he not be there for these important events. It is most likely that the estrangement was responsible though family lore has it that he enlisted in the second regiment because there were relatives already there.

[1] Heads of families at the first U.S. census. Md. By U.S. Bureau of the Census. Washington, 1907. p. 105

[2] John Drewry - his last will.

In the name of God amen, I John Drewroy (Drury) of Saint Mary's County in the State of Maryland being sick & weak of body but of sound & disposing mind memory & understanding. Considering the certainty of death & the uncertainty of the time thereof, and being desirous to settle my worldly affairs,& thereby be the better prepared to leave this world when it shall please God to call me home, do therefore make & publish this my last will & testament in manner from following that is to say..first and princepally I commit my soul into the hands of almighty God, & my body to the Earth to be decently buried at the discretion of my Executor herein after named and after my just debts are paid I devise and bequeath as follows...Item, I give and bequeath unto my beloved wife Ann Drury (Drury) one third part of my real estate during her natural life and likewise one part of my household furniture and stock to her their heirs forever.... It is forth my will that my wife shall have her choice of my stock and furniture to the amount of her thirds...Item I give and bequeath to beloved sons Francis Decalus (Desales) Drury, Joseph Drury & William Drury seven pounds ten shillings current money each to them & their heirs forever..Item I give and bequeath unto my beloved daughter Monica Drewry (Drury) one cow to her and her heirs forever...Item I give and bequeath unto my beloved children Annastania Vepells (Vessels) Susanna Raliy (Raley) Mary Mandley Monica Drewry (Drury) John Christophor (Christopher) Drewry (Drury) Francis Decalus (Desales) Drury Ignatius Drewry (Drury) Joseph Drewry (Drury) & William Drewry (Drury) all the residual & remaining part of my estate both real and personal to be equally divided between my children before mentioned to them & their heirs..Lastly I do hereby nominate & appoint my son Francis Decalus (Desales) Drewry to be whole & sole executor of this my last will & testament disannulling any written wills by me heretofor made ratifying & confirming this and no other to my last & testament in testimony whereof I have hereto affixed my hand and seal this 17th day June 1797
Signed sealed and declared to be the last will & testament of the named testator in the presents of us
her mark   His mark
Aloweser Greenwell   Eleanor (X) Stone   John (X) Drewry (Drury)

[3] Ibid

[4] Tax list of 1777 to Montgomery County, Maryland, Sugarloaf Hundred; Abstract of Wills 1785-1820 Nelson County, Kentucky, NCHS 84

[5] Op Cit

[6] Himmelheber, Peter, Email msg. of 4/9/2007

[7] www.stmarysfamilies.com, Benedict Riley to Susanna Drury – Jesuit Misions

[8] Phyllis Hugo Stager Email posted 4/30/2000, Elizabeth O. Thompson m. abt 1705 & they had Francis 1706, James 1713, Susanna 1714, George 1715, John 1717, Clement 1719, Richard 1721 & Elizabeth 1723.; From research of Theodore L. Brownyard sent to St. Mary's County Historical Society 2/10/2003 Will of William Hayden made 19 July 1732 and proved 6 March 1733/34. Lists heirs wife Elizabeth, sons Charles, William, Francis, James, George, John, Clement, and Richard; daughters Grace, Thomasine, Susanna and Elizabeth.

[9] Email from Robert Dora - 4/25/2001 "I conclude that William most likely came down the Ohio in 1781. They were in Illinois by June of 1782 and the Ohio was difficult then, as now in the spring."

[10] Claims entered in Elizabeth City County, Court Book, p. 19: DREWRY, John, 1781 for 1 bu. Indian meal for troops at halfway house under Col. Dabney pr. cert. from Sam'l. Armistead 2 (pounds)-6; two bundles fodder for Col. Armisteads Legion 15 pounds.

[11] 25 Feb 1797, DA:TH25:046

[12] Brumbaugh, Gaius Marcus, MARYLAND RECORDS VOL I, 1993, Genealogical Pub. Co., Baltimore, p. 333 (marriages) "1795 April 21 Drury, John and Ann Jarbo."

[13] Ann Jarboe listed as head of household in 1790 census for St. Mary's County Maryland, No Ann Jarboe listed in 1800 but Ann Drury listed in 1800 for St Mary's County.

[14] Taylor, George B., Virginia Baptist Ministers, third series

[15] Ibid

[16] Edwards, Morgan, History of the Baptists in Virginia

[17] Ibid; Magazine of Virginia Genealogy vol. 27 No. 1, Early records of Chappawansic Baptist Church, Stafford County. 1766-1844, p. 38

[18] "Minutes of Broad Run Baptist Church, Fauquier Co., Va., 1762-1872." "Genealogical Record" Vol. 7, No. 3, Sept. 1965 through Vol. 9, No. 4, Dec. 1967." Houston Gen. Forum, Houston, Texas.

[19] Steve Driver Email of 5 June, 2013

[20] 200th Anniversary Committee of the Strawberry Baptist association, "The Early Trails of the Baptists", p. 12

[21] Magazine of Virginia Genealogy vol. 27 No. 1, Early records of Chappawansic Baptist Church, Stafford County. 1766-1844, p. 40

[22] Marriage Bonds of Bedford County, Virginia 1755-1810, p. 73, p. 1014;Wigginton, William, Some families of Bedford and Washington counties, Virginia; 12/28/1788 Joseph Drury surety for both

[23] Bedford County Court Order Book 9, p. 333; Bedford County Court Order Book 15, p. 337

[24] Marriage Bonds of Bedford County 22 February 1794, p. 6

[25] Prince William Miscellaneous papers, Virginia archives; Min. 1752-53 – 116

[26] David Wigginton Email 10/14/2007

[27] Courtesy of David Wigginton; original on file, Manuscripts Division, Alderman Library, University of Vriginia, Charlottesville, accession # 52001

[28] "Genealogical Record" Vol. 7, No. 3, Sept. 1965 through Vol. 9, No. 4, Dec. 1967." Houston Gen. Forum, Houston, Texas.

[29] "Minutes of Broad Run Baptist Church, Fauquier Co., Va., 1762-1872." "Genealogical Record" Vol. 7, No. 3, Sept. 1965 through Vol. 9, No. 4, Dec. 1967." Houston Gen. Forum, Houston, Texas.; Monthly meeting. Oct. 22, 1785: Joseph Drury was released from censure, and at his request, he being about to remove his residence, was dismissed to any church of the same faith & order.

[30] A History of Bedford County, Virginia – Jeremiah Hatcher received a license to perform marriages in the Baptist Church 27 June 1785

[31] Ibid – Joseph Drury received a license to perform marriages in the Baptist Church 29 September 1790

[32] Fold3.com, Revolutionary War, Virginia, p. 15 image 10942187

[33] Driver, Steve, Email message of 14 June 2013

[34] Application # 213613 for membership DAR made by Cora Hankins Dean, wife of John George Dean of Nevada, Iowa. Application Date: July 17, 1922 - Approved October 13, 1925

[35] Ibid

[36] Courtesy of Steve Driver

[37] Courtesy of Steve Driver

[38] Davis, Marie, "Davis:" A part of the collection of Clyde and Marie Davis

[39] Courtesy of Steve Driver

[40] Archives of Maryland, census 1776, Lower William and Mary Hundred, Charles County, Maryland; Brumbaugh, Gaius Marcus, Maryland Records Vol. 1, p. 309

[41] Archives of Maryland, Vol. 21, p 345

Chapter Thirteen

Maryland and Drurys in the Civil War

The State of Maryland was in a peculiar situation leading up to and during the Civil War. Neighboring Virginia and other seceding states considered Maryland a sister state and expected she would join with them in their new Confederacy. The attitude of the citizens of Maryland changed over the years leading up to the war. In 1853 a legislative committee reported,

> *"That the two races must ultimately separate, the committee do not doubt. Their separation is the only solution of the political problem to which their present existence together gives rise and there is but one place to which they can remove as a body – and that is Africa. They must get out of the way of the white man, and go where he cannot live."* [1]

But by 1860 the legislature was recommending laws to prohibit any future emancipation of slaves.[2]

Maryland was vital to the Union in several ways. The nation's capital, Washington D.C., was located in Maryland and President Lincoln was determined to prevent it from being located in a confederate state. He could not allow it to be surrounded by enemy territory and cut off from communication with the north. In addition, Baltimore, Maryland, was a major hub where three rail lines converged. The easy movement of troops and vital supplies depended on control of the city.[3]

In many ways Maryland mirrored the attitudes of the country concerning the practice of slavery. The economy of Northern and Western Maryland was more industrial and depended much less on the use of slaves. In addition much of its population had migrated from neighboring Pennsylvania and New Jersey and was opposed to slavery. Typical was the response of a German farmer's wife in the Monocacy valley, who stated when asked,

> *"I would not have a slave. No man works for another with no hope of gain for himself. I would have to spend all of my time watching to force him to do the work required. I would have to provide him with clothing and sustenance no matter how poorly he worked, and be always on the alert to prevent his escape. In consequence I would have no time for my own work."*

Southern Maryland, on the other hand, was primarily dependant on agriculture. The production of tobacco in particular was a heavily labor-intensive process. As a consequence, most southerners, including the Drury families in Southern Maryland, owned slaves, used them on their plantations, and had done so for generations. These basic attitudes were evident from the earliest years of colonization. Puritans and other religious groups who settled in New England, New York, and Pennsylvania mostly held that it was a sin to "own" or enslave another human being. These were not the prevailing ideas in England or in most of the southern colonies. The practice of indenture, where a person was bound or obligated to serve another for a period of time without compensation, was prevalent both in England and in the colonies.

As we mentioned in an earlier chapter, this was often a way for a person to obtain passage to America in exchange for agreeing to work for a certain period of time. The difference between this and an ordinary job was that during the time of indenture servants had no rights other than those granted by their master. During this time they were for all practical purposes slaves. The difference between indenture and slavery was that the servant was obliged to serve only for a definite period of time while the slave was a slave for life.

Indentured servants formed the major part of the unskilled labor force during the late 1600s in Maryland. Conditions improved in England by 1700 and the numbers of people coming to Maryland as indentured servants drastically declined. In the meantime tobacco production continued to increase. To make up for this shortage of labor, planters began to import Negro slaves from Africa. This practice continued in all the southern colonies for the next 150 years. By the time of the civil war there were almost four million slaves spread across the southern states. This division of sentiment had economic as well as cultural roots. For most southern plantation owners the value of their slaves comprised the major portion of their wealth and all of their labor force. Freeing their slaves meant ruin for many and severe hardship for the rest. It would be a major change in lifestyle for everyone.

This divided families as well as the country. Drurys in southern Maryland were completely sympathetic to the confederate states and most of them joined the confederate army and fought for the south. Those in northern Maryland had mixed feelings but many fought for the Union.

Governor Hicks of Maryland publicly told Washington officials that Maryland would remain neutral, but at the same time he privately assured the government that Maryland would supply her quota of troops for the Union Army.[4] President Lincoln, however, was taking no chances. There was considerable sentiment for the confederacy in Maryland. To prevent problems with the populace, Union troops were dispatched initially to Baltimore to quell riots there. Afterward they were to move south preventing any aid to the confederates. Maryland essentially became an occupied country with the Union army even going so far as to establish a confederate prisoner of war camp at Point Lookout.

Because of the fact that Union troops occupied almost all of Maryland during the war, she was spared the devastation suffered by much of the country. This ended in 1862 when General Robert E. Lee brought his army of Northern Virginia into Maryland. He believed that many Marylanders were sympathetic to the southern cause and might support his troops as they marched. In addition the army needed supplies. Most of the territory south of the Potomac had been stripped bare of food and his army was having trouble keeping supplied. Unfortunately this support did not materialize. His entry was in western Maryland where southern support was less prevalent to begin with. In addition, when the inhabitants saw the dirty ragged troops, tired from weeks of fighting, they were even less inclined to join them. For the most part folks either hid inside their houses or watched silently as the troops passed through.

Lee's advance was halted when a pursuing Union Army led by Major General George McClelland attacked his position at Antietam Creek near Sharpsburg, Maryland. Union forces attacked at dawn on 17 September 1862. The engagement raged off and on for the next twelve hours with neither side gaining complete victory. By the end of the day the battle of Antietam, or the battle of Sharpsburg as it was called by the Confederates, became the bloodiest single day battle in American history. Combined casualties on both sides numbered over twenty two thousand. Maryland troops were there on the Union side so it is possible that Drurys were fighting each other.

Union forces attempted to control all the states they perceived as bordering the north but were sympathetic with the south. In addition to Maryland there was also Kentucky where the Union sought to prevent confederate forces from using portions of the state as routes to move troops and supplies, and Missouri whose sentiment was evenly divided.

By the time of the Civil War in 1861, Drury families who were originally from Maryland had moved to Kentucky, Tennessee, Indiana, Illinois, Missouri, and even as far as Texas. No matter where they were when the south seceded, most of them continued supporting the southern way of life.

Two sons of Peter Drury Jr. and his wife Elizabeth from St. Mary's County in southern Maryland joined the confederate forces as musicians.[5] Charles T. Drury from Maryland also enlisted in 1862 at Richmond, Virginia in Company B 2nd battalion of the Army of Virginia. He was a drummer and was also listed on the roll as a musician. [6]

Those unfamiliar with nineteenth century warfare might mistakenly assume that as musicians, soldiers would not see much combat. Nothing could be further from the truth. In both the Union and Confederate Armies musicians were either buglers or drummers. Their job was to initiate and coordinate troop actions during battle. Buglers had a call for each command and sounded them at the direction of their officers. The drummers kept the troops coordinated and moving together. Both were always in the thick of battle.

About this same time two distant cousins, Henry and John Drury, in Washington D.C. volunteered with the Union Army. Cyrus Driver, who we think may have been related to Drury families, also enlisted as a private in Company C of the 2nd regiment of the Maryland Union infantry. [7]

Another family divided by the war was that of Brigadier General Bennett Riley whose father had fought for the Revolution. Even though he died in 1853 nine years before the start of the war, the family could not have generally supported the south. Despite this his son Edward, who was also a West Point graduate, resigned his commission when the war began and joined the Confederate Army. As a trained soldier he was very useful and eventually became a member of General Robert E. Lee's staff. After the war he returned to his home in Buffalo, New York, and is one of the two confederate Veterans buried there.

Several Drury families in Maryland migrated to the central region of the newly established Kentucky Commonwealth starting about 1790. Only a few decades later, children and grandchildren of these Maryland immigrants found themselves divided between allegiances to the Union and the Confederacy. As the Civil War broke out, the Union established its first Federal base south of the Ohio River to help ensure that Kentucky would not fall to the Confederacy. This southern base, Camp Dick Robinson, was established in Garrard County in August 1861. It was named after Captain Robinson, a Union sympathizer, who allowed the Union Army to use his farm as a Union recruitment station in 1861.[8] Camp Robinson became a recruitment location for several Drurys joining the Union Army

Camp Dick Robinson

One example of a Drury becoming engaged in the increasing political division in Kentucky is James Alexander Drury who enlisted in the Confederate Breckinridge guards in 1862. He was 39 years old. His family had owned slaves so this possibly contributed to his decision. Another reason could have been the harsh treatment of citizens in his community by the Union Army in efforts to keep Kentucky from openly joining the Confederacy.

James A. Drury 1862 [9]

155

James, with relatives Charles Girtin, Valentine Girtin (brother and cousin of his wife Mary Ann), and brother-in-law Leonard Mattingly, enlisted with Adam R. (Stovepipe) Johnson's band, then known as the Breckenridge Guards. Later, as the units' effectiveness was recognized, they were joined with the highly-regarded Confederate Cavalry raider, John Hunt Morgan. Thereafter, Breckenridge Guards came to be known as the 10th Regiment Kentucky Partisan Rangers, commanded by Colonel Adam R. Johnson. All joined Company F within a few weeks of each other, beginning with Drury and Mattingly on Aug 19, 1862, at Union County, KY. Also, serving with James, but in Company G, was Francis Sylvester, his youngest brother, then 23 years old.

James' first cousin, James Hamilton Drury, joined as a member of either Company F or Company G, depending on the source of information. After his return home at the close of the war, he was arrested, taken to Henderson, Kentucky, and tried for his life. Adam Johnson, James' commanding officer during the war, was contacted by some of his men who complained that the Yankees were attempting to charge them with stealing horses during the war. On hearing this Johnson returned to Kentucky and testified that they were enlisted men and under orders to impress horses. The cases were dismissed.

Additionally, a few days earlier, on August 15, 1862, another brother–in-law, 30 year old, Leo Joseph Braddock, joined Company F. In all, seven members of the extended family served in the same Regiment. All were the rank of Private, entitling them to monthly pay of $11, raised to $18 in June 1864. The unit saw action in Kentucky and Tennessee and acted as a guide for General John H. Morgan on his raids into Kentucky, Indiana and Ohio. According to inquiries by descendant George L. Drury, James served in the same company with Mr. Bob Lynn, then the only surviving Confederate in Union County in 1936. Veteran Lynn told Mr. Drury that he remembered James A. Drury very well, mentioning that during the war service, James had the nickname of "Penny."

An interesting sidelight is the fact that James may have been with Morgan's raiders during a raid through Perry and Morgan Counties in Ohio where Brown ancestors of later Drury descendants were living. They told stories to their descendants of being frightened and hiding when the raiders came to their farm and of how the soldiers took their supplies. They tell of living for a year on potatoes and buckwheat because there was nothing else left.

Records show that James was wounded and captured on 12 June 1864 at Cynthiana, Kentucky, and sent to Camp Chase in Columbus, Ohio, where he was held until his release 15 May 1865, a month after the end of the war. James contracted Malaria (called Ague) during the war or possibly while he was a prisoner. His pension application stated he had been shot in the arm and shoulder during the battle at Cynthiana.

We see an example of these complicated family loyalties with James' brother-in-law Leo Braddock who fought with him for the confederacy while two of Leo's cousins, Stephen and Francis, fought for the Union. Stephen died at Gettysburg, but Leo's stepbrother Charles Malone served as a Union Spy. [10]

Other Kentucky Drurys were also caught in the political strife of the time, but chose to side with the Union. These included Gordon Drury and his younger brother, Harvey "Harve."[11] Although brothers, the two had strikingly different appearances. Gordon was a blue-eyed, red-haired young man of 22 years. Harve was a dark-haired, dark-eyed teenager. They were still single and working on the family farm when the war began. Both enlisted as privates in the Union Army on the same day, 23 Sep 1861, at nearby Camp Dick Robinson. Both were assigned to Company H, 4th Kentucky Mounted Infantry.

In the fall of 1862, their regiment was stationed at Lebanon, Kentucky. Since it was close to their Washington County home, the brothers apparently decided to go absent without leave to visit the family. Both finally returned to their unit on the same day in November 1862 and were each sentenced to forfeit five dollars pay and serve additional unit duties.

As the 4th Regiment began to move south into Tennessee and Georgia, the brothers' service paths began to diverge. Harve became ill in September 1863 and apparently never returned to combat. He spent several months in a Nashville hospital before being transferred to an Army hospital in Evansville, Indiana. He was medically discharged there in March 1864.

Gordon, however, remained with his unit as they moved into the Georgia area. On July 30, 1864, he was captured near Atlanta by the Confederate forces and spent the rest of the war in prison in Georgia. Upon his release at the end of the war, Gordon was transferred to Camp Parole in Annapolis, Maryland, for processing following his imprisonment and repatriation. He was discharged apparently without any serious medical problems and with "no disability."

Other Drurys in Kentucky, while not fighting in the war, provided equally important services to both sides. Catherine Drury entered the order of Sisters of Charity of Nazareth in 1822. Her sister Anastasia followed in 1824. They were known in religion as sisters Martha and Isabelle. As the war continued, Surgeon Dr. Hewitt urged the Union commander to obtain the services of the Sisters of Charity of Nazareth. Sister Martha set up medical facilities in the old courthouse in Paducah and enlisted the services of several of her colleagues to help. They spent much of the war in Paducah, Kentucky, caring for wounded soldiers from both sides. They received many casualties from such battles as Shiloh, Fort Donaldson, Fort Henry, and Belmont. The doctors in charge praised their efforts and officials were so impressed that President Lincoln sent a personal thank you note and issued an order to the army that none of their members or anything belonging to them was to be molested or harmed in any way.[12]

Drurys in Tennessee also were active. James Drury born in 1836, a son of William Drury (1813 – 1874) and Caroline Johnson (1820 – 1902), served as a private in the Confederate Army in Company 9, second regiment, Tennessee Cavalry. He enlisted in 1861 and died in 1864. He was shot in the head at the battle of Harrisburg, Mississippi, and was buried in a mass grave near Tupelo.

Private James Drury, CSA [13]

James was no doubt enraged by the treatment of his uncle Francis Drury by Union soldiers who came through the area. Francis was a minister and Pastor of the New Harmony Baptist Church. He was no threat to anyone. The tale related to descendants was that the Union army came down Drury's Ridge and stopped at the Drury farm. The Yankee soldiers tied Francis, who was partially crippled, to a tree in the front yard while they searched the house looking for food, especially meat, as well as other valuables. When they found nothing they retaliated by setting fire to one of the upstairs bedrooms. Fortunately, after they left, the family was able to extinguish the fire and save the house. [14]

James' great aunt, Martha Drury Davis, was also an intense southerner. Her family owned slaves, and she was always used to being waited on. She had a difficult time adjusting after the war to a life without them. She was also extremely proud of the fact that her husband, Wade Hampton Davis, was related to Jefferson Davis, the president of the Confederate States of America. One of her sons fought for the Confederacy, but she felt disgraced when two grandsons, George Drury Davis and Berryman Kenchin Davis who ended the war as a major in the 43rd regiment, Missouri volunteer Infantry, joined the Union army and she never spoke to them or their families afterward. [15] They were sons of her son William Davis and his wife Sarah Elizabeth Barnes.

Texas also joined with the southern states when the confederacy was formed. As a new state it was fiercely protective of the rights the states possessed. It held, with the other southern states, that the federal government had no right to dictate whether slavery should be legal or not in the states where its citizens had approved the practice.

Harry Drury, a second generation Kentuckian and another descendant of the Maryland Drurys, was the oldest son of John D. and Elizabeth Sweeney Drury. Harry also happened to be a first-cousin of Gordon and Harve Drury mentioned earlier. At the age of 13, Harry moved with his family from Mercer County, Kentucky, to Robertson County, Texas. Little did anyone know at the time that only eight years later, Harry would be fighting along side his Texas neighbors against many of his cousins that remained in Kentucky.

Harry enlisted at age 21 in 1861 as a private in the 4th Texas Cavalry Regiment, Company K also known as the Eutaw Blues. As was customary for Confederate Cavalry volunteers, Harry provided his own horse, tack, and weapons. A military appraisal of his equipment in 1861 tells us that he had a horse ($65), tack and equipment worth $12, a gun worth $20, and a pistol worth $5.

At the beginning of the war Texas Governor Edward Clark offered the Texas militia organizations to the Confederate army. In order to do this there was a technical mustering out of all the Texas troops and then an immediate reenlistment in the Confederate army. Harry was mustered out only ten days after he enlisted but the unit was immediately designated as the 12th Texas Cavalry Regiment of the confederate Army.[16]

The Twelfth Texas Cavalry served in the Trans-Mississippi as part of Parsons' Brigade throughout the war. Although the men hoped to serve on the east side of the Mississippi River, upon reaching Memphis in May 1862, they were diverted to Little Rock to participate in stopping the Federal advance there. The regiment distinguished itself fighting Federal cavalry during Union Brig. Gen. Samuel R. Curtis' White River Expedition. The Texans' first important skirmish came at the battle of Whitney's Lane on May 19; they also fought in the battle of Cotton Plant on July 7. On August 3, the regiment took part in attacking Curtis' supply line at L'Anguille Ferry and destroyed federal property estimated at half a million dollars. Federal troopers called the Twelfth the "Swamp Fox Regiment," because the men traveled the swamps at night and often attacked Federal positions after dark.

Throughout the war the Twelfth Texas served as scouts and raiders along the west side of the Mississippi River in southeast Arkansas and northeast Louisiana. The regiment's most significant fighting came during the Red River campaign in Louisiana in the spring of 1864. As scouts and raiders, they protected East Texas from Federal soldiers and became one of the best known Texas cavalry regiments in the Trans-Mississippi Department. [17]

The Cavalry was not the only Texas unit to enlist Drurys. Henry Drury, a grandson of the Michael Drury who came to Kentucky from Rutherford County, North Carolina, was a veteran of the Blackhawk war and had moved to Lavaca County, Texas, with his family. When Texas seceded he enrolled in the Twelfth Texas Infantry.

The 12th Infantry Regiment was organized and mustered in Confederate service at Waco, Texas, during the spring of 1862. The regiment was assigned to O. Young's and Waul's Brigade, Trans-Mississippi Department, and saw action in Louisiana and Arkansas. On the afternoon of April 29, the Union forces reached Jenkins' Ferry and began crossing the Saline River, which was swollen by heavy rain. Rebel forces arrived on the 30th and attacked repeatedly. The Federals repulsed the attacks and finally crossed with all their men and supply wagons, many of which they were compelled to abandon in the swamp north of Saline. The Confederates bungled a good chance to destroy Steele's army that regrouped at Little Rock after crossing the river. Drury's prior experience evidently proved useful. We don't know exactly what experiences he had, but his actions during numerous battles helped him stay alive and kept his companions safe. This leadership ability must be why he was later discharged as a first Sergeant.

Missouri was another of the so called border states where, as in Maryland, sentiment both for and against slavery caused problems. Missouri's history during the Civil War was as split as the northern and southern states themselves. From 1861 to 1865, Missouri was torn apart by the Civil War. The conflict brought violent military battles, ruthless guerrilla warfare and a complete upheaval of the state's institutions. Many citizens of the state wanted to side with the North while others were partial to the cause of the South. [18]

Martha Drury Davis, though born in Tennessee, was living in Missouri by 1861 when the Civil war broke out. The fact that they were in Missouri may be part of the reason why two of her grandsons joined the Union army while her son joined the Confederates.

Another Union draftee we find was Clement Drury, a grandson of William Drury and Mary Ann Wootten who came to Illinois from Maryland in 1782. Records show that he was 36 years old in 1864 when he reported for duty as a private with Company C of the 21st regiment Missouri infantry. He is described as being five feet nine inches tall, with a light complexion, blue eyes and dark hair. [19]

His regiment was organized February 1, 1862, from the 1st and 2nd Northeast Regiments Missouri Infantry. It was attached to Dept. of Missouri until March 1862 then attached to the 1st Brigade, 6th Division, Army of the Tennessee. The regiment was active throughout the south during the following years. By 1864 when Clement was drafted, the regiment moved to Nashville, participating in the battle of Nashville. Later they were at Vicksburg, Mississippi, with Grant, then they were sent to New Orleans. [20]

---

[1] Radoff, Morris L., The Old Line State, A History of Maryland 1971, p.73
[2] Ibid
[3] Ibid p, 79
[4] Pollard, Edward A., The Lost Cause, 1866 p. 122
[5] William C. Drury, Private, Co. B, 1st MD Battery, CSA (Chronicles of Saint Mary's, August 1961). Civil war soldiers website - NARA - Private, Co. B 2nd Battalion, Maryland Infantry - Musician.; 1862-1865, Possibly the Charles F. Drury listed in Civil War Soldiers website (NARA) as musician Co. B 2nd Battalion Maryland Infantry.
[6] NARA, combined service records of confederate soldiers, Roll M31
[7] Ibid
[8] Kentucky Historical Society, "Print, 'Head-Quarters at Camp Dick Robinson, Near Branstsville, Kentucky,' 1861," http://www.ket.org/artstoolkit/statedivided/gallery/resources/campdick/campdick_more.pdf
[9] Courtesy of Luke Scheer Jr.
[10] Sheer, Luke J. Jr., James Alexander Drury, unpublished manuscript, 2006
[11] http://www.fold3.com/image/225293705/
[12] Archives of Sisters of Charity of Nazareth
[13] Courtesy of Steve Driver
[14] Driver, Steve, The descendants of John Drury of Macon County, Tennessee, unpublished manuscript, 2007
[15] Driver, Steve, Email of 7/27/2012
[16] Drury, Johnny B., Biography of Harry A. Drury, unpublished manuscript 2012
[17] Bailey, Anne J., "Twelfth Texas Cavalry," *Handbook of Texas Online* (http://www.tshaonline.org/handbook/online/articles/qkt12), Texas State Historical Association
[18] http://www.sos.mo.gov/mdh/civilwar/
[19] www.fold3.com/image/#231597301
[20] en.wikipedia.org/wiki/21[st]_Missouri_volunteer_infantry

Chapter Fourteen

Unplaced Drurys

Families and individuals in this chapter are believed to be part of the Maryland Drurys. Up to now unfortunately they have not been positively connected to John, to Peter, or to their uncle James Drury. In treating each family we will offer our best guess as to where they belong.

Bernard Drury (est. b. 1740)

The only source we have for Bernard is in the diary of Father A. A. Aud reported in a message from Susan Elliot, a descendant of that branch of the family. She says the diary mentions Bernard with a wife Ann as the father of Ignatius Drury, husband of Mary Magdalen Goldsborough. Mary was the d/o Jonathan Goldsborough and Monica.[1] Considering the average age at marriage of 18th century males, an estimate of Bernard's birth is about 1740 to 1745. He could be a grandson of James Drury through an as yet undocumented son or possibly a grandson of the Robert Drury who we think remained in Cecil County.

Members of this family and their relatives were devout Catholics for generations. Richard Coombs, father-in-law of Hilary Drury, Bernard's grandson, moved to Kentucky from North Carolina to be closer to a church. Ignatius and Mary were still in Georgetown as late as 1806 when the couple witnessed the will of James Fenwick.[2] After moving to Kentucky their oldest child, Margaret (1795 – 1865), entered the Convent at "Old Loretto" near St. Charles Church in Washington (later Marion) County, Kentucky, with the religious name of Sister Martina. Her niece Matilda Ann also became a Sister in the Loretto order in 1852. Three other descendants of Hilary became Priests.

Mary Drury moved her family to Kentucky after her husband died in Maryland. The family came first to the Cox's Creek Settlement in what is now Nelson County in 1808. There is no proof for the supposition that Ignatius had something to do with boat traffic on the Potomac River. However Ignatius did seem to be associated with James Fenwick and his partner John Mason who were in the business of shipping goods between America and England. In 1809 Mary petitioned the court to allow her to sell Ignatius' boat to pay bills and provide for her children.[3]

Some time after the move to Kentucky Mary's only son Hilary bought a farm near the site of St. Lawrence Church in Daviess County and moved there about 1830. Hilary and his wife Theresa took his mother Mary to live with them. The new farm was about 70 miles northwest of Cox's Creek, a considerable distance from all his friends and acquaintances. One fact that might have influenced him was that Leonard Knott, who married his sister Mary, had also moved to this area. He would at least have some family nearby.

His marriage to Theresa Coombs was in 1825, and their first three children were born at Cox's Creek. The eldest, Matilda, entered the convent at Loretto in 1852. When she died on 12 Feb 1911 at age 84, her youngest brother Edwin, then chaplain for the Sisters of Loretto, performed the Funeral services. Eliza Jane, their second child, was born probably sometime in 1828. We estimate her marriage to J. Hardy Clements to have been about 1848 or a bit later. The third child, Ignatius Guy, never married and became a Doctor after graduating at the Medical University of Louisville, Ky. He set up practice at Knottsville in 1862 and remained there until his death 4 Sep 1902. The remaining six children married and raised their families in Kentucky. One grandson Celestine Bray, son of Theresa Rose Drury and James William Bray, also became a priest. He was ordained to Priesthood 21 July 1895. He was pastor of St. Rose Church, Cloverport, Ky. for 15 years and then pastor of Holy Cross Church, Louisville, Kentucky. He died 6 Oct 1920. Father Bray is the one who collected much of this data.[4]

We have quite a bit more about Hilary's youngest son, Edwin.

"DRURY, FATHER EDWIN, Father Drury's ancestors were among the Catholic settlers of Maryland in the 17th century. His father, Hilary Drury was born in Maryland in 1799, and came to Kentucky in 1808. (Sister Jamesetta, our present school principal, also traces her ancestry back to Hilary.) Father Drury's mother, Teresa Coomes, was born in Kentucky on Sept. 7, 1797.

Father Drury was born on June 16, 1845, in St. Lawrence Parish, Daviess County, KY. At an early age he entered old St. Thomas Seminary, near Bardstown, and completed his course at Preston Park Seminary (now Bellarmine College campus) in Louisville.

Ordained a priest on June 21, 1872, at the cathedral in Louisville. Father Drury assisted at his home parish until the fall of that year (1872), when he became pastor of St. Francis Xavier Church, Raywick. In the spring of 1874, he bought three acres of land about four miles from Finley and built St. Matthew's station in lower Marion County. In 1907, when the church at Finley was built, the station was closed and only a small cemetery remains to mark the site of St. Matthew's.

On Nov. 11, 1874, Father Drury was appointed second resident pastor of St. Francis of Assisi Church at Chicago (St. Francis), KY. In 1880 he built the first parochial school. In June of 1885 ill health forced Father Drury to resign his pastorate. Upon recovery in late 1886 he became pastor of the Pewee Valley missions, which post he held until his health failed again in 1894. In the fall of 1897 he accepted lighter duties as chaplain at St. Thomas Orphanage, then located in Bardstown, and began giving missions in Peoria, IL. from August 1898 to August 1899 when he began his mission preaching throughout the Diocese of Louisville.

On March 23, 1906, Father Drury was appointed chaplain at the Loretto Motherhouse, Loretto, KY, which office he held until his death at St. Joseph Infirmary (Fourth Street location) on Feb. 2, 1913. He was buried in the Motherhouse Cemetery." [5]

Hilary had two other sisters who married and raised families. Monica married Thomas S. Montgomery and bore him four sons. She moved with her husband to Randolph County Illinois sometime before 1849 and remained there for the rest of her life. Mary Margaret married Leonard Knott and remained in Kentucky. Leonard also moved to Daviess Co. where the village and Precinct of Knottsville was named for him. He was the son of James Knott, a native of Maryland and a pioneer of Nelson County. He came to Daviess County in 1826, and was the first settler in what is now the Village of Knottsville. He first lived one year in a small cabin on the Whitesville Road, and built in Knottsville in 1827. [6]

Zachariah Drury (est. b. 1773)

Zachariah Drury first appears in Kentucky in 1791 on the tax list for Nelson County.[7] He is the earliest documented Drury from Maryland to appear there. He married Mary Jane Molohon, the daughter of James Molohon and Susanna Parsons, on January 12 1797.[8] We can assume with confidence that he was connected with the Maryland Drurys since his bride and her family were originally from Charles County, Maryland. Speculation here gives us several possibilities. His birth in 1773 estimated from the Marion County, Kentucky, census of 1850,[9] places him as a possible third child of Philip and Emerentia "Ann" Drury. However recent findings suggest that Philip's third child could also possibly be Benedict Drury who married Mary Simms in 1810. This is based on land records showing that Benedict had some association with "Dry Docking Addition," part of the original Drury lands in St. Mary's County.[10] Either Zachariah or Benedict would fit there, so neither can be positively placed as Philip's son.

There is also a mention in a letter by William Rodman, 2nd great grandson of Anastasia French Drury, to his brother of a Zachariah Drury who was allegedly a son of Ignatius Drury prior to his marriage to Anastasia French. Unfortunately we have no independent confirmation of such an event. If true this would make Zachariah a bit older than we previously had estimated raising the possibility that his marriage to Mary Jane Molohon could have been a second marriage.[11]

In addition, the following Drurys could be his parents though nothing to date has been established.

Robert Drury (b. by 1733) and Mary Margaret (b. bef 1754). They had no children recorded after 1772.
Nicholas Drury (b. 1738 - d. by 1789) and Monica (b. 1738/1743 – d. aft 1790). Their last recorded child was born in 1772
Enoch Drury Jr. (m. 1770) and Tabitha Graves. Their only recorded child is in 1771.
James Drury Jr. (m. bef 1771) and Sarah had no children recorded between 1771 and 1774
Peter Drury (b. 1740) and Eleanor (m. bef 1771). Their only recorded child was in 1776.
John Baptist Drury (b. aft 1744) and Mary Margaret, Their last recorded child was in 1770.

Richard Drury (m. bef 1770) and Elizabeth. There is a gap in children between 1771 and 1786.

Between their marriage in 1797 and Zachariah's death in 1855 the couple had eight known children, the youngest being Isadore born about 1815. There were probably more that we have not identified.

Michael Drury (ca. 1757)

In originally researching this family there was confusion over the number of men named Michael Drury who had not been positively identified at that time. We start here with Michael Drury (b. ca. 1757). He had two sons, Michael Jr. (b. abt 1778), and John (b. 1796). Michael and his sons came to Kentucky from Rutherford County, North Carolina.[12] Michael Jr. married Susanna Guffey (nicknamed Suckey) in 1799 and had a son, Henry (b. 1800), and a daughter, Mary. After the move to Kentucky, his brother John married Teresa (Treacy) Yates, a daughter of Zachariah Yates and Ann Hayden.[13] Timothy O'Rourke in private communications before his death believed that this family migrated to Carolina from Maryland.

These dates and places eliminate two of the confusing Michaels. These were Michael (s/o) Peter (est. 1736) and his son Michael Jr. (b. 1785). Not only are the dates different, these two men remained in Maryland their entire lives.

Henry (1800 – 1875) married Susanna David (b. 1807) on 8 February 1827 in Washington County, Kentucky, by whom he had 6 children. Henry married second Helen Layton (1829 – 1876) on 16 January 1838 by whom he fathered another eight sons and three daughters. After his second marriage he moved his family to Perry County, Missouri. In 1846 he was confirmed at St. Mary of the Barrens Church in Perry County, Missouri, along with his wife.[14] He took part in the Blackhawk War and by 1853 had moved to Lavaca County, Texas. When the Civil War erupted he enrolled in the 12th Texas Infantry and was later discharged as a First Sergeant. He died in Lavaca County, Texas, at the age of 75. Henry's sister Mary married Charles Vessells on 23 March 1820.

Thomas Theodore Drury (1818)

Thomas' ancestry is a mystery. According to Barnes he married in Ann Arundle[sic] County in central Maryland, yet his life seems to be centered in the town of Ridge in southern St. Mary's County. The marriage notice was printed in the Baltimore Sun, but it does not state where the marriage took place nor where Reverend Lipscomb was located.[15] It is possible they were married in St. Mary's county, but we have no positive proof for either location. He lived and was buried at his plantation called "Portnoy's Oversight" near Ridge.

Portnoy's Oversight

He married Martha Ann Lydaman d/o Andrew Lydaman and "William" Thomas.[16] This raises a question as to _____ Thomas' given name but that is exactly how it was given in the reference cited by Judith Burger. Additional research has discovered that Martha was a daughter of Andrew and his second wife Brittana Thompson.[17] The Lydamans were also from St. Inigoes district in southern St. Mary's County. I have no idea at present of who would be a likely set of parents for Thomas. I suspect that there is at least a generation between Thomas and any of the people we cover in other chapters.

Thomas was a farmer but he also had other interests. He was appointed postmaster of Ridge, Maryland, on 17 Apr 1848.[18] By 1850 the census listed him as a merchant with a small child.[19] He was listed as Constable in the 1870 Census but died by the end of that year. He was 52 years old.[20] [21] [22] [23]

Thomas' son George married Georgeanna Victoria Raley in 1880. Her parents were James Raley (1817- 1875) and Mary Elizabeth Taylor (1836 – 1898). They had ten children between 1883 and 1904. Their daughter Georgia (b. 14 Oct. 1897) died 8 months later in June of 1898. The rest lived long lives.

George also had two older sisters. Elizabeth Indiana Drury was born about 1848 and married William C. Foxwell on 16 February 1871. Her sister Mary Virginia was born about 1852. She is mentioned in her mother's will as Mary Nerderman so her marriage took place before 1889.

Ignatius Drury

There was an Ignatius Drury who married Mary Tenny (some think Taney) in 1800.[24] There is a definite connection here to the St. Mary's County Drurys as shown by the

165

names of the witnesses to their marriage. These witnesses can definitely be linked to St. Mary's County. Some have suggested that this Ignatius was the same son of Ignatius Drury and Anastasia French who later appears in Kentucky about 1810.

Elizabeth Drury (b. bef. 1758)

Elizabeth Drury married Jeremy Gatton in St. Mary's County on 2/14/1773.[25] Assuming she did not marry before the age of 15, we can estimate her birth as not later than 1758. Similarly, Jeremy's birth can be estimated as sometime not later than the early 1750s assuming he was "of age" when he married. Other Gatton family members in addition to Jeremy (Jeremiah) named in 1794 were Thomas, Nicholas, Elizabeth, Mary, Ann, Nancy, and Anastasia. I assume, though without proof, that the Elizabeth in 1794 is Elizabeth Drury Gatton and that at least some of the other Gatton individuals listed are her children.[26] One connection that could be suggested is that she was a daughter of John Drury and Susanna Hayden. Her assumed age is consistent with this assumption. The birth dates of their other children do not conflict, and her marriage at Newtown suggests a residence somewhere in or near Beaverdam Manor where John and Susanna were living. Until more proof is discovered this can only be speculation.

Ignatius Drury (legislator) and William C. Drury

There was also another Ignatius Drury in Washington County, MD. He was a member of the Maryland State Legislature/House of Delegates in 1822 and was a proponent of the "Jew Law" that was being debated. This proposal would give Jews the right to hold office and serve on juries. It was quite controversial at the time.[27]

Ignatius died in Washington County between October of 1824 and August of 1825.

DIED,
On Thursday evening last, at his residence in this county, after a short illness, *Ignatius Drury*, Esq. in the 36th year of his age. The deceased was one of the Delegates from Washington county in the Legislature of Maryland during the session 1822-3; and through life sustained the character of an honest man.
On Friday last, at her residence in this place, after a protracted illness, Miss *Eleanora M'Dannell*.

He had been serving as the administrator of the estate of Benjamin Brown in Washington County, but by 2 August 1825, William C. Drury had assumed administration of this estate. William C. Drury and Ignatius Drury were probably related because of the fact that it was only a few months at most after Ignatius died that we have William taking over these duties. How else would the Brown relatives get another person (and a Drury at that) to take over.

In 1812 Ignatius Drury was Captain in the 10th regiment in Washington County. William Drury was an Ensign in that same regiment. Ignatius became guardian for the heirs of John Lefever on 26 Feb 1817 with one Enoch Drury standing security. On 14 Feb 1824 William Drury stands security for John Haney for the heirs of John Ragan. On 30 Mar 1824 William Drury becomes the guardian of the Ragan children (Shirley, Ignatius, George, Marian, Elizabeth, and Joseph) with Ignatius Drury standing security, and on 4 Apr 1826 (several months after Ignatius died) William becomes guardian to Mariah, Henry, John, Samuel, and Isaac Lefever. I do not think all of this was coincidence. There had to be a close connection.

William Drury

Connections for this William Drury are a complete mystery. His marriage is documented in a database on *Ancestry.com*.[28] His wife is listed there as Ann West with no additional data other than the marriage date of 5 April 1795. Census data has him listed by 1810 still living in the area around Beaverdam Manor with two children.[29]

What follows here is complete speculation with nothing to support it other than possible coincidences. I wonder if this could be the William Drury who was corresponding with George Fenwick in 1811 concerning management of Fenwick's Swamp Island plantation. Census data in 1800 lists John and Stephen Raley, Joseph Stone Sr. and William Stone, Michael Heard, Sary Peacock, who was probably the mother of Jane Drury's husband Zachariah Peacock, Thomas Thompson, and Ignatius Joy as close neighbors. These are all families who have associations and connections with the Drurys. The letter in 1811 mentions that William has two children. So does the 1810 census. The 1810 census also lists one female over 45. We have been assuming that the William who wrote the letter was possibly a son of Philip and Ann Newton. We also have no idea what happened to Ann after Philip died in 1795. The assumption was always that she moved in with Bernard and his family. But what if she decided that a move to Kentucky was not for her. When Bernard left she could have moved in with another son. The problems here are the dates. If William was a son of Philip he could not have been born earlier than 1780. This would make him 15 years old when he married. This would have been highly unusual. How could he support himself and a wife at such a young age? The William Drury of the letter could still be a son of Philip, but he could not be the one here who married Ann West.

Tecla Joy

Tecla Joy wrote her will in 1796 after an apparently long and fruitful life.[30] Her name was spelled as "Teachlea" in her Will. Some say she was born Tecla Drury though obviously we have no idea who her parents were. Her will names Jane Drury as a sister. This is why she is assumed to be a Drury. If this is true then a possible set of parents would be John Drury and Mary Ford.

167

A second possibility not generally considered is that Jane was married to a Drury and was either a spouse or a widow. In that case there would be no way to identify parents of either of them. The will does mention Catherine Joy and a grandson Thomas Joy. We can assume, again without proof, that Catherine was either a daughter or a sister-in-law and that Thomas was Catherine's son.

Jane Drury

There are two other females named Jane Drury who are unable to be connected positively to any of the currently researched Drury families. One is Jane M. Drury who was born in 1822 possibly to Enoch Drury and his second wife Eleanor Joy who married in 1816.[31] Jane married John B. Raley as her second husband and his third wife in 1856. John was born about 1803 in St. Mary's County. He lived on a farm called "The Vineyard"[32] until his death in 1879.

The other is an older Jane Drury who married Zachariah Peacock as his second wife in 1804. One possibility here is that she is the daughter of Philip Drury born in 1777. The Hodges card file lists the name as Joan. As mentioned earlier some researchers have interpreted this as an abbreviated Joannes, the latinized form of John. The names Jane and Joan are close enough in spelling and pronunciation to be easily confused.

Isaac Drewry

In 1674 a list of passengers on board the "Constant Friendship" whose master was William Wheatly, included one Isaac Drewry.[33] Then a warrant was issued in the name of the said William Wheatly for two thousand one hundred and fifty acres of land due to him for transporting the above mentioned passengers into the province to inhabit. The certificate was returnable October 9, next January 12, 1674.[34] Isaac was transported in 1674. [35]

Enoch Drury (1791 – aft 1833)

We know very little about this Enoch Drury. His birth is calculated from an assumed age of 21 when he married Lucy Greenwell in 1812. His birth therefore had to be at least in 1791 or earlier. There were only two other Enoch Drurys in St. Mary's county in that time period. Enoch Drury who married Tabitha Wimsatt died in 1784, and his son Enoch had already married Mary Brewer in 1807. There was another Enoch Drury in Washington D.C. about 1825 but there is no way at present of knowing if they were the same person.

There is no available record to show what happened to Lucy Greenwell Drury, but she had to have died sometime between 1812 when they married and 1815 When Enoch married for the second time to Eleanor Joy a daughter of Ignatius Joy and Dorothy Booth. We know of no children born of this first marriage. Enoch and Eleanor had at least two daughters though proof for this is not solid. They were Jane M. Drury born 31 December 1822 and Susan Drury in 1825.

Jane married John Radford Junior a son of John Radford and Monica French on July 26, 1850.[36] Unfortunately the marriage did not last long. Her husband apparently died before she could give him a child and she remarried to John B. Raley a son of Zachariah Raley and Ann Wilkinson by 1856. Their first child was born in 1857.

[1] *Johnathan Goldsborough Will Abstract, Montgomery County, Maryland 1776 – 1825* - Mary G. Malloy, Jane C. Sweeny, and Janet D. Manuel, Family Line Publications, Westminster, Maryland 1977 p 56; Will mentions daughter Mary Drury; Executor is Ignatius Drury

[2] King, Jackie, *Will of James Fenwick*, Electronic

[3] 6/1809: Mary Drury was granted letters of admin on the estate of Ignatius Drury (Orphan's Court rec Fenwick); 6/1811: Mary Drury admx of Ignatius Drury to sell his vessel and other property for payment of debts (Orphan's Court rec Fenwick)

[4] Bray, Celestine RCP, *Coombs Family from Holy Cross Church* pp 5,6; also Stewart, Dorothy Brown, *Once Upon a Time* pp 154,155

[5] *History of Daviess County, Kentucky*, Interstate Pub. Co. Chicago reprinted by McDowell Pub. Utica, Kentucky 1980 p 620

[6] Op Cit

[7] Ftp//ftp.rootsweb.com/pub/usgenweb/ky/nelson/taxlists/taxes/nelson2.txt, Tax List: *Nelson County Tithes 1785 – 1791, Nelson Co. Ky.*

[8] A copy of Jane and Zachariah's marriage license with James Molohon's (Mollihorne) signature is available on *microfilm Roll 986767* at the Kentucky State Archives in Frankfort, Ky. Bk 111-17; see also Kingdon, Margaret Clark *Washington County Kentucky Marriage Records 1790 – 1878*, p 51

[9] 1850 Census, Marion County Kentucky, image 61

[10] *Chronicles of St. Mary's Vol. 7* p 171, Benedict Drury, Sale of Dryarkins addition and other properties to John Raley (of Gabriel) 3/3/1814

[11] Letter quoted in *History of Roman Catholic Diocese of Owensboro Kentucky*, p 269

[12] Jean Ward <jward@tca.net> Electronic

[13] Thompson, Gerald, *Kentucky Catholic Pioneers: The Rolling Fork Settlement Vol. 1*, McDowell Pub., Utica Ky. 1977

[14] Obrist, Patricia Bishop, Priest's notes, 1846 census St. Mary of the Barrens in Perry County, Missouri

[15] *Baltimore Sun 28 November 1846*, Marriage Notice, Married on 26th inst by Rev R. M. Lipscomb, Thomas T. Drury to Martha A. Lydaman all of St. Mary's County

[16] Andrew Lydaman Will, Liber: gc#2 Folio: 179 ; 8/5/1844, Probate: 1/28/1846

[17] Marsha Barton, <mbb_dcmarva@yahoo.com> electronic

[18] Hammett, Regina Combs, *A History of St. Mary's County, Maryland*

[19] Courtesy of Tom Jennings, *1850 Census 2nd district St. Mary's County 13 Sep 1850*

[20] Will of Thomas T. Drury, Signed: April 1 1870, Proved: November 8, 1870. Liber J.T.M.R. No. 1 p. 287
Last Will & Testament Of Thomas T. Drury
In the name of God Amen.I Thomas Theodore Drury of St. Mary's County in the State of Maryland, being in bad health but of sound and disposing mind memory and understanding, and considering the certainty of death, and the uncertainty of the time thereof, and being desirous to settle my worldly affairs and thereby be the prepared to leave this world when it shall please God to call one hence, do therefore make and publish this my last will and testament, in manner and form following that is to say First and principally I commit my soul into the hands of Almighty-God, and my body to the earth to be decently buried at the discretion of my Executor hereafter named and after my debts and funeral charges are paid I devise and bequeath as follows.
It is my wish and desire that my dear wife Marthay A. Drury shall have my entire estate during her single life after my debts are paid. After the death or marriage of my wife Martha A. Drury it is my wish and desire that my estate Real & personal shall be sold and equally divided between my three children, Elizabeth Indiania Drury and Mary Virginia Drury and George W. Drury and lastly it is my wish and desire that my wife Marthy A Drury and William C Foxwell shall be my administrators.
   Witness my hand and seal April 1st 1870
Test   T. T. Drury (((Seal)))
A.C. Tennisson
Geo. H. Cullison

St. Mary's County to wit: The 8th day of November 1870. The last will and testament of T. T. Drury late of St. Mary's County deceased, being this day presented to the Orphan's Court for probate and no objections being made or caveat filed against the said last will and testament the Orphan's Court for St. Mary's County ordered the same to be put to probate recording to law.

Certified by

J. T. M. Raley Reg. of Wills

For St. Mary's County

St. Mary's County

On the 8th day of November 1870 came A. C. Tennisson & Geo. H. Cullison subscribing witnesses to the aforegoing last Will and Testament of Thomas T. Drury late of Said County, deceased, and made oath on the Holy Evangels of Almighty God, That they did see the Testator sign and seal this Will: that they heard him publish, pronounce and declare the same to be his last Will and Testament, that at the time of his so doing he was, to the best of their apprehension, of sound and disposing mind, memory and understanding and that they subscribed their names as witnesses to the Will in his presence, at his request, and in the presence of each other

Sworn to in open Court

Test   J. T. M. Raley   Register of Wills for St. Mary's County

[21] Burger, Judith A., *Register of Wills, St. Mary's County, Maryland JTMR 1 277-278*

[22] Will of Martha A. Drury, Signed: April 30, 1889, Proved: June 3, 1889, Liber J.B.A. No. 1 p.194

Last will and testament of Martha A. Drury

I, Martha A. Drury of St. Mary's County, being of sound and disposing mind and memory, do hereby make and publish this as and for my last will and testament.

I give, devise and bequeath to my beloved son George W. Drury all of my estate, real, personal and mixed, to him and his assigns forever, provided he pays unto my daughter Mary Virginia Nerderman, two hundred dollars two years after my death without interest.

I will and bequeath to my son in law William Forwell (Foxwell) one dollar, to be paid to him by my son George W. Drury.

As witness my hand and seal, this thirty (30th) day of April eighteen hundred and eighty-nine. (1889)

M. A. Drury

Signed sealed, published and declared by Martha _____ Drury, the above named testatrix as and for her last will and testament, in the presence of us who at her request, in her presence and in the presence of each other, have hereunto subscribed our names as witness.

S. Clarke

R. M. Edwards   J. H. Miles

St. Mary's Co. S.S. ~~~~

On the 3rd day of June 1889 came S. Clarke and James H. Miles, two of the three subscribing witnesses to the aforegoing last will and testament of M. A. Drury, late of Said county, deceased; and made oath on the Holy Evangels of almighty God: that they did see the Testator sign and seal this will; that they heard her publish pronounce and declare the same to be her last will and testament, that at the time of her so doing she was, to the best of their apprehension of sound and disposing mind, memory and understanding; and that, they, together with R. M. Edwards, subscribed their names as witnesses to this Will in her presence, at her request, and in the presence of each other.

Sworn to in open Court. Test

James T. M. Raley, Reg Of Wills for St. Mary's Co. Filed June 3rd, 1889.

[23] Burger, Judith A., *Register of Wills, St. Mary's County, Maryland JBA 1 194-195* Note: The name of the son-in-law Forwell may be Foxwell but if so the x is not crossed

[24] Trinity Church – Georgetown DAR Vol. 47, *Trinity Church Marriage and baptism Records 1795-1805*, April 26, 1800, Married with license Ignatius Drury and Mary Tenny (some think Taney) before the underwritten witnesses: Elizabeth Clark, Leonard Goler.

[25] O'Rourke, Timothy, *Catholic Families of Southern Maryland* – p 34

[26] O'Rourke, Timothy, *Catholic Families of Southern Maryland* – p 99 Communicants at Easter time at St. Inigoes

[27] Papenfuse, Edward C. et. Al., *Archives of Maryland, Historical list Vol. 1*, Annapolis, Maryland; Maryland State Archives, 1990

[28] Dodd, Jordan, Liahona Research, comp. Maryland Marriages, 1655-1850 [database on-line]. Provo, UT, USA: Ancestry.com

[29] 1800 census; 1810 census

[30] St. Mary's County Will books 1791-1805 Vol. JJ2: 161,162

[31] Reno, Linda, Email of 10/1/2007

[32] Dobricky, John, Email of 2/12/2003

[33] The rights due for transportation of the forty three persons mentioned in the list were proved by "Captain William Wheatly before me this ninth day of July 1674",signed Charles Calvert.

[34] MDHR Land office patents, vol. 18, 11, 17, 1-23-1-23, 160

[35] Skordas, liber 18, folio 160

[36] "Maryland Records, Vol. 1, Marriage Licenses of St. Mary's County, Md. 1794-1864, pg. 385", Jane M. Drury & John F. Radford, Jr. Marriage License 7/26/1850.

170

Chapter Fifteen

Collateral Lines

Bowles

George Bowles was born in England, the son of Valentine Bowles. He settled in St. Mary's County, Maryland. According to the will of George Plater, George Bowles was a tenant of his, residing in St. Mary's County on 234 acres of "Hazzard". He married Lillias Watson, who was born in Scotland. They are presumed to be the parents of John Bowles, William Bowles, and Elizabeth Bowles of St. Mary's County. It is known George Bowles had children, some of whom pre-deceased him. George Bowles was named the only heir of his brother John Bowles of Kent County, when he died in 1752, "if he had any heirs still living".[1] Our line continues with their son William who married Elizabeth Gough and died before 1743.[2] John Bowles, son of William and Elizabeth, was born before 1730 and died before 1790.[3]

Donnelly tells us in *Colonial Settlers St. Clements's Bay 1634 – 1780* that "John Bowles married Monica Wootten, a daughter of an unknown Wootten father and his wife Elizabeth whose maiden name was also unknown.[4] For years this statement created the impression that Monica's maiden name was Wootten. Unfortunately this is not correct. The administrative accounts of Charles Daft in 1731 names Monica Daft as a daughter. This account was administered by Isaac Booth and his wife Elizabeth, the widow of Charles Daft.[5] Then in 1756 Elizabeth Booth wrote her will and named Monica Boalds as a legatee.[6] This Will also names a daughter Elizabeth Wootten. This leads us to believe that Elizabeth Spink who had married Charles Daft and later Isaac Booth had also been married at some time prior to 1756 to a Wootten. These documents provide clear proof that the wife of John Bowles was Monica Daft and not Monica Wootten.

Now we begin to approach the connection to our Drurys. John Bowles and Monica Daft had a son, John Baptist Bowles, in 1762. He died in Scott County, Kentucky, in 1819. He married Henrietta Wheatley in Maryland before 1788. But here again we have confusion about Henrietta's maiden name. Some say she was Mary Henrietta Wheatley, a daughter of James Wheatley and Henrietta Norris. But Connie Riley, a descendant, has posted a letter from someone she calls "Sister Mary B" claiming that Henrietta was Henrietta Perkins and listing all their children. The reference states that Mary Jane O'Nan (daughter of Dennis O'Nan and Clarissa Bowles, one of J.B's daughters) stated that her grandmother was Henrietta Perkins and her grandfather was John B. Bowles. The list of children named in the letter is identical to lists derived from other sources. No additional data has surfaced to confirm either assertion. Henrietta evidently died between 1807 when her youngest child, Cecelia, was born and 1819 when her husband John remarried to Sarah Bickett. Cecelia married James Wimsatt Drury in 1825. He was a son of Bernard Drury and Catherine Wimsatt, a daughter of Robert Wimsatt and Dorothy Abell.

Newton

The Newton family has connections to Drurys in both Maryland and Virginia. Newtons were well to do with extensive property both in England and America. According to his will in 1695 John Newton owned large estates in Westmoreland County, Virginia, as well as property in Hull, England and his Carleton and Campbellforth estates in Yorkshire. John Newton, the original immigrant, was born about 1639 at Carleton Manor, Kingston on Hull, Yorkshire. He went first to Maryland about 1660 and then to Virginia by 1672.[7] He married Rose Sturman before 1777. At that time he was referred to as John Newton of Maryland.[8] John apparently was a master mariner but had several large grants of land in Westmoreland and King George Counties. Rose was his fourth wife but the first in America. She was born in England about 1629 and died about 1712/3 in Virginia. Her son, Captain Thomas Newton, inherited all of her property in both Maryland and Virginia.[9]

Captain Thomas Newton (1678 – 1728) lived and died in Westmoreland County. He married twice, first to Elizabeth Allerton, a daughter of Isaac Allerton and Elizabeth Willoughby. She was born and died before 1702. His second wife was Elizabeth Storke, daughter of Nemiah Storke and Betheland Gilson.

They were married in 1702 and had a son, Thomas (1702-1741) shortly thereafter.[10] The given name of Thomas' wife was Katherine though we do not know her maiden name. Thomas had at least two sons, Thomas and Clement. Clement, who died in 1760[11] was living on a plantation called Newton's Rest.[12] A number of his children are mentioned elsewhere and help us to identify connections and relationships between this family and our Drurys.

The most direct relationship comes through the marriage of one of his daughters to Philip Drury in 1770. Philip always referred to his wife as Ann. Researchers over the years have listed her given name variously as Bibianna, or Emerentia, or both. Clement's Will mentions four daughters. It lists Ann, Mary, Bibianna, and Immaranchaner that a number of people have interpreted as creative spelling for Emerentia. All three of the names proposed as Philip's wife are given as legatees in Clement's will of 1770. We know one of them was his wife but not exactly which one. Was it Ann, or Bibianna, or Emerentia?

Yates

The Yates family has several connections to the Drurys in several generations. John Yates was the original immigrant who arrived before 1695. His son Martin, who married Elizabeth Dabridgecourt that year, was born in England about 1666 and died in St. Mary's County, Maryland, in 1724.[13] Martin's son Thomas was born in 1703 and died in 1770. Thomas married Mary French a daughter of John French and Monica whose maiden name is not known. Their daughter Ann married Michael Drury, a son of Peter Drury and Jane Bailey in 1770. This provides our first link between the families.

Another son, Martin (1700 – 1775), had a granddaughter Ann (Anna) Yates who married Francis Desales Drury as her second husband 15 October 1799. He was a son of John Drury (1739 – 1797) and an unknown spouse. Ann had previously been married to James Thompson.

Finally, Ann's younger brother Zachariah (b, 1760) had a daughter Teresa who married another Michael Drury in Kentucky. They married in 1817. This Michael has not been connected to the Maryland Drurys though some connection is thought to exist. He came to Kentucky from Rutherford County, North Carolina.

Wigginton

The Wigginton families of northern Virginia that eventually become associated with Joseph Drury first appear in the mid seventeenth century with William Wigginton who died by 1732.[14] He lived in that part of Stafford County that eventually became Prince William County. One source, Stafford County Tithables (1723-1790), on page 136 lists a William Wigginton on Augustine's run in 1728/9. Consulting a map of this area shows that the run enters Aquia Creek through Government Island that was previously known as Wigginton Island. This land might possibly be the 124 acres of marshland patented in 1730[15] by William's brother Henry Wigginton and surveyed by John Warner.[16]

William and his wife (probably an O'Neal) had at least three sons and three daughters. His son William apparently died before he did. His son Henry (1690-1736) is credited with being the progenitor of the Stafford line of Wigginton. A third son, John (hereafter called John I) is believed to be the originator of the Prince William line who appears on the Brent Town map in Chapter twelve as dwelling twenty four.[17] His sister Ann Wigginton Mason Butler also lives nearby. By 1770 John I has died and his son John (now John II) occupies this property. John II married Elizabeth Farrow a daughter of Abraham Farrow and Sybil Whitledge. Joseph Drury also had property in the Brent Town area not far from the Wigginton plantation. Joseph married John's daughter Sybil Wigginton in 1776 and was closely associated with the Wigginton family. Interestingly, Joseph's wife Sybil had a great uncle William Farrow who had a daughter Ann Farrow who married Samuel Wells. Their Wells descendants connect with Drurys in Missouri in the middle of the nineteenth century.

Wheatley

John Wheatley, one of the first of that name, arrived in St. Mary's County, Maryland, about 1641.[18] By 1648 we find him on what became Batchelor's Comfort, one of half a dozen properties he acquired in St. Mary's County.[19] According to his will[20] he married Elizabeth whose maiden name is unknown. They had nine known children between 1688 and 1704. Their fourth child, Joseph (1694-1739)[21] provides the next step in our journey toward a Drury connection. His widow Martha administered his will though the reported date is confusing. He wrote his will on 15 October 1739. According to Mary Donnelly in *Colonial Settlers, St. Clement's Bay*[22] his widow administered the estate on 17 March

1739. I believe this was probably a printing error when the book was printed. It probably should have been shown as 17 March 1739/40. The three month overlap between the old and new style calendar would account for this seeming impossibility. In other words, Joseph wrote his will in October of 1739. He evidently died shortly thereafter and his wife administered the estate the following spring.

Wheatleys and Drurys have a definite connection through the marriage of Henrietta Wheatley to John Baptist Bowles who were the parents of Cecelia Bowles who married James Wimsatt Drury in 1825. Our problem is that we do not know exactly how Henrietta is connected to the rest of her family. The confusion arises because verifiable source information about Henrietta and her ancestry has not been found up to now. Extensive searching has found no Wheatley with a first given name of Henrietta. This leads to the supposition that Henrietta may be a middle name. Others think she may have been a widow when she married John Bowles. However no likely marriage has been discovered. The closest we can come at present is to say that she was Mary Henrietta Wheatley, a daughter of James Wheatley and Henrietta Norris. James was a son of Joseph and Martha. Others, as we said earlier in discussing the Bowles family, think that her maiden name was never Wheatley, but no proof exists for any of them.

Wimsatt

The Wimsatts and the Drurys were close neighbors in Beaverdam Manor in the mid eighteenth century. Philip Drury was living on "Flower of the Forest" and his neighbor Robert Wimsatt owned "Satisfaction." Both plantations were originally parts of a larger property named "Wimsatt's Frolic."[23] Their children grew up knowing each other and attending the same church so it seems natural that Philip's son Barnard and Robert's daughter Catherine should eventually marry as they did in 1797.[24]

Wimsatts probably arrived in Maryland from their native Wales sometime in the early seventeen hundreds. There was a Richard Wimsatt who died in St. Mary's County by 28 October 1725. He and his wife Sarah had presumed sons Richard and John.[25] Their son Richard was born before 1705 in Wales. He married Teresa Ford about 1729. She was a daughter of Robert Ford and Margaret Bailey.

Their oldest son, Robert, was born in 1732. He took the oath of fidelity during the revolution and was a member of the Maryland Militia.[26] He died in 1794.[27] He married Dorothy Abell about 1762.[28] She was the daughter of Samuel Abell and Eleanor Bryan. Robert grew up in the Roman Catholic tradition and was a member of a Catholic parish. His wife, Dorothy, probably went along because a wife in those times obeyed her husband's wishes. She would have been familiar with religious tension growing up in a household where her father was Anglican and her mother was Catholic.

One well documented example was an incident when Samuel took his son Philip to swear the oath of office to be a county official. Philip embarrassed his father by refusing to take the oath because it was against his religion. Samuel accused his wife of going against his wishes and instructing Philip in the Catholic faith. She replied that, as a dutiful wife, she had never disobeyed him or gone against his wishes, but she had prayed to God that Philip would accept the teachings of her church.

Hayden

The Haydens and Drurys had similar reasons for coming to America. Their support of the Monarchy during the English Civil War caused the loss of their ancestral lands. As Catholics they also suffered persecution because they refused to renounce their Catholic faith and accept the Church of England.

Francis Hayden was born in 1628. He grew up during the war and lost much of his fortune and privilege. He is assumed to be the immigrant to Maryland because no records have been found for him (as of about ten years ago) in English Court or Provincial records.[29] The fifty year old Francis and his wife Thomasin Butler proved his right to a 200 acre tract on 28 April 1678 for transporting himself, his wife Thomasin, and his two daughters Penelope and Mary into Maryland.

Their son William (1674-1732) married twice and was probably the first to be born in Maryland. Later research has posited three marriages for him though this may be problematic. A first marriage to Ann Snowden Rosewell, though undated, would have to have been in his teens and would have been short lived. No children have been ascribed to this marriage. If the marriage was in error then he married first Elizabeth Clements about 1695 when he was twenty one. Hiden states she was the mother of his four eldest children, Grace Herbert, Thomasin Cissell, Charles, and William.[30]

William listed his children in his will of 1732 in what may be presumed to be birth order. When his second (or third) wife made her own will in 1760, depending on whether Ann Rosewell is counted or not, there was no mention of any of the four eldest children or their heirs. This leads to the conclusion that they were by his previous wife and only the eight youngest beginning with Francis were to have bequests in her Will.[31]

Two of their children provide our link to the Drury family. Francis Hayden was born between 1706 and 1709 the eldest of the eight children of William Hayden and Elizabeth Thompson. He married Ann Drury, a daughter of John Drury and Ann Payne, about 1731. There is confusion about Ann Drury's given name. After her husband died in 1848 she remarried to Sebastian Thompson and is listed as Elizabeth Thompson when she administers Francis' Estate. This could be confusion in the records. It is also possible that her full name was Elizabeth Ann Drury and the earlier records only listed the middle name. There is some precedent for this as at times female children were given the names of both paternal and maternal grandmothers. For example, James Drury a great grand nephew of John Drury (husband of Susanna Hayden) named his first daughter Catherine Henrietta, the given names of her female grandparents, Catherine Wimsatt and Henrietta Wheatley. We know Ann's maternal grandmother was Ann Assiter.[32] Following our logic, the mother of John Drury (husband of Mary Ford), though unknown, could have been Elizabeth. Known children of Ann and Francis Hayden were Bernard (1732), James (1734), George (1736), and Francis (abt. 1737).[33]

Our second link is more substantial. The eldest daughter, Susanna, married John Drury the brother of her sister-in-law Ann (or possibly Elizabeth Ann) in 1734. Many of their descendants are well documented in earlier chapters.

Raley/Riley

Drury families have several connections to the Rileys in the eighteenth and early nineteenth centuries. Linking these connections to an overall Riley genealogy in Maryland is complicated by two factors. First, Riley descendants, in researching their ancestry, do not always agree about these various lineages. Second is the fact that the name is spelled sometimes as Riley and at others as Raley. Most researchers agree that these both refer to the same families but it easy to see how confusion could arise.

There were Rileys in St. Mary's County as early as 1688 but solid connections cannot be established between them and later Rileys who marry Drurys. We begin with Zachariah Raley and his wife Ann Wilkinson whose son John B. Raley was born about 1803 in St. Mary's County. He lived on a farm called "The Vineyard"[34] until his death in 1879. John married four times fathering a total of thirteen children. His third wife was Jane M. Drury who he married in 1856. Jane's ancestry is also unclear. Our best guess based on circumstantial evidence is that she was a daughter of Enoch Drury (who we also cannot definitely place) and his second wife Eleanor Joy.[35]

Another connection between the Drurys and Rileys is found with Bennett Riley who served in the Revolutionary War and married Susanna Drury, the daughter of John Drury (1739-1797) and his first unknown wife in 1784.[36] At present we have no idea who Bennett's parents were. A third Riley connection with unknown connections to Riley ancestors is that of Georgina Victoria Raley, a daughter of James Raley and Mary Elizabeth Taylor who married George Winfield Drury, the son of Thomas Theodore Drury and Martha Ann Lydaman.[37] They lived in southern St. Mary's County. At present we have no connection to anyone before Thomas for the Drurys nor to anyone prior to James for the Raleys.

Joy

The Joy family had multiple connections to the Drurys for more than one hundred years. The earliest Joy to arrive in Maryland was Peter Joy (1628).[38] Peter was apparently a carpenter who was indentured to Major John Billingsley[39] about 1652. He married Martha Golson shortly before his indenture was completed. Their son, Peter, was born about 1655. The son married Ann Stone. Peter Jr's grandson Ignatius (1778-1838) married Dorothy Drury (1775-aft 1860), a daughter of Michael Drury. Another connection is with Enoch Joy, another son of Peter Joy and Ann Stone. He married Tecla Drury before 1735. She was an Aunt of Dorothy Drury (1775-aft 1860).

A third relationship was that of Eleanor Jarboe who married Samuel, a son of Philip Drury and Emerentia (Ann) Newton in 1799 though this one is more distant. We trace it from Monica Joy (1663-1707) who was a daughter of Peter Joy and Martha Golson. She married Henry Jarboe one of the sons of Lt. Col. John Jarboe and Mary Tattershall about 1680.[40] They had a son Charles who fathered a son named Joshua (1740-1792).[41] It was Joshua's daughter Eleanor who married Samuel Drury.

In the early eighteen hundreds we have three siblings, Edmund Barton Joy, Eleanor Joy, and Dorothy Rosalie Joy all of whom were connected to Drury families. Edmund married Elpha Isabella Raley the daughter of John Raley and Elefred Drury who is, as yet, not connected to any of the Drury families. Eleanor was the third wife of Enoch Drury and mother of Jane M. Drury mentioned above in the section on the Rileys. Dorothy married Ignatius Randolph Raley a son of Stephen Raley and Sarah whose maiden name may have been Joy.

We also have Ann B. Joy (we don't know her maiden name) whose daughter Elizabeth married Zachariah Peacock in 1797. Zachariah Peacock married a different Jane Drury as his second wife in 1804. This Jane was possibly a daughter of Philip Drury and his wife Emerentia Newton. Ann Joy's will in 1835[42] leaves all her property to Enoch Drury who is also the executor of her estate. This is probably Enoch the father of Jane Drury. John B. Raley (Jane's future husband) was also a witness to the will. Another interesting connection was that Ann Thompson, John Raley's wife at the time, had a brother Joseph who married Elizabeth Drury a daughter of Edward Drury and Granddaughter of Michael Drury who was a brother of Philip mentioned above.

[1] Donnelly, Mary Louise, "Colonial Settlers St. Clements's Bay 1634 - 1780 St. Mary's County, Maryland", p 39
[2] General Index to Wills of St. Mary's County Maryland', Sept 28, 1745 Bold, William Liber T.A. No. 1 Folio 157
[3] General Index to Wills of St. Mary's County Maryland', May 6, 1797 Bowles, John Liber J.J. No. 2 Folio 186
[4] Donnelly, Mary Louise, Colonial Settlers St. Clements's Bay 1634 – 1780 p. 42
[5] 8/4/1731: Admin. accts. of Charles Daft. Distribution to: widow, 1/3. Residue to: Charles Daft, Susanna Daft, Monica Daft. Adm: Isaac Booth and his wife, Elizabeth Booth.
[6] Will of Elizabeth Booth, St. Mary's County Maryland 1/3/1756-2/3/1756. Daughters: Elizabeth Wooten and Mary Booth, all of my personal estate. Daughter: Monica Boalds, 1 shilling sterling. Wit: James Roach, William Combs, James Payne.
[7] Virginia, a guide to the old dominion – May 1940
[8] Virginia Magazine of History and Biography Vol. 1 p 269; quarterly, vol. 4 p 37
[9] Westmoreland County Wills 826/1727 – Newton, Rose, To my son Thomas Newton, land in Virginia and Maryland my late husband Thomas Gerrard left me.
[10] Baldwin, Maryland Calendar of wills, Liber 22 Folio 420
[11] Baldwin, Maryland Calendar of wills, Liber 31 folio 113
[12] Himmelheber, Peter, Papist lands in St. Mary's County, Maryland 1760; Chronicles of St. Marys Vol. 49 #1
[13] www.Stmary'sfamilies.com/wills
[14] Westmoreland County Wills 1729-1748
[15] 1730 patent book c-81, 24 acres of marsh land
[16] Virginia Northern Neck land grants 1694-1737, Gray p 78.
[17] Stafford County Wills book LM, page 185 (1732)
[18] Archives of Maryland Vol. 10, Judicial and Testamentary business of the Provincial Court, 1649-50-1657, William Hand Brown Ed., p 371
[19] Provincial Land Office (patents), 196, 359, 362, 405, 409
[20] Prerogative Court (wills) 4: 388
[21] Prerogative Court (wills) 22: 140
[22] Donnelly, Mary, Colonial Settlers, St. Clement's Bay, p. 239
[23] Himmelheber, Peter, *electronic msg. of 10/02/2010 to Linda Reno concerning survey of Wimsatt's Frolic –" by* ca 1790 both Williams Good Luck and Wimsatts Frolic had been resurveyed into three tracks called Peace & Quietness,

129-acre for Robert Wimsatt {UC:336}; Satisfaction, 191-acres, for Joshua Jarbo {PC:572} and Flower of the Forrest, 95-acres for George Spalding {UC:161}"

[24] Barnes, Robert, Maryland Marriages; census 1800, 1801

[25] Maryland Probate records, Perogative Court Abstracts, 1751-1755. p 35, FTM CD 206

[26] Peden, Henry C. Jr., Revolutionary Patriots of Calvert and St. Mary's Counties, Maryland, 1775-1783, Willow Bend Books, Westminster, Maryland, p. 327

[27] Administrative Accounts – estate of Robert Wimsatt 5/6/1801 liber jj jf 1, pp 196, 197

[28] St. Mary's County wills, book JJ-I Pg. 5-8

[29] Hiden, M. W., The Hiden Family, in Tyler's Quarterly Historical and Genealogical Magazine, Vol. II, Genealogical Publishing Company, 1981, p. 181

[30] Hiden, M. W., The Hiden Family, in Tyler's Quarterly Historical and Genealogical Magazine, Vol. II, Genealogical Publishing Company, 1981, p. 183

[31] Maryland wills Liber 31, Folio 202

[32] Will of Ann Assiter, SMC 11/4/1693-3/20/1693-4; Carr, Lois Green, card file sc4040 - 1166,1695

[33] LDS – Ancestral files (AF) Id: 11057100 and IGI Id: 3029780

[34] Dobricky, John, Email of 2/12/2003

[35] Reno, Linda, Email of 10/1/2007

[36] Bennet Raley -his bible "born to bennet raley and his wife Susanna- John Raley B. June 1 ,1785; Bennet Raley,2d-November 27 1787; Nancy Raley- September 18, 1789; wife Frances Frazier Raley- b. Joseph Raley-January 25, 1796; Elizabeth Raley-b. October 16, 1801

[37] *Baltimore Sun 28 November 1846*, Marriage Notice, Married on 26th inst by Rev R. M. Lipscomb, Thomas T. Drury to Martha A. Lydaman all of St. Mary's County

[38] Archives of Maryland Vol. V pp 405-410

[39] Nugent, Nell Marion, Cavaliers and Pioneers Vol. 1, p 239

[40] This assumes she married two years before her son Peter was born.

[41] Randy Dunavan- <randydunavan@cablelynx.com>

[42] St. Mary's County Wills 1821-1835, book EJM #1, Folio 310

Descendants of Charles Drury

1. Charles Drury (d.27 Aug 1740-Ann Arundle County,Maryland)

sp: UNKNOWN

    2. Sarah Drury (b.Abt 1710)

      sp: Abraham Simmons Jr. (m.Abt 1730;d.Bef 16 Apr 1745)

        3. Abraham Simmons

        3. Beatridge Simmons

          sp: William Simmons

    2. Charles Drury (b.Abt 1712-England;d.by 6/11/1766-Anne Arundle County,Maryland)

      sp: Elizabeth Miles

      sp: Mary (m.Aft 1740)

        3. Charles Drury

          sp: Margaret Childs

        3. William Drury (b.Abt 1750-Washington D.C.)

          sp: Elizabeth Ijams (b.3 Dec 1750;m.17 Nov 1768;d.Aft 1817)

        3. Sarah Drury

          sp: Nercules Courtenay (b.15 Oct 1736-Newrey,Ireland;m.1774;d.21 Aug 1816-Baltimore County,Maryland)

        3. Elizabeth Drury

          sp: Matthew Cooley (m.1774)

        3. Margaret Drury

          sp: John Pindell (m.by 1770)

        3. Ann Drury (b.1745-Anne Arundle County,Maryland)

          sp: Zebediah Wood (b.1743-Anne Arundle County,Maryland;m.10 Sep 1776;d.Abt 1795-Anne Arundle County,Maryland)

        3. Easter Drury

        3. Samuel Drury (b.Aft 1740)

          sp: Ann Ijams (b.2 Jul 1759;m.29 May 1779)

    2. Sophia Drury

      sp: Charles Boteler (d.Aft 1730)

        3. Edward Boteler

        3. Walter Boteler (b.22 Oct 1763;d.22 Feb 1829)

          sp: Jemima (b.1763;d.29 Jan 1831)

    2. Esther Drury

      sp: Nathan Selby (m.1741)

        3. John Selby (b.1745-Prince George County,Maryland)

          sp: Margaret Clagett (m.1771)

    2. Mary Drury

sp: Alice Adney (m.17 Jun 1733)

Descendants of Charles Drury

1. Charles Drury (b.Abt 1712-England;d.by 6/11/1766-Anne Arundle County,Maryland)

sp: Elizabeth Miles

sp: Mary (m.Aft 1740)

- 2. Charles Drury

  sp: Margaret Childs

  - 3. Jerningham Drury (d.1816-Anne Arundle County,Maryland)

    sp: Sarah Hill (m.14 Apr 1790)

  - 3. Charles Drury

  - 3. Joseph Drury

  - 3. Mary Drury

    sp: Van Simmons (m.5 May 1773)

  - 3. Dau Drury

    sp: Welch

  - 3. Henry Childs Drury (b.1797-Anne Arundle County,Maryland;d.17 Feb 1873-Anne Arundle County,Maryland)

  - 3. Samuel Drury

- 2. William Drury (b.Abt 1750-Washington D.C.)

  sp: Elizabeth Ijams (b.3 Dec 1750;m.17 Nov 1768;d.Aft 1817)

  - 3. Elizabeth Drury

    sp: John Green (m.by 1806)

  - 3. William Drury Jr.

    sp: Maria Smith (m.13 Nov 1816)

  - 3. Henry Childs Drury (b.1780-Anne Arundle County,Maryland;d.1854-Anne Arundle County,Maryland)

    sp: UNKNOWN

- 2. Sarah Drury

  sp: Nercules Courtenay (b.15 Oct 1736-Newrey,Ireland;m.1774;d.21 Aug 1816-Baltimore County,Maryland)

- 2. Elizabeth Drury

  sp: Matthew Cooley (m.1774)

- 2. Margaret Drury

  sp: John Pindell (m.by 1770)

- 2. Ann Drury (b.1745-Anne Arundle County,Maryland)

  sp: Zebediah Wood (b.1743-Anne Arundle County,Maryland;m.10 Sep 1776;d.Abt 1795-Anne Arundle County,Maryland)

  - 3. Mary Ann Wood (b.1778-Anne Arundle County,Maryland)

- 2. Easter Drury

- 2. Samuel Drury (b.Aft 1740)

  sp: Ann Ijams (b.2 Jul 1759;m.29 May 1779)

  - 3. Marydell Drury

    sp: Richard Hill

  - 3. William Drury

    sp: Evans

  - 3. Elizabeth Drury (b.Abt 1781;d.Bef 1842-Anne Arundle County,Maryland)

    sp: Samuel Ward (m.23 Nov 1798)

    sp: Lyles

3. Ruth Drury (b.1783;d.21 Jan 1862)

   sp: Benjamin Welch (b.15 Feb 1779-Anne Arundle County,Maryland;m.7 Feb 1804;d.16 Jul 1857-AAC,Maryland)

3. Ann Drury (b.Abt 1785)

   sp: George Gardiner (m.12 May 1826)

3. Mary Drury (b.Abt 1787)

   sp: William Smith

   sp: Humphries

3. Margaret Hill Drury (b.Abt 1789)

   sp: William Hopkins

3. Plummer Ijams Drury (b.Abt 1791)

   sp: Margaret Gannon (m.17 Jan 1814)

3. Samuel Drury Jr. (b.1792-Anne Arundle County,Maryland;d.1867-Washington D.C.)

   sp: Mary Nolan (b.1794-England;m.5 Jul 1815;d.1867)

3. John Ijams Drury (b.Abt 1797)

3. Henry Childs Drury (b.Abt 1797;d.12 Feb 1873-Anne Arundle County,Maryland)

   sp: Mary Ann Owens (b.1802-Anne Arundle County,Maryland;m.1823;d.6 Jul 1870-Anne Arundle County,Maryland)

Descendants of Robert Drury

1. Robert Drury (b.1635-England)

sp: <Unknown>

  2. Robert Drury ? (b.Abt 1660-St. Mary's County,Maryland)

  2. John Drury (b.Abt 1662-St. Mary's County,Maryland;d.by 1724-St. Mary's County,Maryland)

    sp: Ann Payne (b.Bef 1670-St. Mary's County,Maryland;m.Aft 1695)

      3. Thomas Drury (b.(est) abt 1702)

        sp: Mary m.Bef 13 May 1751)

      3. Robert Drury (b.Est 1703;d.1774-,St. Mary's County,Maryland)

        sp: Mary (m.22 Aug 1725)

      3. Ann Drury (b.Abt 1710-St. Mary's County,Maryland)

        sp: Francis Hayden (b.Abt 1706-St. Mary's County,Maryland;m.Abt 1731;d.Abt 1760)

      3. John Drury (b.Abt 1710-St. Mary's County,Maryland)

        sp: Susanna Hayden (b.1714-St. Marys County,Maryland;m.10 Dec 1734)

      3. Peter Drury (b.Est 1715-,St. Mary's County,Maryland;d.1770/1771-,St. Mary's County,Maryland)

        sp: Jane Bailey (m.Abt 1735/1736;d.Bef 1770-St. Mary's County,Maryland)

        sp: Ann Bailey (b.Abt 1735-St. Mary's County,Maryland;m.?)

      3. Tecla Drury (b.1720-St. Mary's County Maryland;d.1796-St. Mary's County Maryland)

      3. Jane Drury (b.by 1720-St. Mary's County,Maryland)

    sp: Mary Ford (m.Aft 1711)

  2. Margaret Drury ? (b.Abt 1666-St. Mary's County,Maryland;d.1726-St. Mary's County,Maryland)

    sp: John Tant (m.1683)

      3. James Tant (d.1717)

        sp: Mary Tattershall (m.by 1701;d.1703)

        sp: Mary Heard (m.by 1705)

      3. Mark Tant

      3. Mary Tant

        sp: Mark Lampton

      3. Ann Tant

        sp: James Manning

      3. Jane Tant

        sp: Robert Thompson

      3. Elizabeth Tant

      3. Winifred Tant

        sp: Vitus Herbert (b.Abt 1700;m.1715/1718;d.1726)

      3. Margaret Tant

        sp: Walter Pye (b.Bef 1695-Charles County Maryland;m.Bef 1717;d.1749-Charles County Maryland)

      3. Susanna Tant

        sp: Richard Thompson (d.Bef 3 Jul 1734)

  2. James Drury ? (b.Abt 1669-St. Mary's County,Maryland)

    sp: <Unknown>

      3. Mary Drury

        sp: Charles Chamberlain (m.by 1705;d.Aft 1750-Virginia)

3. James Drury Jr. (d.bet 3/19/1779 and 5/10/1779-St. Mary's County,Maryland)
   sp: Sarah (Thompson ??)

Descendants of Margaret Drury ?

1. Margaret Drury ? (b.Abt 1666-St. Mary's County,Maryland;d.1726-St. Mary's County,Maryland)

sp: John Tant (m.1683)

- 2. James Tant (d.1717)

  sp: Mary Tattershall (m.by 1701;d.1703)

  - 3. Ann Tant (b.Abt 1701-St. Mary's County,Maryland)

    sp: George Medley (m.by 1723;d.1731-St. Mary's County,Maryland)

    sp: William Williams (m.Bef 12 Jun 1733)

  - 3. John Tant (b.Abt 1703-St. Mary's County,Maryland)

  sp: Mary Heard (m.by 1705)

  - 3. Matthew Tant (b.Abt 1706-St. Mary's County,Maryland)
  - 3. Mary Tant

- 2. Mark Tant

- 2. Mary Tant

  sp: Mark Lampton

  - 3. Mark Lampton (d.Bef 6 Nov 1733-St. Mary's County,Maryland)

- 2. Ann Tant

  sp: James Manning

  - 3. John Manning

- 2. Jane Tant

  sp: Robert Thompson

  - 3. William Thompson
  - 3. Henry Thompson

- 2. Elizabeth Tant

- 2. Winifred Tant

  sp: Vitus Herbert (b.Abt 1700;m.1715/1718;d.1726)

  - 3. William Herbert (d.Bef 1733-St. Mary's County,Maryland)
  - 3. Joseph Herbert
  - 3. Vitus Herbert Jr.

    sp: Elizabeth

- 2. Margaret Tant

  sp: Walter Pye (b.Bef 1695-Charles County Maryland;m.Bef 1717;d.1749-Charles County Maryland)

  - 3. Edward Pye (b.Bef 1717-St. Mary's County Maryland;d.1750-Charles County,Maryland)

    sp: Sarah Edelen (b.18 Feb 1705/1706-Charles County Maryland;m.25 Feb 1735/1736;d.Aft 1758-Charles County Maryla)

  - 3. Jane Pye (b.Bef 1724;d.Aft 1752)
  - 3. Margaret Pye (b.1724-Charles County Maryland;d.7 Jun 1777-Antwerp)
  - 3. Walter Pye Jr. (b.Bef 1725-Charles County Maryland;d.Aft 1788-Charles County,Maryland)
  - 3. Mary Pye (b.Bef 1731-Charles County Maryland;d.1783-Charles County Maryland)
  - 3. James Pye (b.Bef 1732-Charles County Maryland;d.Aft 1752-Charles County Maryland)
  - 3. Robert Pye (b.1734-Charles County Maryland;d.Aft 1752-Charles County Maryland)
  - 3. Ann Pye (b.Bef 1734-Charles County Maryland;d.Aft 1778-Charles County Maryland)
  - 3. Henrietta Pye (b.Bef 1734-Charles County Maryland;d.1775-Charles County Maryland)

- 2. Susanna Tant

sp: Richard Thompson (d.Bef 3 Jul 1734)

Descendants of James Drury ?

1. James Drury ? (b.Abt 1669-St. Mary's County,Maryland)

sp: <Unknown>

    2. Mary Drury

        sp: Charles Chamberlain (m.by 1705;d.Aft 1750-Virginia)

            3. Eleanor Chamberlain (b.1706-St. Mary's County,Maryland)

            3. Mary Chamberlain (b.1714-St. Mary's County,Maryland)

            3. Thomas Chamberlain

                sp: Catherine (b.1697-St. Mary's County,Maryland;m.1737)

    2. James Drury Jr. (d.bet 3/19/1779 and 5/10/1779-St. Mary's County,Maryland)

        sp: Sarah Thompson ??

            3. Stephen Drury (b.1767-St. Mary's County Maryland)

            3. James Drury (c.10 Dec 1771-St. Mary's County,Maryland)

            3. Thomas Drury (b.1774-St. Mary's County,Maryland)

            3. Richard Drury

Descendants of John Drury

1. John Drury (b.Abt 1662-St. Mary's County,Maryland;d.by 1724-St. Mary's County,Maryland)

sp: Ann Payne (b.Bef 1670-St. Mary's County,Maryland;m.Aft 1695)

- 2. Thomas Drury (b.(est) abt 1702)

  sp: Mary Herbert (b.Abt 1710;m.Bef 13 May 1751)

- 2. Robert Drury (b.Est 1703;d.1774-,St. Mary's County,Maryland)

  sp: Mary (m.22 Aug 1725)

- 2. Ann Drury (b.Abt 1710-St. Mary's County,Maryland)

  sp: Francis Hayden (b.Abt 1706-St. Mary's County,Maryland;m.Abt 1731;d.Abt 1760)

  - 3. Bernard Hayden (b.Abt 1732-St. Mary's County,Maryland)

  - 3. James Hayden (b.Abt 1734-St. Mary's County,Maryland;d.Abt 1834)

  - 3. George Hayden (b.Abt 1736-St. Mary's County,Maryland)

  - 3. Francis Hayden (b.Abt 1737-St. Mary's County,Maryland)

- 2. John Drury (b.Abt 1710-St. Mary's County,Maryland)

  sp: Susanna Hayden (b.1714-St. Marys County,Maryland;m.10 Dec 1734)

  - 3. Frances Anna Drury (b.1735;d.between 1802 and 1807-St. Genevieve Dist. Upper la. Territory)

    sp: Joseph Tucker (b.17 Aug 1744-Virginia;m.Abt 1767;d.Bef 12 Jul 1816-St. Genevieve Dist. Upper la. Territory)

  - 3. William Drury (b.1737-,St. Marys,Maryland;d.1801-Prarie du Roche,Randolph County,Illinois)

    sp: Mary Ann Wootton (b.1736-St. Mary's County,Maryland;m.Abt 1758)

  - 3. John Drury (b.Abt 1739-St. Mary's Co.,Md;d.Jun 1797-St. Mary's Co.,Md)

    sp: Unknown (m.Abt 1760)

    sp: Ann (m.21 Apr 1795;d.Aft 1797)

  - 3. Joseph Drury (b.Bef 1750;d.Abt 1806-Bedford County,Virginia)

    sp: Elizabeth (m.Bef 1772;d.Bef 1776-Bedford County,Virginia)

    sp: Sybil Wigginton (b.Abt 1751-Prince William County,Virginia;m.1776)

  - 3. Jeremiah Drury (b.1750-St. Mary's County,Maryland;d.Aft 1800-St. Mary's County,Maryland)

    sp: UNKNOWN

  - 3. Monica Drury (b.Feb 1751-St. Mary's County,Maryland;d.18 Dec 1827-Perry County,Missouri)

    sp: Nicholas Moore Jr. (b.1748-St. Mary's County,Maryland;m.Abt 1779;d.1 Sep 1827-Perry County,Missouri)

  - 3. Mary Drury (b.1753)

    sp: Richard Basil Knott

  - 3. Elizabeth Drury

    sp: Jeremy Gatten (m.14 Feb 1773)

  - 3. Francis Drury (b.Aft 1755-St. Mary's County,Maryland)

    sp: Mary Ann Carpenter

- 2. Peter Drury (b.Est 1715-,St. Mary's County,Maryland;d.1770/1771-,St. Mary's County,Maryland)

  sp: Jane Bailey (m.Abt 1735/1736;d.Bef 1770-St. Mary's County,Maryland)

  - 3. Michael Drury (b.Est 1736-,St. Mary's County,Maryland;d.1826-St. Mary's County,Maryland)

    sp: Ann Yates (b.1743/1755;m.3 Nov 1770)

  - 3. Nicholas Drury (b.1738-,St. Mary's County,Maryland;d.Bef 1790)

    sp: Monica

  - 3. Peter Drury (b.1740-,St. Mary's County,Maryland)

    sp: Eleanor

3. Ignatius Drury (b.1745-St. Mary's County;d.Aft 1800-Nelson County,Kentucky)

   sp: Anastasia French (b.29 Jul 1750-St. Mary's County,Maryland;m.11 Dec 1769)

3. Philip Drury (b.Est 1750-,St. Mary's County,Maryland;d.9 Jun 1795-St. Mary's County,Maryland)

   sp: Emerentia Bibiana Newton (m.4 Sep 1770;d.bet 1795 -1812)

3. Robert Drury ?

   sp: Mary Margaret

3. John Drury ?

   sp: Elizabeth

   sp: Mary Margaret

3. Enoch Drury ? (d.1784-,St. Mary's County,Maryland)

   sp: Tabitha Wimsatt

3. Catherine Drury

3. Mildred Drury (b.1755-St. Mary's County,Maryland;d.by 1831)

   sp: Ignatius Russell (b.10 Mar 1748-St. Mary's County,Maryland;m.1772)

3. Richard Drury ?

   sp: Elizabeth (m.Bef 1771)

  sp: Ann Bailey (b.Abt 1735-St. Mary's County,Maryland;m.?)

2. Tecla Drury (b.1720-St. Mary's County Maryland;d.1796-St. Mary's County Maryland)

2. Jane Drury (b.by 1720-St. Mary's County,Maryland)

sp: Mary Ford (m.Aft 1711)

Descendants of Ann Drury

1. Ann Drury (b.Abt 1710-St. Mary's County,Maryland)

  sp: Francis Hayden (b.Abt 1706-St. Mary's County,Maryland;m.Abt 1731;d.Abt 1760)

    — 2. Bernard Hayden (b.Abt 1732-St. Mary's County,Maryland)

    — 2. James Hayden (b.Abt 1734-St. Mary's County,Maryland;d.Abt 1834)

    — 2. George Hayden (b.Abt 1736-St. Mary's County,Maryland)

    — 2. Francis Hayden (b.Abt 1737-St. Mary's County,Maryland)

Descendants of John Drury

1. John Drury (b.Abt 1710-St. Mary's County,Maryland)

sp: Susanna Hayden (b.1714-St. Marys County,Maryland;m.10 Dec 1734)

— 2. Frances Anna Drury (b.1735;d.between 1802 and 1807-St. Genevieve Dist. Upper la. Territory)

   sp: Joseph Tucker (b.17 Aug 1744-Virginia;m.Abt 1767;d.Bef 12 Jul 1816-St. Genevieve Dist. Upper la. Territory)

    — 3. Peter Joseph Tucker (b.1769-Virginia;d.24 Dec 1845-Perry County,Missouri)

      sp: Christina Hagan

    — 3. Thomas Tudor Tucker (b.1772-St. Mary's County,Maryland;d.1833-Perry County,Missouri)

      sp: Chloe Manning

      sp: Susannah Hagan

    — 3. Mary Tucker (b.1776-St. Mary's County,Maryland;d.20 Jan 1846-Perry County,Missouri)

    — 3. Joseph Tucker Jr. (b.1777-St. Mary's County,Maryland;d.25 Jul 1833-Perry County,Missouri)

      sp: Eleanor Sims

    — 3. Nicholas Tucker (b.1782-St. Mary's County,Maryland;d.13 Oct 1839-Perry County,Missouri)

      sp: Mary Ann Miles

    — 3. Michael Tucker (b.1783-St. Mary's County,Maryland)

      sp: Dorothy Johnson

    — 3. James Tucker (b.1784-St. Mary's County,Maryland;d.28 Feb 1856-Perry County,Missouri)

      sp: Theresa Hagan (b.1787-Prince George's County,Maryland;m.3 Sep 1805;d.Abt 1860-Lavaca County Texas)

    — 3. William Tucker (b.1786-St. Mary's County,Maryland;d.20 Aug 1852-Perry County,Missouri)

      sp: Sarah Ann Hayden

    — 3. John Tucker (b.4 Jul 1788-St. Mary's County,Maryland;d.5 Aug 1856-Perry County,Missouri)

    — 3. Francis Tucker (b.24 Feb 1793-Kentucky;d.12 Apr 1865-Perry County,Missouri)

— 2. William Drury (b.1737-,St. Marys,Maryland;d.1801-Prarie du Roche,Randolph County,Illinois)

   sp: Mary Ann Wootton (b.1736-St. Mary's County,Maryland;m.Abt 1758)

    — 3. Clement Drury (b.1759-St. Mary's County,Maryland;d.1814-Prarie du Roche,Randolph County,Illinois)

      sp: Marie Josephte Provost (b.1769-Prarie du Roche,RC,Illinois;m.1 Aug 1785;d.1833-Prarie du Roche,RC,Illinois)

    — 3. Raphael Drury (b.1763-St. Mary's County,Maryland;d.1835-Prarie du Roche,Randolph County,Illinois)

      sp: Elizabeth McNabb

    — 3. John Drury

    — 3. William Drury

— 2. John Drury (b.Abt 1739-St. Mary's Co.,Md;d.Jun 1797-St. Mary's Co.,Md)

   sp: Unknown (m.Abt 1760)

    — 3. Ignatius Drury (b.1760-St. Mary's Co.,Md;d.Aft 1797)

    — 3. Susanna Drury (b.Bef 1767-St. Mary's Co.,Md;d.Bef 1789)

      sp: Bennet Raley (b.1740-St. Mary's Co.,Md;m.16 Aug 1784;d.Aft 1810)

    — 3. John Chrysostom Drury (b.1766/1771-St. Mary's Co.,Md;d.Aft 1810)

      sp: <Unknown> (m.Bef 1779)

    — 3. Francis Desales Drury (b.Abt 1768-St. Mary's Co.,Md;d.1809-St. Mary's Co.,Md)

      sp: Ann (Anna) Yates (b.Bef 1777-St. Mary's Co.,Md;m.15 Oct 1799;d.1805/1807-St. Mary's Co.,Md)

      sp: Winifred Lowe (b.1777/1779-St. Mary's Co.,Md;m.11 Nov 1807;d.5 Apr 1819-Washington,D.C.)

    — 3. William Drury (b.Abt 1777-St. Mary's Co.,Md;d.26 Feb 1851-Mercer County,Kentucky)

      sp: Elizabeth Lankford (b.1781-Dorchester County,Maryland;m.4 Feb 1799;d.Bef 1819-Kentucky) sp: Elizabeth T. Edwards (b.Abt 1781-Pennsylvania;m.9 Jan 1819;d.7 Nov 1850-Mercer County,Kentucky)

 3. Anastasia Drury (b.1768-St. Mary's Co.,Md;d.Aft 1797)

  sp: Charles Vessels (b.1750;m.1788)

 3. Mary Drury (b.Bef 1782;d.Aft 1797)

  sp: Matthew Mandley (b.Bef 1782;m.Bef 1797)

 3. Monica Drury (b.Bef 1784-St. Mary's Co.,Md;d.Aft 1794)

 3. Joseph Drury

sp: Ann (m.21 Apr 1795;d.Aft 1797)

2. Joseph Drury (b.Bef 1750;d.Abt 1806-Bedford County,Virginia)

 sp: Elizabeth (m.Bef 1772;d.Bef 1776-Bedford County,Virginia)

  3. Mary Drury (b.Sep 1772-Bedford County,Virginia)

  3. Elizabeth Drury (b.1775-Bedford County,Virginia)

 sp: Sybil Wigginton (b.Abt 1751-Prince William County,Virginia;m.1776)

  3. Isaac Drury (b.1777)

   sp: Sarah Dowdy (m.24 Dec 1832)

  3. Rebecca Drury (b.11 Sep 1779;d.Jul 1855)

   sp: Sanders Brown (m.14 Feb 1817)

  3. Sallie Drury (b.1781-Prince Williamco,Va)

   sp: Elijah Russell (m.5 Apr 1813)

  3. John Drury (b.5 Jan 1781-Prince Williamco,Va;d.1858)

   sp: Rachel Dorris (b.1792;m.Abt 1810;d.1858)

  3. George Drury (b.11 Sep 1783-Prince Williamco,Va)

  3. Betsy Drury (b.1785-Prince Williamco,Va)

   sp: ??? Easley

  3. James Drury (b.1785-Prince Williamco,Va)

   sp: Nancy Stith

  3. Nancy Drury (b.1787-Bedfordco,Va)

   sp: ??? Foster

  3. Frances Drury (b.1791-Bedfordco,Va;d.1856-Il)

   sp: Fielden Hankins (b.Abt 1789;m.Abt 1809;d.1883-Il)

  3. Martha Drury (b.3 Jul 1794-Bedfordco,Va;d.23 Aug 1888-Limestoneco,Tx)

   sp: Wade Hampton Davis (b.1796;m.13 May 1813;d.1877-Marysville,Mo)

  3. Lucy Drury (b.8 Nov 1796-Bedfordco,Va;d.11 Jan 1889)

   sp: Josiah Dorris (b.8 Nov 1796-Nc;m.12 May 1816;d.20 Jan 1871)

2. Jeremiah Drury (b.1750-St. Mary's County,Maryland;d.Aft 1800-St. Mary's County,Maryland)

 sp: UNKNOWN

  3. Dau Drury (b.Bef 1790-St. Mary's County,Maryland)

  3. Son Drury (b.1790/1800-St. Mary's County,Maryland)

  3. Son Drury (b.1790/1800-St. Mary's County,Maryland)

  3. Dau Drury (b.1790/1800-St. Mary's County,Maryland)

2. Monica Drury (b.Feb 1751-St. Mary's County,Maryland;d.18 Dec 1827-Perry County,Missouri)

 sp: Nicholas Moore Jr. (b.1748-St. Mary's County,Maryland;m.Abt 1779;d.1 Sep 1827-Perry County,Missouri)

  3. Bede Moore (b.1773;d.1856)

   sp: Verlinda Adams (b.Abt 1779;m.5 Dec 1800;d.10 Dec 1859-Perry County,Missouri)

3. Isadore Moore (b.1771-St. Mary's County,Maryland;d.1842-Perry County,Missouri)

    sp: Eleanor Cooper (b.Abt 1766;m.22 Mar 1794)

    sp: Leah McDaniel (b.Abt 1779-Nelson County,Kentucky;m.Abt 1799;d.6 Feb 1854)

3. James Nicholas Moore (b.1775;d.1853)

    sp: Sarah Quick (b.Abt 1788-St. Mary's County,Maryland;m.10 Apr 1804;d.31 Aug 1869-Perry County,Missouri)

    sp: Susanna Becraft (m.27 Oct 1801)

2. Mary Drury (b.1753)

    sp: Richard Basil Knott

3. Mary Knott (b.1771;d.1852)

3. James Knott (b.1776)

    sp: <Unknown>

3. Susannah Knott

3. Nancy Knott

3. Elizabeth Betsy Knott

3. Clement Knott (b.1780;d.1847)

    sp: Mary Brewer (b.Abt 1784-St. Mary's County,Maryland;m.7 Jan 1802)

2. Elizabeth Drury

    sp: Jeremy Gatten (m.14 Feb 1773)

2. Francis Drury (b.Aft 1755-St. Mary's County,Maryland)

    sp: Mary Ann Carpenter

3. Ann Drury (b.1778-St. Mary's County,Maryland;d.12 Oct 1852-Perry County,Missouri)

    sp: Bernard Smith (b.1772-St. Mary's County,Maryland;m.Abt 1796;d.15 Feb 1847-Perry County,Missouri)

Descendants of William Drury

1. William Drury (b.1737-,St. Marys,Maryland;d.1801-Prarie du Roche,Randolph County,Illinois)

sp: Mary Ann Wootton (b.1736-St. Mary's County,Maryland;m.Abt 1758)

    2. Clement Drury (b.1759-St. Mary's County,Maryland;d.1814-Prarie du Roche,Randolph County,Illinois)

       sp: Marie Josephte Provost (b.1769-Prarie du Roche,Randolph County,Illinois;m.1 Aug 1785;d.1833-PDR,RC,Illinois)

          3. Marie Susanne Drury (b.20 Oct 1786-Prarie du Roche,Randolph County,Illinois)

            sp: Etienne Langlais (m.1 Feb 1799)

          3. Elizabeth Drury (b.6 Oct 1788-Prarie du Roche,Randolph County,Illinois)

          3. Therese Drury (b.2 May 1791-Prarie du Roche,Randolph County,Illinois)

          3. John Baptist Drury (b.1803-Prarie du Roche,Randolph County,Illinois;d.1849-St. Genevive County,Missouri)

            sp: Marie Olympe Placet (b.4 Dec 1804;m.11 Feb 1820;d.19 Dec 1878)

          3. William Drury (b.1796-Prarie du Roche,Randolph County,Illinois)

          3. Ann Jeanette Drury (b.31 May 1798-Prarie du Roche,Randolph County,Illinois;d.1850-Prarie du Roche,RC,Illinois)

            sp: Antoine Barbeau (b.1793-Prarie du Roche,Randolph County,Illinois;d.1845-Prarie du Roche,Randolph County,Illinois)

          3. Ursule Drury

          3. Clement Drury Jr. (b.1801-Prarie du Roche,Randolph County,Illinois)

            sp: Henrietta Godere (b.1805-Prarie du Roche,Randolph County,Illinois;d.1838-Prarie du Roche,Randolph County,Illinois)

          3. Lucille Drury (b.1805-Prarie du Roche,Randolph County,Illinois)

          3. Raphael Drury (b.1808-Prarie du Roche,Randolph County,Illinois)

            sp: Jeanne Blais

            sp: Marie Ann Duclos

    2. Raphael Drury (b.1763-St. Mary's County,Maryland;d.1835-Prarie du Roche,Randolph County,Illinois)

       sp: Elizabeth McNabb

    2. John Drury

    2. William Drury

Descendants of Frances Anna Drury

1. Frances Anna Drury (b.1735;d.between 1802 and 1807-St. Genevieve Dist. Upper la. Territory)

  sp: Joseph Tucker (b.17 Aug 1744-Virginia;m.Abt 1767;d.Bef 12 Jul 1816-St. Genevieve Dist. Upper la. Territory)

    2. Peter Joseph Tucker (b.1769-Virginia;d.24 Dec 1845-Perry County,Missouri)

      sp: Christina Hagan

        3. Christina Tucker (b.1796;d.1845)

        3. John P. Tucker (b.1798;d.1869)

        3. Benedict Tucker (b.1800)

        3. Peter Pierre Tucker (b.1803;d.1847)

        3. Nicholas Peter Tucker (b.1805;d.1853)

        3. Mary Tucker (b.1806;d.1848)

        3. Josiah Tucker (b.1810;d.1880)

        3. Raymond Tucker (b.1811;d.1877)

        3. Elizabeth Tucker (b.1817)

    2. Thomas Tudor Tucker (b.1772-St. Mary's County,Maryland;d.1833-Perry County,Missouri)

      sp: Chloe Manning

        3. Mary Tucker (b.1794;d.1847)

        3. Joseph Tucker (b.1796;d.1847)

        3. John T. Tucker (b.1799;d.1867)

          sp: Sarah Vessels (b.Abt 1800;m.1822)

        3. James Tucker (b.1790)

        3. William T. Tucker (b.1803;d.1854)

      sp: Susannah Hagan

        3. Theresa Tucker (b.1806)

        3. Thomas Tucker (b.1808;d.1841)

        3. Christina Tucker (b.1810;d.1847)

        3. Nancy Tucker (b.1811;d.1847)

        3. Gregory Tucker (b.1816;d.1853)

    2. Mary Tucker (b.1776-St. Mary's County,Maryland;d.20 Jan 1846-Perry County,Missouri)

    2. Joseph Tucker Jr. (b.1777-St. Mary's County,Maryland;d.25 Jul 1833-Perry County,Missouri)

      sp: Eleanor Sims

        3. Charles J. Tucker (b.1799;d.1841)

        3. Elizabeth Tucker (b.1801;d.1850)

        3. Peter Joseph Tucker (b.1802;d.1880)

        3. Mary Tucker (b.1804;d.1826)

        3. Appollonarius Tucker (b.1808)

        3. Joseph Tucker III (b.1810)

        3. Matilda Tucker (b.1813)

    2. Nicholas Tucker (b.1782-St. Mary's County,Maryland;d.13 Oct 1839-Perry County,Missouri)

      sp: Mary Ann Miles

        3. Joseph Leander Tucker (b.1821;d.1870)

        3. Lewis Tucker

        3. Henry Nicholas Tucker (b.1807;d.1874)

3. Hillary Tucker (b.1808;d.1872)

3. Michael Tucker (b.1810;d.1844)

3. Charles Tucker (b.1811;d.1867)

3. Elizabeth Tucker (b.1811;d.1886)

3. John N. Tucker (b.1812;d.1909)

3. Steven Leander Tucker (b.1823)

3. Cecelia Joanna Tucker (b.1825;d.1848)

3. Richard Tucker (b.1826)

2. Michael Tucker (b.1783-St. Mary's County,Maryland)

sp: Dorothy Johnson

3. Anne Tucker (b.1803)

3. Raphael Tucker (b.1804)

2. James Tucker (b.1784-St. Mary's County,Maryland;d.28 Feb 1856-Perry County,Missouri)

sp: Theresa Hagan (b.1787-Prince George's County,Maryland;m.3 Sep 1805;d.Abt 1860-Lavaca County Texas)

3. Susanna Tucker (b.17 Apr 1814-St. Genevieve Dist. Upper la. Territory;d.18 Jan 1901-Perry County,Missouri)

sp: Sylvester Moore (b.25 Dec 1808-St. Genevieve Dist. Upper la. T;m.25 Jan 1831;d.28 Oct 1893-Lavaca County Texas)

3. Elizabeth Tucker (b.16 Sep 1815-St. Genevieve Dist. Upper la. Territory;d.1849-Lavaca County Texas)

sp: William Augustine Cissell (b.13 Aug 1810-St. Genevieve Dist. Upp;m.14 Jan 1833;d.7 Jan 1878-Lavaca County Texas)

3. Mary Tucker (b.17 Oct 1817-St. Genevieve Dist. Upper la. Territory;d.1880-Lavaca County Texas)

sp: Pius Hagan (b.1810;m.29 Jul 1834;d.1860/1870-Lavaca County Texas)

3. Sylvester Tucker (b.11 Dec 1818-St. Genevieve Dist. Upper la. Territory;d.5 Sep 1875-Perry County,Missouri)

sp: Mary Jane McGinnis (b.1824-Perry County,Missouri;m.12 Jul 1841;d.Bef 1868-Perry County,Missouri)

sp: Elizabeth Warren (b.Abt 1845-Perry County,Missouri;m.26 Oct 1868)

3. Vincent Tucker (b.26 Jan 1820-St. Genevieve Dist. Upper la. Territory)

3. Isadore Tucker (b.4 Apr 1821-Perry County,Missouri;d.8 May 1904-Lavaca County Texas)

sp: Isabel Christine Wimsatt (b.5 Jan 1825-Missouri;m.17 Jan 1842)

3. Alexius Tucker (b.11 Oct 1822-Perry County,Missouri;d.26 Apr 1890-Lavaca County Texas)

sp: Sarah Ann Riley (b.2 Mar 1829-Perry County,Missouri;m.6 Feb 1845;d.7 Jul 1888-Lavaca County Texas)

3. Joseph Simeon Tucker (b.17 Feb 1825-Perry County,Missouri;d.13 Jun 1851-Indianola Texas)

sp: Mary Ann Burtles (b.1829;m.18 Aug 1845;d.13 Jun 1851-Indianola Texas)

3. Theresa Tucker (b.5 Oct 1826-Perry County,Missouri;d.7 Jul 1888-Lavaca County Texas)

sp: Joseph Ryan (m.15 Jul 1847)

3. Mary Ann Tucker (b.9 Apr 1830-Perry County,Missouri;d.6 Feb 1914-Lavaca County Texas)

sp: Leo Brewer (b.29 Jan 1827-Perry County,Missouri;m.1 May 1848;d.Bef 1870-Lavaca County Texas)

3. Joseph Tucker (b.9 Apr 1830-Perry County,Missouri;d.2 Oct 1913-Lavaca County Texas)

sp: Malinda Brown (b.31 Jan 1828-Perry County,Missouri;m.16 Oct 1848)

2. William Tucker (b.1786-St. Mary's County,Maryland;d.20 Aug 1852-Perry County,Missouri)

sp: Sarah Ann Hayden

3. Sarah Ann Tucker (b.1816-St.Genevieve District,Upper Louisiana Territory;d.14 Aug 1865-Perry County,Missouri)

sp: Peter Dean (b.12 Sep 1812;m.Bef 1833;d.16 Oct 1884)

2. John Tucker (b.4 Jul 1788-St. Mary's County,Maryland;d.5 Aug 1856-Perry County,Missouri)

2. Francis Tucker (b.24 Feb 1793-Kentucky;d.12 Apr 1865-Perry County,Missouri)

Descendants of John Drury

1. John Drury (b.Abt 1739-St. Mary's Co.,Md;d.Jun 1797-St. Mary's Co.,Md)

sp: Unknown (m.Abt 1760)

── 2. Ignatius Drury (b.1760-St. Mary's Co.,Md;d.Aft 1797)

── 2. Susanna Drury (b.Bef 1767-St. Mary's Co.,Md;d.Bef 1789)

    sp: Bennet Raley (b.1740-St. Mary's Co.,Md;m.16 Aug 1784;d.Aft 1810)

    ── 3. John Raley (b.1 Jun 1785-St. Mary's County,Maryland)

    ── 3. Benedict L. Raley Jr. (b.27 Nov 1787-St. Mary's Co.,Md;d.9 Jun 1853-Buffalo,New York)

        sp: Ann Combs (b.1794/1801-St. Mary's Co.,Md;m.15 Jan 1816;d.INT 1820 (1820/1840)-St. Mary's Co.,Md)

        sp: Arabella Israel (b.Abt 1805-Philadelphia,Pennsylvania;m.1834)

    ── 3. Ann "Nancy" Raley (b.18 Sep 1789-St. Mary's Co.,Md)

        sp: William Bliss (m.1812)

        sp: Benjamin Lawson

── 2. John Chrysostom Drury (b.1766/1771-St. Mary's Co.,Md;d.Aft 1810)

    sp: <Unknown> (m.Bef 1779)

    ── 3. Elias Drury (b.1786-St. Mary's County,Maryland)

        sp: Ann (b.Abt 1784-Maryland;m.3 Jan 1804;d.1833)

        sp: Anastasia Cain (b.1799;m.3 Feb 1834;d.Bef 1854-Hardin County,Kentucky)

    ── 3. John Drury (b.Dec 1789-St. Mary's Co.,Md;d.Aft 1810)

    ── 3. Robert Drury (b.5 Apr 1792-St. Mary's Co.,Md;d.Aft 1810)

    ── 3. Mary Drury (b.1794-St. Mary's Co.,Md;d.Aft 1810)

── 2. Francis Desales Drury (b.Abt 1768-St. Mary's Co.,Md;d.1809-St. Mary's Co.,Md)

    sp: Ann (Anna) Yates (b.Bef 1777-St. Mary's Co.,Md;m.15 Oct 1799;d.1805/1807-St. Mary's Co.,Md)

    ── 3. Mary Ellen Drury

    ── 3. Ann Caroline Drury

        sp: John Dunbar Sanner (m.25 Jan 1824)

    sp: Winifred Lowe (b.1777/1779-St. Mary's Co.,Md;m.11 Nov 1807;d.5 Apr 1819-Washington,D.C.)

── 2. William Drury (b.Abt 1777-St. Mary's Co.,Md;d.26 Feb 1851-Mercer County,Kentucky)

    sp: Elizabeth Lankford (b.1781-Dorchester County,Maryland;m.4 Feb 1799;d.Bef 1819-Kentucky)

    ── 3. John D. Drury (b.Betw 1811 - 1812-Mercer County,Kentucky;d.Between 1869 - 1870-Robertson County,Texas)

        sp: Elizabeth Sweeney (b.Abt 1822-Kentucky;m.5 Jan 1840;d.Between 1855 - 1858-Robertson County,Texas)

        sp: Martha J. White (b.Abt 1838-Georgia;m.13 Jul 1859)

        sp: Nancy Elizabeth "Louise" Gregg (b.13 Jan 1839-Tennesse;m.9 Apr 1864;d.6 May 1919-McLennan County,Texas)

    ── 3. Joshua Drury (b.Abt 1817-Kentucky;d.1892-Washington County,Kentucky)

        sp: Sarah Martin (b.1820;m.14 Aug 1838;d.1887)

    sp: Elizabeth T. Edwards (b.Abt 1781-Pennsylvania;m.9 Jan 1819;d.7 Nov 1850-Mercer County,Kentucky)

    ── 3. Mary Drury (b.Aft 1820-Nelson County. Kentucky;d.1854-Daviss County,Kentucky)

        sp: Leonard Knott (b.Abt 1797-Nelson County,Kentucky;m.19 Jul 1819;d.1854-Daviss County,Kentucky)

    ── 3. Indiana Drury (b.1822-Kentucky)

    ── 3. Harvey A. Drury (b.Abt 1823-Kentucky;d.Aft 1860-Texas)

        sp: Martha Inman (b.Abt 1826-Kentucky)

── 2. Anastasia Drury (b.1768-St. Mary's Co.,Md;d.Aft 1797)

    sp: Charles Vessels (b.1750;m.1788)

        3. Eleanor Vessels (b.23 Mar 1788-St. Mary's County,Maryland)

        3. Mary Vessels (b.14 Mar 1790-St. Mary's County,Maryland)

        3. Anna Vessels (b.3 Mar 1793-St. Mary's County,Maryland)

   2. Mary Drury (b.Bef 1782;d.Aft 1797)

     sp: Matthew Mandley (b.Bef 1782;m.Bef 1797)

   2. Monica Drury (b.Bef 1784-St. Mary's Co.,Md;d.Aft 1794)

   2. Joseph Drury

sp: Ann (m.21 Apr 1795;d.Aft 1797)

Descendants of William Drury

1. William Drury (b.Abt 1777-St. Mary's Co.,Md;d.26 Feb 1851-Mercer County,Kentucky)

    sp: Elizabeth Lankford (b.1781-Dorchester County,Maryland;m.4 Feb 1799;d.Bef 1819-Kentucky)

        2. John D. Drury (b.Betw 1811 - 1812-Mercer County,Kentucky;d.Between 1869 - 1870-Robertson County,Texas)

            sp: Elizabeth Sweeney (b.Abt 1822-Kentucky;m.5 Jan 1840;d.Between 1855 - 1858-Robertson County,Texas)

                3. Harry A. Drury (b.Abt 1840-Mercer County,Kentucky)

                3. Mary Drury (b.1840-Mercer County,Kentucky;d.Unknown)

                3. Martha Jane Drury (b.Abt 1841-Mercer County,Kentucky)

                3. Elizabeth F. Drury (b.Abt 1843-Mercer County,Kentucky)

                3. Indiana Drury (b.8 May 1846-Mercer County,Kentucky;d.3 Jun 1889-Hood County,Texas)

                3. Willis D. "W.D." Drury (b.28 Jul 1848-Mercer County,Kentucky;d.Aft 1910-Callahan County Texas)

                3. William Drury (b.Abt 1850-Mercer County,Kentucky;d.Unknown)

                    sp: Febie A. ( ) Drury (m.1869)

                3. John A. Drury (b.21 Sep 1852-Mercer County,Kentucky;d.11 Mar 1929-Graham,Carter,Oklahoma)

                    sp: Martha Ann Stroud (b.7 Feb 1847-Batesville,I,Arkansas;m.27 Jun 1878;d.26 Feb 1935-Duncan,Stephens,Oklahoma)

                    sp: Louisa Ellen Roe (m.21 Jan 1871;d.Bef 7 May 1873-Robertson County,Texas)

                    sp: Alice Hada Williams (b.Abt 1857;m.7 May 1871(Div))

                3. Joseph Upton Joshua Drury (b.16 Dec 1854-Calvert,Robertson,Texas;d.3 Sep 1924-Healdton,Carter,Oklahoma)

                    sp: Mary Ford (b.Between 1854 - 1858-Texas;m.17 Jun 1876;d.Between 1880 - 1888-Erath,Hood,Texas)

                    sp: Lillie Jane Sessions (b.14 Jun 1866-Randolph,Bibb,Alabama;m.6 May 1888;d.23 Feb 1952-Ardmore,Carter,Oklahoma)

            sp: Martha J. White (b.Abt 1838-Georgia;m.13 Jul 1859)

                3. Thomas W. Drury (b.Abt 1859-Robertson County,Texas)

            sp: Nancy Elizabeth "Louise" Gregg (b.13 Jan 1839-Tennesse;m.9 Apr 1864;d.6 May 1919-McLennan County,Texas)

                3. Charles D. Drury (b.23 Mar 1865-Texas;d.28 May 1929-Robertson County,Texas)

                3. James Drury (b.Abt 1869-Texas;d.Abt 1882-Limestone County,Texas)

        2. Joshua Drury (b.Abt 1817-Kentucky;d.1892-Washington County,Kentucky)

            sp: Sarah Martin (b.1820;m.14 Aug 1838;d.1887)

                3. Gordon Drury (b.1839-Washington County,Kentucky;d.1921-Washington County,Kentucky)

                    sp: Violet (b.1847-Washington County,Kentucky;m.Abt 1865)

                3. Merrit Drury (b.1841-Washington County,Kentucky;d.1925-Washington County,Kentucky)

                    sp: Martha (b.1845-Washington County,Kentucky;m.Abt 1860)

                3. Harvey Drury (b.1843-Washington County,Kentucky;d.1922-Washington County,Kentucky)

                3. Nancy Elizabeth Drury (b.1846-Washington County,Kentucky;d.1925-Washington County,Kentucky)

                3. William Drury (b.1848-Washington County,Kentucky;d.1879-Washington County,Kentucky)

                3. Grandville Drury (b.1852-Washington County,Kentucky;d.1900-Washington County,Kentucky)

                3. Martha Ellen Drury (b.1857-Washington County,Kentucky;d.1925-Washington County,Kentucky)

                3. James Earl Drury (b.1858-Washington County,Kentucky;d.1907-Washington County,Kentucky)

                3. Dorinda Drury (b.1862-Washington County,Kentucky;d.1893-Washington County,Kentucky)

                    sp: William H. Drury (b.1847-Henderson County,Kentucky;m.1881)

                3. Sarah Catherine Drury (b.12 Feb 1867-Washington County,Kentucky;d.14 Nov 1948-Washington County,Kentucky)

                    sp: George Thomas Cornish (b.1867-Washington County,Kentucky;m.10 Jun 1885;d.1923-Washington County,Kentucky)

                3. Julia Ann Drury (b.1870-Washington County,Kentucky;d.1937-Washington County,Kentucky)

    sp: Elizabeth T. Edwards (b.Abt 1781-Pennsylvania;m.9 Jan 1819;d.7 Nov 1850-Mercer County,Kentucky)

2. Mary Drury (b.Aft 1820-Nelson County. Kentucky;d.1854-Daviss County,Kentucky)

    sp: Leonard Knott (b.Abt 1797-Nelson County,Kentucky;m.19 Jul 1819;d.1854-Daviss County,Kentucky)

       3. James I Knott

       3. Mary E. Knott

         sp: John Haynes

       3. Margaret M. Knott

       3. Unknown Knott

2. Indiana Drury (b.1822-Kentucky)

2. Harvey A. Drury (b.Abt 1823-Kentucky;d.Aft 1860-Texas)

    sp: Martha Inman (b.Abt 1826-Kentucky)

       3. Sarah Drury (b.Abt 1844-Mercer County,Kentucky)

       3. William H. Drury (b.1847-Henderson County,Kentucky)

         sp: Martha Evelyn Byrd

         sp: Dorinda Drury (b.1862-Washington County,Kentucky;m.1881;d.1893-Washington County,Kentucky)

         sp: Alice Mask (b.1859;m.29 Dec 1893)

       3. James Drury (b.Abt 1849-Mercer County,Kentucky)

       3. Margaret Jane Drury (b.1860;d.1949)

         sp: William Edward Sharp (b.1851-Texas;m.3 Jan 1886;d.1924-Texas)

Descendants of Joseph Drury

1. Joseph Drury (b.Bef 1750;d.Abt 1806-Bedford County,Virginia)

sp: Elizabeth (m.Bef 1772;d.Bef 1776-Bedford County,Virginia)

   2. Mary Drury (b.Sep 1772-Bedford County,Virginia)

   2. Elizabeth Drury (b.1775-Bedford County,Virginia)

sp: Sybil Wigginton (b.Abt 1751-Prince William County,Virginia;m.1776)

   2. Isaac Drury (b.1777)

     sp: Sarah Dowdy (m.24 Dec 1832)

   2. Rebecca Drury (b.11 Sep 1779;d.Jul 1855)

     sp: Sanders Brown (m.14 Feb 1817)

       3. Patsy Brown (b.17 Nov 1817)

       3. Samuel Brown (b.12 Dec 1818)

       3. Polly Brown (b.12 Jan 1820;d.1912)

         sp: Robert Hankins (b.14 Apr 1819;m.11 Sep 1845;d.15 Dec 1889)

   2. Sallie Drury (b.1781-Prince Williamco,Va)

     sp: Elijah Russell (m.5 Apr 1813)

   2. John Drury (b.5 Jan 1781-Prince Williamco,Va;d.1858)

     sp: Rachel Dorris (b.1792;m.Abt 1810;d.1858)

       3. Polly Drury (b.4 Jul 1811)

       3. William Drury (b.18 Jul 1813;d.1870/1880-MacOn Co,Tn)

         sp: Caroline Johnson (b.1820;d.1902-MacOn Co,Tn)

       3. Elizabeth Drury (b.26 May 1817)

       3. Lucinda Drury (b.30 Mar 1819)

       3. Delila Drury (b.8 Jul 1821;d.1850-MacOnco,Tn)

       3. Stephen Drury (b.1 Oct 1823)

       3. George Riley Drury (b.1827;d.1885-MacOnco,Tn)

         sp: Lucinda Meador (d.1855)

         sp: Alzia Pipkin Reagan

       3. Francis Millard Drury (b.1828;d.1901-MacOnco,Tn)

         sp: Elizabeth Shrum (m.1852;d.1856)

         sp: Elizabeth Jane Leath (b.1840;m.1858;d.1902)

       3. Martha Drury (b.1834)

   2. George Drury (b.11 Sep 1783-Prince Williamco,Va)

   2. Betsy Drury (b.1785-Prince Williamco,Va)

     sp: ??? Easley

   2. James Drury (b.1785-Prince Williamco,Va)

     sp: Nancy Stith

   2. Nancy Drury (b.1787-Bedfordco,Va)

     sp: ??? Foster

   2. Frances Drury (b.1791-Bedfordco,Va;d.1856-Il)

     sp: Fielden Hankins (b.Abt 1789;m.Abt 1809;d.1883-Il)

       3. Deborah Hankins (b.1811-Tn)

         sp: John Hays

3. Jane Hankins (b.1816-Ky)

   sp: Morris Merrick

3. Davis Hankins (b.Abt 1818)

   sp: Abigail Elmore

   sp: Julia Ann Henderson

3. Wesley Hankins (b.27 Jan 1818-Ky)

3. Emily Hankins (b.1823-Ky)

   sp: Jonathan Hayes

3. Andrew Jackson Hankins (b.10 Mar 1824-In;d.27 Feb 1913-Ok)

   sp: Lydia Ann Pennington (b.22 Oct 1826;m.28 Aug 1845;d.25 Jan 1885)

3. William Hankins

3. Nimrod Hankins

2. Martha Drury (b.3 Jul 1794-Bedfordco,Va;d.23 Aug 1888-Limestoneco,Tx)

  sp: Wade Hampton Davis (b.1796;m.13 May 1813;d.1877-Marysville,Mo)

3. William Davis (b.6 Feb 1814-Smithco,Tn;d.9 Jul 1875-Nodawayco,Mo)

   sp: Sarah Elizabeth Barnes (m.6 Apr 1837)

3. Nancy Davis (b.Mar 1817;d.Dec 1831)

3. Smithen Hamilton Davis (b.9 Sep 1819-Breckenridgeco,Ky;d.26 Mar 1894-Thayer,Mo)

   sp: Rhoda Jane Moreman (m.19 Apr 1846)

3. Elizabeth Davis (d.16 Aug 1848)

   sp: Thomas Groves

3. Hiram Davis (b.14 Feb 1821-Breckenridgeco,Ky;d.15 Jul 1895)

   sp: Mary Jane Broyles (d.14 Feb 1918)

3. Martha Jane Davis (b.29 Sep 1828-Sumnerco,Tn)

   sp: Elijah Johnson

   sp: George Washington Long

3. James Wade Davis (b.8 Apr 1830-Marionco,Il)

   sp: Martha Simpson Faulkner

   sp: Martha Ann Robinson

2. Lucy Drury (b.8 Nov 1796-Bedfordco,Va;d.11 Jan 1889)

  sp: Josiah Dorris (b.8 Nov 1796-Nc;m.12 May 1816;d.20 Jan 1871)

3. Hiram Cassity Dorris (b.25 Jan 1818-Smithco,Tn;d.1847)

   sp: Elizabeth K. Fulkerson (m.25 Nov 1841)

3. Wiley Howell Dorris (b.1820-Smithco,Tn;d.1843-Plattco,Mo)

3. Presley Alexander Dorris (b.8 Nov 1822-Smithco,Tn;d.19 Nov 1901-Alturas,Ca)

3. Carlos Jefferson Dorris (b.Sep 1824-Smithco,Tn;d.8 Dec 1907-Alturas,Ca)

3. Sarah Catherine Dorris (b.8 Aug 1826-Smith Co.,Tn;d.4 Mar 1894-Cottage Grove,Or)

   sp: John Porter (b.11 Sep 1821-Howard Co.,Mo;m.11 Jul 1844)

3. Letha Parlee Dorris (b.1829-Fultonco,Il;d.1854-Humboltco,Ca)

3. Cyrus Grundy Dorris (b.4 Jan 1831-Fultonco,Il;d.17 Oct 1903-Alturas,Modocco,Ca)

   sp: Elizabeth Barnes (b.8 May 1844;m.22 Aug 1860)

3. Parthena H. Dorris (b.16 May 1833-Fultonco,Il;d.1912)

   sp: Preston Hays

   sp: Francis Payne (m.26 Jan 1855)

3. Columbus Dorris (b.16 Apr 1837-Fultonco,Il;d.31 Dec 1875-Siskiyouco,Ca)

   sp: Rachel Cyrus (m.24 Oct 1864)

3. Amanda Melvina Dorris (b.1838-Fultonco,Il;d.1854-Humbolt Sink,Ca)

Descendants of Peter Drury

1. Peter Drury (b.Est 1715-,St. Mary's County,Maryland;d.1770/1771-,St. Mary's County,Maryland)

sp: Jane Bailey (m.Abt 1735/1736;d.Bef 1770-St. Mary's County,Maryland)

- 2. Michael Drury (b.Est 1736-,St. Mary's County,Maryland;d.1826-St. Mary's County,Maryland)

  sp: Ann Yates (b.1743/1755;m.3 Nov 1770)

  - 3. Edward Drury (c.15 Dec 1771-St. Mary's County,Maryland;d.1819/1820-St. Mary's County,Maryland)

    sp: UNKNOWN

  - 3. Joshua Drury (c.2 Feb 1774-St. Mary's County,Maryland)

  - 3. Dorothy Drury (b.1775-St. Mary's County,Maryland;d.Aft 1860-St. Mary's County,Maryland)

    sp: Ignatius Joy Jr. (b.1761/1763-St. Mary's County,Maryland;m.11 Jan 1807;d.16 Mar 1838-St. Mary's County,Maryland)

  - 3. Mary Ann Drury (b.1785-St. Mary's County,Maryland;d.Aft 1825-St. Mary's County,Maryland)

    sp: Rhodolphus Gibson (m.Bef 1812)

    sp: Joseph Leonard Johnson (b.1775-St. Mary's County,Maryland;m.22 Sep 1812;d.1833-St. Mary's County,Maryland)

  - 3. Michael Drury Jr. (b.1785-St. Mary's County,Maryland;d.Bef 1823-St. Mary's County,Maryland)

    sp: Catherine Johnson (b.1791-St. Mary's County,Maryland;m.30 Aug 1813)

  - 3. Catherine Drury (b.1795/1800-St. Mary's County,Maryland)

  - 3. Sarah Marthalina Drury (b.1799)

    sp: John Johnson (b.1784;m.9 Jan 1819;d.1860)

  - 3. George Drury (b.Bef 1800-St. Mary's County,Maryland)

- 2. Nicholas Drury (b.1738-,St. Mary's County,Maryland;d.Bef 1790)

  sp: Monica

  - 3. Leonard Drury (b.1759-St. Mary's County,Maryland)

  - 3. Bennett Drury (c.17 Apr 1768-St. Mary's County,Maryland)

  - 3. Mary Drury (c.2 Sep 1770-St. Mary's County,Maryland)

  - 3. Joseph Drury (c.2 Sep 1770-St. Mary's County,Maryland)

    sp: UNKNOWN

  - 3. Monica Drury (c.4 Oct 1772-St. Mary's County,Maryland)

    sp: Joseph Herbert (m.9 Feb 1795)

- 2. Peter Drury (b.1740-,St. Mary's County,Maryland)

  sp: Eleanor

  - 3. Jesse Drury (c.22 Sep 1776-St. Mary's County,Maryland)

  - 3. Wilfred Drury (c.24 Jan 1779-St. Mary's County,Maryland)

    sp: Nellie Baily (m.9 May 1799)

- 2. Ignatius Drury (b.1745-St. Mary's County;d.Aft 1800-Nelson County,Kentucky)

  sp: Anastasia French (b.29 Jul 1750-St. Mary's County,Maryland;m.11 Dec 1769)

  - 3. Dorothy Drury (b.1771-St. Mary's County,Maryland;d.Abt 1850-Daviss County,Kentucky)

    sp: John H. Payne (b.14 Feb 1769-St. Mary's County,Maryland;m.20 Oct 1794;d.24 Mar 1846-Daviss County,Kentucky)

  - 3. Ignatius Drury (b.1773-St. Mary's County,Maryland;d.betw 6/1833 - 8/1833)

    sp: Harriet Redding (m.5 Dec 1799)

    sp: Deborah Thorne (m.Bef 1817)

  - 3. Charles Drury (b.7 Feb 1776-St. Mary's County,Maryland;d.1852)

    sp: Emily Thorne (b.1783-St. Mary's County,Maryland)

    sp: Elizabeth Leach (b.1782-St. Mary's County,Maryland)

3. Elizabeth Drury (b.1782-St. Mary's County,Maryland;d.1866-Nelson County,Kentucky)

    sp: Charles Burkham Jarboe (b.1785-St. Mary's County,Maryland;m.1805;d.12 Jun 1866-Daviss County,Kentucky)

3. Monica Drury (b.1785-St. Mary's County,Maryland;d.12 Jun 1866-Nelson County,Kentucky)

    sp: Charles Warren (b.27 Sep 1782-St. Mary's County,Maryland;d.4 Apr 1868-Nelson County,Kentucky)

3. Mary Ellen Drury (b.19 Jun 1787-St. Mary's County,Maryland;d.2 Feb 1858-Washington County,Kentucky)

    sp: William Hogan (b.27 Oct 1788;m.1 Jan 1814;d.17 Jun 1854-Washington County,Kentucky)

3. Ann Drury (b.1789-St. Mary's Co.,Md;d.31 Dec 1857-Baltimore)

2. Philip Drury (b.Est 1750-,St. Mary's County,Maryland;d.9 Jun 1795-St. Mary's County,Maryland)

  sp: Emerentia Bibiana Newton (m.4 Sep 1770;d.bet 1795 -1812)

3. Bernard Drury (b.1771-,St. Marys County,Maryland;d.26 Jul 1819-,Washington County,Kentucky)

    sp: Catharine Wimsatt (b.1775-,St. Mary's County,Maryland;m.7 Nov 1796;d.23 Mar 1838-,Marion County,Kentucky)

3. Tecla Drury (b.1772-,St. Mary's County,Maryland;d.Aft 1811-St. Mary's County,Maryland)

    sp: Allen Norris (b.Bef 1772-St. Mary's County,Maryland;m.7 Jan 1811;d.Aft 1811-St. Mary's County,Maryland)

3. Zachariah Drury ? (b.1773-St. Mary's County,Maryland;d.1855-Nelson County,Kentucky)

    sp: Mary Jane Molohon (b.Abt 1769-Maryland;m.12 Jan 1797)

3. Samuel Drury (b.4 Feb 1775-,St. Mary's County,Maryland)

    sp: Eleanor Jarboe (b.2 Nov 1768-St. Mary's County,Maryland;m.21 Oct 1799)

3. Emerentia Drury (b.1777-,St. Mary's County,Maryland)

3. Jane Drury (b.1779-St. Mary's County,Maryland;d.Bef Oct 1813-St. Mary's County,Maryland)

    sp: Zachariah Peacock (c.21 Mar 1773-St. Mary's County,Maryland;m.11 Feb 1804)

3. Clement Drury (b.Abt 1784-St. Mary's County,Maryland)

    sp: Ann Cissell (b.1785-St. Mary's County,Maryland;m.29 Jan 1803;d.Bef 1811-St. Mary's County,Maryland)

    sp: Dorothy Boyd (m.5 Jun 1811)

3. Male Drury (b.1780/1790)

3. John Drury (b.bet 1790 - 1795-,St. Mary's County,Maryland)

2. Robert Drury ?

  sp: Mary Margaret

3. Dorothy Drury (c.19 May 1770-St. Mary's County,Maryland)

3. Ann Drury (c.5 Apr 1772-St. Mary's County,Maryland)

2. John Drury ?

  sp: Elizabeth

3. John Drury (b.Dec 1766-St. Mary's County,Maryland)

  sp: Mary Margaret

3. Mary Drury (b.Jan 1768)

3. Elizabeth Drury (b.Oct 1770)

2. Enoch Drury ? (d.1784-,St. Mary's County,Maryland)

  sp: Tabitha Wimsatt

3. Alathair Drury (d.1807-St. Mary's County,Maryland)

3. Aloysia Drury (c.3 Apr 1771-St. Mary's County,Maryland)

3. Elizabeth Drury (c.20 Dec 1772-St. Mary's County,Maryland)

3. Eleanor Drury (c.6 Feb 1774-St. Mary's County,Maryland;d.Abt 1799)

    sp: Philip Abell (b.1772-St. Mary's County,Maryland;m.24 Dec 1796;d.11 Aug 1811-St. Mary's County,Maryland)

3. James Drury (c.9 Apr 1776-St. Mary's County,Maryland;d.Bef 19 Mar 1793-St. Mary's County,Maryland)

3. Winifred Drury (b.1 Apr 1777-St. Mary's County,Maryland;d.17 Feb 1856)

        sp: James Thompson (b.betw 1770-77-St. Mary's County,Maryland;m.23 Dec 1805;d.14 Mar 1846)

    — 3. Frances Drury

    — 3. Mary Drury

    — 3. Enoch Drury Jr. (d.4 Nov 1817-St. Mary's County,Maryland)

        sp: Mary Brewer (b.1786;m.27 Nov 1807)

— 2. Catherine Drury

— 2. Mildred Drury (b.1755-St. Mary's County,Maryland;d.by 1831)

   sp: Ignatius Russell (b.10 Mar 1748-St. Mary's County,Maryland;m.1772)

    — 3. Eleanor Russell (b.26 May 1773-St. Mary's County,Maryland)

    — 3. Phillp Russell (b.15 Sep 1775-St. Mary's County,Maryland)

    — 3. Allusia Russell (b.24 Dec 1777-St. Mary's County,Maryland)

    — 3. Charles Russell (b.1783-St. Mary's County,Maryland;d.1816-St. Mary's County,Maryland)

        sp: Monica French (b.1796-St. Mary's County,Maryland;m.10 Aug 1812;d.1850-St. Mary's County,Maryland)

— 2. Richard Drury ?

   sp: Elizabeth (m.Bef 1771)

    — 3. Peter Drury ? (c.7 Nov 1771-St. Mary's County,Maryland)

        sp: unknown (m.by 1793)

        sp: Ann Hayden (m.23 Jan 1816)

        sp: Mary Cox (m.29 Dec 1828)

    — 3. Richard Drury Jr. (b.Bef 1786-St. Mary's County Maryland;d.Aft 1827-St. Mary's County Maryland)

        sp: Jane Blair (b.Bef 1791-St. Mary's County Maryland;m.9 Jan 1806;d.Aft 1827-St. Mary's County Maryland)

sp: Ann Bailey (b.Abt 1735-St. Mary's County,Maryland;m.?)

Descendants of Nicholas Drury

1. Nicholas Drury (b.1738-,St. Mary's County,Maryland;d.Bef 1790)

sp: Monica

    2. Leonard Drury (b.1759-St. Mary's County,Maryland)

    2. Bennett Drury (c.17 Apr 1768-St. Mary's County,Maryland)

    2. Mary Drury (c.2 Sep 1770-St. Mary's County,Maryland)

    2. Joseph Drury (c.2 Sep 1770-St. Mary's County,Maryland)

      sp: UNKNOWN

        3. Joanna Drury (c.7 Feb 1787-St. Mary's County,Maryland)

        3. Joseph Drury (c.5 Apr 1789-St. Mary's County,Maryland;d.1859-St. Mary's County Maryland)

          sp: Mary Ann Dixon (m.22 Jul 1823;d.Bef 1840-St. Mary's County Maryland)

    2. Monica Drury (c.4 Oct 1772-St. Mary's County,Maryland)

      sp: Joseph Herbert (m.9 Feb 1795)

Descendants of Michael Drury

1. Michael Drury (b.Est 1736-,St. Mary's County,Maryland;d.1826-St. Mary's County,Maryland)

sp: Ann Yates (b.1743/1755;m.3 Nov 1770)

    2. Edward Drury (c.15 Dec 1771-St. Mary's County,Maryland;d.1819/1820-St. Mary's County,Maryland)

      sp: UNKNOWN

        3. John Thomas Drury (b.1796-St. Mary's County,Maryland;d.Aft 1870)

          sp: Susanna Greenwell (b.Abt 1801;m.19 Jan 1824)

          sp: Ann Priscilla Joy

        3. Dorothy Drury (b.1799-St. Mary's County,Maryland;d.Aft 1860-St. Mary's County,Maryland)

          sp: Joseph Pilkington (b.Abt 1780-St. Mary's County,Maryland;m.24 May 1841;d.1850/1860-St. Mary's County,Maryland)

        3. Elizabeth Drury (b.Bef 1800-St. Mary's County,Maryland)

        3. Julia Ann Drury (b.Bef 1821-St. Mary's County,Maryland;d.24 May 1885-St. Mary's County,Maryland)

          sp: Bennett Greenwell (b.1786-St. Mary's County,Maryland;m.23 Apr 1838;d.27 Jan 1863-St. Mary's County,Maryland)

    2. Joshua Drury (c.2 Feb 1774-St. Mary's County,Maryland)

    2. Dorothy Drury (b.1775-St. Mary's County,Maryland;d.Aft 1860-St. Mary's County,Maryland)

      sp: Ignatius Joy Jr. (b.1761/1763-St. Mary's County,Maryland;m.11 Jan 1807;d.16 Mar 1838-St. Mary's County,Maryland)

        3. Ignatius Summerfield Joy (b.20 May 1812-St. Mary's County,Maryland;d.4 Aug 1887-St. Mary's County,Maryland)

          sp: Mary Edley Morgan (b.1837-St. Mary's County,Maryland;m.1 Feb 1853;d.1912-St. Mary's County,Maryland)

        3. Elizabeth Joy (b.1813-St. Mary's County,Maryland;d.1850/1860-St. Mary's County,Maryland)

          sp: Henry Hilton Jr. (b.1806-St. Mary's County,Maryland;m.7 Aug 1841;d.1850/1860-St. Mary's County,Maryland)

        3. John Michael Joy (b.1821-St. Mary's County,Maryland;d.Aug 1883-St. Mary's County,Maryland)

          sp: Eleanor Johnson (b.1830-St. Mary's County,Maryland;m.18 Jan 1853;d.1860/1870-St. Mary's County,Maryland)

          sp: Amanda Ann Mattingly (b.29 Jul 1838-SMSC,Maryland;m.10 Jan 1870;d.21 Jun 1897-St. Mary's County,Maryland)

    2. Mary Ann Drury (b.1785-St. Mary's County,Maryland;d.Aft 1825-St. Mary's County,Maryland)

      sp: Rhodolphus Gibson (m.Bef 1812)

      sp: Joseph Leonard Johnson (b.1775-St. Mary's County,Maryland;m.22 Sep 1812;d.1833-St. Mary's County,Maryland)

        3. William Peter Johnson (b.29 Jun 1813-St. Mary's County,Maryland;d.16 Dec 1892-Lewisport,Hancock County,Kentucky)

          sp: Lucretia A. Jarboe

        3. Ann Johnson (b.Abt 1815)

        3. John Lewis Johnson (b.17 Apr 1817;d.6 Jan 1890)

          sp: Elizabeth Dorothy Payne (m.21 Nov 1843)

        3. Joseph Leonard Johnson Jr. (b.22 Feb 1819;d.16 Mar 1901)

          sp: Martha Ann Payne (m.12 Jan 1847)

        3. Michael Hilary Johnson (b.Abt 1822)

        3. Richard B. Johnson (b.1825)

    2. Michael Drury Jr. (b.1785-St. Mary's County,Maryland;d.Bef 1823-St. Mary's County,Maryland)

      sp: Catherine Johnson (b.1791-St. Mary's County,Maryland;m.30 Aug 1813)

        3. Edward Drury (b.1814-St. Mary's County,Maryland)

        3. Rose Anna Drury (b.5 Apr 1815-St. Mary's County,Maryland;d.5 Oct 1885-Rockport,Indiana)

          sp: Alfred Hall (b.1812;m.1838;d.Oct 1861-Rockport,Indiana)

        3. Eleanor Drury (b.1817-St. Mary's County,Maryland)

    2. Catherine Drury (b.1795/1800-St. Mary's County,Maryland)

    2. Sarah Marthalina Drury (b.1799)

sp: John Johnson (b.1784;m.9 Jan 1819;d.1860)

- 3. Mary Priscilla Johnson (b.27 Dec 1819)

    sp: Enoch R. Evans

- 3. Uriah Johnson (b.25 Mar 1821;d.23 Apr 1896)

    sp: Clarissa "Clara" Eleona Shircliffe (b.14 Jan 1828;m.13 Jan 1847;d.17 Nov 1895)

- 3. Joseph Stephen Johnson (b.26 Dec 1825)

- 3. Thomas Johnson (b.Abt 1827)

- 3. Eleanor Johnson (b.1829/1830)

- 3. Hillery E. Johnson (b.22 Apr 1832)

- 3. William Edward Johnson (b.Apr 1836)

- 3. Martha Johnson (b.1837/1838)

- 3. John T. Johnson (b.1839)

2. George Drury (b.Bef 1800-St. Mary's County,Maryland)

Descendants of Ignatius Drury

1. Ignatius Drury (b.1745-St. Mary's County;d.Aft 1800-Nelson County,Kentucky)

sp: Anastasia French (b.29 Jul 1750-St. Mary's County,Maryland;m.11 Dec 1769)

- 2. Dorothy Drury (b.1771-St. Mary's County,Maryland;d.Abt 1850-Daviss County,Kentucky)

  sp: John H. Payne (b.14 Feb 1769-St. Mary's County,Maryland;m.20 Oct 1794;d.24 Mar 1846-Daviss County,Kentucky)

  - 3. John Payne (b.30 May 1799-Prince George's County,Maryland)

  - 3. Ignatius Payne (b.27 Aug 1801-Prince George's County,Maryland)

  - 3. Cornelius Payne (b.28 Aug 1803-Daviss County,Kentucky;d.3 Feb 1835-Daviss County,Kentucky)

    sp: Mary M. Payne (b.28 Apr 1805-Daviss County,Kentucky;m.4 Nov 1823;d.15 Dec 1871-Daviss County,Kentucky)

  - 3. Dennis Henry Payne

  - 3. Charles Payne (b.1809-Prince George's County,Maryland)

- 2. Ignatius Drury (b.1773-St. Mary's County,Maryland;d.betw 6/1833 - 8/1833)

  sp: Harriet Redding (m.5 Dec 1799)

  - 3. Mary Ann Drury (b.2 Nov 1801-District of Columbia)

    sp: James E. Bowling (b.1792-Faquier,Virginia;m.7 Mar 1818;d.22 Oct 1848-Baltimore,Maryland)

  sp: Deborah Thorne (m.Bef 1817)

  - 3. Milburn Drury

  - 3. George Francis Drury

  - 3. William Drury (b.1817;d.20 Nov 1833-Nelson County,Kentucky)

- 2. Charles Drury (b.7 Feb 1776-St. Mary's County,Maryland;d.1852)

  sp: Emily Thorne (b.1783-St. Mary's County,Maryland)

  - 3. Catherine Drury SCN (b.31 Mar 1805;d.16 Aug 1890)

  - 3. Anastasia Drury SCN (b.1812-Nelson County,Kentucky;d.17 Mar 1875-Nelson County,Kentucky)

  - 3. James Drury (b.1823-Washington County,Kentucky)

  - 3. George Drury

    sp: Elizabeth McClain

  - 3. Robert Drury

    sp: Rose Carrico

  - 3. Pius Drury

    sp: Mary Blandford

  - 3. Mary Drury

    sp: Stephan Theodore O'Bryan (b.1801-Nelson County,Kentucky;m.5 Oct 1829;d.Aft 1860)

  - 3. Matilda Drury

    sp: Martin O'Bryan (b.1810-Nelson County,Kentucky;m.5 Oct 1830;d.1839-Davies County,Kentucky)

  - 3. Martha Drury

    sp: John Robert O'Bryan (b.21 Jan 1811-Nelson County,Kentucky;m.1848;d.Aft 1880-Davies County,Kentucky)

  - 3. Susan Drury (b.1816;d.1841-Nelson County,Kentucky)

    sp: James Wehlan

  - 3. Mahala Drury (b.1821;d.1896)

  sp: Elizabeth Leach (b.1782-St. Mary's County,Maryland)

- 2. Elizabeth Drury (b.1782-St. Mary's County,Maryland;d.1866-Nelson County,Kentucky)

  sp: Charles Burkham Jarboe (b.1785-St. Mary's County,Maryland;m.1805;d.12 Jun 1866-Daviss County,Kentucky)

- 2. Monica Drury (b.1785-St. Mary's County,Maryland;d.12 Jun 1866-Nelson County,Kentucky) sp: Charles Warren (b.27 Sep 1782-St. Mary's County,Maryland;d.4 Apr 1868-Nelson County,Kentucky)

    3. Harriet Warren

      sp: Pius Montgomery

2. Mary Ellen Drury (b.19 Jun 1787-St. Mary's County,Maryland;d.2 Feb 1858-Washington County,Kentucky)

  sp: William Hogan (b.27 Oct 1788;m.1 Jan 1814;d.17 Jun 1854-Washington County,Kentucky)

    3. Ignatius Hogan (b.Abt 1815)

    3. Mary Hogan (b.18 May 1816-Washington County,Kentucky;d.7 Mar 1897-Daviss County,Kentucky)

      sp: John H. Rodman (m.1836)

    3. Ann Hogan

    3. William Hogan

    3. Christine Hogan

    3. Helen Hogan

    3. Elizabeth Hogan

    3. Matilda Hogan

2. Ann Drury (b.1789-St. Mary's Co.,Md;d.31 Dec 1857-Baltimore)

Descendants of Philip Drury

1. Philip Drury (b.Est 1750-,St. Mary's County,Maryland;d.9 Jun 1795-St. Mary's County,Maryland)

sp: Emerentia Bibiana Newton (m.4 Sep 1770;d.bet 1795 -1812)

+ 2. Bernard Drury (b.1771-,St. Marys County,Maryland;d.26 Jul 1819-,Washington County,Kentucky)

  sp: Catharine Wimsatt (b.1775-,St. Mary's County,Maryland;m.7 Nov 1796;d.23 Mar 1838-,Marion County,Kentucky)

  - 3. Robert Drury

  - 3. John Drury

  - 3. Benedict W. Drury (b.13 Jan 1799-St. Mary's County,Maryland;d.1844-Union County,Kentucky)

    sp: Mary Ann Miles (b.8 Sep 1805;m.Bond 27 Jan 1823;d.24 Oct 1842-Union County,Kentucky)

  - 3. Maria Drury (b.1801-St. Mary's County,Maryland;d.19 Sep 1822-Nelson County,Kentucky)

  - 3. Ann Clare Drury (b.1801-St. Mary's County,Maryland)

  - 3. Sarah Drury (b.1802-St. Mary's County,Maryland;d.31 Jul 1824-Nelson County,Kentucky)

  - 3. James Wimsatt Drury (b.9 May 1803-,St. Mary's County,Maryland;d.13 Dec 1852-St. Charles County,Missouri)

    sp: Cecelia Bowles (b.15 Oct 1807-Scott County,Kentucky;m.26 Jan 1826;d.6 Aug 1852-St. Charles County,Missouri)

  - 3. Catherine Drury (b.1804-,St. Mary's County,Maryland;d.7 Nov 1827-,Washington County,Kentucky)

    sp: Clement Molohan (b.1789-St. Mary's County,Maryland;m.22 Nov 1824;d.29 Apr 1852-Hickman County,Kentucky)

  - 3. Ignatius Drury (b.27 Oct 1806-,St. Mary's County,Maryland;d.9 Jul 1887-,Union County,Kentucky)

    sp: Lydia O'Nan (b.5 Mar 1811-,Henry County,Kentucky;m.3 Aug 1830;d.1881-,Union County,Kentucky)

    sp: Catherine M. O'Nan (m.8 Nov 1883)

  - 3. Elizabeth Drury (b.1810-St. Mary's County,Maryland;d.1824-Nelson County,Kentucky)

  - 3. William W. Drury (b.Abt 1814-Washington County,Kentucky)

    sp: Elizabeth E. Hardisty (b.Abt 1815-Kentucky;m.3 Mar 1835;d.22 Mar 1863-Union County,Kentucky)

    sp: Mary E. Hardisty (b.Abt 1817-Kentucky;m.20 Dec 1863)

  - 3. Joseph Drury (b.3 Jun 1816-Washington County,Kentucky;d.16 Feb 1879-Union County,Kentucky)

    sp: Harriet Griffith (b.1819-Marion County,Kentucky;m.22 Oct 1839;d.1854-Union County,Kentucky)

    sp: Mary Hetty Hardesty (b.20 Jun 1830-Union County,Kentucky;m.13 Apr 1855;d.16 Feb 1879-Union County,Kentucky)

    sp: Sarah Ann Fraine (b.Abt 1826-Kentucky;m.25 Jan 1864)

+ 2. Tecla Drury (b.1772-,St. Mary's County,Maryland;d.Aft 1811-St. Mary's County,Maryland)

  sp: Allen Norris (b.Bef 1772-St. Mary's County,Maryland;m.7 Jan 1811;d.Aft 1811-St. Mary's County,Maryland)

+ 2. Zachariah Drury ? (b.1773-St. Mary's County,Maryland;d.1855-Nelson County,Kentucky)

  sp: Mary Jane Molohon (b.Abt 1769-Maryland;m.12 Jan 1797)

  - 3. John Drury (b.1798-St. Mary's County,Maryland)

    sp: Mary Yates

  - 3. Lucy Drury (b.1799-Washington County,Kentucky;d.30 Jan 1873-Perry County,Missouri)

    sp: Henry P. Phillips (b.1797-Maryland;m.23 Oct 1823;d.10 Mar 1884-Perry County,Missouri)

  - 3. James Drury (b.1800)

    sp: Mary Leake

  - 3. Ellenor Drury (b.1802)

  - 3. Francis Drury (b.1806-Washington County,Kentucky;d.1866)

    sp: Juliann Gough (b.1800;m.3 Nov 1827)

  - 3. William Drury (b.1814)

  - 3. Isadore Drury (b.1815)

    sp: Elizabeth Green (b.1825-Marion County,Kentucky;m.by 1842)

2. Samuel Drury (b.4 Feb 1775-,St. Mary's County,Maryland)

  sp: Eleanor Jarboe (b.2 Nov 1768-St. Mary's County,Maryland;m.21 Oct 1799)

2. Emerentia Drury (b.1777-,St. Mary's County,Maryland)

2. Jane Drury (b.1779-St. Mary's County,Maryland;d.Bef Oct 1813-St. Mary's County,Maryland)

  sp: Zachariah Peacock (c.21 Mar 1773-St. Mary's County,Maryland;m.11 Feb 1804)

2. Clement Drury (b.Abt 1784-St. Mary's County,Maryland)

  sp: Ann Cissell (b.1785-St. Mary's County,Maryland;m.29 Jan 1803;d.Bef 1811-St. Mary's County,Maryland)

  sp: Dorothy Boyd (m.5 Jun 1811)

2. Male Drury (b.1780/1790)

2. John Drury (b.bet 1790 - 1795-,St. Mary's County,Maryland)

Descendants of Enoch Drury ?

1. Enoch Drury ? (d.1784-,St. Mary's County,Maryland)

  sp: Tabitha Wimsatt

    2. Alathair Drury (d.1807-St. Mary's County,Maryland)

    2. Aloysia Drury (c.3 Apr 1771-St. Mary's County,Maryland)

    2. Elizabeth Drury (c.20 Dec 1772-St. Mary's County,Maryland)

    2. Eleanor Drury (c.6 Feb 1774-St. Mary's County,Maryland;d.Abt 1799)

      sp: Philip Abell (b.1772-St. Mary's County,Maryland;m.24 Dec 1796;d.11 Aug 1811-St. Mary's County,Maryland)

    2. James Drury (c.9 Apr 1776-St. Mary's County,Maryland;d.Bef 19 Mar 1793-St. Mary's County,Maryland)

    2. Winifred Drury (b.1 Apr 1777-St. Mary's County,Maryland;d.17 Feb 1856)

      sp: James Thompson (b.betw 1770-77-St. Mary's County,Maryland;m.23 Dec 1805;d.14 Mar 1846)

        3. Maria Thompson (b.1806/1810-St. Mary's County,Maryland;d.1845/1850-St. Mary's County,Maryland)

          sp: John B. Raley (b.1803/1804-St. Mary's County,Maryland;m.12 Feb 1828;d.1879-St. Mary's County,Maryland)

        3. John B. Thompson (b.1813;d.Aft 1850)

          sp: Mary Louise Tarleton (b.2 Apr 1819;m.11 Nov 1839;d.9 Sep 1844-St. Mary's County,Maryland)

          sp: Ann Maria Bean (b.1820;m.3 Feb 1845)

        3. Elizabeth Thompson (b.1816-St. Mary's County,Maryland;d.Aft 1860-St. Mary's County,Maryland)

    2. Frances Drury

    2. Mary Drury

    2. Enoch Drury Jr. (d.4 Nov 1817-St. Mary's County,Maryland)

      sp: Mary Brewer (b.1786;m.27 Nov 1807)

        3. Elizabeth Drury (b.1819-St. Mary's County,Maryland;d.Aft 1850-St. Mary's County,Maryland)

          sp: Joseph Thompson (b.1809-St. Mary's County,Maryland;m.2 Nov 1841;d.Aft 1850-St. Mary's County,Maryland)

Descendants of Thomas Theodore Drury

1. Thomas Theodore Drury (b.1819-St. Mary's County,Maryland;d.by 8 Nov 1870-St. Mary's County,Maryland)

sp: Martha Ann Lydaman (b.3 Aug 1825-St. Mary's County,Maryland;m.28 Nov 1846;d.5 May 1889-St. Mary's County,Maryland)

- 2. Elizabeth Indiana Drury (b.1848)
- 2. Mary Virginia Drury (b.1852)
- 2. George Winfield Drury (b.12 Feb 1853-St. Mary's County,Maryland;d.8 Aug 1911-St. Mary's County,Maryland)

  sp: Georgeanna Victoria Raley (b.1859-St. Mary's County,Maryland;m.1880)

  - 3. Mary Edith Drury (b.29 Jan 1883)
  - 3. Cora Elizabeth Drury (b.27 Aug 1885)
  - 3. Theodore L. Drury (b.24 Jun 1887)
  - 3. Clarence Desrubes Drury (b.14 May 1890)
  - 3. James Raub Drury Sr. (b.12 Aug 1891)

    sp: UNKNOWN

    - 4. James Raub Drury Jr. (b.1918)

      sp: Alice

    - 4. Donald F. Drury

      sp: UNKNOWN

  - 3. Joseph Clyde Drury (b.23 Jun 1894)
  - 3. Nettie Anastasia Drury (b.6 Aug 1895)
  - 3. Georgia Esstill Drury (b.14 Oct 1897;d.Bef 1900-St. Mary's County,Maryland)
  - 3. George Lloyd Drury (b.8 Feb 1901)
  - 3. Mary Lillian Esstill Drury (b.13 Oct 1901)

Descendants of Bernard Drury

1. Bernard Drury (b.Abt 1740-St. Mary's County,Maryland)

sp: Ann

    2. Ignatius Drury (b.Sep 1773-St. Mary's County,Maryland;d.Bef 1808-St. Mary's County,Maryland)

      sp: Mary Magdalen Goldsborough (b.1761;m.Sep 1793)

        3. Margaret Drury (b.1795-St. Mary's County,Maryland;d.21 Oct 1865-Loretto,Washington County,Kentucky)

        3. Hilary Drury (b.3 Dec 1799-St. Mary's County,Maryland;d.6 Aug 1872-Davies County,Kentucky)

          sp: Theresa Coombs (b.1807-Davidson County,Kentucky;m.1825;d.fall 1878-Davies County,Kentucky)

            4. Matilda Ann Drury (b.18 Jun 1826-Davies County,Kentucky;d.13 Feb 1911)

            4. Eliza Jane Drury

              sp: J. Hardy Clements

            4. Ignatius Guy Drury (b.18 Nov 1829-Davies County,Kentucky;d.4 Sep 1902-Davies County,Kentucky)

            4. Mary Eleanora Drury

              sp: James R. Mattingly

            4. Richard Theodore Drury (b.8 Feb 1832-Davies County,Kentucky;d.1852-St. Mary,Kentucky)

            4. Mary Margaret Drury (b.17 Oct 1836-Davies County,Kentucky)

              sp: James Robert Spaulding (m.1860)

            4. Theresa Rose Drury (b.7 Nov 1839-Davies County,Kentucky;d.12 Feb 1901-Davies County,Kentucky)

              sp: James William Bray (b.15 Nov 1834;m.15 Nov 1861;d.23 Feb 1901-Davies County,Kentucky)

            4. William Francis Drury (b.29 Jan 1843-Davies County,Kentucky;d.1941-Davies County,Kentucky)

              sp: Matilda Genevieve Mattingly (m.Nov 1872)

            4. Edwin Drury (b.6 Jun 1845-Davies County,Kentucky;d.2 Feb 1913)

        3. Monica Drury

          sp: Thomas Montgomery

             4. Ignatius Bernard Montgomery (b.1822-Randolph County,Illinois;d.Bef 1880-Perry County,Missouri)

              sp: Martina Cissell (b.18 Dec 1832-Perry County,Missouri;m.9 Oct 1849;d.27 Dec 1906)

            4. Charles H Montgomery (b.1825-Kentucky;d.Aft 1860)

              sp: Elizabeth Philomene Cissell (b.19 Jul 1837-PC,Missouri;m.10 Jan 1854;d.15 Oct 1905-Perry County,Missouri)

            4. Thomas Leander Montgomery (b.27 Jun 1828-Kentucky;d.23 Nov 1880)

              sp: Victoria Ferdinanda Cissell (b.16 Mar 1843-PC,Missouri;m.2 Oct 1860;d.28 Jan 1874-Perry County,Missouri)

            4. William Albert Montgomery (b.14 Aug 1833;d.3 Mar 1852)

    2. Rebecca Drury (d.1838-Hardin County,Kentucky)

Descendants of Michael Drury

1. Michael Drury (b.Abt 1775)

sp: Susanna Guffey

- 2. Mary Drury (b.1795)
- 2. Henry Drury (b.23 Jan 1800-Rutherford County,North Carolina;d.29 Dec 1875-Lavaca County,Texas)

  sp: Susanna David (m.8 Feb 1827;d.betw 1833 and 1837)
    - 3. James William Drury (b.20 Jun 1826-Hardin County,Kentucky;d.7 Jun 1905-Oluste,Oklahoma)

      sp: Ann Jane Thigpen (b.16 Sep 1836-Louisiana;d.7 Mar 1896-Oluste,Oklahoma)
    - 3. Elizabeth Drury (b.2 Aug 1827-Hardin County,Kentucky;d.28 Mar 1901-Wilson County,Texas)

      sp: John Baptist Howe (m.7 Sep 1845)
    - 3. Nancy Ann Drury (b.10 Jul 1829-Johnson County,Indiana;d.22 Jan 1906-Burnet County,Texas)

      sp: William Ezechial Shuford (m.1849)
    - 3. John Drury (b.1 Jan 1832;d.9 Apr 1846-Perry County,Missouri)
    - 3. Lucretia Drury (b.26 Dec;d.2 Apr 1834)

  sp: Helen Layton (b.3 Apr 1829-Washington County,Kentucky;d.21 Jan 1876-Lavaca County,Texas)
    - 3. Peter Severian Drury (b.14 Feb 1839-Perry County,Missouri;d.22 Feb 1839-Perry County,Missouri)
    - 3. Lucretia Ellen Drury (b.4 Jul 1840-Perry County,Missouri;d.16 Aug 1847)
    - 3. Henry Francis Drury (b.4 Jun 1842-Perry County,Missouri)
    - 3. Frances Josephine Drury (b.6 Jun 1844-Perry County,Missouri;d.22 Apr 1845)
    - 3. Charlemagne Drury (b.29 Jan 1846-Perry County,Missouri;d.15 Aug 1887-Lavaca County,Texas)

      sp: Cornelia Jane Brown
    - 3. John Baptist Drury (b.15 Nov 1848-Perry County,Missouri)
    - 3. Benjamin Franklin Drury (b.3 Mar 1851-Perry County,Missouri;d.11 Oct 1875)
    - 3. Thomas Benton Drury (b.15 May 1853-Lavaca County,Texas;d.1 Oct 1864)
    - 3. Daughter Drury (b.6 Nov 1856;d.6 Nov 1856)
    - 3. Joseph C. Drury (b.24 Nov 1858-Lavaca County,Texas;d.13 Feb 1861-Lavaca County,Texas)
    - 3. Michael Emmett Drury (b.9 Sep 1861-Lavaca County,Texas;d.20 Dec 1905-Wood County,Texas)

      sp: Ann Elizabeth Livingston
- 2. John W. Drury

  sp: Teresa Yates (m.21 Jan 1817)
    - 3. Henry Drury (b.Abt 1819)
    - 3. Jerome Drury
    - 3. Nancy Drury
    - 3. Victoria Drury
    - 3. George Washington Drury (b.19 Apr 1829)

Descendants of Zachariah Drury

1. Zachariah Drury (b.1773-St. Mary's County,Maryland;d.1855-Nelson County,Kentucky)

sp: Mary Jane Molohon (b.Abt 1769-Maryland;m.12 Jan 1797)

  2. John Drury (b.1798-St. Mary's County,Maryland)

    sp: Mary Yates

  2. Lucy Drury (b.1799-Washington County,Kentucky;d.30 Jan 1873-Perry County,Missouri)

    sp: Henry P. Phillips (b.1797-Maryland;m.23 Oct 1823;d.10 Mar 1884-Perry County,Missouri)

      3. Austin Phillips (b.1824-Kentucky)

      3. John Zachariah Phillips (b.1830-Kentucky;d.2 Sep 1853-Perry County,Missouri)

      3. Martha Ann Phillips (b.1831-Kentucky)

      3. Henry Phillips (b.1833-Kentucky;d.Apr 1867-Perry County,Missouri)

        sp: Mary Josephine Tucker (b.16 Feb 1840-Perry County,Missouri;m.12 Nov 1857;d.14 May 1893-Perry County,Missouri)

      3. Mary Jane Phillips (b.1 Jan 1834-Kentucky)

      3. James Lafayette Phillips (b.1836-Kentucky)

      3. Louis B. Phillips (b.1838-Hardin County,Kentucky;d.Bef 1906-Missouri)

  2. James Drury (b.1800)

    sp: Mary Leake

  2. Ellenor Drury (b.1802)

  2. Francis Drury (b.1806-Washington County,Kentucky;d.1866)

    sp: Juliann Gough (b.1800;m.3 Nov 1827)

      3. Charles Drury (b.28 Feb 1829-Union,Kentucky)

      3. Henry Absolom Drury (b.28 Apr 1833-Union,Kentucky)

        sp: Louise Frances Utley (m.14 Mar 1862)

      3. Francis Ignatius Drury (b.31 Jul 1835-Union,Kentucky;d.1875)

        sp: Eliza Jane Boarman (m.1 Apr 1869)

  2. William Drury (b.1814)

  2. Isadore Drury (b.1815)

    sp: Elizabeth Green (b.1825-Marion County,Kentucky;m.by 1842)

      3. Mary F. Drury (b.1843)

      3. William Zachariah Drury (b.1847)

      3. Charles Henry Drury (b.1849)

      3. Sarah E Drury (b.1853-Marion County,Kentucky)

      3. Josephine Drury (b.1858-Marion County,Kentucky)

Descendants of Peter Joy

1. Peter Joy (b.1665;d.1740)

sp: Ann Stone (b.1699-St. Mary's County Maryland;m.Bef 1701;d.by 5/1/1747-St. Mary's County Maryland)

  2. Charles Joy (b.1701-St. Mary's County,Maryland;d.1778-St. Mary's County,Maryland)

    sp: Unknown

      3. Charles Joy Jr.

      3. Thomas Joy

      3. Peter Joy

      3. Robert Joy

      3. Elizabeth Joy

      3. Sarah Joy

        sp: Stephen Raley

          4. Ignatius Randolph Raley (b.1793-St. Mary's County,Maryland;d.1843/1850-St. Mary's County,Maryland)

            sp: Dorothy Rosalie Joy (b.27 Feb 1794-SMSC,Maryland;m.10 Feb 1822;d.29 Jan 1884-St. Mary's County,Maryland)

      3. Ann Joy

        sp: Edward Stone

          4. James Stone

          4. Charles Stone

          4. Sarah Stone

  2. Enoch Joy (b.by 1715-St. Mary's County Maryland;d.by 8/20/1746-St. Mary's County)

    sp: Tecla Drury (b.1720-St. Mary's County Maryland;m.Bef 1735;d.1796-St. Mary's County Maryland)

      3. Enoch Joy Jr. (b.1742-St. Mary's County)

        sp: Rebecca

          4. Henrietta Joy (b.Bef 1774-St. Mary's County,Maryland)

          4. Thomas Joy (b.Abt 1777-St. Mary's County,Maryland)

            sp: Eleanor

              5. William Thomas Joy (b.Sep 1819;d.1906-Washington,D.C.)

              5. Joseph Joy (b.1801;d.1877)

          4. Catherine Joy (b.Bef 1776-St. Mary's County,Maryland;d.Aft 1820-St. Mary's County,Maryland)

            sp: Thomas Mooney Brewer (b.Bef 1778-SMSC,Maryland;m.31 Dec 1798;d.1813/1820-St. Mary's County,Maryland)

      3. Ignatius Joy (b.Bef 1768-St. Mary's County,Maryland;d.29 Mar 1827-St. Mary's County,Maryland)

        sp: Dorothy Booth (b.Bef 1773-St. Mary's County,Maryland;m.Bef 1788;d.1829-St. Mary's County,Maryland)

          4. Edward Joy (b.1778-St. Mary's County,Maryland;d.10 Mar 1857-St. Mary's County,Maryland)

            sp: Mary Ann Goddard (b.1816-St. Mary's County,Maryland;m.7 Jan 1833;d.1866-St. Mary's County,Maryland)

          4. Edmund Barton Joy (b.1792-St. Mary's County,Maryland;d.Bef 15 Dec 1864-St. Mary's County,Maryland)

            sp: Ann Saxton (b.1794/1803-St. Mary's County,Maryland;m.4 Feb 1818;d.1832/1840-St. Mary's County,Maryland)

            sp: Elpha Isabella Raley (b.1816-St. Mary's County,Maryland;m.14 Jan 1842;d.1858/1860-SMSC,Maryland)

          4. Dorothy Rosalie Joy (b.27 Feb 1794-St. Mary's County,Maryland;d.29 Jan 1884-St. Mary's County,Maryland)

            sp: Ignatius Randolph Raley (b.1793-St. Mary's County,Maryland;m.10 Feb 1822;d.1843/1850-SMSC,Maryland)

          4. Eleanor Joy (b.1794/1800-St. Mary's County,Maryland;d.29 Jun 1884-St. Mary's County,Maryland)

            sp: Enoch Drury (b.Bef 1791-St. Mary's County,Maryland;m.4 Jan 1815;d.Aft 1833)

              5. Jane M. Drury (b.31 Dec 1822-St. Mary's County,Maryland)

                sp: John Radford Jr. (m.26 Jul 1850;d.1850/1856-St. Mary's County,Maryland)

                    sp: John B. Raley (b.1803/1804-St. Mary's County,Maryland;m.1856;d.1879-St. Mary's County,Maryland)
                └ 5. Susan Drury (b.1825-St. Mary's County,Maryland;d.1910-Baltimore,Maryland)
            4. Samuel Joy (b.1808-St. Mary's County,Maryland;d.Aft 1842-St. Mary's County,Maryland)
                sp: Rebecca Leach (b.1810-St. Mary's County,Maryland;m.11 Jan 1831;d.Aft 1842-St. Mary's County,Maryland)
            └ 4. Jane Joy (b.Bef 1817-St. Mary's County,Maryland;d.Aft 1820-St. Mary's County,Maryland)
        3. Charles Joy (d.1783/1784-St. Mary's County,Maryland)
        3. Athanasius Joy (b.1745-St. Mary's County,Maryland;d.Aft 1779-St. Mary's County,Maryland)
            sp: Anna Diana Thompson (b.Bef 1752-St. Mary's County Maryland;m.Bef 1767;d.1778-St. Mary's County Maryland)
            4. Mary Joy (b.Bef 25 Mar 1767-St. Mary's County,Maryland)
            4. Philip Joy (b.Bef 19 May 1771-St. Mary's County,Maryland;d.1817-St. Mary's County,Maryland)
                sp: Elizabeth Joy (b.17 May 1768-St. Mary's County,Maryland;d.Bef Nov 1816-St. Mary's County,Maryland)
            4. Aloysia Joy (b.22 Sep 1776-St. Mary's County,Maryland;d.Aft 1778-St. Mary's County,Maryland)
            4. Ann Leonard Joy (b.Bef 1778-St. Mary's County,Maryland)
            4. Aloysius Joy (b.Bef 24 Jan 1779-St. Mary's County,Maryland)
            └ 4. Elizabeth Joy
    └ 3. Peter Joy
2. Mary Joy (b.Abt 1710-St. Mary's County,Maryland;d.Bef 1780-St. Mary's County,Maryland)
    sp: John Raley (b.1705/1710-St. Mary's County,Maryland;m.Bef 1735;d.Bef 19 Sep 1746-St. Mary's County,Maryland)
        3. John Raley (b.1735-St. Mary's County,Maryland)
            sp: Henrietta Greenwell
            4. Sarah Raley (c.20 Jul 1777-St. Mary's County,Maryland)
            4. John Raley (b.1755-St. Mary's County,Maryland;d.1834-St. Mary's County,Maryland)
                sp: unknown
                5. Ann Nancy Raley (b.1795-St. Mary's County,Maryland;d.1844-St. Mary's County,Maryland)
                    sp: James Goldsborough (b.1800-St. Mary's County,Maryland;m.28 Jul 1821;d.1839-St. Mary's County,Maryland)
                5. John Raley (b.1795/1800-St. Mary's County,Maryland;d.1832-St. Mary's County,Maryland)
                5. Mary Raley (b.1800-St. Mary's County,Maryland;d.Aft 1826-St. Mary's County,Maryland)
                    sp: Richard Stone (b.Abt 1800-St. Mary's County,Maryland;d.1826/1832-St. Mary's County,Maryland)
                sp: Elefred Drury (b.1770-St. Mary's County,Maryland;m.13 Jun 1807)
                5. Alley Raley (b.Bef 1808-St. Mary's County,Maryland)
                5. Monica Raley (b.Bef 1808-St. Mary's County,Maryland)
                5. Obediah Raley (b.Bef 1808-St. Mary's County,Maryland;d.Aft 1831-St. Mary's County,Maryland)
                5. Caroline Raley (b.1810-St. Mary's County,Maryland;d.Aft 1870-St. Mary's County,Maryland)
                    sp: George W. Latham (b.1799-St. Mary's County,Maryland;m.20 Nov 1830;d.1860/1870-SMSC,Maryland)
                5. George Francis Raley (b.by 1810-St. Mary's County,Maryland;d.Aft 1862-St. Mary's County,Maryland)
                    sp: Mary Elizabeth Spalding (b.1822-SMSC,Maryland;m.12 Jan 1839;d.Aft 1850-St. Mary's County,Maryland)
                5. Thomas Raley (b.1815-St. Mary's County,Maryland;d.Bef 1860-St. Mary's County,Maryland)
                5. Elpha Isabella Raley (b.1816-St. Mary's County,Maryland;d.1858/1860-St. Mary's County,Maryland)
                    sp: Edmund Barton Joy (b.1792-SMSC,Maryland;m.14 Jan 1842;d.Bef 15 Dec 1864-St. Mary's County,Maryland)
        3. Peter Raley (d.1742/1749-St. Mary's County,Maryland)
        3. Ann Raley (b.1738-St. Mary's County,Maryland)
        3. Benedict Raley
        3. Eleanor Raley
    sp: Lazarus Ross (m.Aft 1746)

      3. Lazarus Ross Jr.

         sp: Jane Cox (m.20 Nov 1780)

           4. Lazarus Ross III (b.1782-Virginia;d.1865-Grant County,Indiana)

      3. Rebecca Ross (d.1812-Clark County,Indiana)

         sp: Willouhby Nugent (m.by 1772;d.1812-Clark County,Indiana)

2. John (Baptist) Basil Joy (b.by 1726-St. Mary's County Maryland;d.1776-St. Mary's County Maryland)

   sp: Mary Hazel (b.1731-St. Mary's County Maryland;m.Bef 1746;d.1755-St. Mary's County Maryland)

   sp: Sarah Greenwell (b.Bef 1739-St. Mary's County Maryland;m.Bef 1762;d.1778-St. Mary's County Maryland)

2. Anthanatius Joy (b.Bef 1727-St. Mary's County Maryland;d.1779-St. Mary's County Maryland)

2. Ignatius Joy

   sp: Joan

     3. John Joy (b.1735-St. Mary's County,Maryland)

     3. Enoch Joy (b.1740-St. Mary's County,Maryland)

     3. Ann Joy (b.1741)

        sp: John Raley

     3. Anthanatius Joy (b.1745-St. Mary's County,Maryland)

2. Sarah Joy (b.Bef 1733-St. Mary's County Maryland)

   sp: Samuel Harris

   sp: John Nevitt

2. Elinor Joy (b.Bef 1733-St. Mary's County Maryland)

Name index

Jane 52, 58, 59, 168
Jane M. (1822) 168, 176
Jeremiah 71
Jerningham 62, 64
Jesse 109
Joan (Jane?) 119, 121, 122, 177
John 154
John (1739) 53, 71, 82, 93, 140
John (1781) 145
John (1796) 164
John (s/o Philip) 119, 122
John (1665?) 23, 39, 42, 43, 71
John Baptist 75, 93
John Chrysostom 71, 82
John D. 158
John H. 100
John Jr. 44, 52, 71, 91, 140,
   166, 176
John Thomas 100
John William 100
Joseph (1751) 53, 72, 140, 149
Joseph (1816) 120
Joseph (1770) 98
Joseph Benedict 126, 127
Joseph Benedict Jr 127
Joseph Levi 98
Joshua 99
Julia Ann (1801)102
Leonard 93, 98
Louis Mason 67
Lucy (1796) 147
Mahala 105, 106
Mamie Elizabeth 99
Margaret (1669?) 23, 46
Margaret 125
Margaret (1795) 161
Maria (1801) 120
Martha (1794) 146, 158, 160
Martha Joanna 127
Mary (d/o James) 44, 45
Mary (d. 1729) 20
Mary (1618?) 20, 39, 61
Mary (d/o Charles 1776) 106
Mary (d/o Enoch) 109
Mary (d/o Hilary) 161
Mary (1753) 53, 72, 140
Mary (d/o John (1739) 71, 87,
   140
Mary (1772) 141
Mary (1770) 98
Mary (1799) 123,125
Mary (1853) 127
Mary Ann (1801) 105
Mary Elizabeth 66
Mary Ellen (1787) 107, 135
Mary Lillian 127

Mary Lucinda 101
Mary Margaret 163
Matilda 106
Matilda (1827) 162
Michael 54, 73, 93, 99, 118
Michael (1757) 164
Michael (1785) 164, 172, 173
Michael Jr. (Miley) 103
Milburn 105
Mildred 76, 110
Miriam E. 127
Monica 72, 87
Monica (d/o Hilary) 163
Monica (1785) 107
Monica (1772) 98
Nancy (1789) 146
Nicholas 54, 55, 73, 98, 109
Peter 44, 52, 54, 72, 115
Peter Jr. 54, 55, 73, 109
Peter M. 125
Peter W. 126
Philip 54, 93, 115, 119, 135,
   136
Philip C. 100
Philip Maguire 101
Pius (s/o Charles 1776) 106
Plummer 64
Raphael 135
Rebecca (1779) 144
Rebecca (1812) 123, 126
Richard 45
Richard (s/o Peter) 78, 123
Richard (imm) 21, 23
Richard Ignatius 100
Richard Jr. 123, 126
Robert (m 1825) 44
Robert (1619) 23, 24
Robert (1634) 21, 23, 24
Robert (1660) 23, 28, 38, 40
Robert (d. 1625) 22
Robert (London) 23
Robert (1798) 120
Robert (s/o Peter) 54, 93, 111
Robert Barton 98
Robert Barton Jr. 99
Robert V. 102
Rose Anna 103
Sabra Ann 99
Samuel (A.A.) 62, 66
Samuel (1775) 119, 121
Sarah (1802) 120
Sarah (1615?) 20, 39, 61
Sarah (1782) 144
Sarah Marthalina 73, 74, 104,
   137
Sophia (1718?) 20, 39, 61

Stephen (1767) 45
Susan (1816) 106
Susan (1798) 123, 125
Susanna 71, 83, 176
Susanna (1854) 127
Tecla 44, 52, 57, 168, 177
Tecla (d/o Philip) 119, 121
Theresa Rose 162
Thomas (1774) 45
Thomas (est 1702) 44, 52, 58,
   93
Thomas Foley 127
Thomas Harry 101
Thomas Theodore 52, 164, 165
Wilfred 109, 137
William 167
William (1604) 23
William (1629) 19
William (1638) 19, 93
William (1737) 53, 55, 71,
   109,135
William (1777)71, 86
William (1786?)119, 122
William (1814)120
William (1750)62
William (1817) 105
William (1867) 100
William (1804) 123, 125
William 19, 21, 23
William A. (1860) 127
William Albert 101
William C. 138, 167
William Elbert 127
William H. (1825) 125
William Henry 126, 127
Winifred (1777) 109, 110
Zachariah 119, 120, 135, 163,
   176

Dryden
   Ann 110

Duff
   Mary 58

Dunbar
   Mary Ann 125

Dyer
   Martha E. 126, 127
   William S. 127

223

Hillery E. 104
John 104, 137
John Lewis 103
John T. 104
Joseph Leonard 73, 103
Joseph Leonard Jr. 103
Joseph Stephen 104
Leonard 99, 103, 104
Martha 104
Mary Priscilla 104
Mattingly Gibbons 101
Michael Hilary 103
Richard B. 103
Thomas 104
Uriah 104
William Edward 104
William Peter 103

Joy
Ann Priscilla 100
Dorothy Rosalie 177
Edmund Barton 177
Eleanor (m 1816) 168, 177
Elizabeth 177
Enoch 177
Enoch (bef 1715) 57
Ignatius 168, 177
Ignatius Jr. 102
Ignatius S. 103
John Michael 103
Mary E. 126
Peter 57, 177
Peter Jr. 177
Sarah 177

K

Kerse
John 43

Knott
Basil 72
Leonard 161, 163
Richard 140

L

Lacey
Georgeann 99

Lampton
Mark 49

Layton
Helen 164

Leach
Elizabeth 106

Leigh
Mary Jane 126

Long
Elizabeth 99
George Henry 99
Mary Ann 98
Monica (Mocky) 98

Longmore
William Hugh 127

Lydaman
Andrew 165
Martha Ann 52, 165

M

Malone
Charles 156

Mandley
Matthew 140

Manning
John 48

Mason
John 161

Mattingly
Amanda 103
Leonard 155

McClain
Elizabeth 106

McNabb
Archibald 135
Elizabeth 135

Medley
George 47

Merriken
Christian 19
Hugh 19
John 19

Metcalf
Sibyl 142

Miles
Elizabeth 21, 39, 61

Mills
John 56
Susanna 110

Molohon
Clement 120, 121
James 163
Mary Jane 135, 163

Montgomery
George 107
Pius 107
Thomas S. 163

Moore
Nicholas 53, 72

Morgan
Mary 103

Murray
John 54

N

Newton
Bibianna 115
Clement 115, 172
Gabriel 136
Ignatius 123
John 172
Thomas 115, 172

Nolan
Mary 66

Norris
Allen 121

O

O'Brien
Mary Ethyl 105
John Robert 106
Martin 106
Stephan Theodore 106

Stone
    Ann 57, 177
    Francis 126
    James (1841) 126
    James H. 126
    Dr. Joseph 126

Sweeny
    Elizabeth 158

T

Tant
    John 23, 46
    James 47
    Matthew 47

Tarleton
    Mary 110
    Rhodolphus 110

Tattershall
    Lawrence 47, 48
    William 47

Taylor
    Mary 165, 176

Tennison
    Maria 104

Tenny
    Mary 166

Thomas
    David 141
    Elizabeth 52
    Elizabeth (w/o William
        Hayden) 58, 71

Thompson
    Brittana 165
    Elizabeth 110
    Henry 49
    James 110
    Jane 49
    John B. 110
    John Basil 110
    John Basil Jr. 110
    Joseph 110
    Julianna 125
    Maria 110
    Tecla 44, 57
    William 49

Thorne
    Deborah 105
    Emily 106

Tillard
    William 64

V

Van Reswick
    John 127

Vessells
    Charles 164

W

Warren
    Charles 107
    Harriet 107

Wathen
    Anastasia 110

Wheatley
    Etta 171, 174
    Joseph 174

Whitledge
    Sibyl 173

Wigginton
    Henry 173
    John 173
    John (f/o Sibyl) 142
    Sarah 142, 143
    Sibyl 141, 173
    William 173

Wilkinson
    Ann 110, 168, 176

Williams
    William 47

Wimsatt
    Catherine 119, 174
    James 109
    Richard 174
    Robert 119
    Tabitha 109

Wise
    Ann Marie 126
    James 126
    Samuel 126
    William 126

Wood
    Charles 99
    Zebedee 62

Y

Yates
    Ann 99, 172, 173
    John 172
    Martin 172, 173
    Teresa 164, 173
    Thomas 99, 172
    Zachariah 164, 173

Young
    Elizabeth 46

Bibliography

A History of Bedford County, Virginia

A History of The Roman Catholic Diocese of Owensboro, Turner Publishing Company

Abercrombie, Janice L. and Richard Slatten, *Virginia Revolutionary Publick Claims*, Iberian Pub. Co., Athens, GA, 1992

Abstracts of the Administrative Accounts of the Prerogative Courts of Maryland 1715-1718

American Genealogical-Biographical Index (AGBI)

Ancestry.com, 1900 Census St. Mary's County, Maryland

Andrews, M.P.,*Ter'y History of Maryland Vol I*

Andrews, Mathew P, *A History of Maryland*

Anne Arundel County Inventory and accounts

Archives of Maryland on line: Assembly Proceedings 20 Sept. – 18 Oct., 1694 Vol. 19

Archives of Maryland, census 1776, Lower William and Mary Hundred, Charles County, Maryland

Archives of Maryland, Kent Co. Court Proceedings 1645-1656

Archives of Maryland, Proceedings of the Court of Chancery 1669-1679 Vol. 51, 67

Archives of Maryland, Vol. 78

Archives of Sisters of Charity of Nazareth

Austin, Helen <austinart@aol.com> 118 Ryan Crest Lane, Decatur, Alabama, 35603

Bailey, Anne J., "Twelfth Texas Cavalry," *Handbook of Texas Online* (http://www.tshaonline.org/handbook/online/articles/qkt12), Texas State Historical Association

Barnes Robert, *Maryland Genealogies Vol. 1*

Barnes, *Maryland Marriages 1655-1850*

Bedford County Court Order Book 9

Beitzel, Edwin Warfield, *History of the Jesuit missions of St. Mary's County*

Beitzel, Edwin, *Calendar of events St. Mary's County in the American Revolution*, St. Mary's County Bicentennial Commission

Bennet Raley -his bible

Blackwell, Claude G., *Proceedings of the Orphan's Court of St. Mary's County*,

Boles, David, Barth-Hickey Ancestry

Bossy, John, Reluctant Colonists: The English Catholics confront the Atlantic, p 158 in Quinn, David B., *Early Maryland in a Wider World*, Wayne State University Press Detroit, Mi. 1982

Bozeman, John L., *History of Maryland, Vol. 1*

Bray, Celestine RCP, Coombs Family from Holy Cross Church, Louisville, Ky.

Bruce, Philip Alexander, *An Economic History of Virginia*, Macmillan 1896

Brumbaugh, Gaius Marcus, *Maryland Records Vol. I* 1993, Genealogical Pub. Co., Baltimore

Brumbaugh, G.M. *Maryland Records---Vol. II, State of His Lordship's Manor*, Genealogical Publ. Co., Baltimore, Md, 1985

Burger, Judith A. Will of John Bailey d. 1712 Register of Wills, St. Mary's County, Maryland

Burger, Judith A. Will of Peter Drury d. 1770 Register of Wills, St. Mary's County, Maryland.

Carr, Lois Green and Walsh, Lorena, S., The Planter's Wife: The experience of white women in Seventeenth Century Maryland in *William and Mary Quarterly* 3rd series Vol. 34 # 4

Carr, Lois Green, {excerpt from MSA sc54094 0306-3}

Catholic Record Society, Miscellanea V, London 1909

Chronicles of Saint Mary's, August 1961

Chronicles of St. Mary's Vol. 7

Church of Latter Day Saints Family History Library Film 1254514

Claims entered in Elizabeth City County, Court Book

Cockburn, George, Rear Adm., to Vice Adm. Sir Alexander Cochrane, July 19, 1814

Coldham, Peter Wilson, ("marriage register of Rev. David Love")

Conrad, Glenn R. Some Maryland Germans who settled in Louisiana

Cook, Michael L. & Bette Ann, A Pioneer History of Washington County, Kentucky

Cotton, Jane Baldwin, *Maryland Calendar of Wills, Vol. 1*

Creek, Jan, E-mail msg 11/6/98

Cronin, William B., The disappearing Islands of the Potomac pp 128-129, JHU press, 2005

Crowl, Philip D., The revolution and after: 1774-1789, *The Old Line State: A History of Maryland,* Morris L. Radoff, Ed., Hall of Records Commission State of Maryland, Annapolis 1971

Crowley, Kitty, lookup volunteer: St. James Church Records

Crumrine's History, http://www.chartiers.com/pages/articles/dunmore.html

Cryer, Leona, *Some Johnsons of Southern Maryland* -- Gateway Press, Baltimore Md. 1991

Culver, Francis B., Ed. Society of Colonial Wars in Maryland Vol. 2

Daughters of the American Revolution ID Number: 70926

Davis, Marie, "Davis:" A part of the collection of Clyde and Marie Davis

Dean, Cora Hankins, Application # 213613 for membership in the DAR

Death Notices from the (Baltimore) Sun 1851-1853 v. 1

Dobricky, John <john.dobricky@gmail.com>

Dodd, Darcy, http://www.bayweekly.com/year00/issue8 18/life8 18.html, Inside Southern Anne Arundel's Stately Homes

Donnelly, Mary Louise, Colonial Period Tenants and Owners of Beaverdam Manor 1998

Dora, Robert, 7th great grandson of Robert Drury

Driver, Steve, Email of 5 June, 2013

Driver, Steve, "The descendants of John Drury of Macon County," Tennessee, unpublished manuscript, 2007

Drury, Francis Eugene Sr. World War I Draft Registration Card, 1917-1918

Drury, Johnny B., "Biography of Harry A. Drury," unpublished manuscript 2012

Drury, Leonard, Pension Application # 15035 dated 10/10/1832 issued in Jackson Twp., Stark County, Ohio

Early Catholic Cemetery Listings of Washington, Nelson, and Marion Counties, Kentucky, West Central Kentucky Family Research Association, McDowell Pub., 1984

Economic Aspects of Tobacco http://www.tobacco.org/history/colonialtobacco.html

Edwards, Morgan, *History of the Baptists in Virginia*

Elizabethan Recusants and the Recusancy Laws: www.elizabethan-era.org.uk/elizabethan-recusants-recusancy-laws.htm

Elton G. R., Contentment and discontent on the eve of colonization p. 112 in Quinn, David B., *Early Maryland in a Wider World*, Wayne State University Press Detroit, Mi. 1982

en.wikipedia.org/wiki/21st_Missouri_volunteer_infantry

Family History Library Film 1254514 NA Film Number T9-0514

Family Tree Maker CD 206, Maryland Probate Records, Prerogative court Abstracts 1737 – 1744

Fausz, J. Fredrick, Merging and Emerging Worlds: Anglo-Indian Interest Groups and the Development of the Seventeenth Century Chesapeake in Colonial Chesapeake Society,

Fenwick, Laverne M., The confiscation of British Property in Maryland in Chronicles of St. Mary's V.5 # 7 (July 1957) Resurveyed map of Beaverdam Manor

Fold3.com, Revolutionary War, Virginia

Francis Eugene Drury, Sr. World War I Draft Registration Cards

Frederick County Docket Books, 1780

Fresco, Jesuit Missions

Fresco, Margaret. K., *Marriages & Death in St. Mary's Co., Md. 1634-1900 –* Supplement

Froude James Anthony, History of England from the fall of Woolsey to the defeat of the Spanish Armada 1870

Genealogical Record" Vol. 7, No. 3, Sept. 1965 through Vol. 9, No. 4, Dec. 1967." Houston Gen. Forum, Houston, Texas. "Minutes of Broad Run Baptist Church, Fauquier Co., Va., 1762-1872."

Graham, Michael, Meetinghouse and Chapel in Colonial Chesapeake Society Ed. Lois Green Carr, Phillip D. Morgan and Jean B. Russo

Green, Margaret Morris on Drury Family Genealogy Forum: http:genforum.genealogy.com/drury/messages/810.html

Greer, George C., *Early Virginia Immigrants, 1623 – 1666*

Grun, Bernard, *The Timelines of History*, Simon and Shuster 1971

Hale, Nathaniel Claiborne, *Virginia Venturer: A Historical Biography of William Claiborne 1600 – 1677*. 1951

Hawke, David Freeman, *Everyday life in Early America* Harper 1988

Henretta, James et al. "Margaret Brent: A Woman of Property " in *America's History* 3rd Ed. Worth 1997

Hierarchia Catholica Medii et Recentioris Aevi, Volume 8

History of Daviess County, Kentucky

History of Tobacco, Boston University Medical Center http://academic.udayton.edu/health/syllabi/tobacco/history.htm#industry

History of Union County, Kentucky

Horn, James, Adapting to a New World: A comparative study of Local Society in England and Maryland 1650 – 1700, in Colonial Chesapeake Society, Ed. Lois Green Carr, Phillip D. Morgan, and Jean B. Russo p 152

Hotten, John Camden, *The Original Lists of Persons of Quality ... and Others who went from Great Britain to the American Plantations - 1600 - 1700* (London 1874)

http://en.wikipedia.org/wiki/Battle_of_Bladensburg#cite_note-Elting206-9

http://www.royal.gov.uk/HistoryoftheMonarchy/KingsandQueensofEngland/thetudors/ElizabethI.aspx

Index to Marriages and Deaths in the (Baltimore) Sun 1837-1850

Index to Maryland Colonial Judgments, Liber II 1669 – 1672

Innes, Arthur D., *A History of England: The British Empire Vol. II* Macmillan 1913, and Lunt, William Edward, *History of England* Harper & Brothers 1945

Inventories & Accounts 33.321 (8/20/1746 – 10/7/1746)

Jones, Mary Josephine, "Hardin Co, KY marriages (1793 to 1850)" compiled by for the Ancestral Trails Historical Society

Keddie, Neil, St. Mary's County Wills

Kelly, Quakers in the Founding of Anne Arundel County

Kentucky Historical Society, "Print, 'Head-Quarters at Camp Dick Robinson, Near Branstsville, Kentucky,' 1861," http://www.ket.org/artstoolkit/statedivided/gallery/resources/campdick/campdick_more.pdf

Kentucky State Archives Frankfort, Ky. microfilm Roll 986767 Bk 111-17

Kingdon, Margaret Clark, *Washington County Kentucky Marriage Records 1790 – 1878*

Klapthor, Margaret Brown, Southern Maryland in the War of 1812 in "The Record" April 1965, Charles County Historical Society

Krumpleman, Dorothy Payne, Photo of Archbishop George Thomas Montgomery

Land Office Unpatented Certificate of Survey, SM #141

Land Office, Maryland State Archives, Land Patents, Vol. 19

Land Records of Prince George's County, MD

Land, Aubrey C., The Planters of Colonial Maryland, in *Maryland Historical Magazine* Vol. 67 # 1

Loker, Aleck, *A Most Convenient Place – Leonardtown Maryland 1650-1950*

Magazine of Virginia Genealogy vol. 27 No. 1, Early records of Chappawansic Baptist Church, Stafford County. 1766-1844

Main, Gloria, Tobacco Colony

Marriage Bonds of Bedford County, Virginia 1755-1810

Marriage Index: District of Columbia, Delaware, Maryland and Virginia, 1740-1920, FTM CD #399

Maryland Archives, viii

Maryland Calendar of Wills Vol 8 1738-1743

Maryland Gazette, August 4, 1814, Letter entitled "Movements of the Enemy"

Maryland Gazette, Baltimore, June 20 and July 21 1786

Maryland Genealogical Bulletin Vol. 2

Maryland Historical Magazine Vol. 1 No. 80 (Spring 1985)

Maryland Probate Records, Calendar of Wills, Vol. 13

Maryland Probate Records, Prerogative Court Abstracts 1733-1738

Maryland Probate Records, Prerogative Court Abstracts 1738-1744

Papenfuse, Edward C. et. Al., *Archives of Maryland, Historical list Vol. 1, Annapolis, Maryland*; Maryland State Archives, 1990

Maryland State Archives, Georgetown University Special Collections

Maryland State Archives; Maryland Indexes; (Chancery Papers, Index); 1713-1787

Maryland State Archives, S 1161-1-7 1/4/5/44, inventory of Mr. Moses ADNEY, AA, 13 Feb 1732 & 18 Oct. 1733, by Alice, w/o Chas. Drury

Menard, Russell R., 1705 Tract Map of St. Mary's County, in *Chronicles of St. Mary's*, Vol. 21 # 5 (May 1973)

Menard, Russell R., British Migration in Colonial Chesapeake Society, Ed. Lois Green Carr, Phillip D. Morgan, and Jean B. Russo

Muster Rolls and other Records of Maryland Troops in the American Revolution 1775-1783" Volume XVII

Muster Rolls and other Records of Maryland Troops in the American Revolution 1775-1783" Volume XVIII

NARA catalog ID 570910

Nash, Mary Lou, Email message of 8/21/99

National Society of the Daughters of the American Revolution, Genealogical Abstracts of Revolutionary War Pension files Vol. 1

Nelson Co., KY Cemeteries

Nelson County Deed book bk. 2

Nelson County Tithes 1785-1791, Nelson Co., Ky.

New York Daily Times, 6/11/1853

Newman, Harry Wright, *Anne Arundel Gentry Vol. I*, 1970

Nolan, John S., The militarization of the Elizabethan State in Journal of Military History Vol. 58 No. 3 (7/1994) <http:// www.jstor.org/stable/2944132>

Norfolk Order book 1657-1668

Nugent, Nell Marion, *Cavaliers and Pioneers* Books 1 and 2

O'Rourke, Timothy, *Catholic Families of Southern Maryland*

O'Rourke, Timothy, Colonial Source Records: Southern Maryland Catholic Families

Obrist, Patricia, Dora, Robert and Drury, Donald, Remember the Drury Family Vol. II

Obrist, Patricia Bishop, Priest's notes, 1846 census St. Mary of the Barrens in Perry County, Missouri

Olson, Mary M., *St. Patrick Catholic Church History and Records, Stithton, Hardin County, Kentucky, 1831-1920*, McDowell Publishing Company, Utica, Kentucky, 1999

O'Neill, Gary, e-mail

O'Rourke, Timothy, *Maryland Catholics on the Frontier*, Brefney Press, 1981

Peden, Henry C. Jr., *Maryland Deponents Vol. 1*

Peden, Henry C. Jr., *Revolutionary Patriots of Anne Arundel County, Maryland*

Peden, Henry C. Jr., *Revolutionary Patriots of Baltimore Town and Baltimore County Maryland 1775-1783*, Family Line Publications, Silver Spring, Maryland, 1988

Perrin, W. H., *Kentucky Biographical Sketches* Vol. V

Pollard, Edward A., *The Lost Cause*, 1866

Prerogative Ct. (Test. Proceedings), 27 (MdHR 983), p. 38 Film 3299, Pt. 2, Liber IX, Folio 451, 452, 453

Prince George's County Land Records 1739-1743 Liber Y

Proceedings of the Council of Maryland 1692 –1694

Proceedings of the Provincial Court of Maryland 1666-1670

Radoff, Morris L., *The Old Line State: A History of Maryland* 1971

Ramey, *Immigrant Ancestors of Maryland*

Ransom, Linda Lawson Typed papers outlining family tradition

Record of the County Militia" Washington County, Kentucky

Reno, Linda, electronic, msg of 8/13/2010

Reno, Linda, St. Mary's County Wills

Rent Rolls, Chronicles of St. Mary's, Vol. 21, No. 5

Risjold, Norman K., *Chesapeake Politics 1781 – 1800*, Columbia University Press 1978

Rogers, *History of Agriculture and Prices in England*, Vol. V

Roth, Marilyn, email message of 10/20/2000

Saint Mary's County Balances and Distributions - 1/16/1790

Schlesinger, Arthur M., Maryland's share in the last Inter Colonial War, *Maryland Historical Magazine*, Vol. 7

Selby, Lois, email message 12-27-1998

Sheer, Luke J. Jr., James Alexander Drury, unpublished manuscript, 2006

Shoemaker Sandy, Where Maryland Began…The Colonial History of St. Mary's County 2000

Simons, Katherine E., Obituary of Louis Mason Drury 1910-2004

Sisters of Charity of Nazareth Archival Center, P.O. Box 3000, Nazareth, KY 40048

Skinner, V. L. Jr. *Abstracts of the Administration Accounts of the Prerogative Court of Maryland Libers 6-10, 1724-1731*

Skinner, V. L. Jr., *Abstracts of the Inventories and Accounts of the Perogative Court of Maryland 1674-1718*

Skordas, Gustav, *The Early Settlers of Maryland 1633-1680*

Smith Ernest, *Religion under the Barons of Baltimore* 1896

Smith, Sarah B., *Historic Nelson County, Its Homes and People*, 1982

St. James Parish records, Anne Arundel County, Maryland

St. Mary's Beacon, Leonardtown Maryland

St. Mary's County Land Office,

St. Mary's County Levy Court Records 1829 – 1877

St. Mary's County Historical Society, research of Theodore L Brownyard

St. Nicholas Church Burials Patuxent River Naval Air Station St. Mary's County, MD, NAS project E38

Stanwood, Owen, The Baron of Saint-Castin and the Transformation of the Northeastern Borderlands, Michigan State University, *French Colonial History* Vol. 5

Stevenson, Thomas, *The Dry Docking Farm* (Private Pub.) 2001

Stewart, Dorothy Brown, *Once Upon a Time*

Storey, L. E., http://worldconnect.rootsweb.com/cgi-bin/igm.cgi/op=DESC&db=lestorey.htm

Taunt, John, Will Abstract, 17th Oct., 1702

Taylor, George B., Virginia Baptist Ministers, third series

The Chicago Daily Tribune

The Dreamboat that ran aground - U.S. policy towards Venezuela 1955-1960

The Early Trails of the Baptists" 200th Anniversary Committee of the Strawberry Baptist association

The Holy Bible, King James Version

Thomas, James Walter, *Chronicles of Colonial Maryland*, Google Books

Thompson, Gerald, *Early Kentucky Catholic Pioneers - The Rolling Fork Settlement Book I*

Tippett, Ben, Journal book A in 1790

Trigger Bruce G. ed., *Indians of North America*, Smithsonian Institute, V. 15

Trinity Church Marriage & Baptism Records 1795-1805

Twigge, Graham, Plague in London: Spatial and temporal aspects of mortality in Endemic diseases in London, in Center for metropolitan working papers series No 1 1993, Ed. John L. Champion.

U.S. Congressional Documents and Debates, 1774-1875, A Century of Lawmaking for a New Nation

U.S. Congressional Documents and Debates, 1774-1875. Bills and Resolutions, House of Representatives, 13th Congress, 3rd Session. (Library of Congress)., A Century of Lawmaking for a New Nation

United States Department of State Washington, D.C

US Census St. Mary's County, Maryland 1850

US Census St. Mary's County, Maryland, 1790, 1800, 1810

Virginia Archives, Prince William Miscellaneous papers

Virginia Revolutionary Publick Claims, Abercrombie, Janice L. and Richard Slatten., Iberian Pub. Co., Athens, GA, 1992

Wallace, Johnson and Muir to Ridgely, September 30 1786, Ridgely family papers, Maryland Historical Society

Walsh, Lorena, Community Networks in the early Chesapeake, in Colonial Chesapeake Society, Ed. Lois Green Carr, Phillip D. Morgan, and Jean B. Russo

Washington County, Kentucky Court Order Bk. "D"

Washington D.C. City Directory 1864

Webb, Benjamin J., *A Centenary of Catholicity in Kentucky*

White, Virgil D., *Index to Revolutionary War Service Records Vol. I: A-D*, The National Historical Publishing Co., Waynesboro, TN., 1995

Wigginton, David, Email 10/14/2007

Witmer, Dennis, <dawitmer@aol.com>

Wright, F. Edward, *Maryland Militia, War of 1812, Vol. 5, St. Mary's and Charles Counties* 1983

www.Stmary'sfamilies.com

Zimmer, Jackie, "An Industrial revolution in St. Mary's County" in Southern Maryland – this is living